Forbidden Territory
and
Realms of Strife

Forbidden Territory
and
Realms of Strife

The Memoirs of
JUAN GOYTISOLO

Translated by Peter Bush

VERSO

London · New York

This edition first published by Verso 2003
© Juan Goytisolo 2003
Translation © Peter Bush 2003
First published as *Coto vedado* (1985) and
En los reinos de taifa (1986) by Editorial Seix Barral
© Juan Goytisolo 1985, 1986

The moral rights of the author and translator have been asserted

1 3 5 7 9 10 8 6 4 2

Verso
UK: 6 Meard Street, London W1F 0EG
USA: 180 Varick Street, New York, NY 10014–4606
www.versobooks.com

Verso is the imprint of New Left Books

ISBN 1–85984–555–X

British Library Cataloguing in Publication Data
Goytisolo, Juan
Forbidden territory and realms of strife: the memoirs
of Juan Goytisolo
1. Goytisolo, Juan 2. Authors, Spanish – 20th century –
Biography
I. Title
863.3'4

Library of Congress Cataloging-in-Publication Data
A catalog record for this book is available from the Library of Congress

Typeset in Garamond by YHT Ltd, London
Printed in the UK by The Bath Press

Contents

Prologue to the Verso Edition

What reasons can lead an already mature author to extend his work as a novelist into the arena of autobiography? I suppose these must differ according to the ethical concerns and preoccupations of the individual writer. I myself had but two. After I had finished the novel *Landscapes after the Battle*, I read a handful of memoirs by older or contemporary Spanish writers, then put aside a narrative project that was already fermenting and began to write *Forbidden Territory*.

What is marketed in Spain as memoirs has nothing in common with what I understand to be autobiographical writing. Spanish memoirists are frequently forgetful: though prolix in elaborating incidents and anecdotes concerning their peers, they maintain a cautious silence in respect of the most intimate aspects of their own lives and, above all, avoid like the plague any examination of their consciences and recognition of mistakes which might call them to account. While some collect reminiscences and detail of little or no interest—I'm thinking of Franco's poet laureate José María Pemán's *My Lunches with Important People* which doesn't even relate the menus—others direct poison darts at their enemies whether real or imagined, while simultaneously they fashion a portentous, if not pontifical, image of themselves. Anything which might harm or betray such an image is carefully swept under the carpet. Perhaps Catholic tradition, and its exonerating sacrament of confession, explains that reluctance to reveal the secrets and errors of one's ways, and that of the Reformed Churches, where such a thing does not operate—with the corollary that it favours personal reflection—accounts for the outstanding succession of auto-biographies in the English language, from Samuel Pepys to Frank Harris and Oscar Wilde.

Mario Vargas Llosa once remarked how, whilst the Spanish love to tell their life-stories to perfect strangers on train journeys yet resist putting them on paper or frequently lie when so doing, the English are usually most reserved in the presence of strangers yet devastatingly sincere when confronting the challenge of the blank page. The autobiographical text, as I conceive it, hardly exists in Spain: the only one I recognised when I embarked on the adventure of the two volumes brought together in this edition was the work of Blanco White which I myself translated from English into the mother tongue of the man who described himself as a "self-banished Spaniard". In short: I tried to plug one of the many gaps in Spanish literature. If I had been a British author I would not have tried to compete with so many distinguished predecessors or I would have done it differently, through recourse to parody, as in the autobiographical fiction of *Landscapes after the Battle*, or, more recently, *A Cock-Eyed Comedy*.

The other reason was more personal: the need to explain the wherefore of a literary vocation, shared with my two brothers, and the change this underwent after *Count Julian*. I think the trauma of civil war and family unhappiness were decisive in respect of the first: the protective cupola collapsed and left the three of us orphans without maternal warmth and with an aged, sick father who lacked authority and was unable to offer any guidance. The second is clarified by a reading of *Realms of Strife*, especially the final pages, focused on my stay in Tangier, when the idea of the 'betrayal' of Count Julian took seed. From that date, I think that my novels and works of literary or socio-political reflections speak for themselves and do not require any autobiographical complement. Personal facts, facets and circumstances appear in filigree in the fictions of *State of Siege* and *A Cock-Eyed Comedy*. But the task undertaken in these two volumes begins and concludes with these pages. Since then my private life lacks interest and any addition to the latter would in my view be pointless.

Juan Goytisolo
Marrakesh, 2 December 2001

FORBIDDEN TERRITORY

*La lucidité est la blessure
la plus rapprochée du soleil.*
RENÉ CHAR

· PART 1 ·

THE WRITING OF genealogies, according to the ironic narrator of Biely's *Petersburg*, comes down to tracing the origins of well-to-do families right back to Adam and Eve. Beyond this important, undeniable discovery, the foliage and branches of maternal and paternal family trees do not usually extend—with the possible exception of a few aristocratic families—into that original limbo going by the pompous name of the dark night of time. In my case, I am an offshoot on both sides of exemplary bourgeois stock; the information that I obtained during my childhood about my ancestors does not go beyond the first half of the nineteenth century. This did not prevent my father, in one of those dreams of greatness that always acted as a prelude to one of his disastrous enterprises, from fashioning a family coat of arms that comprised, if I remember rightly, fleurs-de-lys against a red background. He traced the shield himself on parchment that gleamed from its frame on the verandah of our house in Torrentbó and was, he said, irrefutable proof of our noble lineage. On those long summer evenings that favored the evocation of the intimate details and long-lost anecdotes of family life, my uncle Leopoldo would greet the explanation of our so-called family shield with a wry, skeptical smile: no sooner had his brother turned his back than he would confide his suspicions that Great-grandfather's journey of no return from Lequeitio to Cuba, where he went as a youth and quickly made a fortune, was perhaps the result of his need to break from an environment hostile because of the initial stigma of his birth as a bastard. Why otherwise had this triumphant success settled down with such pomp in Catalonia and not in his native Basque country? That alienation and rupture from the rest of the family is and will always be a riddle. In any case, he would conclude, the shield and noble origins were products of my father's wild fantasy: our Basque forebears were but country gentlemen.

Whatever the truth of the matter, Great-grandfather Agustín, whose imposing, lordly image presided over the ghostly collection of Torrentbó portraits during my childhood, had become one of the magnates of the Cuban sugar industry thanks to his merciless exploitation of a cheap, abundant labor force: namely, the slaves. The way in which he amassed enormous capital over a few years reveals his harsh, authoritarian character, endowed with the ambition and pride that go with power—a man entirely convinced of his rights. As the owner of the San Agustín sugar refinery in the municipality of Cruces, next to Cienfuegos, he also acquired numerous properties on the island and in the metropolis. We owe to the orderly habits of his son Antonio the preservation of a real archive of documents—personal letters, bills, checks, commercial correspondence, receipts, photographs—which would enable a historian interested in the business practices and way of life of a prosperous family of Spanish settlers in South America to unearth the ideology, beliefs, aspirations of the old sugarocracy and the impact on them of the political vicissitudes of the colony, from the first independence struggles and abolition of slavery to the events that culminated in the blowing up of the *Maine* and the direct intervention of the United States. From the letters sent to and from Cuba one can reconstruct Great-grandfather's hectic movements between Barcelona, Havana, and Cienfuegos; his decision to entrust the care of the refinery and other interests on the island to his son Agustín, while my grandfather-to-be Antonio and "little Trina" settled into their luxurious accommodations on their properties and estates in the principality of Catalonia; his wife's numerous ailments, which she, Great-grandmother Doña Estanisláa Digat y Lizarzaburu, eased only by devout practices and religious feelings. The reader can get an idea of the effect the belated discovery of these papers produced in me by leafing through the pages of *Señas de identidad* and, especially, the first chapter of *Juan sin tierra*. The family myth, carefully nourished by my father, vanished forever after the naked revelations of a world of abuse and robbery, outrages hidden behind pious phrases, excesses and violence beyond belief. A constant, repressed feeling of guilt, an obvious residue of a long-since defunct sense of Catholic morality, was added to my already heightened awareness of the iniquities of Spanish society and the irrevocably parasitic, decadent, and vacuous world to which I belonged. I had just discovered Marxist doctrine and its detailed descriptions of the crimes and privileges of the bourgeoisie matched perfectly the reality evoked by those faded bundles of letters.

That is how at the age of twenty-three or twenty-four I became a fellow traveler of the clandestine Communist party—coinciding, to be true, with one of my father's financial disasters, which brought us to the brink of ruin. My decision owed as much to a hasty reading of the pamphlets and books that began to circulate undercover in Spain as to the conclusive evidence I found for their theories in the daily life, history, and ups and downs of my own family. I then lived through the Cuban revolutionary process, which was initiated a few years later. It was a liberating experience, historically sanctioned by the past crimes of my family, and my enthusiastic participation would soon help me to cast off my heavy burden of guilt. The letter included in the last chapter of *Juan sin tierra* is authentic although I made a few changes in transcription to adapt it to the novel. I still retain others that are equally wounding and accusing.

Without any wish to labor the matter, just to arouse the emotions that they stirred in me, I will copy those whose eloquence will free me of the need to comment.

Cienfuegos, Sep. 5, 1873

Dear Don Agustín Goytisolo
Dear master, this letter is to inform you that yesterday the 24th i gave young Agustín 300 gold pesos to give me the letter and he say that he can't give it me i no use to you because of my illness as your honor know and i hope your honor speak to him about this i with Vizente and he keeping me, paying my sickness costs and i hope your honor tell young Agustín to give it me to see if I move somewhere else where i get better since i very sick and if your honor want to make sure of this just ask people you can trust in nothing more to say may god bless you, little Trinidad and the rest of your family, your servant Factora Goytisolo.

Remember your honor that you promised me the letter and when i see how your honor delayed i got into debt but they still not give it me. I not know what to do and if you want me work in the fields and sleep on the ground you tell me that be my reward for toiling i hope and hope you and the Virgin of Charity will send me the letter your servant girl F.G.

Cienfuegos, July 30, 1882

Dearest sir with the deepest sense of sorrow i write to give you the sad news of the loss of your beloved black Cándido, my beloved husband, who passed on to a better life on the 23rd of this month and just as the loss of his likeable character has plunged friends and family into terrible grief i am convinced that you will suffer equally and i beg you to pray for him and to this end i put myself at your disposition and pleasure May God preserve you for many years
Ceferina Goytizolo

Cienfuegos, April 22, 1884

Dear Don Agustín Guaitisolo
My dear friend, I hope this letter find you and all your family enjoying perfect health and that your life is all happiness. Blessed be little Fermina Trina Luisita Josefita may God be with her for a thousand years and i give thanks to your son Agustín for the favors he bestows on me in a misfortune which befell me and from which he, after God, has saved me and please call your servant who would much rather see you than write to you and please answer this letter so i may kiss it in place of yourself who is not my master but my father.
Vicente Goitisolo

But I am anticipating a reading that took place many years later. During the summer holidays in my early school years, the glorious past of my father's family was centered above all on the rather faded tobacco-colored photographs that were evidence of their magnificence and splendor. The scenes of the refinery—the sugarcane train with the Goytisolo and Montalvo nameplate, its trucks ready for the crop, the sugarhouse and the stores, the dwellings of the blacks, the machine room where the sugar was purified—and Great-grandfather's substantial possessions—the Cienfuegos mansion, the sumptuous Moorish residence he had built on the Barcelona Ensanche, his establishment on the Plaza de Cataluña at present owned by the Bank of the Basque Country were graphic proof of a greatness that even if faded could confer and still did confer on my father an immanent sense of superiority. The bound collection of the old *Ilustración Española y Americana* with its wealth of prints of the period, engravings and daguerreotypes, contributed to the development of my simple-minded fantasies within the parameters of space and history that framed the family epic. The colonial images of Cuba, the rebels' clothes and appearance, mass farewells to the volunteers embarking for Havana are an integral part of a kaleidoscope of memories that are closely linked to my childhood. The myth of Cuban adventure would thus assume for me, until adolescence erupted, the form of a paradise lost, of an Eden glowing before my eyes only to vanish afterwards like a mirage.

In Cuba Grandfather Antonio had married the daughter of rich settlers of Anglo-Menorcan origin: the sweet, pure, distant Catalina Taltavull y Victory whose puberty portrait reveals a melancholy resignation to her fate. After selling off the West Indian heritage, the Taltavulls also settled in Barcelona where my grandmother's brother led a life of ostentatious leisure that was heavily criticized by the parallel branch of the family. In *La Habana para un Infante difunto* Guillermo Cabrera Infante, while listing the inhabitants of the block of flats in which he was brought up by his parents and brother, mentions an Afro-Caribbean called Tartavul who must in reality have been a Taltavull descended from some slave belonging to my other paternal great-grandfather and entered in the register under his master's name as was the custom at the time. These Goytisolos and Taltavulls still exist in Cuba and my brother José Agustín was photographed with one of them who by chance bore the same name as me. In 1962 during a brief visit to the town of Trinidad, near Cienfuegos, I heard of another Juan Goytisolo, famous for his magical arts, who had just taken refuge in the hills apparently fleeing the fury of some husband he had deceived.

It is much easier to reconstruct the Barcelona life of my Basque-Cuban family: one can add to Grandfather Antonio's well-organized documents and letters the decanted memories of the peaceful summertime reminiscences of my father, his brother Leopoldo, and sister Catalina in the house in Torrentbó. From their endless gossip in the garden or on the verandah, I know that my great-aunt Trina, a formidable mustachioed

Catholic spinster, who looked like a guardsman according to Leopoldo, lived surrounded by a small band of curates and canons. They accompanied her in her life of leisure and benefited from her generous charity. In their decorative lapdog role, they would come to her society gatherings, give her an arm when she crossed the street and obsequiously hold her sunshade. In this way, Uncle jokingly concluded, these pious leeches inherited all her wealth when she died. Aunt Catalina would pretend not to hear his comments and, stretched out on her eternal chaise longue, would mumble and count her rosary beads. The useless, extravagant life of Great-uncle Juan Taltavull was also the object of much comment and speculation: on one occasion in a typical fit of megalomania he had reserved a special train for his guests in order to entertain them in his luxurious mansion in Caldetas. He and Aunt Angeles had lived a leisurely life on their income and, as this diminished, they gradually sold off their property until they reached the uncomfortable, if not desperate, state in which I met them: imprisoned in a huge elegant flat on the Rambla de Cataluña, incapable of sustaining the extravagant follies to which, in their misfortune, they had become accustomed. Both died after the war and I only met two of their four children: Aunt Mercedes and a male, Juanito, who followed in his father's erring footsteps to the shame and scandal of his family. In the dining room at Torrentbó hung a child portrait of Great-uncle Juan ridiculously dressed in a tight jacket and dark underpants, seated on a kind of red stool or bench: his furtive, scowling expression, the solemnity and effort on his face, the suspicious nervousness of his position could lead an evil-minded observer to suppose that the artist had caught him in the humble act of defecation.

The figure of Grandmother—parallel and symmetrical in the unchanging order of pictures that decorated the room—in no way resembled him. Catalina Taltavull reveals the image of a gentle, delicate adolescent girl, condemned by the patriarchal code of the society in which she lived to the shadowy existence of a faithful, obedient partner, the victim of a relentless succession of births that would prematurely destroy her life. Grandfather Antonio made her pregnant with great regularity and she left him ten heirs, both male and female, when she died in childbirth at the age of thirty-seven. As a widower, her husband devoted himself with Christian resignation to the careful management of his wealth and the strict upbringing of his children. While his brother Agustín took over the patrimony in Cuba and sold off the Cruces refinery, which was costly and unproductive after the great political and economic changes wrought by the independence struggle and the North American invasion, he spent his time maintaining an elevated social position against the gradual erosion of time and the changes in his fortunes, since he lacked his father's drive and infallible business sense. A large part of the correspondence at the beginning of the century is taken up by relations with Cuba. One letter from his lawyers just after the end of the war with the United States gives a revealing insight into the state of mind of one segment of the wealthy classes after the shock of Spain's defeat and the threat of radical revolution led by the rebels: "even when the country is being slowly rebuilt and there are still many hotheads talking of machetes and gunfire and terrifying children, the positive fact remains that the country is advancing. Large companies are changing hands every day and foreign money will soon revive life and well-being in the fields of Cuba watered by so much blood and tears. Whatever the future of the country politically speaking, if the Americans intervene one way or the other in its destiny, it will prosper."

Although the exchange of letters with Cuba becomes infrequent after the division of property between the two brothers, the documents concerning Spanish life still present considerable interest. They allow us to recreate the daily existence of a wealthy, conservative, rigidly pious émigré back from South America. His behavior, feelings, and ideas fill me and have always filled me with deep antipathy. His proverbial miserliness—vouchsafed by all who knew him—allowed only one exception and that was in the sphere of religion. When Uncle Leopoldo commented that he preferred to spend his money on parties and mistresses like Uncle Juan Taltavull to ruining himself as "others" did for love of the Church, the dart was clearly aimed at this wasted largesse. Such exceptional generosity was not altogether disinterested: like a good merchant's son, he pursued a rate of profit that if not immediate and tangible was at least metaphysical. In payment for his faithful, assiduous service to the ecclesiastical cause, Pope Leon XIII had deigned to grant a plenary indulgence *in articulo mortis* to him, his relatives, and descendents for three generations. The certificate bearing his photograph, stamp, and signature gleamed pompously from its frame on the wall at Torrentbó. Although one can echo my uncle's rather pedestrian view that absolution of sins, whose benign cloak protected me (whatever my crimes) from the punishment of hell, must have cost him a small fortune, the tremendous rewards of eternity were infinitely more worthwhile to a believer like my grandfather. To secure eternal happiness for oneself and for one's family assumed the proportions of a highly profitable investment. The rigidities of a favorable social system were extended beyond the present like the paradise dreamt of by Egyptian nobles buried in the Valley of the Dead, whose hypogea contain the most beautiful drawings of the life of plenty—flowing with food, drink, servants, and offerings—that awaits them when they depart from this world. To reproach him for such foresight—a real insurance policy against death for himself and his family—would be otiose and unseemly and a shocking example of ingratitude.

Grandfather's severe, haughty character, his sad life as a widower, the insistence with which he submitted his sons and daughters to the rigors of a harsh, religious education are clear from his correspondence with them during their years as boarders with the Jesuits or nuns of the Sacred Heart. The religious manuals of the time, which were compulsory reading for my aunts and uncles during their summer holidays, reflect a curious Manichaean conception of the world divided between God and evil, much closer to Genesis than to the Gospels, and are far more revealing than any analysis of the ultramontane thought of our ruling classes during the Restoration. A much-handled copy of a *Prayers to St. Joseph*, which I just happen to have with me as I write these lines, meticulously gathers together a series of miracles in which Divine Justice fulminates indiscriminately against freethinkers, blasphemers, trade unionists, Republicans, masturbators, and enemies of the Pope: "In one town there was an example of Heaven taking revenge. At about midday the priest was taking Holy Communion to a sick man. After leaving the church he walked in front of an inn where there were three men seated at a table. Two got up and took their hats off as they saw the most holy sacrament. The third man, rather than imitating them, began to mock them, and, as an example of his courage and wit, he blasphemed horribly against Jesus Christ and the Virgin Mary. Hardly had the wretched man uttered his blasphemy than he fell unconscious to the ground in the presence of his terrified companions. A doctor was called, so was the parish priest, but all to no avail: on three separate occasions the priest came to confess the dying man, but always in vain. That blasphemy was his last word on earth. He shook with horrible convulsions for ten hours; delirious, he cut his tongue with his own teeth and then expired. ... Another individual who was very fond of reading immoral newspapers saw his daughter, dressed in white about to go to a neighboring village where the bishop was administering the sacrament of Confirmation; flew into such a rage that he tore off her veil, snatched away the bouquet she was carrying and shut her up in a room. After a few days a wild horse ran through the village without hurting anyone, went in the thoughtless father's house, knocked him down, and stamped on him till he was dead."

A man of order worried by the convulsions that shook Barcelona on the eve of the *Semana Trágica*, my grandfather enthusiastically supported the repressive policies of Antonio Maura against the agitators and revolutionaries who dared to disturb the social order. I recently found among his papers a letter, dated 1 February 1904, on the official stationery of the President of the Council of Ministers in response to my grandfather's of which there is unfortunately no copy. Maura thanked him sincerely for his kind support: "From the growing number of letters of encouragement which I receive daily from people of all social classes, I can see that upright moral public opinion is gaining ground and this spurs me on to finish the work I have begun." This unholy exchange of opinions between my grandfather and the grandfather of my friend, Jorge Semprún—as I said to him when I shared this amusing find with him—would perhaps have been interpreted by Santiago Carrillo, the former general secretary of the Spanish Communist Party, if he had known of it when Semprún broke with the Party and I unwittingly became involved through a letter I published in *L'Express*, as a distant antecedent of our evil alliance aimed at undermining the unity of the organization and the morale of its members. This surprising link between the two grandfathers—seen after an interval of almost eighty years from the privileged vantage point of our different political experience—strikes me as one of those chance events in history that often lead people to believe in the presence behind the scenes of a sly, mocking genius skilled in the art of paradox and the subtle use of irony.

In the second decade of the century the correspondence decreased in size till it dried up completely. Grandfather's final years in his mansion on calle Mallorca are thus lost to the realms of conjecture and gossip: the university studies of his elder sons, marriages, summer holidays in Tor-rentbó, the slow, implacable decline from wealthy patrician to greedy, mean financier, reduced by the natural inertia of life to an empty, dec-orative existence. The date of his death coincided with the betrothal of my father and apparently delayed for a few months the celebration of the wedding. The classic family cycle of success, splendor, and decline, already evident in his old age, must have filled him with bitterness and anxiety. The sharing out of his still considerable fortune among his ten sons and daughters, and their lack of ambition and fighting spirit, augured a dif-ficult period of uncertainty in an era characterized by social mobility and political upheavals. When the bond that held them together disappeared, his heirs would quickly disperse: their coexistence in the anachronistic mansion, already dwarfed by the surrounding flashy apartment blocks of the Ensanche, would soon become expensive and useless. While some married and set up homes, others, like Leopoldo, Luis, and Montserrat, sought out pleasant modern flats suited to their tastes and needs. The Moorish villa was sold and soon disappeared under the demolition gang's hammers, swept away by the wave of property speculation in those years that would change forever the peaceful, romantic appearance of the city.

If any of my aunts and uncles played an important role in my child-hood, most of them quickly disappeared or appeared fleetingly in the shadows like a group of bit-actors. My memories of Aunt Rosario, her husband, and her children are almost entirely bound up with my first experience of life, when their family and ours lived as refugees in the village of Viladrau during the war. I have a hazy picture of Aunt María, a widow with seven children: a visit with my mother to a rather Gaudí-style house in calle Dominicos in the upper reaches of Bonanova. I never

met Aunt Magdalena: sick and neurotic, because of her protracted suffering, she had got addicted to drugs and died in a clinic when I was a
child. Her brothers and sisters would avoid mentioning her and all I know
about her I learned indirectly or in whispered conversations. I once discovered in Torrentbó a little book of hers much underlined in pencil: its
title, *The Deceptions of Morphine*, suggests that it was recommended to her
by a doctor during one of her cures. The work, which was supposed to
warn of the dangers of drug abuse, included the "divine" Marquis de Sade
in a strange list of famous addicts: so this first mention of the creator of
Justine and Juliette reached me through that pseudomedical prose riddled
with lies and errors. It had the predictable result of arousing in me a
strong desire to get to know his life and work, which were portrayed with
such unhealthy fascination by the horrified propagandist. Uncle Joaquín,
who qualified as a doctor like Leopoldo, emigrated to Argentina before I
was born, after his marriage had been roundly condemned by our family
because of his wife's humble origins. Once there he devoted himself with
sudden, unsuspected energy to an enormous cattle-farming enterprise
until he made a fortune that elevated his economic status well above his
brothers' and sisters'. The hardships of civil war and the shortages in the
Republican zone supplied him with a pleasant opportunity to remove the
stain on the family honor with regular shipments of food supplies to his
father, brothers, and sisters who received them like water in the desert. He
was given a hero's welcome when he, Aunt María, and our cousins arrived
in the port of Barcelona in the late forties. The whole family came to
embrace the ex-black sheep and my father, forgetting his active role in
dispatching him to Patagonia, held him up as a paragon of virtue, an
example to be followed. While he and his brothers struggled as best they
could through the hard times of postwar Spain and the decline in their
fortunes, the reviled Joaquín emerged strengthened from the test, an
object of respect and admiration. My father, whose obsession with the
dangers of Communism at times bordered on the pathological, encouraged us to make our fortunes far from Europe, learning from the
experience and advice of Great-grandfather's worthy rival in the quest for
glory and adventure. Uncle Joaquín and his wife took only moderate
pleasure from their revenge and overwhelmed us all with their affection
and simplicity.

Grandfather Antonio's younger offspring, Ignacio and Montserrat, also
made sporadic appearances in my childhood. Ignacio was an industrial
engineer and inventor of patented improvements to the railway system.
During the war he had become a passionate supporter of Franco and had
heated discussions with Leopoldo when the latter forecast the inevitable
defeat of the Germans after the battle of Stalingrad. Montserrat belonged
to an entirely different world from that of her brothers: with neither

mother nor father, she adopted an independent, carefree style of life, the very opposite of the puritanical piety that had dominated her upbringing. She smoked, drank, was a pioneer of the Charleston, split skirts, and sunbathing before marrying, in her thirties, one Federico Esteve with whom she settled in Majorca before the civil war. I remember them visiting the house in Pablo Alcover to ask my father (in his capacity as elder brother) for permission to marry. The marriage turned out to be very unhappy and, after years of suffering and humiliation, finally led to her ruin.

I will write later about Uncles Leopoldo and Luis and about Aunt Catalina: all three played their part in my life's development. The rest of the paternal stock—twenty or so cousins who included or include a Salesian father, an Opus Dei worthy, a missionary in Chad, and a Marxist worker-priest—will also emerge in these pages as required by the narration of the facts. While the idea of the family has for years ceased to have any meaning for me, the strangeness of our surname and a purely atavistic reflex action can explain my mania for consulting the telephone directories of the cities I visit in the vague hope of happening upon a remote member of the clan. However, except for Mexico City and New York, I have never discovered any trace of distant relatives by this means. My connection with the Goytisolos, beyond the circle of my brothers and sister, has in the last decades been a product of chance: in the first place, there was a strange non-meeting with a Madame of my name in a Marrakesh hotel because of a telegram dated in Bordeaux from this most mysterious lady cancelling her and her companion's reservations on the same day as I arrived; this caused understandable confusion and the incredulous comment of the hotel manager convinced that the message was mine and that I was pulling his leg—"vous ne me ferez pas croire tout de même, Monsieur, qu'un nom pareil court les rues!" There was the equally unlikely but real, tangible poster advertising a Goitisolo brandy displayed, to my amazement, in a window in the Great Bazaar of Istanbul, by a Turkish trader who was a fan of Atlético Bilbao and an admirer of all things Basque. As I do not suffer from hallucinations and had not smoked kef, I only had to stand for a few seconds with my nose pressed against the shop window set out with Basque national flags before I was convinced that it was true.

IMPERCEPTIBLY, THE SIGNS *accumulate. Scattered insidiously, treacherously, at irregular intervals, as if spaced out deliberately to make it difficult for you to read them. Not just the physical deterioration you hardly notice in daily life, the greater efforts required in all the routines and petty rituals, not even the anger and surprise, the instinctive rebellion—quickly suppressed—when you are suddenly confronted with a faded photograph from your youth: rather the brutal blow that strikes, at a carefree, happy moment, smashing through plans and calculations, and delivers you without defenses to awareness of inevitable decrepitude.*

You are driving, for instance, at daybreak through a quiet, luminous countryside, along a peaceful, almost deserted side road and have forgotten, in fact, as you later discover, that it is Friday the thirteenth and that you are also in French département *thirteen: all of which anyone remotely superstitious could interpret, albeit mistakenly, as an act of provocation. You brake at the stop sign by the junction with the main Saint Rémy-Tarascon road in response to a call from a middle-aged individual carrying a battered old suitcase on the other side of the crossroads: he wants a lift to a nearby town and once you realize it's on your route, you cross the road, after a brief exchange of words, forgetting even to look left, and suddenly hear a violent screech of brakes, seconds before the crash reduces your car to a sad heap of scrap metal. You stagger out of your car, confront the truck driver's waxen face, contorted by fear, an innocent bearer of a warning from destiny and Arab into the bargain. You say a few soothing words to him in his own language and then listen as he stammers out—not at all surprised by the fact that this seemingly injured European speaks his language—a half-whispered recitation of the* Kulchi fi yid Allah *and other respectful formulas from the Scriptures interwoven with exclamations of thanksgiving. An unlikely dialogue on the glass-strewn road. You don't yet feel any pain from the thumbnail that is hanging off, as you notice the indirect cause of the accident running off at top speed, suitcase on shoulder, and the shopkeeper at the crossroads lets you telephone the friend with whom you were staying and then pockets the price of the call without a murmur. Only confusion at your presence in this hazy, ghostly world, an object of the pity or idle chatter of the inevitable spectators, next to the aged, skinny figure of the helpless Moorish fruit-transporter who, after the shock, is also striving to establish the simple facts of the case—what damage, whose responsibility, the need to inform his boss, while you await the arrival of the police.*

Or fifteen months later in the course of a sentimental journey to a region you have written about, after visiting the lonely, rural landscape, the setting for the plot of one of your novels, returning to the spot as the guilty man always revisits the scene of his crime, engulfed by a noisy, high-spirited throng of fans who have come from every corner of the province to witness, like you, the cruel, expiatory ceremony of the penning of the bulls. You perch on the wooden barrier in the lower square in Elche de la Sierra, through which the beasts will soon pound with their retinue of oxen and farmhands to a chorus of shouts and exploding fireworks, running away, attacking, climbing, delighting, and exciting the motley crowd; you move away from the human swarm, walk on up the street with your friends behind the rear guard, toward the parish church, trying to predict from the screams and hastily beaten retreats when the horns will come back from the square, the fenced-off square where the bulls will be fought and executed hours afterward in the bloody, collective ritual: after a long wait, you go down a side street that has been barricaded off, deaf to the warnings of your friend from Albacete who knows the lay of the land better than you—the length of the walk to the church, the lack of refuge points and barriers over which to climb in case of dire necessity—intent on reaching the stockade where the bulls are kept: you get to the opening onto the square and from the gap in the upright, wooden palisade, assess the difficulty of clambering in without drawing the attention of one of the animals, which already excited by the exploding firecrackers and the noise of sticks and clubs is pawing the ground, gazing stubbornly at the exit, anxious to attack, break through, and take revenge on the wily gang of boys who mock and mistreat it; you look for a safe place on your left as the beast lowers its head, charges quickly at the opening in the fence, and thunders past the farmhands, you hear the cries of terror when it catches one of them in full flight, throws him on the floor, gouges the body with its horns, and then abandons him for dead, facedown, and continues its outraged chase; again you hear the uproar announcing the second bull and notice your neighbors sneak away and climb up the barricades on the right, hauled up by the people above them; for a second time, you cling rashly to the left corner, trapped between a wall and the vertical logs of the barricade; suddenly you realize that the bull has crossed the opening and instead of moving forward to attack those speeding off into the distance, it has turned round and is squaring up to you, barely two meters away; it stares at you for endless moments, just time for you to consider calmly, in pure amazement, the unthinkable situation you are in: your back to the corner, no way of getting over the barricades, aware of the absurdity of the scene, in suspense, your mind in a thick fog of disbelief; you try slowly to move toward the gate, convinced it is impossible this is really happening to you, that you are the protagonist in some sort of daydream, the usual, nightly, opaque, exhausting, persistent nightmare; yet you feel the blow from its head that knocks you down, drags you on your face across the ground; all notions of time and place disappear, seconds, unimaginable seconds, no panic, no pain, no anxiety, only, only, only an overwhelming sense of unreality; you then hear a friendly cry, your name howled rather than shouted out, moments before anonymous hands pull you up by your arms, sit you up, rescue you; as you look up, you can see Abdelhadi between the horns of the bull, hoisted up like an empty carton by the furious beast, about to be flung backward by a toss of its head until, whipped by youths after a brief, spectacular fall to the ground, the animal gets up, forgets your savior, half turns and races, enraged, after the gang. There is movement, concern, belated, untimely offers of help from those huddled around you and Abdelhadi; you are almost flown through the air to the nearby first-aid post, both wanting with the wounded pride of someone who has just tripped in public to stop people from taking pity, to be removed as quickly as possible from their curious gaze; you grasp at once, far from the surrounding bustle, the grotesque, comic twist of fortune that has hit you on exactly the same day as a wretched spur-of-the-moment torero died impaled on a bull's horns in the ring at Albacete in front of millions of future televiewers; you are determined to hide this humiliation from Monique, especially from her, before it is consumed, digested, exorcised, days, weeks, months, or years later, thanks to that slow, gradual, internal process leading secretly to the act of writing; you are identified, treated, your bumps and bruises disinfected with Mercurochrome and cotton and like sleepwalkers acknowledge the admiring homage of a corporal in the Civil Guard, witness to the accident, who slaps Abdelhadi on the shoulder several times, tries in vain to communicate with him, and then turns to you and clumsily formulates his compliment: your friend, though an Arab, is noble and brave.

Just like a frustrated mother after an unwelcome miscarriage wishes to overcome her trauma and impatiently searches for a suitable opportunity to become pregnant again, you suddenly feel in the bedroom where you are recovering from the blow the violent urge to write rise up after months of sterility, the urgency and need to write, express yourself, not to allow all that you love, your past experience, emotions, what you are and have been, to disappear with you, determination to fight tooth and claw against oblivion, that black abyss with open jaws that lies in wait, you well know, around any corner, to capture the precious gift of life, the human miracle, the reluctant concessions of existence and reality, you delight in your five senses' confirmation that the daily portent is being extended, that a chance postponement allows you to be yourself, sudden, repeated floods of memories, flashes in the pan, snapshots, will-o'-the-wisps, an intoxication with seeing, touching, smelling, stroking, evoking the past, History, histories, the linking of facts, imponderables, circumstances that have changed you into this misused body stretched out on your back on the bed in the narrow room where you are staying, a moment relived now almost two years later at the touch of a pen when you begin to order your impressions and feelings, shape them on the blank page, abridged reminiscences, like waves breaking, subject to your wandering memory, imperative to tell others and yourself what you were and are not, whom you might have been and have not become, to clarify, correct, complete the reality elaborated in your successive fictions, the single book, the Book you have been creating and re-creating for twenty years and as you invariably note, at the end of each of its chapters, that you still have not written.

THE SHADOWS AND darkness on my mother's side are even deeper. Grandfather Ricardo rarely mentioned them and Grandmother Marta's confidences, heard as a child, have largely been erased from my memory. I know for certain that my great-great-grandmother was Andalusian, was called doña María Mendoza and wrote a novel, *The Silver Bars*, inspired by the stories of Sir Walter Scott: we kept a copy of the book bound in red in the house on calle Pablo Alcover but my curiosity never tempted me to read it. There was also a portrait of her, a lady of severe, majestic appearance, although infected by the gift or insane desire to write. Novel and portrait disappeared when my father died or perhaps before, victims of the confusion of those years; furniture and belongings were moved from the house and the family scattered everywhere. The vestiges of the past were annoying interferences in my youth and it was only later that I thought again about that possible, distant, genetic transmitter of the literary vocation that would mark my life and my brothers'. Who was she, what was she like, why did she write? And other such questions, unanswered and lost in the limbo of oblivion.

When I was three or four I did see my great-grandmother, her daughter-in-law, in her mansion in Pedralbes: she was dressed in mourning and wore yellowish, perhaps dyed, ringlets above her ears. Her name was Pastor, she came from military stock and had been widowed by José María Vives y Mendoza, a notary with humanist leanings. This great-grandfather possessed a historical-military library, some volumes of which—Latin dictionaries, an illustrated chronicle of the *almogávares*—ended up in our house. Grandmother Marta used to tell us stories from the career and service record of members of the family, and describe her feelings as a child when the cornet sounded and the guard formed to welcome their arrival at the barracks. Her family's legalistic, military traditions had, however, very little in common with the anomalous, rebellious, Catalan nationalist attitudes of her brother, the poet and translator Ramón Vives Pastor. My great-uncle Ramón, as I indirectly discovered much later, had led a bohemian existence in his youth, dedicated to literature, dandyism, and dissipation. Contemporary accounts present him as a skeptical, passionate character: his Catalan version of the *Rubáiyát* of Omar Khayyám is dedicated to his lover, the Irish Bertha St. George, *filla tristoia i dolça d'aquella verda Erin, esclava, com ma terra, d'una llei opressora*. The translation, based on the one by the French Orientalist and diplomat M. Nicolas had a prologue by Joan Maragall and includes some lines that I used to read with enjoyment through discreet recourse to the dictionary when at the end of my schooling I began to lose my religious faith:

Vaig enviar mon ànima vers el llunyà Invisible
les lletres a l'altra Vida per a que em confegís,
i, poc a poc, a mi va retornar passible,
dient: "Jo soc mon proper Infern i Paradís."

Muller: no vui que preguis per mi. Déu fa son do
sens que se li demani, i els vels del seu perdó
i sa misericordia, inmensos com el mar,
*cobriran, sense veures, els grans pecats d'Omar.**

His hostility to religion and militant nationalism must have caused a scandal even in the liberal, cultivated milieu where he was brought up. Grandmother Marta often spoke of him: the jokes he used to play when they were children, his trip to Geneva where he went in search of a cure for the tuberculosis that would drag him years later to the grave. He had thrown a piece of paper on the ground there, in the middle of the street, and a passerby had reproached his carelessness, unworthy of a civilized country, and invited him in a friendly manner to pick it up. It is one of the few anecdotes I remember and was always accompanied by the comment: the Swiss are very clean and tidy. Some of his books were on the shelves in the bookcase in the hall in Pablo Alcover, in French, Castilian, and Catalan: a beautiful edition of *La regenta* was among them. There was also a pile of folders full of his manuscripts. With the cruel indifference of a child, I had used the blank side of the pages to draw and scribble, so condemning his dramatic works to destruction and to oblivion. When I think now of my action, it surprises me to realize that, even in my unconscious state, I was capable of such a lamentable deed: of dealing a crushing blow to the precious object of his efforts and reducing to ash the testimony and justification of one life. But, incredibly, at home we hadn't been inculcated with the slightest respect toward his writings. Apart from Grandmother's string of family anecdotes, nobody referred to him, from

---

* I sent my soul far to the Invisible
to search out the message from the After-life:
And soon my soul calmly returned
to tell me: "I am my own Heaven and Hell."

Woman: I don't want your prayers. God will
have his way without them, and the power
of his forgiveness and pity, vast like the ocean,
will cover over Omar's great sins and not notice them.

which I deduce an attitude of reproving caution. Those who knew him—
my mother, Aunt Consuelo—had died or kept a prudent silence like
Grandfather. As for my father, I know that he professed a frank, stubborn
antipathy toward him. His Catalan nationalism and bohemianism were in
direct opposition to my father's traditionalist convictions, his sentimental
attachment to things Basque and liking for patriotic values; then there
was the irrational ingredient, the suspicion voiced on several occasions,
times when he was looking for a universal cause for calamities and misfortunes, that Great-uncle Ramón had been the source of the tubercular
meningitis that had killed my brother Antonio at the age of seven, before
I was born. This fact, and his unrestrained dislike for Grandfather Ricardo
for reasons that I will later reveal, explain why his relationship with my
mother's family was at best cold and distant. The work and memory of
Ramón Vives were damaged beyond repair in that domestic atmosphere
traumatized by the disaster of war in years of vertical salutes and imperial
language, attachment to religious norms and eternal essences, a sacrificial
victim of circumstances in which the mere mention of his name was
upsetting, and they were abandoned unprotected to the caprice of an
irresponsible, ignorant child. My unhappy contribution to his second
death fills me today with sadness and embarrassment. Little, very little,
survives of the work of this rebel thrust by an untimely birth into a
society traditionally hard on dissidents and whose harsh therapy in times
of crisis would find an unfortunate complicity within the heart of his own
family. His *Notes poètiques*, subtitled *Poesia és llibertad*, printed at the
beginning of the century, have never reached my hands and I know
nothing about them apart from the odd passing reference by his nephew,
my mother's first cousin, Professor Josep Calsamiglia. In spite of that, the
few details I have to construct his history and character convert him into
one of the few ancestors with whom I feel affinity and a moral closeness
beyond the fortuitous, uncertain ties of blood, an affinity stained in his
case with remorse and melancholy. The writing destroyed and torn to
shreds by me as a child has perhaps unconsciously infected me and insidiously emerged in all I have written and write. Whether true or not, the
idea of that possible transmigration consoles me for my unredeemable
action, which it transforms into a rebirth if not a gentle form of afterlife.

The same aura of mystery envelops the life and personality of my Aunt
Consuelo. My mother's younger sister was also blessed with a luminous
beauty; her expression, captured in a number of photos, reveals a defenseless fragility barely disguised as modesty and charm. She was fond of the
violin and had lessons in interpretation until she could play tunefully. She
wrote a delicate poem on Maurice Ravel, which was published in the
magazine *Mirador* and jealously guarded by Grandfather among his
papers. Her records of Bach, Mozart, Schubert, Brahms, Debussy, pre-

served in an album that came to us after the war, put me in contact for the first time with the peaceful realm of music; but, although she died when I was nine years old, I never got to see her. Before I was born, she had married the lawyer Eusebio Borrell and was widowed without children. This short-lived marriage and the nature of the disease that finished off her husband were never mentioned in the family circle. A portrait of the couple, taken in front of one of the monuments of the first Universal Exhibition, I'm not sure whether on the paseo de San Juan or in the Ciudadela Park, reveals him as one of those individuals with bland, shrinking features who, for some mysterious reason, are so plentiful in the ranks of the petty bourgeoisie of Barcelona. As a result of his premature death, Aunt Consuelo had gradually lost her sanity. When I began to open my eyes and notice what was happening around me, she never came to our house and was probably already confined to a nursing home. During the civil war, her parents took her into the flat where they sought refuge after the militia requisitioned the Pablo Alcover mansion. There, the bombing raids of Franco's planes, sirens, terror, shortages swept away her last traces of lucidity. After the conflict, she was shut up again and died soon afterward of an illness the nature of which I am ignorant. I can only remember her funeral, which I attended with my brothers and sister, wearing a black arm band. Although Uncle Eusebio's family lived in the same district of Bonanova where we were brought up, and we passed his house daily—a dark, damp villa at the top of calle Anglí—on our way to the Jesuit school, for some unknown reason we had no contact with them. My grandparents referred to the other mother-in-law by the nickname of Shorty and the pejorative character of the term added to this strange distancing suggests that some bitter, unresolved contention existed between the two families. Were there also political motives, linked to possible Catalan leanings or the possibility, suggested by my father, that Uncle Eusebio had passed on to his wife some shameful, incurable disease? Again as in the case of Ramón Vives, the erosion of time and death of contemporaries prevent any certain answer. When I read history books, the intrepid sureness with which their authors establish what happened thousands of years ago produces in me an insuperable sensation of incredulity. How is it possible to reconstitute a remote past if even the most recent past appears to be sown with doubts and uncertainties? The darkness over the destiny of a good part of my family illustrates perfectly to me our powerlessness to discover and exhume after a few years the tangible reality of what happened.

Grandfather Ricardo's branch of the family offers less variety and melodrama: originating apparently from the Ampurdán, it includes among its members the lawyer and publicist Gay de Montellá, the author of a number of works on legal matters. Who his parents were or what they did is a memory he took with him to the grave. Grandfather had two brothers, Víctor and Laureano, whom I got to know before the war: they dressed with austere elegance and ceremoniously took off their hats as they entered the house. I couldn't say, however, exactly when they died: both left family, and Aunt Lola, the widow of one of them, used to visit us with her offspring in the forties. She was a baroque lady covered in cosmetics, whose figure is associated in my memory with a world of porcelain jugs and tasselled lampshades. Her children and nephews and nieces bore their difficult, precarious existence with dignity: but social decline hurt their pride and good manners. Grandfather was in their eyes the wealthy man of the family but, so far as I understand, they rigorously observed the rule against complaining or testing out his very doubtful feelings of generosity. These distant relatives gradually deserted the family sphere: the last time I saw them at home, at the end of my school career, was when they came to say hello on the pretext of the departure of one of them to seek his fortune in the kinder, more prosperous land of Venezuela.

The gradual, definitive eclipse of my mother's side was especially important for my brothers and me because of our future status as writers. To answer the question so often repeated in recent years of why don't we write in Catalan, I feel compelled to spell out the circumstances in which our life as a family developed. While grandparents Marta and Ricardo spoke that language to each other, they addressed us in Spanish on the express instructions of my father. Although Grandmother had taught us some nursery rhymes and often mixed up expressions and phrases from both languages, at home—with my father and Eulalia—and at school—in class and with friends—we only used Spanish, an impoverished, diluted Castilian as I later discovered, when I extended the circle of my acquaintances and friendships beyond the insipid, conventional Barcelona bourgeoisie. Under strong pressure during the several years in which the "language of the Empire" had by decree to be cultivated, Catalan survived with difficulty in the intimacy of people's homes. A fruit of this would be my meagre knowledge of the language beyond the polite formulas, greetings, and swear words that I learned every summer from the Torrentbó peasants. Father, from the nirvana of his anti-Catalan phobia, would delight in contrasting the lineage, distinction, and euphony of the language of Castile—the resonant sonority of its toponomy—Madrigal de las Altas Torres, Herrera del Duque, Motilla del Palancar—with the plebeian coarseness of some grotesquely pronounced Tarrasas, Mollets, or Hostafrancs in order to round off his most singular course in comparative etymology and phonetics with the obligatory reference to the mysterious beauty of the term *luciérnaga* as opposed to the miserable obscenity of the local *cuca de llum*. For one reason or another, the truth is that my mother tongue—vanished forever with my mother—became with her death deeply alien to me: a language within which I would move uncomfortably and could hardly read fluently until, once I was established in France, I took the trouble to study it in my spare time in order to get to know its works without using a dictionary. Thanks to that effort I can now enjoy reading writers like Foix, Ferrater, or Rodoreda, but after almost thirty years of remoteness everyday common phrases do not spring easily to my lips.

In the present period of "linguistic normalization," my situation—like that of my brothers and a dozen or so friends and writers—is marginal, on the outside, in a double sense. In Madrid we are mistakenly thought of as Catalans, as Alberti is Andalusian, Bergamín is Basque, or Cela is Galician. But our colleagues and compatriots quite rightly do not welcome us into their midst to the extent that our basic activity—writing—links into a language and culture different from the ones they identify with. Spaniards in Madrid and Castilians in Barcelona, our location is ambiguous and contradictory, threatened with being ostracized by both sides and yet enriched through this mutual rejection by the precious gifts of mobility and rootlessness.

As proof, my own case: the inclination toward one or other language by a potentially bifid writer is not the exclusive result of individual free choice but rather the result of a series of social and family conjunctions that are grasped later. The early disappearance of my mother, the conservative, religious Franco-ist milieu in which I was reared, were no doubt essential factors in my insertion into a culture that, fifty years earlier, Uncle Ramón Vives had termed "oppressive." But, more significant than that historical determinism in favor of one of the languages in the field is, in my case, the passionate relationship I developed from the day when, far from Spain and Catalonia, I discovered that it was my true country and the object simultaneously of love and hate. My late passion for Castilian culture and language, already suffered by a series of writers who developed their masterpieces in conflict with them, by dint of bitter inner turmoil, was at once a lustral identity bath and defense mechanism against the emptiness of a lengthy exile. To say that I did not choose the language but that I was chosen by it would be the simplest way of conforming to the truth. The wavering between two cultures and languages is fairly similar to the child or adolescent's sensual and emotional indecision: dark, underlying forces will one day channel his future erotic orientation without his consent. The blind impulse toward the male physical form will thus be as mysterious as the one that will lead him to fall in love forever with a language fit for Quevedo or Góngora. A choice that is all the more meaningful and valuable for being expressed in a forum or meeting of cultures, the clash of which implies ideas of crossbreeding, bastardy, and contingency. Castilian in Catalonia, Frenchified in Spain,

Spanish in France, a Latin in North America, *nesrani* in Morocco, and a Moor everywhere, as a result of my wanderings, I would soon become that rare species of writer not claimed by anybody, alien and opposed to groupings and categories. The family conflict between two cultures was the first indicator, I now think, of a future process of dynamic breaks and tensions that would put me outside the bounds of abstract ideologies, systems, or entities always characterized by their self-sufficiency and circularity. The fruitfulness of all that remains beyond entrenched walls and fields, the vast domain of latent aspirations and silent questions, the fresh, unfinished thinking, the interchange and osmosis of cultures would gradually create the sphere in which my life and writing would develop, on the edge of values and ideas that were castrating rather than sterile, linked to the notions of creed, country, State, doctrine, or civilization. Nowadays, when Hispanic bluster daily reproduces celebrations of our artistic and literary glories in small, medium, or large regions of the land, the silence, alienation, and emptiness that envelop me and several others, far from saddening me, convinces me that the opposition loyalty/root-lessness in relation to language and country of origin is the best indicator of aesthetic and moral value fortunately beyond the reach of the organizer of Homages. Freedom and isolation will be the reward of the creator immersed to his eyebrows in a multiple, frontierless culture, able to migrate as he pleases to the pasture that suits him yet never settling for any. The intimate civil war of my sexuality and language, perhaps the prelude to my literary and phallic orality, was directed underground through the cultural conflict fought by my family. After the death of my mother, the ground was to remain clear, but the victory of Spanish, returning boomerang-like, occurred a good few years after my youthful dedication to writing: it was the work, not of an imagined partheno-genesis of Catalan, but of a temporary but necessary defense against the cunning Gallicist invasion. My stubborn conquest of a language intensely proud of its difference took place then in dialectical opposition to the fertile stimulus of other languages: without this dynamic interrelation with French, English, or Arabic at the rich crossroads of several opposed cultures, I would not have been able to contribute my modest, respectful homage to the Archpriest of Hita in the here and now of Djemaa el Fna.

A WARENESS OF THE *complete inanity of the enterprise: amalgam of your motivation and inability to make up your mind about your aim and would-be destination: a lay substitute for the sacrament of confession?; an unconscious desire to justify yourself?: to make a statement that nobody asks you for?: a statement for whom, from whom?: for you, everybody else, your friends, enemies?: the wish to make yourself better understood?: to awaken feelings of affection or pity?: to feel yourself accompanied by future readers?; to struggle against the oblivion of time?; purely and simply an exhibitionist impulse?: impossible to answer these questions and yet attack the task, the daily torture of confronting the page, putting your life on the drawing board, the unmentionable material reality of your body, not the one hidden by masks and disguises in daily ritual farce, projection of a false image aimed at the gallery, inopportune guest who usurps your voice and contracts it in the endless muttering of a ventriloquist, no, the other one, which within hours, days, weeks, scared, bent, on its knees, defenseless like a fetus, will repeat the sucking gestures and mannerisms, internal feeding, a polymorph of the distant maternal cloister, the silent, proscribed truth, deprived of the power of speech, that other ego whisked out of the sight of their neighbor or of themselves by those aspiring to the tinsel of fame, spokesmen for future power reason dogma ideology, not daring to bring into public gaze their desires great or small, the misery, disloyalties that litter the sinuous path of their lives with pebbles, competing for a History that excludes and destroys histories, professional swindlers or bemedalled pachyderms, counterfeiters, at any rate, of a past subject to considerations of long-term strategy of petty self-interest, even if it is not submitted, when they take up their pen and strike the official, hieratic pose of their glorious portraits to a merciless lobotomy operation.*

To be distinguished from them, what they leave out, half-truths, two weights and two measures, forgetful memoirs, grotesque hagiographies, inner, private censorship in order to concentrate on what is most painful and difficult to express, what you haven't yet said to anybody, an odiously vile or humiliating memory, the bitterest blow in your life: to find in the internal resistance to laying it bare the moral canon of your writing, that bull's horn that is not simply metaphoric but real, as real as the one that dragged you along during the celebration of the encierros, a metaphor, like those of Don Quixote, lived from within, not wind-mill-giants nor basin-helmets, a total fusion of both levels in the material text, a deliberately accepted risk of being turned over and gored, no external sanction if you miss the mark, only the wounding awareness of your infringing the rules of your personal game, of not being up to the effort required, of throwing in the towel half-way, pitifully unfaithful to yourself and everyone else.

SCENARIO: AN AGED mansion in the Bonanova district, number thirteen calle Raset. A house since demolished, the long, narrow garden of which was terraced down to the Vía Augusta, separated by an enormous ditch from the open stretch of the Sarriá train, between the Muntaner and Ganduxer stations. You remember its appearance because you often ran around there on the way to your school-friend's house: an ugly, ramshackle building, which is also preserved in some family photos taken before you were born. You do not, however, retain any memory of your stay there: according to your calculations, it must have been short, since at the age of three or four you had already moved to the Tres Torres, to number forty-one in a street to be rebaptized in the postwar period with the name of Pablo Alcover.

Time: date of birth was the fifth of January 1931. Although the exact time it happened is recorded on the certificate of baptism, you have forgotten and are not interested in finding out. It probably happened at dusk or well into the night: during your childhood your parents would say that you were a present from the Three Kings of the Orient and you thought you belonged to the day of the Magi until some public document straightened you out years later. As you don't have too much faith in the stars or in their possible influence over our destiny, this lack of precision on the moment you came into the world does not cause you any concern. Your Capricorn character is beyond doubt, and in some popular books on that subject you easily recognized various traits and elements of your character. But, instead of investigating the influence of the planets or giving yourself over to the electronic science of some Astroflash, you prefer to invent, like the Archpriest of Hita, a fantastic ancestor from Venus with the help of Al Biruni or Alí Abenragel. Cured of your father's obsession with distinguished lineages, you find it infinitely more agreeable to manipulate at will the jovial compilations of ancient astrological treatises. Venus-Zuhara, whose cheerful, libidinous patronage would mark with her stamp those born in lands of Islam, would be the best antidote against the obstinacy, self-absorption, and harshness of your official sign and a plausible explanation for the irreducible rigor of your dichotomy.

Prehistory: eventually restored through photographs seen in childhood and, sometimes, later lost from sight. In the first place, the wedding photo: unusual portrait of the couple who twelve years later would procreate you. He's standing up, wearing a morning coat, slim, mustached, incredibly young: no similarity to the sick, worn-out old man you would later know. She's sitting on a sofa, wearing a snow-white veil and bridal gown, caught in the glory of her unfaded beauty. The man's hand resting protectively on her shoulder. A serious, absorbed expression on the woman's face, perhaps distant or removed from the ancestral rite that she was fulfilling.

The wardrobe and mirror behind them both similarly reflect them from a tangent: the aquiline outline of the bridegroom, invested with a certain intellectual air by the light, metallic frame of his spectacles; the soft, gentle silhouette of the betrothed, captured in a pose whose daring spatial harmony we could describe as à la Velázquez were it not for the absence from the picture of the anonymous author of the photograph.

Surprise: the material nature of the love between those two beings, visible in the careful, punctilious trouble with which the portrait-painter, your father, fixes the serene beauty and expression of the eternally mysterious youthful woman, as if, foreseeing her sudden disappearance, he was unconsciously collecting proof of that future existence soon to be swept away.

Blurred images of the Torrentbó terrace, its eucalyptus trees, balustrade, pond with frog-mouthed fountains, the stone bench, the extravagant, rustic pavilion. Her, always her, still her, in half boots, long loose skirt, summer bodice and blouse, her carefully gathered-up honey-colored hair.

Sometimes, Pedralbes, with Aunt Consuelo in the enormous garden of orange trees or on the tennis court, radiant, confident, spontaneous, with a racquet in her hand, happy and windswept.

Later: the short-lived family trinity.

Antonio, the firstborn, thus baptized in Grandfather's honor, alone or with her, at the age of six or seven, in his blue-and-white sailor-suit, looking as if he has received Communion, just a bit proud and arrogant and, at a distance, fragile, awkward, unreal, retrospectively pathetic.

Enlargements dispersed by the monotony of time, framed in purple or grey card: images of the twenties, hoops, bicycles, toys, mutual affection, smiles, derisory testimony of the suddenly incomplete trio.

First experience of grief, to which your parents' loss of affection for and rejection of the loving practice of photography no doubt date back.

T HE OPAQUE LIMBO *of childhood: tunnel darkness broken momentarily by patches of light, fleeting images: fixed by chance in a tender, adaptable mind or simply a product of some later, now forgotten process?: an irregular, slow succession of black-and-white and color pictures painfully rescued from the mists of my dreams and then projected by a magic lantern: difficult to link them together in the right order, insert them in the place they happened and endow them with possible meaning: seminal nucleus of future memories or a passing impression captured in shadows?: avoiding, above all, tricks and traps, anachronisms that lie in wait, the temptation of a palimpsest interpretation: merely sifting the sparks of light, the voltaic arc created by the break in the electric circuit, picking them out of the shapeless, porous night caught in the bubble of their modest splendor.*

A parallel between the scarcity of the first images that you retain and your experience on the night when you absorbed an enormous dose of majoon dissolved in a glass of mint tea: sitting in a café by the fortress in Tangier, surrounded on your long trip by soothing cardplayers and the becalming aroma of kef while a ridiculous television broadcast a muted version of the political-cum-bullfighting disquisitions of an overweight announcer from your species. Nothing at the beginning except for waves, currents, rushes to the brain that either intermittently or in syncopation crossed its yielding surface, gently unifying it, as if under the burning breath of the sirocco. Awareness of the importance of the moment, the palpable material nature of the place, your central presence in the weft. Then, suddenly, a rapid, almost hurtling succession of literary images: similes, tropes, daring verse, dazzling, airborne metaphors, light feathery levitation, slow gliding, dizziness, furious flights. An ecstasy of concepts, sinuous baroque, captivating phrases, coiled up snakes: the creative paroxysm of someone who has scaled the peaks of poetic art but realizes the avaricious precariousness of his gifts. Then the metaphors overlap, rest on each other, combine with maddening rapidity, flow liquid through your fingers, rival Góngora's light subtlety: they appear, gleam, burst, mock your efforts at retaining them, drag you along with them tied to their tail. Attempts to set buoys, scatter pebbles in that feverish flux, gradually becoming frenetic, provoke only verbal collisions, semantic fractures, sudden derailings. Powerless, you will see how the brilliant display of words vanishes like a firework. Nothing, absolutely nothing, remains of it: sparkles, verses, genial inventions rush into oblivion. Your brain is present at the procession and constant replacing on its murky surface of dozens of miraculously forged masterpieces and, just like those overrefined dreams that hardly leave a tattered web when you wake up, so your fleeting control of the creative mechanism like a child's distant awareness of the adult world is reduced to a few words and images emptied of all meaning, mere indicators of a previous chain, now lost. The floating names of Góngora and Borges, rising up like small islands after an endless night beset by anguish and exultation; the childish remnants and snapshots, similarly free from context and seam, must be, in both cases, the sad vestige of impressions and facts whose extreme poverty completely rules out any attempt at interpretation.

I MAGES FILTERED AS if through a skylight: you are sitting in the dark on the floor of a room, possibly under the dining room table, and, from your hiding place, you look at the adults moving about and talking in the kitchen, clearly visible, unaware of this future description of the scene and the tiny presence of an observer. The memory could perhaps relate to your first home in calle Raset or, more likely, to some family visit to Great-grandmother in her Pedralbes villa.

Summer holidays in Llansá: while he is swimming toward the small island or headland opposite, she sits on the beach reading a book or newspaper. You are playing with your younger brothers, you make sandpies and castles, you join in a neighbor's frustrated attempts to get going a kind of float that he has invented but it lets in water everywhere and finally capsizes. Neighbors' conversations around your mother: Mr. and Mrs. Isern, Pascualín Maisterra's parents, and, as you will discover later in Mexico, the family of Ramón Xirau, the writer.

Trips in the buggy with Ciscu as far as the Font de Gat in Pedralbes. Visits to the grandparents, Marta and Ricardo, in their house in the nearby calle Doctor Roux. The exact distribution of the rooms in your memory, the jagged layout of the garden. Sometimes you sleep there and, when they take you to see your mother, who has just fallen ill with dropsy, you are told you have got a baby brother. You go into the room where the baby is sleeping and pinch him, unsure whether you are curious or envious, you want to be certain, you say, that "he's real."

You have learned how to feel yourself and, when alone, you usually slip your fingers along your groin and caress your penis. One day your mother catches you, gently moves your hand and tells you you shouldn't do it. The wet nurse feeds Luis and, often, if you bother her, she laughs, squeezes her breast and splashes you with her milk. One day, José Agustín and Marta dress you up in a big skirt and you enter the dining room in Pablo Alcover in the disguise; your father's reaction is unexpected and energetic: he pulls the skirt off you and smacks the guilty parties. Someone said you might die through lack of air. The idea terrifies you and for a few moments you take deep breaths in and out so as not to risk the same unhappy fate as Antonio. When you go to bed, you gasp and pray to the holy Guardian Angel asking him to protect you.

Your father has bought a grey DKW and is learning to drive in the Tres Torres district. His instructor tells him to pull the grey knob up and down and Marta and José Agustín laugh in the backseat: take your nob out, put it back in. You go to the convent run by nuns of St. Teresa's Order in calle Ganduxer built by Gaudí: Mother Delfina gives you sweets and, on the way home, maids and the girls accompanying the infants talk about Paquita Marín: a very beautiful girl, in a higher form at the school, who sings *Rocío*, flirts with the boys, uses powder and lipstick. Expressions of admiration and horror. Someone asks you if you want to be her boyfriend and you proudly say yes please.

Friends of the house: Ciscu and his buggy; Paquita the dressmaker; Miss María Boi. Family conversation about the English working week, the war in Abyssinia, Gardel's tangos. As you are being fussy over your food, your father puts you on a fruit diet: after the first minutes of euphoria, you are in tears demanding the previous diet. One day you go to Torrentbó in the DKW, sitting on the front seat on your mother's knee. As the car twists round the slope at San Vicente de Montalt, your father is distracted, momentarily loses control of the steering wheel, and crashes against a plane tree. Your head hits the windshield, you suffer deep cuts on your skull, forehead, the bridge of your nose: scars that will mark you forever. A vague memory of shouts, pain, your mother crying, the chemist's shop and chemist who fainted when he saw you. The return to Barcelona, bandaged up, surrounded by toys and pampered: sitting on the floor, with your presents, you have the pleasant impression of being king of the world.

The wooden chalet in the Gulf of Puigcerdá: the meadows, streams, cows, unmistakable smell of cowpats and grass that would come back to you a long time afterwards, in the Haute-Savoie, during the shooting of a film written by Monique. Walks through the town, the lake, the Cabrineti square, an excursion to the frontier spot of Bourg Madame. A Sunday Mass, the sermon of which will be the object of mysterious commentaries. Uncle Ignacio comes to see you and you hear for the first time on his lips the sinister name of the *rabassaires* and the ominous initials, FAI.

IN SPITE OF the atmosphere of disruption and agitation, my memories, which are confused until then, seem to get clearer and settle down at the beginning of 1936. My family lived in the house in Pablo Alcover and, while my mother went about her domestic chores, my father would leave very early in the morning for the ABDECA office—the Barcelona Gum and Fertilizer Company—of which he was the main shareholder and whose factory was in Hospitalet. After the trauma of Antonio's death, I think that both their lives followed a pleasant, calm routine. Marta, José Agustín, and I went to the St. Teresa school, and the Galician maid took over care and responsibility for Luis. To an outside observer, we were the typical bourgeois family of the time: an economy model car, involvement in a small industrial enterprise, a rented villa in the Tres Torres district, a brand-new chalet in an upmarket residential area in Puigcerdá. I cannot say for sure whether the comfortable, unpretentious channels of that existence corresponded to my parents' taste and aspirations. After getting a degree in the Chemical Sciences my father had sought a way to combine his undoubted talent and inventiveness in that field with a much more doubtful skill at running a business: unlike his brothers Leopoldo and Luis—the latter, handicapped by his deafness—he aspired to be a man of action, an off-shoot worthy of the Cuban stock begun by the tough, tenacious lad from Lequeitio. Although I haven't any reliable evidence, I presume that things weren't going badly for him at the time: our style of life was not extravagant like that of the already bankrupt prodigals of the family, but probably suited its nature and needs. He really swung between two opposite extremes: a rather Prussian love for an austere, orderly way of life and an impatient thirst for fame, to rival grandfather's exploits, which swept away all the restraints and caution of his usual miserliness and led him to invest money rashly in absurd, risky ventures. His first forays into industry had worked successfully, but the world economic crisis and the violent unrest during the Republic soon caused him problems. At this time, in the key year of 1936, which opens the doors to my story, my father was, in purely social terms, a decent employer of longstanding right-wing persuasion, ready to ride out the storm that would finally be unleashed over the country with unprecedented violence to the misfortune of him and everybody else.

I think my mother's position is more problematic. Daughter of a family in which the liberal professions abounded, with a greater concern for the world of culture, she had adapted without any apparent difficulty to life with a man whose intellectual interests and ambitions were quite at variance with her own. The titles of housewife, model consort, mother of four were absolutely in line with all that traditional society represented by her husband expected of her but did not entirely fit in with her emotional sensibility and insatiable desire for books. The placid image of the still youthful woman with her elegant hairstyle, wrapped round with a fur boa, captured in a portrait in the passage in the Pablo Alcover house does not express in its hollow conventionality the deeper, more complex reality that is, however, revealed by the list of her favorite books. While my father was unaware of the existence of literature until the publication of my first novel, *Juegos de manos*, hit him like a cold shower, my mother, perhaps with the help of her uncle the poet, had created for herself a vast, out-of-the-ordinary literary culture. When at the age of nineteen or twenty I began, dictionary in hand, to explore the array of French books that made up her library, their content—plays, novels, memoirs, volumes of poetry—and the catalogue of authors—Proust, Gide, Ibsen, Anouilh— showed me the range of a passion that, in its turn, would have a decisive influence on my life. A new image of her as a secret, solitary reader, in a typical bourgeois household full of children shouting and constant to-ing and fro-ing, replaced the one made up till then of incoherent memories and shallow recollections. The young woman who gave birth to me, suckled me, looked after me, my brothers and sister, externally bound to her role as mother of a family, was she the same one who, as I would discover much later through the confidences of one of her cousins, had secretly written a text entitled *The Wall and Madness*, the morbidity of which made a strong impression on her?* What was the relationship between the two? How could the second, hidden existence have tolerated the pedestrian, mediocre life of the first? The compromise between the two must have been real, since I can see nothing to indicate that she endured marriage and domestic life as an annoying burden. She had probably fashioned for herself an inner, spiritual life where she could take refuge through writing and reading. My father and the rest of us were no doubt the pillar of her life: but it was a life with its hiding places, havens for rest and meditation, pleasant, protective shade.

The build-up of political, social, and economic factors that polarized the February election campaign from one end to another and gave an overwhelming victory to the Popular Front candidates must have shaken the foundations of my family's peaceful routine. My father was a Catholic monarchist with a gut opposition to Catalan nationalism not only to the radical branch of Macià and Companys but also to the moderate one of Prat de la Riba and Cambó: he had voted for the right-wing coalition of the CEDA as a lesser evil. I can remember the day when, after a Mass in the Josephine convent, I went with my parents to the local electoral college, situated in a house on the corner of Ganduxer, close to the Vía Augusta. As we went in, someone was giving out propaganda for the left-

---

* Mentioned in a letter to Monique written about 1962.

wing parties and my mother refused it in a dignified fashion. "He was really disappointed," they said afterward in the DKW. Unfortunately, I do not remember any detail of the intense months of agitation that preceded the military uprising and the outbreak of the revolution.

In June we went to our chalet in Puigcerdá and the adults' mood of anxiety impressed even a child my age. As I found out later on, my father had planned to send us to France in order to be able to defend his interests in the factory knowing that we were in a safe place but for some reason the plan was not carried through. Later on, the sick, ruined man inexorably associated in my memories with the Viladrau period would continuously lament this mistake that had had such disastrous consequences for the family. The closeness of the frontier, he would say, could have saved his wife from the destiny that awaited her. The idea that it would soon be over, that things would soon be sorted out, decided their return to the lion's mouth: bloody, gun-ridden Barcelona in the hands of the ideals and excesses of revolutionary struggle. On the return journey, a militia control stopped the car to inspect their papers and, after the brief questioning, my parents commented ironically that the group leader, when he got the identity cards, had looked at them upside down.

Days afterward we were in Torrentbó with my mother and the maid. Uncle Ignacio followed the course of events from there with his wife and children, but vanished one morning with his family after hurriedly hiding the holy objects from the chapel in an ivy hedge. On the surface things had not changed: we played in the garden, read "Mickey Mouse," said our prayers; only María's whispered words about the Antichrist and my parents' discussions hinted at the abnormal situation. Mossèn Joaquim, the chaplain from the church of Saint Cecilia in Torrentbó, sometimes came to see us. He was an open, friendly man who chatted to my mother on the verandah and, as he said goodbye, would give us his hand to kiss. Once, to our great surprise, he appeared in the house grotesquely dressed as a civilian, wearing a beret to hide his tonsure: he was going away, he said, and had come to say goodbye. My mother handed him some money and a parcel of food for the journey and, when she was wishing him good luck and he, in turn, was blessing us, I noticed that María was crying. Mossèn Joaquim disappeared into the depths of the wood and was not seen again by any of his parishioners. Although he had asked us to pray for him and no doubt we did, he was immediately caught as he tried to escape and died soon afterward, a victim of an extremist gang.

Our maid's apocalyptic prophecies were fulfilled: the last issue of "Mickey Mouse" had come out splashed in the black-and-red colors of the FAI; churches were burning one after another as under the Roman Empire. From the garden pavilion we observed the lorry of the "reds" parked next to Saint Cecilia, the thick column of smoke rising over the tiny white building. Had someone been gossiping mischievously about our family chapel? Although the hypothesis, later formulated by my father, does have some grains of truth, the fact is that our chapel, completely visible from the place the arsonists were, would have been a tempting target without the need for any informers. Whether the result of chance or careful planning, when minutes later the men from the lorry suddenly burst into our garden we were terrified. María was sobbing: her favorite book was a religious primer made up of biographies of child saints and perhaps she was inwardly flirting with the exciting possibility of approaching martyrdom. My mother, who had looked out of the window when the invaders got the farmers to open the chapel door, was ordered (at revolver-point) to withdraw to her living quarters. We took refuge on the verandah and listened to shouts, hammering, and voices. My mother kept us quiet and the maid was silently telling her rosary beads.

In spite of the fact that there are some dark spots and gaps in my memory of how this episode developed, I well remember the moment after the intruders left and we ventured into the garden to see the damage. The marble statue of the Virgin, the work of Mariano Benlliure, had been knocked down from the altar and was lying outside the chapel with its head knocked to pieces by a mallet. A variety of liturgical objects was still burning on a bonfire. In marked contrast to our sorrow, the farmer and his family were examining the destruction impassively, in silence.

The events I have just related took place in my father's absence. When he finally reappeared after we had waited in a state of nervous tension and anxiety, it was with an escort of two bodyguards: Clariana and Jaume. I found out later that they both carried FAI cards and, in exchange for a hefty reward, assured his physical well-being and freedom against the threats to which he was subject. Every day they went with him to the factory and, in Torrentbó, they slept in the house and watched over the peace and quiet of the family. Jaume was a nice, dark young man whose natural ways and open character at once won my heart. He always carried a revolver, which he would show me and let me touch when he walked with me to the Lourdes and Santa Catalina wells. Alongside his kindness and patience with children, he displayed a strange, admirable respect for the beliefs of others: one day he discovered the black box in which Uncle Ignacio, in his rush to depart, had hidden the chalice and paten in case of a possible militia raid. He informed my mother of his find and advised her to look for a better hiding place. This act of trust increased his standing with all of us. As for me, I think that for the first time in my life I experienced a passion that could be described without exaggeration as amorous toward someone totally outside my family. Jaume's presence, his warm simplicity, our wanderings through the wood, the immense prestige his revolver bestowed on him in my eyes, embellish the images of that summer full of changes and surprises until the day when, for some reason, we were forced to abandon Torrentbó and move into a more modest house in the neighboring town of Caldetas.

Was the position of the house the decisive factor in the move?—its isolation and vulnerability in those dangerous times were obvious. Or was it requisitioned, as I heard later, to accommodate refugees from the Basque country?* Whatever the reason, autumn passed in the house in Sentema opposite the small hot-water spa on the edge of the *riera*. Our new home had a terraced garden at the back climbing the slope of the mountain to the ruined tower of els Encantats. María Boi was still with us, but her untimely religious fervor in a period of furious anticlericalism worried my mother deeply. Had she tried to win us to the idea of martyrdom, as I was later told, or was there some other weighty reason to justify her sudden sacking? Although I cannot answer with any certainty the fact is that she vanished from our sight overnight. My mother aired her empty room and her only comment was that it smelt badly.

It was our first year without school and we spent most of the time in the garden or in the street. The effects of the war were still not evident at home: we had regular meals prepared by two servants. María was always singing *Rocío*; the other preferred *María de la O*. My mother taught me to read and I eagerly went through my geography books. One day, I was looking at the map of Europe with her and she asked me which country I preferred. I pointed at the enormous pink mass of the Soviet Union and she said curtly, "No, not that one." Another time, my father was visited by the committee that was running the factory: a group of five or six men who awkwardly kissed the "lady's" hand, talked a while very noisily, and then started drinking. When they left, one was tottering, and the lavatory was full of vomit. While my father apologized to his wife for the incident, she was indignant and I could hear them at a distance arguing loudly.

A few months passed and we returned to Barcelona. We were back at the house in Pablo Alcover where some foreign soldiers, probably members of the International Brigades, were lodging on the top floor. There I heard the whispered news of my father's arrest (why? by whom?) and his subsequent release thanks to the timely intervention of the trade-union leaders from his factory. They came for him at night, as he later told me, but he had foreseen the danger of the *paseos* and used to sleep in our grandparents' house, preferring to give himself up to the legal authorities. His stay in prison was brief, but he fell ill after he left. The doctors diagnosed pleurisy and he went into Dr. Corachán's clinic.

From then on we visited him daily with my mother, walking through

---

* According to a recent account by the farmer's son, José Antonio Aguirre, president of the Basque government, and his family stayed in the large house for several months.

the Tres Torres district. The clinic had an enormous leafy garden where we played for hours waiting for her to return from the room where they were caring for him. My brothers, sister, and I still didn't know how serious the illness was and, particularly, the method used to cure it: the infection of the initial pneumonia had forced the doctors to drain the pus from the pleurisy by putting a rubber tube between the pleura and an orifice in the ribs. For years, my father stayed in bed or was semi-immobilized by that terrible pipe sunk into his chest and leading to the glass jar into which his humors poured. This new image of my father was only imprinted on my memory in Viladrau; but, gradually, it spread to the one forged in my childhood—that of a man who was active although getting on and whose difference of age with my mother did not seem alarming—and destroyed it altogether. The admiration and respect I felt for him were thus damaged irreparably. The despondent, prostrate figure, hypostatically united to the pipe and the jar of pus, began to fill me with an unjust but real feeling of repugnance. Imprisoned by cotton wool, bottles of medicine, bandages, jars of fluid in a room smelling like a hospital, that pathetic man in no way fulfilled my idea of a father's role or acted as a possible source of support. Without recourse to hyperbole or any retrospective manipulation of the facts, I have long since reached the conclusion that, months before my mother's departure, the protective family shell had begun to shatter around me.

The reason for our move to Viladrau also remains somewhat obscure. The mountain air, no doubt recommended to my father by his doctors, could provide one key. The growing difficulties over supplies in Barcelona, the street battles between rival factions, the first bombings by Franco's planes, and finally the presence there of Uncle Ramón and Aunt Rosario could be other reasonable explanations to throw light on the choice of that summer holiday village set in the skirts of the Montseny mountain. According to my calculations, we must have moved in the autumn of 1937: first to a dark, damp villa, with a garden covered in yellow leaves; later, to a much smaller house where we only occupied the top floor. The building was part of a group of four houses that shared a garden: the owner, an octogenarian smallholder who cultivated the adjoining land, would later be the butt of our jokes and mischief. We had bid farewell to Conchita, and María Cortizo, the Galician servant, cooked and did the household chores while my mother acted as nurse and looked after us as best she could. Downstairs lived a woman named Angeles, accompanied by her daughter: the former used to complain to us about everything, especially the way she was persecuted by her sister, Encarnación, a strong, stout woman, married to a Madrid taxi driver and whose only son, Saturnino, looked abnormal because of slight hydrocephalus and a squint. Encarnación and her husband lived in the house next door and one night we heard shouting and cries for help after which we saw Angeles appear bleeding and dishevelled, blaming her sister for the attack. The rest of the neighboring properties were big villas with stone walls: we soon stealthily penetrated one that was unoccupied; another one, which took up a whole block, was the provisional shelter for the Archive of the Kingdom of Aragon.

Our life in Viladrau that winter prolonged the holiday period that had started a year and a half earlier. The shortages began to make an impact and I remember my mother going round the nearby farmhouses in search of food. During my father's illness, the factory committee paid his salary regularly; but the money was gradually losing its value and as the war advanced and the situation in the Republican camp got worse, the ancient barter economy reappeared. We would go with my mother and brothers and sister to visit Aunt Rosario's family in her flat in the main square in the village or we would walk round the outskirts, taking the road to Espinelves, the path to la Noguera, or one of the shortcuts that curled down to the hidden springs nearby. We often got together to play hide-and-seek with other children in the spacious garden of the Bioscas' villa or we would go to their house for a Charlie Chaplin film show from a Baby Pathé projector. I can remember a soirée of film and poetry when a pathetically enraptured bard declaimed poems by Gustavo Adolfo Bécquer. At home, I read the illustrated stories my mother gave me and I began to draw and write "poetry" in an exercise book. My future career as a writer was thus inaugurated at the age of six: the lines poured out and, once adorned with my own scribbled illustrations, I was quick to show them to visitors with a precocious tingle of pride.

While I write these lines, I am trying to hold steady the few, faithful memories of my mother: the time she had an argument with father—I don't know why—and she wiped her nose with her handkerchief; the day I was feeling abandoned by her and said that I would like to fall ill too, since she was entirely absorbed in caring for her husband, and, unable to restrain herself, she gave me the smack I deserved; the afternoon at my aunt and uncle's when I learned of the accident in which cousin Paco, Aunt María's son, had lost a leg, cut off by a tram while he was roller-skating: Aunt Rosario asked me to tell her only about "some bad news," without giving any specific detail of what it was about and, while my mother got dressed and ran with me to her house, I selfishly enjoyed my momentary power over her gradually suggesting, in my own way, all I knew about the drama.

Until then the civil war and its disasters had distant, indirect repercussions on my consciousness. The small colony of well-off Barcelona bourgeois lived in Viladrau provisionally on the margin of the conflict and maintained a public attitude of prudent neutrality. Only a few ironic comments—the obligatory reference to the fact that Bono, a well-known ladies' hairdresser who had also taken refuge in the village, was picked up weekly by an official car in order to do the hair and beautify the wives of government and *Generalitat* ministers—allowed one to read their real feelings. But, out of earshot of any indiscreet listeners, tongues would be unleashed. At night, we used to be visited by Lolita Soler, a woman in her forties, a gaunt spinster from a monarchist military family, who had lived the siege of Madrid before being evacuated to Catalonia to be stranded like us in that isolated mountain spot. Her bloodcurdling tales of murders, executions, deportations, heroic martyrdoms, recounted in whispers so that we children could not hear her, mingled with encouraging news of the other side's progress, which she apparently intercepted via a crystal radio on the Burgos wavelength. Her tribulations and adventures—which my family thought were exaggerated—aroused endless discussions in the dining room, which continued long after her departure. The precarious situation in which my grandparents lived, the helplessness of Aunt Consuelo, shut up with them in a flat on the Diagonal, the ever more frequent bombing of the city, intensified my mother's state of anxiety, and she was already overwhelmed by four children and a sick husband with no hope of a quick cure. In a letter, which my sister found years after, she told her parents of her fear and worry because of a lack of news after an air attack. Every two or three weeks she would get on the coach that took her to the railway station of Balenya and, after spending the day with them and doing a little shopping, she would return to Viladrau at night. These ever so brief visits did not stop her worries, however, and after several months they became a kind of ritual.

On the morning of 17 March 1938, my mother started her journey as usual. She left home at daybreak and, although I know the tricks that memory and its fictitious recreations play, I retain a clear memory of looking out my bedroom window while that woman, soon to become unfamiliar, walked with her coat, hat, and bag, toward the definitive absence from us and from herself: destruction, emptiness, nothing. It no doubt seems suspicious that I should wake up precisely on that day and that, forewarned of my mother's departure by her footsteps or the noise of the door, I should have got up to watch her leave. However, it is a real image and for some time it filled me with bitter remorse: I should have shouted to her, insisted that she give up the visit. It was probably the fruit of a later guilt mechanism: an indirect way of reproaching myself for my inertia, for not having warned her of the imminent danger, and for not attempting the gesture that, in my imagination, could have saved her.

My memory of the frustrated waiting for her to return—my father's growing anxiety, our comings and goings in search of news to our aunt and uncle's house or to the village coach stop—is much more reliable.

Two days of tension, anticipatory anguish, unbearable silence, visits from our uncle and aunt, Lolita Soler's sobbing, a round of whispered conversation in my father's room until that sad St. Joseph's holiday when the three brothers and sister were brought together on the outside staircase that descended to the garden and Aunt Rosario, with occasional feeble interruptions from Lolita Soler, told us about the bombing, its victims, how she too had been caught, very seriously injured, leading us gradually, like the bull that has just been stabbed by the matador and is now pushed skilfully by his team onto its knees so that he can finish it off with one quick thrust, to the moment when, her voice drowned in tears, ignoring the other woman's pious protests, uttered the unutterable word, leaving us in a state of bewilderment not because of the grief immediately expressed in sobs and wails but rather the inability to accept the brutal truth, still untouched by the bare reality of the fact, and especially its definitive, irrevocable nature.

How her death happened, in exactly which place she fell, where she was taken to, at which moment and in what circumstances her parents identified her is something that I have never known nor will I ever know. The unknown woman who disappeared suddenly from my life, did so discreetly, far from us, as if to temper delicately the effect that her departure would inevitably have, but at the same time thickening the shadows which would envelop her in the future and turn her into a stranger: the object of guesswork and conjectures, incomplete explanations, and doubtful, undemonstrable hypotheses. She had gone shopping in the center of the city and was caught there by the arrival of the airplanes, near where the Gran Vía crosses the Paseo de Gracia. She was a stranger, also, to those who, once the alert was over, picked off the ground that woman who was already eternally young in the memory of all who knew her, the lady who, in her coat, hat, and high-heeled shoes, clung tightly to the bag where she kept the presents she had bought for her children, which the latter, days afterward, in suits dyed black as custom ruled, would receive, in silence, from the hands of Aunt Rosario: a romantic novel for Marta; tales of Doc Savage and the Shadow for José Agustín; a book of illustrated stories for me; some wooden dolls for Luis that lay scattered round the attic forever untouched by my brother.

The empty black bag: all that remained of her. Her role in life, in our life, had finished abruptly before the end of the first act.

O NLY TWENTY YEARS *later—during the preparations for the editing of Rossif's film,* Mourir à Madrid, *the day you and some French friends were viewing a series of Spanish and foreign news and documentary films on the civil war—did the horror that dominated her last moments impose its sharp outline on your consciousness. A weekly news film from the Republican government, in its denunciations of the enemy's aerial attacks on defenseless civilian populations, shows the results of the one suffered by Barcelona on that unforgettable seventeenth of March: alarm sirens, noisy explosions, scenes of panic, ruins, destruction, desolation, cartloads of corpses, hospital beds, wounded comforted by members of the government, an endless line of bodies laid out in the morgue. In the foreground the camera slowly pans the victims' faces and, soaked in cold sweat, you suddenly realize the harsh possibility that the face you fear may suddenly appear. Fortunately, the absent one, with a sense of elegance and modesty, hid in some way to spare you the traumatic, ill-timed reunion. But you were forced to rush from your seat, go to the bar, drink a glass of something, just the time necessary to hide your emotion from the rest and discuss the film with them as if nothing had happened.*

The bond linking that death and the meaning of the civil war would not be apparent to you until the day when, now interested in politics, you began to be fascinated by eye-witness accounts and books on the recent history of Spain. Your religious and family education in the forties had succeeded in breaking the link between the two events. On the one hand, after the collective rosary that followed supper, you quickly prayed in a mechanical, routine fashion three Lord's Prayers for the eternal rest of the absent one's soul; on the other hand, you accepted without any reservations whatsoever the official version of the conflict as rehearsed by radio, newspapers, teachers, relatives, and all around you: a crusade undertaken by healthy, patriotic men against a Republic stained by all kinds of crimes and abominations. The stark, undeniable reality that your mother had been the victim of your side's strategy of terror, a product of cold, hateful calculation, was ignored by your father and the rest of the family. The setbacks the former suffered— imprisonment, illness, widowhood—were, according to him, the work of a band of enemies generically labelled as "reds." Deprived of its context, clean and disinfected, your mother's death was thus transformed into a kind of abstraction that, although it exempted the real guilty ones from their responsibility, emphasized conversely for you the unreal confusion of their fate. Although the ease with which this whitewashing operation was carried out may seem suspicious, the closed, conservative circle in which you live, the silent complicity of your home, the difficulty in getting objective information, clarifies yet again the uncritical acceptance of the facts. It was only at university, when you befriended a student with ideas hostile to the regime and, thanks to him, got to know the books that told the story of the civil war from an opposite point of view, that the bandage fell from your eyes. Imbued with crude but refreshing Marxist principles—hostile to the reactionary values of your class—you began to focus on the events you experienced marginally from childhood from a very different perspective: Franco's bombs—not the innate evil of the Republicans—were directly responsible for the break-up of your family.

To tell the truth—apart from that belated feeling of historical indignation— the early date of your mother's departure took from her exit any real degree of grief. What was snatched from you then would weigh heavily on your destiny, but the consequences of your orphanhood would only appear later: alienation from the father figure, insipid religiosity, lack of patriotism, an instinctive rejection of any kind of authority, all the elements and features that later would fix your character are no doubt closely related to that state. However, to the extent that the attachment to your mother vanished with her, you can say quite truthfully that rather than her son, the son of a woman who is and always will be unknown to you, you are a son of the civil war, its Messianism, cruelty, and anger: of the unhappy accumulation of circumstances that brought into the open the real entrails of the country and filled you with a youthful desire to abandon it forever.

You remember now, in the light of what you have just written, the episode with the axe: the destructive rage that overpowered you one morning in Barcelona, a few months after the war, when you were wandering through the house along with Luis.

At the back of the garden, in the space between the garage and a room used as a junk room, there were two cubbyholes for storing wood and coal beneath the space under the staircase that led to the terrace on the first floor. The junk room was crammed with furniture belonging to the family, awaiting, you suppose, the probable move to Torrentbó. You can remember a number of sofas, armchairs, consoles, corner shelves covered in dust and cobwebs where you used to hide to play at ghosts, happy in the midst of that mixture of valuable objects and broken or useless bric-a-brac. This spot had been transformed into your favorite hiding place when you came back from school until the day when, out of temper or whim, you took the axe from the woodpile and with your brother's help proceeded to destroy its contents with ferocious enthusiasm.

Piece of furniture after piece of furniture, with no quarter given, you began to cut legs, arms, backs, chop tables, rip the stuffing out of chairs, break decorations, pull springs, bash chairs, possessed by a cheerful, absorbing sense of inspiration that you would not meet again, you think today, except in the act of creation, the exultant vandalism of adult writing: the pleasure of exorcising the symbols of a society, the conventions of a code suddenly perceived as an obstacle; an intense desire for vengeance against an ill-formed universe; the effusive, primeval impulse linked to the binomial of creation-discreation. What meaning can be given to this sudden, excited, enjoyable act of two brothers who were normally calm yet suddenly possessed by a destructive rage whose ultimate explanation was beyond them? A protest, accumulated anger, a desire to retaliate? Or boredom, pure lack of awareness, an attempt to imitate the grown-ups? The original cause of the scene, the swiftness and audacity of its execution, will always be an enigma impossible to resolve. You will then focus your memory on the image of those small boys who, with the blows of the axe, liberate in some way a mysterious inner energy, perhaps the unconscious, secret desire to make their voices heard.

MARKED OUT BY the holy signs of mourning, we were the object of much weeping and sympathy. The daily visits of consolation soon became a ritual: Aunt Rosario, her husband and our cousins, Lolita Soler, friends, or just acquaintances from the colony took their turns in my father's bedroom, worried by the helpless state of the sick widower with four children. From now on, who was going to look after us? The question was not posed directly but could be discerned on the anxious, verging on aghast, expressions of his devotees. My father's illness, moreover, required constant care and it was necessary to have recourse to the services of a nurse. Someone mentioned a "right-wing" midwife who had also taken refuge in the village and a few days afterwards old Josefina, a massive, thickset woman with coarse features, settled down with her suitcases and belongings into a spacious room in the front of the house.

Strangely, I do not retain any image of my father during the days following the catastrophe. He stayed shut up in his room while the visitors came and went at his bedside preaching Christian resignation or mumbling the rosary. My brothers, sister, and I, after our shock and despair at the news had gone, got by as best we could and began to savor the advantages of our absolute freedom. At first our black-dyed clothes distanced us from our mates. Some village lads pointed at us and made jokes about our disguise. Any possible attempt on my part to play the victim and win the pity of others was thus a deplorable failure. Life—with its growing difficulties—war—with its suite of horrors—continued their usual course indifferent to and removed from my family's drama. We escaped instinctively from the atmosphere that reigned at home and went off far to play with the village children and organize expeditions to the hills in search of chestnuts.

The general shortage of food became more pronounced: shops and grocery stores lacked the most basic goods and displayed windows and counters empty except for a few odd sweets, cleaning cloths, brooms, and other unnecessary leftover objects. Without reaching starvation point, our family diet worsened daily. María, the servant, would often come back with her bag full of turnips and greens: the only articles sold in the market. The parcels that arrived from time to time from Argentina or France—sent by Uncle Joaquín and our relations in the Gil Moreno de Mora family—were a real feast. We opened them at home or in Aunt

Rosario's flat and shared out their contents—sugar, coffee, chocolate, tinned meat, condensed milk—with the same restrained anxiety with which the authors of a dangerous, daring raid later share out their booty. Then the deficiencies in the post and the frequent loss of parcels forced us to search out other sources of supplies: direct purchase from the peasants, the breeding of domestic animals, happy fruitful hunting through garden plots and chestnut trees.

A hunter from the neighboring area of Puigtorrat would often be around at home with the spoils of his forays: hares, partridges, and squirrels. One day he even brought a strange, skinned animal that, in spite of his denials and protests of good faith, turned out to be a vixen. In the periods of greatest scarcity, Marta, José Agustín, and myself would steal watercress or the stalks of wild marrow from the edge of the cultivated fields or would spread out fanwise through the nearby chestnut trees until the cries and threats of the owner or tenant put us to flight. In the attic, we bred rabbits and a dozen hens: their eggs, mixed with greens or marrow leaves, comprised the usual dish for our lunch or supper except on those happy days when we received food from France or Argentina. The chestnuts—raw, boiled, or roasted—were the second source of sustenance. Consequently, and perhaps as a result of the scares I had when getting them, I have always hated them and have not tasted them since the war ended and we left Viladrau.

As soon as she moved in, Josefina the nurse had elaborated a strategy aimed at domination based on a pretense of motherly affection, and on cunning and intimidation. Her first victim was Lolita Soler: her repeated visits to the widower's bedroom singled her out in her eyes as an immediate rival and Josefina dispatched her rapidly after a violent row. After removing that awkward presence, she began to adopt with us the role of the caring mother: in the dining room, in front of my father, she used to sit me on her lap and embrace me tightly with lots of kisses and tender, loving gestures. Luis's indifference to her endearments irritated her and, when alone, she was quick to reproach him for it. She had also taken charge of the running of the kitchen and she used the few items there for her own benefit: in spite of her robust constitution and good color, she pretended to suffer from continuous "weakness" and did not stop eating throughout the day. Thinking she was indispensable to my father, she gradually intensified her pressure on him. During the rosary after supper and the prayers for my mother, she exhibited extreme piety, which soon seemed hateful to us. Her attempt to replace my mother, evident in many details, no doubt finally opened my father's eyes, despite his prostrate, dependent state. Did she perhaps hint clumsily at some sexual advance that could only repulse him, obsessed as he was by his wife's memory? Or did she somehow suggest to him the suitability of remaking his life, of looking for an adoptive mother for those poor orphans? Her crude ways, hypocritical behavior, and coarse, obscene physical appearance did not favor her plans for conquest. But something must have happened between them since my father, taking strength from his weakness, suddenly threw her out of the house. I can remember Josefina's tears as she saw her dream destroyed. Still hoping for some possible intervention by us, she tried in vain to win us to her cause: now living away from us, she got me to her lodging with the bait of some sweets and tried to wheedle from me news of my father's health and temper. But from then on he forbade us to have any contact with her. One day when we spotted her in the distance, on the way to the market, José Agustín and I sang an indecent ditty to her, and she went into a fury, insulted us, and threw large stones after us.

After she left, Lolita Soler and my uncle and aunt resumed their visits. My sister, Marta, now carried out the onerous duties of nurse to my father and looked after him patiently. The room's bitter smell, the cannula and stained cotton wool, the spittoon, bedpan, and jar of pus created for me on the other hand a circle around the invalid that was difficult to cross. When I went to bed, I furtively touched the thin outstretched hand with my lips and, as far as possible, tried to avoid his outpourings and embraces. The rosaries and Lord's Prayers that we prayed together in his room were the most trying moments in the day. One night when he was reading us a passage from the gospel that makes reference to an ass accompanied by its jenny, this last word sent us into inexplicable fits of laughter. My father was forced to interrupt his reading and in a rage he ordered us out of the room. I remember that as a result of this incident I spoke for the first time of my lack of affection for him, I am not sure whether alone or to one of my brothers or my sister. The idea of being adopted by Uncle Joaquín and accompanying him to Argentina captivated me for some time. Moving in with any member of the family seemed more desirable than living with that sad, embittered man whose grief and frustration I did not share. On another day, I suddenly entered my room and found him sitting on my bed, crying, with my mother's photograph in his hand. Ashamed at discovering something I did not wish to see, I quickly tiptoed out, without uttering a word. Today, this lack of filial pity and understanding of course seems shocking to me. The tests to which my father had been submitted went beyond the limits of his endurance and did not deserve my attitude of rejection. I do not wish to absolve myself in any way but, to explain my behavior at the time, one would have to consider my tremendous disappointment when I realized that the all-powerful, magnificent character praised to the heavens in my mind as a child was not only a flesh and blood being like the rest but senile and helpless to boot. The spite that followed my disillusion should clarify to an extent the precocious, unjust manifestations of cold detachment.

Around this date—the summer or autumn of 1938—I experienced my first sexual emotions. Until then I was completely ignorant of the matter; not even contact with domestic animals had taught me like other children. The time when, at one of the farmhouses near the village, I saw a goat give birth, I accepted my mother's explanation that it had swallowed a sandal and was ejecting it, to the point that, many years later, I related the anecdote to my brothers and sister without realizing my gullibility nor the simplicity of the deceit. In the attic, I would similarly keep a watch on the rooster's attacks on the hens and armed with my rod of justice, I would pursue the supposed perpetrator of these insults. Still my ingenuousness did not stop me, José Agustín, and a gang of kids from playing at showing each other our parts and, with our penises out, dancing a kind of conga to the cry—incomprehensible to me—of "girls, do you want to have a stroke?" My brother declared that he had let María caress him and one day he showed us an enormous damp patch on the front wall of the house, the product, he said, of a militia man who went out with the servant. The mental image of the individual pissing had an indelible impact on me: when I found out later that one of the boys in the gang held down our neighbors' abnormal, hydrocephalic son and urinated over his head, the news overwhelmed and excited me. I went down to the garden anxious to repeat the deed and, when I didn't come across the child, I spat and pissed outside the door to his house, filled with a passionate emotion, the dark causes of which would flower in my writing much later. As for my imaginary victim, I didn't hear of him again: Encarnación and her family moved to another village and their house stayed shut until we left Viladrau.

I do not propose to interpret this violent outburst in the light of my present experience—that is, as a possible forerunner of my future sensuality—but to situate it in the context of immediacy and innocence in which it took place. My desire to physically humiliate the backward, squint-eyed boy was a spontaneous, isolated act that did not rouse in my mind any guilt feelings and soon fell into semi-oblivion. Sometime after, on one of those evenings organized by Lolita Soler and my uncle and aunt, a priest came in civilian dress and, before celebrating mass and giving communion to the adults, he called me to his side and said he wished to hear me confess. Although I followed to the letter his instructions and searched out, bewildered and confused, anything that might give cause for reproach, I never conceived the idea of establishing a connection between that act and the nebulous notion of sin. I evoked or invented some theft or fib and received absolution from that man without feeling any emotion. The concentration and sorrow of the communicants, the priest's Latin, the getting up and kneeling down, the blows to the breast I had forgotten once the war had begun seemed like a mere charade lacking meaning or substance. At the end, the adults ordered us to keep quiet about it. Above all, said my father, not one word to the servant.

Although María had always behaved most discreetly, Lolita Soler and my family distrusted her as a red. On Saturdays and Sundays she went out to dances with militia men, she had won a UGT or PSUC badge in a *tómbola*, and I well remember that, when she commented on the news from the front with us, she said: "With Durruti dead, the war's lost." During Christmas, her pessimism intensified. While my father, Lolita Soler, and my uncle and aunt hardly disguised their joy, she, the poor, illiterate woman who believed in the cause of the Republic and generously offered her body to the soldiers, rightly suspected the arrival of difficult times for her, and she obsessively repeated the legends about the Moors. Her stories—of rapes, chopped-off ears, heads kept in rucksacks for their gold teeth—unearthed in fact under the gloss of antirebel propaganda the old Hispanic phantasmagoria forged in the centuries of the ill-named Reconquest. As for many Spaniards of my generation, the term "Moor" was associated, from an early age, with vague, disturbing images of violence and terror. It would be necessary for twenty years to pass before I overcame the imprints of that period and succeeded in establishing a fruitful personal relationship with the Arab world in its triple dimension of space, body, and culture, a relationship that would soon be transformed into the central axis of my life. Sometimes, in my wanderings through the Islamic world I have thought remorsefully and affectionately about that humble woman from Carballino whose ancestral fantasies, anchored in my subconscious and then doubly exorcised, both in life and writing, would become the source that would later nourish the Moorish inspiration of my work. The ways that make us what we are are tortuous and unpredictable: for my part, I do not have the slightest doubt that in my move toward and sympathy for the Life unto Islam, the fascinated imaginings of the servant I listened to as a boy played through unpredictable twists and turns that initiatory, baptismal role destiny had mysteriously conferred on them.

T HE FRONT WAS getting closer to us: the road had filled
up with soldiers on foot and on horseback, official
vehicles, motorcycles with sidecars, Supply Corps lorries. Then we could
see from our windows long, interminable strings of prisoners of war file
by; their guards rounded them up like cattle outside the local parish
church and gave them their watery rations. Exhaustion, illness, despondency were painted on all their faces: they left behind them a trail of
defecations, dirty paper, and empty tins. Lolita Soler and Aunt and Uncle
watched them go with tears in their eyes and tried to furtively give them a
crust or some other help. José Agustín and I dared to talk to them and we
presented one with a cigarette made from dried maize leaves. A small
nationalist reconnaissance plane appeared one morning and a captain took
his pistol out of its holster and fired a few shots well-seasoned with curses
and oaths at it. Our father told us Barcelona had been liberated by Carlist
troops.

The village provided daily scenes of panic and disorder. Cars packed
with refugees, lorries stuffed with soldiers, passed through heading north
followed by hundreds of people on foot, all dirty and unkempt, soldiers,
civilians, children, old men and women, all loaded with suitcases and
bundles, absurd bits of lumber, saucepans, furniture, an absurdly outlandish sewing machine, a diaspora of insects after the death of the queen
or the unexpected destruction of the ants' nest. There were the wounded
carried on stretchers, cripples on crutches, arms in slings. The nationalists
had just cut off the railway line and José Agustín announced that he had
seen a dead body. Some officers visited us one afternoon. After making
himself comfortable in the dining room, the captain noticed the existence
of a chicken coop in the attic and, with remarkable brazenness, invited
himself to dinner. María sacrificed a couple of hens and, while my father
strove to maintain an empty conversation with his guests, one of the latter
inspected the house curiously and displayed a sudden interest in Aunt
Consuelo's violin case. He insisted on examining the instrument, plucked
the strings, said that his aide was fond of music. After the meal they said
goodbye politely and, belying our fears, did not take anything. The following day, however, the doorbell rang loudly and there was the orderly.
The captain had asked him to requisition the violin, he told us; but he was
thinking of deserting and begged us to help him. Rather than carry out
his orders, he wanted to remain hidden in our house awaiting the arrival

of the nationalist troops. My father agreed to his request. The last Republican soldiers were evacuating the village and there was no longer any risk that the officer would retrace his steps to find out where his subordinate had got to. The deserter's name was Veremundo Salazar, and he came from the Rioja area: he hid in the attic for the whole morning waiting for the sudden appearance of the scouts of the enemy army. We could hear the muffled, intermittent echo of gunfire. The reconnaissance planes continued their flight northward. After a few hours, Veremundo came down from his hiding place, gave us a yellow-handled campaign knife, and bid us farewell. My father had forbidden us to go out but, soon after, without asking his permission, José Agustín and I slipped out to the garden. One of our neighbors had come out to have a look as well and she told us that the village now belonged to "our fellows."

We heard the bells ringing and ran to the plaza. The entire colony of Barcelona refugees seemed to have agreed to meet there: men and women in tears embraced and kissed each other, waved flags, cheered Franco, intoned the "Oriamendi," gave free rein to their emotions. My uncle and aunt with my cousins were also exultant, in ecstasy. Somebody wore a red beret and was surrounded by admirers. They had thrown open the doors of the church the Republicans had converted into a warehouse. People were discussing whether the Carlists or the Falangists would arrive first.

These were busy days, full of changes: new money, food supplies, speeches and hymns broadcast over the loudspeakers. Wearing blue shirts and red berets, José Agustín and I had queued for hours outside the Social Welfare offices where they distributed free fizz and omelette sandwiches. The military were camping in the mansion that had been a shelter for the Archive of the Crown of Aragon: they kept bags of beans and sugar there and, taking advantage of the carelessness or the blind eye of the Supply Corps, a neighbor and I filled two saucepans with their precious contents. My father dared to venture briefly out of the house and made friends with two NCOs: an Italian, Mr. Lupiani, and the man we called "Sergeant Fatty." While we played with cartridge cases, he spoke to them of his widowhood, the misfortunes of life under red domination, his traditionalist, Catholic views. One day he invited them to lunch and, at the end of the meal, perhaps strengthened by their dashing military presence, he sacked María. The red housemaid, bedmate of Communists and militiamen, obeyed the sentence of the court without a murmur of protest. Dejected and flushed, she went off to her room to collect her wretched belongings and put them in a bag: not one of us, still sitting in front of the dishes she had cooked and served, got up to say goodbye or show her any sign of sympathy. With her bag over her back, resigned to her fate, she disappeared forever from our sight.

What happened to her in those days of merciless control and repression, when arbitrary arrests and denunciations were an everyday occurrence? Did she try to find a job in Barcelona—a difficult task lacking as she did references or recommendations from a family that was "beyond reproach"? Did she go back to her own village to suffer misery and hunger? Did she suffer reprisals like so many other women and go through the humiliation of purging courts, spoonfuls of castor oil, and sinister head-shaving? A feeling of retrospective shame overwhelms me as I write these lines. I think it is incredible that even as an eight-year-old I experienced no remorse or shame at that contemptible settling of accounts. Our María served as the sacrificial goat to the real sufferings of my father: yet she had in no way been responsible for them. Of all the unpleasant, sad episodes in the war, this one is no doubt the most difficult to digest.

Mr. Lupiani had created a children's brigade of the Falange and, in his baritone voice, with his chest proudly puffed out, he would teach us to stand to attention, salute, march in step. We sang verses of "Cara al sol," the hymn of the Youth Front: "with ranks closed, strong and warlike, our troops go forward to the morning that promises us our country, justice and bread." A village boy who had received a corporal's stripe would strut in front of us with his uniform and beret. The priests had reappeared also in full dress: they celebrated Mass in the parish church and I received catechism classes from Mossén Rovira to prepare myself for Communion.

Outside these religious and military activities, we enjoyed complete freedom. Schools were not yet open: we walked along the Espinelves road still littered with vehicles either burnt out or reduced to scrap metal; we hunted birds with slingshots and ganged up with the village children. We looked like real savages. I remember the day a large car stopped next to us and a lady offered Luis and me some almost rotten oranges. We refused to take them and the vehicle's occupants resumed their journey surprised and upset. Our dirty, neglected appearance had led them to mistake us for two beggars.

Our favorite pastime consisted of visiting deserted villas and slipping inside them. Our extreme thinness allowed us to get between the bars and, after several fruitful incursions, we brought together an important booty: toys, books, and, especially, a collection of stamps from all the countries in the world; I tried to decipher their origins at home, comparing them with the colored prints in my geography book. José Agustín was becoming an expert in breaking and entering until we were spotted by a neighbor or nosey passerby who reported us and we were severely punished by my father.

I have no memories of my First Communion administered by old Mossén Rovira. On Sundays we went to the parish church with our aunt and uncle and one day the bells rang loudly and there was a long thanksgiving sermon: the war was over! The bare victory communiqué from

Military Headquarters in Burgos passed from lip to lip. Lolita Soler was beside herself about Franco: Spain needed men like him! Mr. Lupiani taught us the words of "Carrasclás":

> With Azaña's mustache
> we'll make brooms
> to sweep the barracks
> of the Spanish Falange

One Sunday, in the parish church, my heart missed a beat: my mother was kneeling on the prayer cushion in one of the front benches. Her hair, profile, and head were lowered in an act of meditation. Emotion held me in suspense: should I go and suddenly appear before her? Would she recognize me after so much time? What would we say to each other? When she got up to receive Communion, the spell vanished: it was a different woman. I felt almost relieved of my fears of this unexpected meeting and since then I think I have never dreamt about her again.

ABDECA shareholders drove from Barcelona to visit my father: they brought presents for us, wore Carlist and Falange badges. Friendly countries: Italy, Germany. Enemies: France, our eternal foe. England? Yes, England as well. What about Russia? The worst of all. You shouldn't even think of mentioning Russia!

Ever since María had been fired, my father had been looking for a maid. We went to see a possible candidate, Julia, who had worked in Aunt María's house before the war and could be trusted. She had spent the last two years in a farmhouse on the outskirts of Viladrau bordering on an estate belonging to the writer Marià Manent. Julia adapted immediately to life with my father. From then on, until her death, she lived with us as part of the family, with only one condition: she had to change her name to Eulalia, since the mention of her real name was painful to the widower. Soon afterward, this woman with red hair and smooth white skin from Aragon, age indefinite, would stay in our house for a probationary period, which, as a result of the bonds that gradually linked us together, in fact lasted a quarter of a century.

Now is not the time to talk about her: the important role played by Eulalia in the lives of myself and my brothers, her complex, contradictory personality, her immense goodness and affection for us, her favorite haunts, caprices, phobias, flirtations require separate treatment. The family whose service she entered, although known to her since before the war, displayed the wounds and scars of the conflict in that spring or summer of thirty-nine: a sick, suspicious, apprehensive widower whose health, although well on the way to recovery, demanded distressing treatment; a fourteen-year-old girl and three boys brought up in a wild state, without any strict code of behavior. Her generosity, self-denial, and intuitive genius helped her to ride out the situation and overcome the obstacles. Her presence during our last few months in Viladrau was discreet and sensible. To tell the truth, I hardly remember what she was like.

Grandmother Marta reappeared that summer. She dressed in mourning as we did, but carefully avoided talking about my mother or the circumstances of her death. She would come for a walk with us to the outskirts of the village and under the chestnut trees and by the fountains we met other families belonging to the colony, dressed to the nines, as if they had not experienced the war. One gentleman would take off his Panama hat when he passed us and we would jokingly tell Grandmother that he was in love with her and wanted to be her fiancé. José Agustín had gone to Barcelona to prepare for his entrance exams for the *bachillerato*, and my father was getting ready to return as well to take charge of ABDECA. Luis and I spent a few more weeks with our grandmother in Viladrau and one day we caught the bus and the Balenyà train: the carriages were packed with people, soldiers, Falangists, heavily laden women. I was excited by the novelty of the journey and sang the verses of "Carrasclás" in chorus with a group of Flechas, the Falangist youth.

Y<small>OUR</small> L<small>EZAMIAN EXCITEMENT</small> *was coming to an end: that desire to fan and stoke the fire of your words to make their union more furious: the pure gleam of the coals had gradually gone out and the last embers hardly shone from the barren ash: in spite of all, the agitation continued, invented new kinds of orgasm, filled your head with sparks: inductions and currents, yielding and malleable, captured as purely visual images: showy structures, fleetingly displayed like spidery Bengal flares or threatening Congolese orchids: the majoon cast you out of yourself, from the tiny café near the fortress where you had just composed and erased your* Soledades *surrounded by peaceful smokers of kef, nebulous domino addicts, sleepy cardplayers: with the absurd television screen Spanishing on in the background, perfectly framed suddenly there for all to see: you, your double, the creator of give-and-take, in the company of an unknown giant of a man, dark-skinned with a walrus mustache, both embracing, climbing like vines, in a splendid copulation: surprise, shock, incredulity at seeing yourself in such an awkward spot, you continue being yourself and yet someone else, split in two, duality, inner agony, gradually a sense of shame: on the sly you look at your neighbors to see if they recognize you, they attack your attitude, censure the brazen joy: desire to cover the screen with a hand like an ingenuous censor at a school cinema, to cut off the electricity, to flee in confusion into the street: to slip off, to stride down the hill, stop an empty taxi, the square, Hammadi restaurant, give the driver the address on the rue Molière, gaze at the pointless movement of people while you ride, pay for it, get out, get your key from the porter, open up, get in the lift, your flat, the lights, corridor bedroom, collapse on your bed: to the Arab cemetery or ghost that will be the scenario for the longest night in your life: the punctual date with the dead you left behind, the conclave of ghosts: a succession of family settings in which they, the absentees, attend to their business dressed as they dressed before, patiently waiting for their turn, for the explanation that is continuously deferred: your father, Alfredo, Grandfather, Eulalia: the garden in Pablo Alcover, the lemon tree beneath which Father used to rest, the kitchen, the dark austere passageway, the horse chestnut tree: or else Torrentbó, the verandah, eucalyptus trees, terrace, Father reading, Grandfather's creased suit, Alfredo with his hoe over his shoulder, Eulalia's weak, unmistakable voice: meeting, recognition, appearance foreseen for some time, your relationship with Monique cleared up, while you wandered and got lost in your search for majoon or hashish, en route to that elusive tribunal of the dead whose decrepitude you did not witness and of which, as they crouched in the shade, they did not fail to remind you: confrontations, mutual recriminations, insidious guiltiness: real people, an oneiric topography, present alternating with sudden leaps backward.*

The only significant exceptions already cleared from your subconscious: the woman who died in the bombing and the hated village of Viladrau.

You can now evoke the time at the beginning of the sixties, when you interviewed for L'Express one of the political prisoners freed by Franco thanks to the international campaign for amnesty. Twenty and a bit years in the Burgos jail, with no horizon beyond the distant square of sky and the close, too close walls of his cell. After getting out, problems of adapting his vision to intervening spaces: dizziness, sickness, headaches behind the eyes. An even worse lack of adaptation to the new reality not assimilated in his subconscious. During the first months in prison, he had dreamt regularly of open spaces: his house, the village, people and places he knew as a free man. Then, surreptitiously, this ozone layer had rarefied until it disappeared: he stopped recalling the world outside the prison when he slept. If he dreamt about his mother, his mother was in prison. If he imagined his village, it was a village behind bars. The prison had penetrated his inner being and allowed him no escape whatsoever. The girls he had known in his youth, heroines of his nocturnal libido, always performed in a prison setting. The military tribunal's punishment thus won after many years an absolute victory: not only a prison for the body, but likewise for mind, imagination, and fantasy.

The destructive power of reality over his dreams still haunted him retrospectively after sixteen months of free movement. The new girlfriends he went to bed with were invariably prisoners in the murky, elusive world of his nightmares. The prisons where he had rotted—bars, walls, courtyards, warders—maintained a cruel force. A hermetic, unassailable camp with no possibility of escape, his inner world remained anchored in prison.

Only by ceasing to dream in this prison, after weeks, months, or years, would our man reach the end of his torture: the opening up of the oppressive space, dilution of stubborn images, the incorporation of new experiences. At the end—a misty mirage—the wonderful promise of freedom.

Strategies common to dream, memory, and oblivion. The decisive importance of time in their development. Wasting activity, insidious erosion finally transformed into devastating routine.

Like the obscene, persistent image that, by dint of masturbating thereupon, gradually loses its power to provoke, the impression of the painful act or the bitter memory fades away without our realizing in an empty atmosphere of boredom and insensitivity. The last taunts of frustration, the brief dull pain, will be the well-known reminder of our enormous fagocytic capacity: patches of history dominated by dream or nightmare and progressively replaced in dreams by new areas of reality.

Nevertheless a mysterious spread of light and shade: the arc light that arbitrarily bathes scenes in your life and leaves others in a discreet darkness from which you cannot rescue them.

Viladrau, to which you have not returned nor will you ever, expelled forever from the fantasy of your dreams and, in spite of that, clear in your memory, reconstructed in your imagination while you write, square inch by square inch, house by house. Beyond dream, memory, oblivion: a simple page in this book that— once printed, torn from you—will not enter your thoughts again.

WHEN I GOT back to Pablo Alcover, the house seemed smaller and was full of people. Once again we lived on the left side of the ground floor and, now that the Russian volunteers had disappeared, Miss Esther, owner of the property, established herself on the top floor with her half-caste servant. The reds had cut down the cypress hedges that divided the garden and in their place had built a two-roomed hut in the back that we used as a lumber-room, store, and playroom. Our grandparents and Eulalia lived with us and the house was also a meeting place for a number of people more or less linked to the family, whom we had lost sight of during the war: Paquita the dressmaker; Ciscu the buggy driver; Luis's Galician maid with her husband and daughter; the mother of Matías, the ABDECA chauffeur. From the start of term in October, José Agustín and I went to the Jesuit school in Sarriá and Marta to the one run by the nuns of the Sacred Heart.

But my real life, with its comings and goings, reading, hiding places, haunts, would continue to be the house.

At times, with the help of the very few photos of the period, I have tried to reconstruct our busy day-to-day existence in those first squalid postwar months. My brothers and I unfailingly appear badly dressed—I'm always wearing castoffs—with my hair cut almost to nothing, dirty knees, holes in my shoes, a strange mixture of orphan and street urchin. Our social status was confusing because of its ambiguous, imprecise character: we were surrounded by pupils from bourgeois families but the experience, manners, and clothing of everyone else were clearly different from ours. The Viladrau period—with the rather wild freedom we had got used to, a precocious fondness for reading, a liking for solitary life, self-taught habits—separated and would always separate me from the rest of my friends. Although the school life we were entering tended toward uni-formity and discipline, the centrifugal attraction of our tribal existence was more forceful and won out in the end.

No doubt my father got by with the wage he earned from the factory but, whether because of the general poverty of the time, or the gap left by my mother in the running of the household, or a combination of the two, we did not live comfortably. The food distributed through the official ration cards was meagre and of poor quality. Matías, the chauffeur, sometimes took us to Torrentbó and we would come back loaded with sacks of potatoes or yams. On schooldays, Eulalia would fill our thermoses with bread soaked in milk or flour mixed with milk. I remember that we used to go to the dairy with her and if the owner had used up his stocks, we had to be satisfied with a tasteless, deceptively white liquid. Sugar disappeared and had to be replaced with saccharine. During that year, bread got worse: the bread sold in bakeries was small, heavy, as hard as stone. To get your teeth into it, you had to soak it. Chocolate tasted of carob beans and it was impossible to buy coffee.

Given the lack of chickens and rabbits, which were confiscated at check-points on the roads into the city, my father had decided to raise guinea pigs. In the garden, between the garage and the shed, he laid out wire fencing behind which the rodents began to propagate. Every day we ran to catch them and hand them over to Eulalia. Cooked in cornmeal, they were our daily diet for some time: Matías, his mother, the housekeeper, and the dressmaker enthusiastically joined in the feast.

The inhuman poverty that oppressed the country affected even the upper classes. We were warned at school against a typhoid epidemic and classes were suspended for a few days. As Luis and I spent a long time every day playing with the guinea pigs, we were soon infested with parasites. Eulalia and Matías's mother oiled our hair and carefully removed the fleas and nits. The day after, my father took us to the hairdresser who clipped the three of us like sheep with a lot of good-natured joking.

This period of plagues, repression, and poverty was dressed for the outside world in fake tinsel and elation: the end of the struggle, the victory of the "good guys" were depicted at home and school in almost mystic terms.

Uncle Ignacio had brought a record of the caudillo's voice: after winding up the old gramophone, we listened to it at dusk, vaguely uplifted. World war had broken out and our visitors talked about it endlessly. In general, German victories were greeted enthusiastically; only Uncle Luis and Uncle Leopoldo expressed reservations. I had got used to reading the newspapers and I excitedly followed the incidents in the conflict: the Danzig Corridor, Poland, the Maginot Line, the Siegfried Line. I plotted the movement of troops on my maps, I found the battle zones, put markers on the ports that sheltered the rival armadas. A great passion for history was gradually added to my initial interest in geography. From then on they would be my favorite subjects until the much later discovery of literature.

Franco, José Antonio, the Martyrs, the rich, drunken beat of the "Bride-groom of Death." At the school of St. Ignatius, before breaking ranks in the playground, we hummed a song of which I remember only one verse and its strident chorus:

War against the fatal sickle
and the destructive hammer
long live our caudillo
and Imperial Spain!

One day, dressed in blue shirts and red berets, we walked down from the top of Sarriá to the center of Barcelona: Count Ciano had arrived! Under the fathers' energetic batons we shouted until we were hoarse, waiting for him to appear in an open car: thousands of arms raised, children's mouths opened, flags, music, emblems, a theatrical apotheosis. The recipient of so much fervor walked slowly before us, bellicose, hardened, erect, apparently indifferent to the cheers and applause: exemplary standard bearer, Roman consul, and gladiator, herald of the new Holy Empire. Immersed in the crowd, the boy with the shaved head was unaware of his outstanding record of service, the punishing skill of his rapid aeronauts. He also greeted, automatically, his pose as a Great Man, a titanic Forger of the Future while the loudspeakers broadcast the "Cara al sol" and those present applauded, went on applauding the processional chariot of heroes, as it became tiny, diminished in the distance.

The experience of the three war-years created a distance between me and my classmates that was difficult to bridge. There was no common ground where my interests, worries, tastes could mesh with theirs. While the majority of them had lived through the conflict within the national territory and proudly showed off their appearance and good manners, I had already felt the true harshness of life: their childishness, sociability, affected ways were totally incompatible with my love of solitude and reading contracted in Viladrau. Except for geography and history, in which I immediately shone to the point of correcting my teachers, at least mentally, my marks were usually average. At recess, I would retreat to some corner or hidden spot with a novel or an illustrated geography book. Efforts to make me play football always failed miserably. In the annual psychopedagogical reports they made to parents, the fathers would anxiously emphasize my isolation, lack of enthusiasm for games, disinterest in my classmates, my furtive reading. My odd appearance, reserved character, and surliness did not help to integrate me into the class. Referring to the excessively long sleeves of a jacket that was already quite old, one of these elegant, refined boys had remarked sarcastically: "You're so young, are you already inheriting?" This comment left me with a feeling of humiliation and helplessness and intensified my misanthropy. The childish hobbies of my schoolmates, their social code, which I did not share, brought me back to my personal world: the house in Pablo Alcover, playing with Luis, talking to Eulalia, reading the newspapers, a voracious hunger for the facts, photographs, and prints in my encyclopedia. About that time, I heard a friend of my father, to whom I shall refer later on, relate a dramatic family incident that happened in Canada some years before: his three daughters lived through the war in a luxury boarding-house—a kind of Gothic castle with turrets and battlements—and the youngest and most beautiful of the sisters was killed in a fire. When I left school, walking down calle Anglí, I would repeat the exotic details of the drama to pupils from the neighborhood, attributing them to my own family. A precocious, obviously compensatory mania for story telling thus became one of the main features of my character for some time. The desire to shock, to be admired, to exalt myself before my companions would then force me to write my own stories, taking advantage of the summer holidays in Torrentbó. Meanwhile, a victim of my own timid, antisocial ways, I ingenuously sought out opportunities to astonish others with sudden demonstrations of largesse or daring. My grandmother used to leave her purse in her room while we were eating, and I would use any pretext to leave the table and casually pinch her money: first, five peseta notes; then, twenty-five peseta notes—a big amount in those days. With the fruit of my thefts, I used to walk up Calle Mayor in Sarriá and go to the sweetshop that still belongs, I believe, to the Catalan poet I most admire today, the surrealist J.V. Foix. There, my grandmother's notes were exchanged for big bags of sweets, which, once at school, I gave out condescendingly to my peers. This lavish generosity—highlighted by the fact that my own lack of pleasure in sweets kept me, scornfully, on the edge of the subsequent scramble—earned me interest and friends and flattered my feelings of vanity and revenge. I remember the day one of the fathers, seeing the floor covered with candy wrappers, asked whom they came from: I got up from my seat and invented a birthday party for a member of the family. The priest accepted the explanation and, with a lordly gesture, typical of those times, ordered the cleaner—a pupil of humble origins who did not pay his matriculation and was responsible for cleaning the classrooms—to sweep them up in front of all of us before the start of the lesson. The boy obeyed without blushing and I fear that nobody in the room blushed on his behalf.

This same eagerness to make myself stand out before my peers in spite of my secretive, introspective nature involved me later on in a distressing episode that would make me hate the school forever. The math teacher, Mercader, left the room for a few minutes and when he came back an informer told him that the rule of silence had been broken; Mercader insisted on knowing who caused the din. A few students in the first rows raised their hands and, anxious to put on airs in front of the others, I raised my arm without noticing that I was the only one to do so in that part of the room. Mercader asked me whom I had talked to: as my action was pure bravado and I hadn't exchanged a word with anybody, I sat there with my lips sealed. My rebelliousness caused amazement and I was punished by having to stand during recess with my face to the wall on the right of the blackboard. The incident seemed to be forgotten when somebody—perhaps the teacher himself—noticed the word *Mercado* written on the wall followed by a swear word. Annoyed, looking serious, he tried to find out who the guilty person was and, seeing that nobody was forthcoming, he suspended break until further notice. Somebody was suspected—a pupil named Masnou—whom Mercader had told off a few days before; but the boy denied that he had written the words. As I had sympathized with him when we were leaving the classroom, he deduced, wrongly, that I was doing so out of remorse, and to shift the blame from himself, he accused me. Next day the priest who was Director of Studies called me to his office and asked me to write the word *Mercado* on a sheet of paper. Although I denied any involvement in the matter, he dwelled on my incredible refusal to reveal the name of the pupil I talked to, my punishment of facing the wall just where the graffiti appeared, and on how ugly and hateful in God's eyes was stubbornness in deception. Stupidly trapped in my own game, I entrenched myself in a pitiful silence. There was no way to prove anything and, consequently, I received no punishment. But from then I felt some teachers bore a grudge against me and my reaction was to lose interest in my studies. Reports on my behavior and my examination scores suffered the effects at once. When, a year later, my brother José Agustín had a personal quarrel with the tutor of his class, my father, very sensibly, decided that the place was not for us and enrolled both of us in the school run by the Christian Doctrine Brothers in the Bonanova district.

The injustice I had suffered, provoked by a chain of events for which I was partly responsible—the manly deed of raising my hand for the gallery although I had not been making a din; my silence and apparent guilt; my inopportune concern for the boy accused of the graffiti revealed to me the close relation that can exist between our acts and their consequences that, once set in motion by them, turn us into sorcerer's apprentices. Hurt by the suspicions of which I was the object and mortified by my own stupidity, I decided to be more cautious and controlled in the future. Although I had learned from the experience, the distress it caused did not disappear. Being accused of something I had not done—a theft, lie, crime—would henceforth become a repeated, obsessive motif of my nightmares. Even today, I am still haunted by dreams of persecution from time to time: I am in the hands of Franco's police or of the KGB. I don't know whether this adult mental script goes back to the spontaneous childish gesture of raising my hand or is the product of a later insidious feeling of guilt. Whatever its source, the many-episoded, monotonous tale of the nightly trial began early in my life and, like those eternal television serials consecrated by public success, forty years later, does not seem to be coming to an end.

At the beginning of July, after the examinations, we moved to Torrentbó. Immediately after the war my father had bought the undivided parts of the estate allotted to his brothers and from then on he was the owner of the entire farmhouse and its land. The changes suffered during the period it gave shelter to President Aguirre after the fall of the Basque country were not serious: although scattered about, dusty, full of cobwebs, most of the furniture and belongings were recovered. The extreme penury of the period and the abundance of a cheap, passive labor force, inspired in my father the idea of setting up a modest farm with some livestock. After drawing up new contracts for grape-picking with the wine producers and organizing the collection and sale of the cork from the cork oak woods, he concentrated on two objectives: the breeding of cows, pigs, rabbits, and chickens and the cultivation of all the agricultural produce that was scarce in Barcelona and commanded very high prices on the black market. Alternating irrigated and dry land; cultivating each properly; clearing hills, mines, and streams; planting fruit trees; fertilizing, sowing, and harvesting; selecting, buying, and caring for animals; all needed the presence of a factotum expert in such matters. In our first postwar summer holidays in Torrentbó, the hardworking, wise, responsible, versatile man prepared to shoulder the enormous task of establishing the model farm was named Don Angel, and on our arrival he was introduced as a paragon of virtue. A veterinarian, a traditionalist, and a Catholic, the new overseer held all the cards necessary to seduce my father. He too had suffered the drama and persecutions of the red period and his wife, seriously ill as a result, was recovering from her illness near Badalona. In his small portable library—which, on his departure, he mysteriously left behind—books of religious devotion and books dedicated to the Carlist struggle rubbed shoulders with dog-eared manuals from his years of college study and works on the feeding and care of cattle, pigs, and horses. At my father's suggestion, he had also bought dozens of rabbits and hens to feed the family every day and, not satisfied with putting them in the coops and barns, he put some in rooms on the floor where we were going to live. When we arrived, Don Angel moved their lordships to the lower floor where the laborers slept, and the landing and rooms next to the chapel had to be cleaned out. But neither his nor my father's enthusiasm were dampened as a result: sitting in the garden, together they planned new improvements and developments before burying themselves in the revision of the voluminous book of accounts.

I can remember Don Angel in his role of the perpetually busy man, walking across the terrace with some tool, giving the laborers their orders, putting right some botched job. He had an enormous range of responsibilities and had to be constantly vigilant: unblocking pipes, changing the cows' straw, swilling out the pigsties, watering the rows of potatoes, getting the buggy ready, harnessing the mule, giving the rabbits their grass. To satisfy my father, he had planted a number of prickly pears in the wood next to the house and used the fertilizers he had suggested for both dry and wet lands. Despite this determination, when their carefully made plans were put into practice they met with a worrying succession of obstacles and unforeseen problems. There was a myxomatosis epidemic that suddenly wiped out the rabbits; several cows stopped producing milk; the vegetables and greens did not respond as they should have to the use of new chemical products. These setbacks—and the hesitations they provoked— seem now from a distance very similar to those that overwhelmed Bouvard and Pécuchet and put an end to their ambitious plans. The distance between Don Angel's plans and their meagre results became a subject of conversation in the family. Eulalia, with her innate suspicion and solid peasant instincts, had elaborated almost scornfully a series of comments on him that gradually damaged his prestige. Hardworking? A lazybones! The interest and diligence he displayed in the presence of my father disappeared as soon as my father's back was turned. Forewarned by her, my brothers and I would catch don Angel stretched out enjoying a peaceful siesta under some tree. In the fields his incompetence was notorious and the laborers did not seem to feel much appreciation for his tiresome exaltation of Carlist ideals. Such useless idleness finally disabused my father and as, to cap it all, the accounts didn't square and the supposed profits were inexplicably transformed into new expenses, the fantasy reign of Don Angel came to an abrupt conclusion. My father decided to get rid of him and entrust the running of the farm to a true family of smallholders.

The manager of one of the adjacent properties wanted to work for us and my father reached an agreement with him. Although indelibly stained by a discreet red past, he had, however, looked after his master's estate during the war and this respect of his for other people's property, added to the fact that his only daughter was the fiancée of a hardworking, right-wing Catholic lad, gave him an aura of respectability. The Rat— this was the nickname by which he was known in the village, in spite of his reddish drinker's complexion and considerable paunch—at once displayed his skill and diligence: the farm's general appearance improved; the crops prospered. Things might have continued on the right track with him and his son-in-law, but the restlessness and itching for experimentation that always niggled away at my father fatally predisposed him toward new adventures.

After he had resolved our immediate problem, our lack of fats and protein, with the domestic breeding of guinea pigs, his anxious mind sought other spheres to conquer. The first stage was his discovery of a dye from juice extracted from walnut shells. He intended to market it commercially, baptized it "walnut paint," and daubed it on the walls of several rooms until, convinced of their ugliness, he gave up on it. Later on, his great liking for prickly pear cacti and their fruits, which he had taught us to pick with pliers at daybreak, led him to concoct a hair cream with a vegetable substance from their leaves. After the typhoid outbreak and the plague of fleas, we once more wore our hair short as was the fashion then and, like all other boys, we used to stick it down every day with dabs of Lucky Strike. After concocting some suspicious looking mixtures and brews, my father decided not to try them out on somebody else's head, but to experiment first upon himself: his already greying hair immediately acquired a gentle greenish hue. But he was not a man to lose heart over such trivialities. He assured us that his mixture strengthened the roots of the hair, stopped it from falling out, and made it look natural. Fortified by the experiment on himself, he insisted on extending it to the family: one morning, despite my tears and protests, he decided to grease my hair with his product. I had to give in, weeping, and at school the strange color of my hair immediately roused my companions' curiosity. The butt of their jokes, I shut myself in the toilet in a rage and furiously soaped my hair until all trace of the wretched invention was gone.

Unfortunately my father—gradually hemmed in by his shareholders in the management of ABDECA and eager to prove his business acumen to himself and everyone else—did not always come up with such simple, cheap schemes. All it took was a catalyst to bring out his secret desire to emulate the spectacular economic successes of Great-grandfather. Two or three years after the end of the war, a scientist with ideas and interests similar to my father's began to come to our house. I shall call him Dr. Roset. Bald, bespectacled, untidily dressed, also beset by digestive problems, he belonged to a well-known family and had lived for several years in Canada: there he had separated from his wife, and now he lived with his two twenty-year-old daughters. They were fair-haired and exceptionally beautiful and their visits with us to the Caldetas beach had the effect of a tidal wave on the bathers. Dr. Roset was a fanatical anti-Communist, and already at that date he had predicted the manufacture of destructive weapons capable of annihilating once and for all the Bolshevik system in Russia. His political ideology and firm religious beliefs naturally inclined my father very much in his favor. As a result, his ambitious plans in the field of plant bacteriology—a new method of inoculating plants aimed at stimulating growth and greatly increasing the number of fruit—were immediately greeted with great enthusiasm. With my father's money, he rented a dilapidated house on the Paseo de Santa Eulalia in Sarriá and set up the bacteriological laboratory where he carried out his experiments. His youngest daughter, my sister, and two of our cousins worked there, in their white coats inoculating soy plants with the contents of his little tubes. As a layman in matters of chemistry and natural sciences, I cannot judge whether the enterprise had any rational basis. In the opinion of some close observers who are better informed than I am, neither my father nor Dr. Roset were on the wrong lines in the practical application of their analyses. However, between the analysis and commercial viability stretched a hazardous path that was very difficult to follow given the austere, precarious state of the market. Since the capital necessary for large-scale promotion was lacking, my father's laboratory could never be anything more than an amusing but costly family toy. After the first tests in the garden in Sarriá, Dr. Roset and my father extended their experiments to the fields and furrows of Torrentbó. Ignoring the fear and suspicions of the farm-manager they sowed enormous amounts of soy on dry lands: some had been inoculated, some hadn't. Marta, my cousins, and the doctor's daughter had been photographed in their white coats holding up a plant pot in each hand. Just like the advertisements for a miraculous hair lotion in which the first image of a horrible, decrepit bald head is followed by another image of the same person, smiling, hairy, amazingly handsome, the half-dead plant on the right was contrasted with the healthy, tall, leafy plant on the left, all attributed naturally to the wonderful virtues of inoculation. But the indisputable results in Sarriá were less impressive in Torrentbó. The differences between plants in height, thickness, and number of seed-bearing pods were often nil. In some cases, to the consternation and dismay of Dr. Roset and my father, the inoculated plants were clearly inferior. This disturbing mystery, welcomed by the impassive farmer with a slightly ironical look, was clarified for me by his son-in-law Alfredo, many years later. Upset by the conceit and apparent omniscience of Dr. Roset—who was naturally contemptuous toward the traditional peasant methods of cultivation—the Rat had amused himself by maliciously changing some of the labels and tags, putting the inoculated sign on the plants that hadn't been inoculated and vice versa. I am not sure whether this cruel trick did or did not precipitate the end of the enterprise. Faced with the impossibility of expanding the market beyond the boundaries of Torrentbó, the bacteriological laboratory had become a hindrance, and after several lethargic years and considerable financial losses, my father decided sensibly to shut it.

My description of my father's obsession with eccentric, even preposterous, undertakings has perhaps inevitably been ironic. I have not done justice to his creative intuitions, to the interest he always showed in the harmonious development of nature's resources, to his real, if modest, contribution to our knowledge and defense of the natural habitat. My father often wrote for the scientific magazine of the Jesuit fathers of Barcelona and, as I was told later by an expert in these matters, his articles, apparently influenced by Teilhard de Chardin, were stimulating and innovative in the context of this mediocre period. From childhood, he strove to bring us up with a respect for a certain ecological balance threatened, he would say, by mechanization and progress. His hatred for artificial ingredients, preservatives, and the manipulatory strategies of the food industry put him in the vanguard of the present movements toward natural foods and natural living. What my adolescence took for manias— his linking of tobacco and cancer, his hostility to prolonged sunbathing, and the pernicious effect of additives and coloring—were eventually proved to be undeniable facts. My father had also, in his way, the misfortune to live in an adverse family climate. His tastes and enthusiasms, unshared by his children, condemned him in turn to a distressing isolation. My personal world, given over passionately to books, the rather petulant fifteen-year-old decision to become a novelist, must have been as strange and alien to him as his failed ventures and scientific disquisitions were to me. These differences of vocation and interests, combined with some traits of character completely opposed to mine, did not favor our mutual understanding. His lack of insight, his blindness in relation to his children met with our parallel blindness and lack of sympathy. My father sincerely believed that by giving up ideas of remarriage and trying to give us a brilliant future, he was sacrificing himself for us. This future— projected by him toward science or business—responded, of course, to his aspirations, not to ours. Although he modified his attitude as time passed—when forced to accept my role as a writer, he dreamt I would at least have a brilliant, successful career—the impossibility of making him accept the true nature of my life doomed from the outset any pretense of dialogue. Our short, infrequent encounters in his last years teetered along under the pious cover of deceit. As we could not discuss crucial matters, our conversation was reduced to a string of commonplaces. Any revelation of my religious agnosticism, Marxist ideas, sexual behavior would have been an unbearable blow to him. It would have been gratuitously cruel to lead the conversation around to any of these topics. Condemned to dissimulation, I remained emotionally distanced from him, not worrying too much about his sad, frustrated life, mentally prepared for the time when he would disappear completely. Only after he was dead, after the unexpected meeting with him, alive, real, almost flesh and blood, the night I was delirious after taking too much majoon, could I judge him more objectively and even experience an outburst of unsuspected tenderness for him.

Before we left Viladrau, our grandparents put Aunt Consuelo back in the nursing home where she had previously been cared for, and they moved in with us on the ground floor on Pablo Alcover. Their presence was scarcely felt in that average-size badly arranged house, which already contained six people counting adults and children. Grandmother Marta had not yet shown the first signs of absentmindedness, and she fulfilled the usual functions of the Catalan *iaia*. She used to take Luis to the infants' school at the top of calle Anglí and, at home, she read him, with inexhaustible patience, the little books in the *Marujita* collection that we both consumed so voraciously. Grandfather Ricardo entertained himself with the help of the daily papers and, weather permitting, used to sit and rest at the end of the garden. Both lodged in the room at the front of the house next to the office: a room filled by a huge plate-glass wardrobe in front of which my parents had their photo taken on their wedding day, a matching double bed, and a bureau in the top drawer of which she put her purse. I could not say if my first raids on the latter began then or after we returned from our second summer in Torrentbó. I probably filched something every once in a while and my regular extractions—once or twice a week—began at a later date.

I slept alone in the library-office, on a divan squashed between the wall and a piece of furniture: after going to bed I could see my grandparents slip into their room and listen to their chatter and prayers until they put out the light. One night, when the whole house was in darkness, I had a visitor. Grandfather, wearing his long white nightshirt, came up to the head of my bed and made himself comfortable on the edge. In a voice that was almost a whisper, he said he was going to tell me a story, but began straightaway to tickle me and cover me with kisses. I was surprised by this sudden apparition and above all by its furtive character. "Let's play," Grandfather would say and, after putting out the bedside lamp by which I sometimes read before falling asleep, and which I had switched on upon hearing his footsteps, he stretched out by my side on the bed and gently slipped his hand down my pajamas until he touched my penis. His touch was upsetting but I was paralyzed by fear and confusion. I felt Grandfather leaning over my lap, first his fingers and then his lips, the viscous trickle of his saliva. When after several unending minutes he seemed to calm down and sat down again on the edge of the bed, my heart beat rapidly. What was the meaning of all this playing around? Why did he make a kind of groaning sound after fingering me? I had no answers and while the unwelcome visitor tiptoed back to the adjacent room where Grandmother was sleeping, I lay there for a while sunk in a state of anxious confusion.

Grandfather Ricardo asked me to keep it a secret and during the day nothing in his behavior would allow one to guess that that peaceful old man sitting with his newspaper in the shade of the chestnut tree was the same person who the night before had got into my bed, all sniggers and tickles. At night, he walked through my room with Grandmother. But, half an hour later—just long enough for her to fall asleep and for the house lights to go out—he repeated the previous night's visit. Unable to react to the new situation he was imposing on me, I pretended to fall into a kind of trance while he masturbated me with his hand and lips: this time he had switched on the light and the idea of seeing him kneeling next to my bed was more than I could take. I don't know how often Grandfather came back to paw me on the warm June nights that preceded the summer and our trip to Torrentbó. Five, ten times? I adopted the ingenious strategy of sleep and so avoided the spectacle of his repeated, annoying fingerings.

Weeks later, in a small grove of carob trees next to the gardens in Torrentbó, I told José Agustín what had happened. We had been discussing Grandfather's character in general terms—his meticulous hygiene, reserve, and stinginess—when the desire to tell him about my recent, embarrassing experience overcame my instinctive shyness. When I finished the story, fearing the likely complications if it was spread further, I begged my brother not to repeat a word of it. If Grandfather resumed his tricks when we returned to Barcelona, I added, I would contrive by myself to disappoint him.

With this in mind I piled a stack of books up by my bed on the night of our return. My grandparents went through my room as usual and, when the lights went out, I remained awake, crouching down, several encyclopedia volumes within reach of my hand, ready to throw at the intruder as soon as he showed up. But Grandfather gave no sign of life and, greatly relieved, I finally went to sleep with my small and now useless throwable library. The next day, after school, José Agustín said that Father wanted to speak to me. I went up to the small terrace above the garage where Eulalia used to hang out the washing. My father sat on a wicker armchair looking serious and forbidding and he asked me at once whether the incident with Grandfather was true. I said it was and his cold, gaunt, hawk-nosed features sharpened and stood out even more like those of a bird of prey. He did not attempt to hide the hatred he felt for his father-in-law, and he explained that this nasty vice of his was a crime against nature and had already ruined his promising career. As I found out then, my grandfather had held an important position in provincial government before the war, until he was caught touching a young lad and relative in a changing-room at the spa in San Sebastián near Barcelona. People wanted to lynch him, my father said approvingly. They took him in handcuffs to prison, like a criminal, and when we went to see him with Grandmother and your mother, they cried tears of shame while he was silent and didn't even try to apologize. More and more excited, my father related in detail the disgrace and stigmas the guilty man had brought upon himself and his family: early retirement from the Town Hall; public dishonor; a perpetual stain on the good name of the family. Out of respect for my mother, he had had to swallow his disgust at that effeminate behavior and lack of virility; but this latest exploit was more than he could endure and his punishment should really teach him a lesson.

I don't know what was said in the interview between the two men, which no doubt took place on the same day I talked to my father. That afternoon, my grandparents packed up their personal belongings and, under the righteous, reproving gaze of their son-in-law, went to live in a small sublet villa about three blocks from home. Their departure, humiliating for both of them, coincided, I think, with the sudden worsening of Grandmother's health. From then on, they both ate lunch and dinner with us, but returned to their new house after rosary and evening prayers. Without taking into account the effect his behavior might have on his mother-in-law, my father did not bother to hide the aversion he felt for the guilty man, the greatest cross he had to bear, he would say sighing deeply. This systematic, persistent, small-minded persecution would continue over twenty years until they both died almost simultaneously. Conscious that he held all the cards, my father came up with a thousand ways to humiliate him. Forced to tolerate him for material reasons—ever since his forced departure from his job with ABDECA and the failed experiment with the bacteriology laboratory, most of our family's income came from the pension and savings of his father-in-law—he made him pay for that fact with an anger that rightly infuriated Eulalia and was often counterproductive. In 1951 when he flung himself into his last and most disastrous adventure with the latest Nazi boy wonder, he did so by coercing Grandfather, almost blackmailing him, into selling a boardinghouse he owned. Instead of elevating us to the heights of opulence, as he trustingly believed, the proceeds from the sale disappeared, as if by magic, into the bottomless pocket of a certain Calvet, who was persecuted by the Belgian police because of his shady dealings with the Germans.

The tension provoked by this fact and, in general, the incessant harassment that preceded it have been described by Luis in his novel *Antagonía* and I won't linger on it. Like many old married couples, my grandfather and father had created for themselves a small private hell whose routine allowed them to survive. The constant bitterness of the one and the cowed resignation of the other were the daily bread of life in

Barcelona: a distressing element, whose intolerable repetition was a decisive factor in my hatred of the place. To move away from home, the district, the city: all my brand-new student plans centered on the idea of escape. The day I finally broke loose, I already lived outside mentally. When you go away it is because you have already left.

The incident with grandfather and the reaction it aroused in the family certainly had a traumatic effect upon me. My father's visceral hatred of homosexuals—Grandfather provided the nearest loathsome example—sometimes reached morbid extremes. He once related with great satisfaction to José Agustín—who wasted no time in repeating to me—that Mussolini ordered the summary execution of "all queers." Although at that time I had not the slightest idea about my future sexuality, the news, rather than exciting me, filled me with unease. Of course, I thought that Grandfather's behavior toward me was reprehensible; but his punishment, cheerfully trumpeted around the house, awoke my sense of injustice and earned my condemnation. Mussolini's crude therapy must have been mentioned by my father, just as a simple piece of information, in the presence of my grandfather, who accepted it without protest—as usual. His submission to other people's judgments, his passive acceptance of his pariah state as natural, his inability to react against the attacks he continuously suffered much later provoked in me tremendous pity for him. His compulsive pederasty, shamefully hidden for decades, had been lived out as a secret tragedy: a vice condemned by the religion he believed in and the society that surrounded him. Since he did not have the moral temper necessary to control it, he had no choice but to offer his head to the executioner's axe each time he had the misfortune to give in to it and was then exposed to public pillorying. The memory of this self-contempt resulting from the scorn of others, of the shame that was accepted and transmuted into inner guilt, weighed very heavily in my decision to affirm my destiny whatever the cost, and to set everything out clearly for myself and others. When Monique published her first novel, entitled *Les poissons-chats*—a work that describes the love of the heroine for a homosexual—Grandfather Ricardo read it, two or three years before he died, and was terribly shocked. Luis told me how he had explained in tears that the passions explored in the book were a hateful sin, that he had suffered from them throughout his life, and that whenever he yielded to them he had most deeply offended God. The idea that I might follow in his tracks, that I too might resign myself to a miserable, broken existence was the best antidote for my doubts and hesitations when, not entirely surprisingly, I found myself in the contradictory position of enjoying an intense emotional relationship with Monique and discovering the physical happiness I had not felt till then with a Moroccan construction worker living temporarily in France. With wise timing death saved my father from this final cruel blow: the realization that his secret fears, perhaps his darkest forebodings, had finally been expressed in me.

My grandmother began to suffer from loss of memory around the time I started to steal regularly from her purse. She was constantly forgetting where she had left things, she looked for them time and time again even in the most unlikely places and, if after turning the whole house upside down, the object that had gone astray did not appear, she would rush from one end of the passage to another like a madwoman, saying that she had gone out of her mind and mumbling like a spell the prayer to Saint Anthony:

> If you seek miracles, look:
> death and horror banished,
> poverty and the devil fled,
> the leprous and the sick healthy . . .

Her disturbed state got worse after our return from our second summer in Torrentbó, and I felt partly responsible. The twenty-five peseta notes that vanished mysteriously from her purse kept tormenting her. But it was here; I left it here with the keys only this morning . . . Grandfather would listen to her patiently, and, much to my relief, diverted any suspicions about theft into possible mishaps in the street, when she took Luis to school or came back from her meditations in church. These scenes, which followed the rhythm of my stealing, did not make me excessively remorseful. From the start, I had latched onto the precious immunity her absentmindedness provided me and used it in the most brazen manner. While Grandmother searched the house with her black oilskin bag under her arm, trying to recall where she had put the blessed note, I calmly stroked it in my pocket, thinking about the packet of sweets with which I would amaze my fellow pupils after the almost daily call at the wonderful Foix sweetshop. Grandmother no doubt suspected me as the probable thief; but rather than accuse me and show me up, she preferred to heap the blame on herself and put the losses down to her disorder and forgetfulness. Sometimes she asked me to recite the supposedly miraculous prayer along with her and I did so without any hesitation, proud of my lack of vulnerability. This shocking lack of any moral sense, almost certainly a fruit of our precocious experience of war, was to affect collectively each of the four children: we would all have, at one moment or another in our life, to struggle fiercely against it, to impose a norm of personal honesty, in a long, exhausting conflict whose outcome was unsure. As far as I am concerned, I did not forge my own code of strict integrity in fits and starts, but much later: far from home and in opposition to the values of our milieu, from the day I began to take an interest in politics where I also discovered a particular kind of trickery and deception. But I find my own unexpected lack of compassion much more surprising than our early amoral attitudes. My grandmother's infinite goodness, her self-denial for us, her boundless patience, the succession of tragedies that marked her life were not considered at all from the moment I decided to swipe from her purse. I can remember with a retrospective sense of shame the day that, no doubt fearing one of the forays I liked to carry out during lunch, excusing myself from the table on the pretext of going to the toilet, she sat down with her oilskin bag, and I was furious at seeing my plans foiled and insisted that she take it out as a matter of good manners and respect for the other guests. Grandmother obeyed me with tears in her eyes and as she left to put her purse in the usual place, she muttered in her distress, "Just as you wish, love, just as you wish."

Aunt Consuelo's death in the nursing home, the conflict between my father and her husband, the rushed move to the new abode far from the rest of the family, were certainly the main causes of Grandmother's mental disturbance. But her knowledge of the facts, of the reasons for their expulsion from our house is and always will be a mystery to me. Did my father or grandfather tell her what happened? Or else, as I sometimes think, had she noticed herself when Grandfather deserted their bed on those nights and slipped into the room next door with intentions that could be no secret to her after his previous arrest and imprisonment? Did she have to resign herself to her husband's final, painful act of madness, perhaps suffering in silence his kissing and titters in their grandson's bed? In its turn, had her more or less certain awareness of all this set off the defense mechanisms of her own dementia? What is certain is that she soon added a mania to her absentmindedness, her real or supposed wayward-ness, and her loss of sense of direction. When I discovered it, I was really perplexed. She collected and rummaged through the garbage. At home she had begun, much to the consternation of Eulalia, to collect the skins of fruit and other leftovers, hoarding them carefully in her bag. She would walk to and fro in the garden loaded down with rubbish, aimlessly, until my father or grandfather told her to sit down. We children spied on her while she stirred up the garbage can and once when she was caught starting to hide some scraps, she lifted a piece of orange peel to her face and explained, as if playing a joke on me: "Look, I've got a mask!" But the initial, ambiguous excitement we felt as we stalked her soon changed to dismay when Grandmother extended the radius of her activity and began to poke furtively into the trash of the whole neighborhood. She had been so neat and tidy in her black hat and suit and obsessed by the idea of washing her feet before leaving the house—she would say that death might catch her in the street, like a woman she once met, with dirty ankles. Now she walked around in a terribly slovenly state: her hair was dirty and dishevelled, her stockings sagged, and her slippers were full of holes. When I spotted her one day in the distance crouching over a garbage can, my heart gave a turn: she looked like a beggar. Grandfather and Eulalia would nag at her affectionately, but in vain: she should look after herself better and leave the trash in peace. What would the neighbors think of her? Grandmother was silent or she would laugh: she was teetering on the brink. When we went to Torrentbó in the summer she stayed in Barcelona with her husband. One day she caught the train to Caldetas to come and see us. Although she knew the route perfectly well, she got lost when she left the station on the way to the *riera* and reached home flushed, out of breath, without money or purse, accompanied by some strangers who had taken pity on her when they saw her lost and alone. She had to be escorted back to Barcelona like a naughty girl who had run away. She spoke incoherently and seemed ridiculously scared that Grandfather Ricardo would scold her.

On our return to Pablo Alcover at the start of term we suddenly discovered her absence. Without us knowing, my father and grandfather had taken the difficult but inevitable decision to intern her in the nursing home where Aunt Consuelo had been. The death of her two daughters and the family tension created by her husband's behavior had swept away the last traces of her sanity, suddenly and indiscriminately removing all her memories. She had eternally sacrificed herself to the good of others and was incapable of thinking of herself. The successive blows that had rained down on her left her unprotected, with nothing to cling to. Although I don't discount the natural inclination to madness present on my mother's side of the family, hers was instead the product of an exceptionally bitter destiny and her almost total inability to fight back: she left the stage on tiptoe, with "shush" on her lips, so that we could enjoy the party peacefully without her.

The unhappiness common to almost all the women in my family and their patient acceptance of their lot show, with astonishing clarity, the truth of the arguments and positions of the feminist movement. Why were they always cast in the role of victims? A passiveness inherent in the supposed "feminine condition" or rather, as they themselves would say on acceding to the use of words, the necessary consequence of the pressures of society? Our grandparents Marta and Ricardo had lived in parallel form through a mutually oppressive situation without being able to help each other: traditional, Catholic, Spanish morality would finally crush both of them.

I only saw Grandmother once more, months later, on the day Eulalia and I went to visit her in the suburban nursing home where they looked after her. The description of this melancholy encounter in *Señas de identidad* spares me the painful task of recalling it in detail here. For those who haven't read the work, I shall just note that grandmother didn't recognize me and that, after exchanging a few polite phrases with Eulalia and myself, she returned to the opaque world that protected her from her unhappiness, where, mistress of a vast void, she undoubtedly lived a better life.

Since the disappearance of Don Angel, our summers in Torrentbó had assumed a regular scenario: the same curtains, the same dialogue, the same actors, the same ritual. Aunt Catalina, my father's eldest sister, moved with her two daughters into the bedrooms next to the chapel and with the help of an old Navarrese servant, La Genara, her family cooked and ate, separate from us, in the dormer rooms on the top floor. Widowed quite some time ago by a husband she never mentioned—as if shrouding him in a cloud of unrelenting, implicit disapproval—she devoted all her time and energy to two main preoccupations: her prayers and the persnickety care of her delicate health. Forced to divide her day between her medicines and her worship, she followed a timetable that was as necessary, absorbing, and exact as those usually imposed in barracks or boarding schools in order to stiffen the resolve of the recruits or pupils. The range and antithetical character of her pains demanded the regular consumption of a series of medicines each of which was usually aimed at overcoming the damaging effect of the previous medicine: the potion she took for her liver apparently had a negative impact on her stomach, which needed as a result a brew that, unhappily, damaged her kidneys for which she then needed a special pill, which in turn ... In between her brews and concoctions, syrups and drugs, Aunt Catalina fitted a tight schedule of prayers and pious acts that were sometimes part of the daily routine and sometimes linked to the calendar of saints' days: rosaries, hymns to the Trinity, novenas, prayers for indulgences, and a litany of lesser prayers to the blessed and saintly she particularly worshipped. Fermín de Urmeneta's journalistic contributions to the *Diario de Barcelona* similarly filled her with ecstasy. Don Fermín, a man with a powerful imagination, had specialized, in a manner of speaking, in the subject of the Holy Spirit and, with enviable fertility, assembled new facts, data, and refinements on the object of his ethereal passion. "What a wise man!" she would say in awe, "Have you read his latest article on the Paraclete?" Although she was assisted by her servant and eldest daughter from bedroom to terrace, from dining room to verandah, Aunt would end every day in a state of exhaustion, deprived of a pleasing, well-deserved solace from her innumerable duties and aches and pains. Stretched out on the chaise longue, with her eternal rosary of black beads in her hand, she remained absorbed in the computation of her prayers and pills while Genara and Eulalia discussed their affairs, podding beans or peas into a basket in the shade of the eucalyptus trees in the garden.

Uncle Leopoldo's visits were equally regular but much shorter: the Rat or Alfredo would pick him up at the station in Caldetas and he would come up the *riera* in the buggy with the bag where he kept his books as well as the tobacco, sausage, and olive oil reserved for his own personal consumption. My father's impulse in offering the house to his brothers and sisters would have been really selfless and praiseworthy if he hadn't spoiled it, as was often the case with him, by imposing mean restrictions and petty reminders on his generous largesse. In order to avoid getting a reputation as a sponger, Uncle would arrive in Torrentbó with samples of slightly rancid, "off" sausages, which he would dress himself in the kitchen, under Eulalia's severe and disapproving gaze. His rather cynical, bachelor spirit of independence, his original, outlandish ways, his lack of respect for convention and ignorance of good manners made him a pleasant, attractive person. He was a fixed star in our summers and his delight in evoking his childhood or displaying his knowledge of geography and astronomy, his skill in dishing out gossipy anecdotes, which, but for him, would have remained in oblivion, granted him a leading role in our family's imaginary world. Under a variety of names and disguises, he would appear in one of my novels and in my brother Luis's trilogy, fixed forever in the heart of a literary enterprise whose existence he would be unaware of.

The passion we shared for geography soon took shape in long, interesting conversations about places and territories that neither of us had ever seen. He was selfish, comfort-loving, and sedentary but, although he detested anything new that required an effort on his part and had hardly set foot outside Catalonia, Uncle Leopoldo spoke excitedly, with a dazzling display of detail, about the Peruvian altiplano and the Argentinian pampa, the climate of Zanzibar and the subsoil of Angola. Following his advice, I acquired a voluminous picture atlas, illustrated with plates and photographs, which was my favorite reading matter for two or three years. Thanks to this, I soon memorized the size, population, capital, main cities, legal status, and natural riches of every country in the world. Our chats would range from the orographic makeup of the Caucasus to the French colonial settlements in India or the South Pacific. Uncle spoke about Numea or Pondicherry as if they were well-known spots where he used to spend his weekends. Convinced that Europe would end up in ruins, whatever the result of the war, he tried to shape my destiny by encouraging me to live far away from the continent. Each of the territories

or states described in the book received its share of his attention. Nigeria
and the Congo offered the European colonizer a vast panoply of natural
riches, but the heat and humidity dominating their weather should discourage me from living there; Brazil had obvious advantages: large
stretches of uncultivated land, a cheap, diligent labor force, a language
that could easily be learned, the welcoming, open nature of the inhabitants; in Cuba and Argentina our relatives could help me get started after
I had arrived. But a trip along the Niger River, with its vast plantations
of cotton, groundnuts, sorghum, and rice, outdid in appeal every place
already considered: the hippopotami, canoes, oleaginous palms, pictures of
the native women collecting coconuts aroused my uncle's enthusiasm.
"Did you see their breasts?" he smiled mischievously. "They look like real
melons!" But the imaginary journeys with which he compensated his
becalmed state of inertia had brought him a few problems and headaches
before I was born. Uncle Leopoldo had inherited a fair amount of money
on the death of Grandfather Antonio and, allowing himself to be swept up
by his nomadic fantasies, he had invested part of it in shares in exotic
companies from which he never recovered a cent. But misfortune, far from
restraining him, had increased his theoretical interest and thirst for
knowledge about distant countries and locations. As he was unable to
embark on adventures because of his age, he said, he wanted to pass on to
his nephews his frustrated vocation as a migrant: "Did you read the report
on the Ecuadorian volcanoes? Pichincha, Chimborazo, Cotopaxi. Oh, if
only I were your age!"

His knowledge of astronomy was equally remarkable. Under the
August night sky, when the stars shone like embers gently stirred by the
freshening breeze, Uncle would examine the firmament as if he owned it
and would patiently teach us to decipher the constellations. As I looked
up, Archer, the Two Bears, Cassiopeia, the Valley of the Lyre gradually
stood out, clear and bright, in the midst of the confused flickering of the
galaxies. Thanks to my uncle, I discovered the infinitude of the cosmos
and our tiny presence within it. When I was assailed by my first religious
doubts a few years later this awareness of the ridiculous smallness of the
earth played a vital part in them: did the inhabitants of a lowly, secondary
star really deserve such a lot of attention from their Maker? What absurd
idea had led the Latter to sacrifice Himself so gratuitously for them? Was
his ridiculous choice from that dense, sparkling swarm pure chance or
caprice? Why just us and not the rest?

Together with this seductive penchant for geography and astronomy,
Uncle Leopoldo also had opinions and characteristics that distinguished
him from the rest of his brothers and sisters. He was an Anglophile, didn't
believe in the Germans' victory, and when he defended his ideas against
my father and Uncle Ignacio, all three would end up in a temper,

insulting and reproaching each other. In our conversations after lunch or in the evenings on the verandah, he would bring out and show off the family's skeletons, much to my father's annoyance. Fixing his glasses on his enormous Basque nose, he would describe the uselessness and extravagance of the Taltavulls, Grandfather Antonio's pompous views, the pigeon-brain of one of our cousins. His sister's piety was often a target for his shafts and darts. Did she really think that a Hail Mary, mumbled mechanically, half asleep, would redeem the blessed souls in purgatory from millions of years of suffering? The emphasis he gave to his words and his sarcastic expression had the virtue of riling our aunt: her face, which was usually bloodless and pale, suddenly went beet red.

On Sundays and public holidays we took the buggy to the church in Torrentbó. Aunt Catalina and my father always made themselves comfortable in the front pews, next to the four or five well-to-do people from the settlement, while my brothers and I, next to the peasants in the back pews, listened to the timeworn sermons on modesty in female dress and the immoral spectacle on the beaches. Mossén Luis spoke with his eyes half-closed, but watched his parishioners' behavior out of the corner of his eye; once he called our neighbor's daughter to task for partially baring her elbow, and he demanded she leave the House of God immediately. After the service, the young people usually walked back while my father and aunt exchanged obsequious greetings with the wealthy widow of the Garí banking family and her escort of noble ladies. On Fridays, the priest would come to our house and celebrate Mass in the chapel: afterwards there was breakfast with the altar boys, at which Mossén blessed the food, and we waited with our heads lowered for the cue to throw ourselves at the toast.

With our cousins María and Carmen we went to the beaches in Caldetas and Arenys de Mar or else, equally loaded down with picnic baskets, we hiked to the top of the nearby mountains or walked through the woods as far as the Corredó well and hermitage. On the way, we picked fruit from the fields and were often insulted by the peasants. Apart from these weekly excursions we remained within the boundaries of the farm; depending on the season we looked for almonds, cherries, figs, or grapes to break the monotony of our daily diet. Now that he was no longer managing ABDECA, my father didn't have the use of the company car and our journeys with him or our uncle or aunt were in the buggy. This was usually driven by the Rat but after his daughter had married Alfredo, his son-in-law would often replace him. He was a strong, handsome young man and would later become a good friend.

At home, we read, played mah-jongg or croquet, bathed in the pond, chased after our dogs. José Agustín and I had frequent quarrels and, since he had age on his side, I tended to seek protection from the grown-ups and adopt the nasty role of tattletale. His unfortunate position as the firstborn—and always unfavorably compared by my father to the brother who had disappeared prematurely—throws enough light on the psychological difficulties he would meet later in life. In that period, his misbehavior was typical of his age and our fights always ended quickly without any grudges or enmity. Luis preferred to play with the children of the neighboring peasant-farmers, and Marta and my cousins talked about movie stars and had written a fan-letter to one of them asking for an autographed photo.

The summer holidays followed an unchanging rhythm, the only new developments occurring a few years later: my scribbling excitedly in notebooks in the naive belief that I was writing novels and my equally frenetic and assiduous masturbating on the eruption of puberty.

The content of my reading matter had been changing during my years at school: my liking for the little books in the *Marujita* series was followed by the discovery of Elena Fortuny's characters—Uncle Rodrigo, Celia, Cuchifritín—and then straight on to *Emil and the Detectives* and, especially, the illustrated series of the *Adventures of William*, probably the best of its kind. My interest in Jules Verne and Salgari came rather later: it was a direct result of my visits to the local cinemas where they showed adventure films and, in any case, did not last very long. At the age of fourteen, on the advice of my Uncle Luis, I had begun to get absorbed in the study of history books: biographies of Queen Victoria and Marie Antoinette, the enormous bound volumes of Lafuente's *History of Spain,* a *History of the Girondins* translated from French, Spengler's *Decline of the West*. In the summer, I lingered over the marvellously engraved pages of the old *Spanish and South American Illustrated Magazine* and alternated these samples of a world that fascinated me—of emperors and czars, assassinations, colonial activities, and royal weddings—with a careful survey of books and chronicles referring to the last war, generally written by Spanish correspondents who witnessed it. Uncle Luis was cut off from all communication because of his deafness. To speak to him, you had to roll up a magazine like a tube and shout through it into his outer ear. He was an avid reader of autobiographies and memoirs, copies of which were arranged in neat rows in the living room of the bachelors' flat he shared with Leopoldo. As I gradually lost my penchant for geography and my affection for exotic journeys, I sought out books and magazines that corresponded to this new direction my curiosity took. Thanks to Uncle Luis, I acquired in the space of two or three years a vast, heterogeneous, disjointed knowledge of areas of European history. The endless lists of capitals, rivers, mountains, cities, and natural produce of the entire world that had amazed my geography teachers were now replaced by lists of dynasties, linked conflicts, wars, battles, defeats recited by me at the first opportunity with all the timing and aplomb of a parrot. My prodigious memory and an absurd appeal to my vanity turned me for some time into one of those intolerable know-it-alls rightly hated by masters and pupils alike. When by some trick of memory I go back to that time, the very temporary, ephemeral confusion of our identities leaves me really confused. This life as an insincere poseur started at the age of fourteen or fifteen and lasted beyond adolescence. My facility for storytelling as one way of compensating for family traumas soon expanded into an adjacent area: during the long summer holidays, I would pour these more or less imitative dreams and fantasies onto paper to form a string of historical and adventuresome nonsense.

My fertility in this vein was extraordinary. Seated at the desk on the upstairs verandah in Torrentbó I composed without any corrections in a state of delirious enthusiasm. The dual influence of films and my knowledge of geography can clearly be seen in one of my manuscripts that was recovered years later and now resides in a private collection at Boston University. My sister used to buy the film magazines of the time and to avoid the tiresome, annoying business of describing characters, I got the idea of cutting out photos from them and sticking them on the pages of my exercise book with simple captions indicating their identities. This device—the discovery and use of which would no doubt have modified the novelistic art of such conscientious authors with an eye for detail as Balzac and Galdós—allowed me to get on with the ins-and-outs of the exploration of the Amazon, which I was describing, without worrying about useless character sketches or tedious particulars. I was a most precocious author of photo-novels and was also pioneering a way into that soon-to-be-fashionable world of behaviorist narrative. No commentaries or digressions—straight to the point! With a similar facility and enthusiasm, I wrote a sentimental novel about Joan of Arc and introduced some anachronisms into it. I am unsure if they were unconscious or not but they would now no doubt be greeted by the most prominent critics as examples of a daring, outspoken desire to innovate: rather than die on Bishop Cauchon's bonfire, she died on Robespierre's guillotine after a dramatic confrontation with him. I have a much vaguer memory of my other fifteen-year-old creations: I think there was one about the French Resistance to the Nazis, another with new scenes in the life of Kit Carson, in an episode of my own making. The films shown in the two Sarriá cinemas that I visited regularly with Luis were a source of second-rate ideas, characters, and settings for the proliferation of plots. Fortunately any notion of originality and plagiarism was not yet part of my personal literary baggage.

Once the work was completed, with a rapidity worthy of Corín Tellado, I implacably subjected my cousins to the reading test. I did not realize what torture I was inflicting on them until the evening of a special free dinner for the residents of Our Lady of Guadalupe College in Madrid University. After dinner we were led into the lounge where I believed, in my innocence, that there would be a brief speech from the writer-star of the unexpected banquet while we had coffee, but once the doors were discreetly closed at a perverse signal from the director, the brief speech turned into the interminable declamation of a drama the end of which could have belonged to that marvellous Chekhov tale: the hurling of a paperweight or similar weighty object that smashes with exquisite precision on the magpie head of the dramatist-novelist and interrupts forever the wonderfully soporific development of the third act. Wary now as a result of my own experience, I never again erred into this horrific abuse so common among literary people of deliberately imprisoning a captive audience. The practical application of the rule of "If you read me, I'll read you" is such an important advance for the Republic of Letters that I think it should appear, as a mandatory precept, in the first article of its Constitution.

Not one of my teachers or masters played a role in the development of the literary tastes I have just mentioned. My reading evolved exclusively within the family, without the slightest connection with what they taught or tried to teach us at school. The idea of giving us texts of the classics to read rather than stuffing our heads with dates of births and deaths and the titles of their many works had not yet even penetrated the brains of the ignorant, small-minded priests in charge of our literature classes. The only book that deserved the honor of being read in class throughout my secondary school life was a volume of Father Coloma's stories, in my last year with the Jesuits. We didn't even get that at the Bonanova school: the good brothers of the Christian Doctrine referred body and soul to the learned critical judgments and proven knowledge in the subject of Guillermo Díaz Plaja. Considering the educational system we suffered, it is not surprising that my love and interest in literature derived from other sources: first, Uncle Luis's advice and then my mother's library. Self-taught like almost all the men and women of my generation, my culture, which was tentatively shaped, would for a long time retain the mark of the prejudices, gaps, and insufficiencies of a barren, sunbaked Spain choked by the censorship and rigors of an oppressive regime. It is very significant that the books I would soon rush upon would be almost without exception by foreign authors. I read the novels that I devoured between eighteen and twenty-five either in French or in the second-rate translations that were smuggled in from Buenos Aires. The teaching handed out at school not only made me hate our literature—which was transformed into a collection of pedantic glosses and banal analyses—but also convinced me that there was nothing there worth getting to know. While consuming works by Proust, Gide, Malraux, Dos Passos, or Faulkner, I maintained an Olympian ignorance of our Renaissance or Golden Age. I even thought that Cervantes' universal reputation was suspect: flattered and praised to the skies by the school textbooks, the *Quixote* had to be a boring, tedious book. Intoxicated by Voltaire or Laclos, I felt no interest in the madness of the old *hidalgo* from La Mancha. I was twenty-six and living in France when I decided to look at the book and was thrown off my saddle, like Saul on the road to Damascus: those execrable school manuals were right. With a mixture of passion and anger I then threw myself at the work of our classical authors—anxious to regain the time wasted by my false educators. My amorous relationship with some of them was established immediately but, as I realized at once with rage, at the wrong time: like a youth who tastes the ineffable delight of intercourse after a long virginity, I had through my own fault been deprived of the most intense enjoyment. My exaggerated youthful prejudice against anything Spanish led me astray in this area as in so many others. I find this mistake the most difficult to forgive of the mistakes I made as a result of my narrow school training.

After my father changed our school in the autumn of forty-three I stayed in the one in Bonanova until the end of my secondary schooling. Five years whose monotony and lack of significance are expressed as much in the sparse memories as in the very slight traces they left in me. Unlike the period from the death of my mother to the senility and internment of my grandmother—a stretch of about four years from which I have very exact reminiscences and to which my memory often returns—what came afterwards seems superficial and distant, a simple change of skin abandoned by someone else on the side of the road. Nothing that was said or happened in the classrooms influenced my life directly or indirectly. That life continued developing on its own, anchored in the family circle, essentially self-taught. When I began to masturbate at the onset of puberty, the incredible new pleasure casually discovered on a summer's day became one of the centers, if not the epicenter, of my life. This potential for enjoyment sited in my body overwhelmed at once, with raw strength, the religious or moral speeches that stigmatized it. In bed, in the bath, at Torrentbó, I regularly surrendered to respect for a material law that, for the space of a few seconds, confirmed me in my isolated, private existence, my irreducible separation from the rest of the world. However, I do not mean that traditional Catholic doctrine on sex, which was drummed into us in classrooms, confessionals, pulpits, religious manuals, made no impression on me. The idea of sin—of mortal sin with its hair-raising consequences—tortured me for several years. Dozens of times, kneeling opposite one of the local parish or church priests, I confessed my guilt and tried to reform myself. I knew full well that hours or days later that vital source of energy bursting out of me would impose its law and would imperiously destroy the fragile framework of precepts that condemned it in vain. Aware of this I escaped the reproaches of the same confessor or spiritual director by regularly changing my church and confessional in a kind of hide-and-seek, the absurdity of which was only too obvious. Although my expressions of piety were forced and my religious beliefs were fragile and lukewarm, the fear of the torture and punishments of hell besieged me for some time. Threats based on the sixth commandment, from preachers and printed in pamphlets like those by Monsignor Tihamer Toth, had a potentially traumatic effect on adolescents in the heat of puberty who listened to or read about the supposed physical and moral ravages of the impure act, a mere foretaste of the eternal, subtle, and most refined tortures awaiting them in life after death. Like all Catholic boys of my and many previous generations I was subject to the harsh test of Saint Ignatius's Spiritual Exercises in the famous refuges belonging to the order, in my case, the ones in Manresa and Sarriá. The precise, detailed, exact description of these by James Joyce—and before him the descriptions by Blanco White of the ones carried out in a cave in Seville by Father Vega, who was clearly imbued with the techniques of manipulation favored by disciples of the Loyola order, at that time temporarily abolished—spares me the task of expounding them to my readers. In *Portrait of the Artist as a Young Man* and Blanco's *Autobiography*, which I translated in part into his native language, my readers will find point by point, trick by trick, example after example of the theatrical development and dramatic stage-managing repeated decades afterwards for me and my companions, with the same inertia with which companies lacking a new repertoire routinely embrace the eternal, profitable revival of *Don Juan Tenorio* each year as All Souls' Day approaches. The ridiculous excesses of one of the orators had a counterproductive effect on me. In spite of the hysterically issued terrestrial and extraterrestrial threats, the secret, enjoyable, absorbing masturbations continued with almost daily refinement.

The grotesque nature of that impossible-to-observe rule—aimed, as in the case of ecclesiastical celibacy, at forming a guilty conscience readily submissive and yielding to the higher or worldly interests of the Church in Rome—was soon proved to me the night or morning I experienced my first nocturnal pollution after abstaining from masturbation for several days as a result of a distressing confession. My awakening, with an erect penis and a sticky patch on my pajama trousers, filled me with terror. What had happened? Had I touched myself without noticing while I slept? Or had someone slipped into my bedroom and repeated Grandfather's nasty antics? Confused and not knowing where to turn, I decided the next night to sleep behind a locked door and with my tight swimsuit on to avoid any direct contact with my hand. But the heat of the night, combined with the unsatisfied lust of my body and the pressure of the material, again provoked the predictable leakage, to my amazement. The conviction that it was a natural act and hence outside the morbid scrutiny of my confessors gradually dawned on me. Together with the panic that the discovery of penicillin aroused among the guardians of Catholic morality—expressed by the brothers of the Christian Doctrine in a desperate affirmation of the existence of varieties of germs of venereal origin that were *resistant to penicillin*—this conviction soon rid me entirely of guilt and gave their sermons on youthful chastity a necessarily ridiculous aura.

As I said, my real life was still centered at home: my reading, novelettish stories, daydreaming, masturbations. School—its courses, studies, breaks, classmates, teachers—was merely a parenthesis in my experience that was closed as soon as I crossed over the leafy garden presided over by the order's founder and reached the Paseo de la Bonanova. My relationship with the brothers and teachers responsible for teaching the different disciplines was always distant and impersonal. While I write, they reappear before me faded by oblivion and the passage of time: the rather harrowing executioner's face of Brother Vicente, whose horrible expression and gesticulations as he described the inevitability of death convinced me that he suffered, as rumor had it, from epileptic fits or some nervous disorder; the smiling face of "Clémens," slight yet and energetic, with a small Hitler-style forelock or toupée, a lovely person although he worshipped the Nazis whose salute he forced on the class to the cry of *Heil Hitler*—he cried like a child on the day of his hero's suicide in the bunker; Brother Pedro's face, fussy and maternal like a broody hen—he had the arduous task of rebuffing on cyclostyled sheets almost the whole of world philosophy—sometimes with strange ad hominem arguments, whether it was Rousseau's effeminacy, or Nietzsche's madness—in the name of the principles, as solid as they were eternal, of the doctrine elaborated by Aristotle and St. Thomas of Aquinas.

The memory of the grey, blurred mass of my fellow pupils is even more amorphous. With one or two exceptions I didn't see them again after leaving school and, to tell the truth, I never took too much interest in them. Around the age of fifteen or sixteen, I became increasingly aware of the economic decline of our family because of my father's unfortunate business enterprises and the gap between our domestic straits and social pretensions. This decadence, symbolized not only by the gradual worsening of our style of life but also by the air of wear, decay, and age that fell over people and things in the Pablo Alcover house, led me for the first and only time in my life to try to make friends, although I knew we had very little in common, with two boys whose social position was much higher than mine, with the illusory hope of being integrated into a society I imagined to be seductive and brilliant. For one or two years, a pathetic, hypocritical boy by the name of Juan Goytisolo tried to imitate the elegance of dress, adopt the distinguished manners, and copy the affected mannerisms and accent characteristic of that fauna so typical of Barcelona—the "playboys of the Diagonal." Pretending to be a member of the set, he attended one or two society gatherings at which his timidity and lack of social graces showed him in his true colors: he couldn't dance, court the well-to-do girls, talk about luxury cars, or even move his body with youthful self-confidence or affected indolence. The feeling of failure and inability to adapt to that milieu left him confused and depressed. But the bitterness didn't last long: the hollow petulance of the two fellow pupils whom he had taken as models in a desire for social success convinced him at once of his mistake. The life of this copycat, snobbish double was fortunately short and its reproduction in the odd photo in grown-up clothes—stiff, awkward, and serious—provokes in me today when I look at it mixed feelings of pity and sarcasm.

Having abandoned my frivolous illusions I returned to the secrets, anguish, and conflicts of the family orbit. I continued to be an uneven pupil, well-endowed, according to my teachers, for the study of history, grammar, and languages, and, on the other hand, weak if not hopeless in science and mathematics. My ineptitude and lack of interest in the latter were total and absolute and convince me of the truth of the old saying that when all is said and done, understanding is a matter of taste. Luckily for me, a friend in my year with whom I often talked in the playground and on the walk home confronted the same problem from the opposite direction. Highly intelligent and able in the areas of physics and mathematics, he reacted with indifference to the subjects that appealed to my curiosity. A friendship that was very beneficial for both of us developed from the mutual revelation of our respective qualities and deficiencies. While I wrote my friend José Vilarasau's essays, he gave me a generous helping hand in the subjects I hated. By helping each other, we managed to finish our crippled *bachillerato* without too many mishaps.

Vilarasau was also the first person in whom I dared confide my religious doubts. We had gradually exchanged some thoughts on the subject and outside the classroom Brother Pedro's supposed philosophical disquisitions were the target of our jokes and ridicule. Both of us thought the Creator's goodness and omnipotence somewhat problematic and contradictory. When we formulated some of our objections to an anonymous list of questions set by the brother to facilitate moral consultations, he suspected we were the authors and began to keep an eye on us. But my school years were coming to an end and the artificial, second-rate, petty world where my wretched tutors had tried to imprison me would soon vanish without a trace. *Time which passed, pricked them like bubbles over the surface of the water/breaking their miserable tyranny*, wrote Luis Cernuda. Like him, I remember them today, as I write, *smiling in my sorrow*.

Final snapshots of Pablo Alcover: cypress hedges, wild rose-trees, bougainvillea in flower, langorous honeysuckle, a horse chestnut tree, an old man reading or nodding off under the shadow of the lemon tree. Territories patiently acquired through usurpation: my father's, Eulalia's, Grandfather's. A steady process of deterioration: a carless garage, a defunct heating system, new, unrepairable faults. The inside got darker and darker: anemic light bulbs, penny-pinching illumination, furtive shadows wandering along the ghostly corridor. My father, in his slippers and white coat, preparing his strange potions, stirring the yogurt with a spoon. Grandfather, in his corner, reading the newspaper, always trying to pass unnoticed, occupying the least space possible. Eulalia, sitting in the dark in the kitchen in order to save electricity, listening to the ever-weaker heartbeats of the house, sounding out its decay, fatigue, asthenia, the ominous signs of its decrepitude: my father's endless warfare against Grandfather, griping, manias, mumbled rosary beads, the stifling enclosure of petty passions, senility, gradual deterioration. Equally there were changes in the young people that ruined and aged it: Marta, a woman, ready to get married; José Agustín, a university student and about to leave us to follow his studies away from home; Luis and I, still tied to school, but ready also to take flight, as it sadly felt, to flee from that house that was falling down around us, partition by partition, wall by wall, ceiling by ceiling. The poor Aragonese servant, made pregnant by the master of the house where she served, unmarried mother of a boy who was always introduced as a nephew, forced to emigrate to Catalonia, to experience changing houses and getting the sack, putting up with the shortages and difficulties of the war, Julia forever transformed into Eulalia, the jealous custodian of three boys whom she would get to love like her own children, ignorant, wise, pathetic, generous, turned, as a result of circumstances, from the central position her strength of will and character gave her among us, into a lucid, fatalistic witness of the decrepitude of things and people: worried at seeing us disappear one after the other, left alone, with two old men, in a ruined, broken-down house, on the lookout for the illness that was silently destroying her, forerunner of the Sphinx to which she euphemistically alluded when there was some misfortune in the family. Leaks, flaking paint, voracious mice, hungry wood-worm, coughing, spitting, decadence, decline: the images, sounds, impressions of my last years in Pablo Alcover, Barcelona, and Spain, ready to leave for wherever, my foot in the stirrup of an as yet imaginary horse. It was a wait punctuated by sudden evasions until the grace or blessing of my final departure. The memory of what I abandoned ceased to belong to me a good long time before I really left: the end of the story, the three deaths, would be beautifully integrated by Luis, with the passage of time, in the literary space of *Antagonía*.

IT ALL HAPPENED *as you had predicted: like an ephemeral, unstable house of cards, the collapse of one would bring down the rest.*

There was Luis's phone call bringing the bad news you had feared: Grandfather was dying, just a matter of hours according to the doctor, you should catch the first plane if you wanted to be at the funeral. Forty-eight busy, intense hours,* in a country where your name already figured on the black list, sidelong glances from the border police, an unwelcome, inopportune guest, attacked in print by the pack, a discreet watch kept on you, behind you a persistent shadow whose discordant movements clearly indicated that it didn't belong to you. Yours had stayed behind when you left for Spain where you returned like a ghost, an individual with a profession, civilian status, residence, place and date of birth fixed in his passport, but deprived by decree of a real identity: the possibility of writing, publishing, expressing yourself in public, meeting friends without fear of compromising them. An unearthly, shadowless, shrunken Hoffmannesque character.

In spite of all you arrived in time to witness Grandfather's Catholic death, fortified, as the death notice read, by spiritual support and apostolic blessing: his confession with a young priest whose dialogue with the moribund man, audible in the next room because of the latter's deafness, seemed like a short farce or comic sketch. Well, Don Ricardo, you are very old and you must start getting ready. Getting ready? Why? How old are you, eighty? Oh, a lot older! And then Grandfather's pleasure as he received the holy oils, convinced as he was that he was being treated with a new, efficient remedy for the eczema that tormented him. Good, the pomade! Brothers and sister sat in the next room while Eulalia and Father, hidden, silent, scared, conscious that the Sphinx she evoked had finally arrived, waited for the denouement in their respective corners with a touching helplessness.

Five months later, on August eighth, it was Father's turn, on his deathbed, looking at you but already not recognizing you, eaten up, wasted to the bones by the illness's implacable advance. Eulalia in her room surrounded by the presents sent to her by Monique, enclosed in her distress, replying in monosyllables to your digressions and questions. Still you could read the silent question that pursues her and that she cannot put into words: what would she do now if the old ones left her?; and especially what would happen to her in that empty, condemned house? The Sphinx already knew the address: just when it was least expected, whenever

---

* The entry and departure days stamped on your passport 4 March 1964 and 6 March 1964.

she felt like it, she might prowl through the district and repeat the visit.

At midnight, the nurse whispered to you to come to the bedroom: your father lay with his eyes open, death rattles and gasps alternated more and more slowly, his lips hardly opened. The spongy unreality of moments without emotion, a feeling of being split in two. You went to the ceremony of the washing and preparation of the corpse to be handed over to the funeral undertakers: the lids were lowered over the fixed, seemingly dazzled gaze of the dead man; Marta's precise, rapid gesture as she removed the gold ring before the hand became rigid. The ridiculous ceremony in the Sarriá parish church, solemn farewell to the mourners, procession of black cars toward the cemetery, stopping in front of the luxurious pantheon where your family's remains rot. Feelings of horror at that mausoleum, your place reserved in it: a firm decision not to allow yourself to be buried there. Visitors with their condolences, an anxious conversation about the state of Eulalia, the intolerable oppression of the decaying scene of your childhood, desires to flee, catch the plane, get to the Prat airport, departure stamped by suspicious police, verification of the assertion of the Pueblo *slanderers of a name more popular in police stations than in bookshops.*

Regular news, through Luis, of Eulalia's cancer, first in Paris, then in Saint-Tropez, finally in Morocco. The selfish, cowardly resolve to continue your wanderings, even though the end is near and definite: the unbearable idea of confronting the terrified, defenseless woman, being forced to hide the reality of her pain, laughing to cheer her up, looking pleased, making up a rosy, happy future for her, lying to remove the grimace that doesn't make it to a smile and sticks in a motionless, stiff, desperate grin. Tetuan, Xauen, Al Hoceima, Meknes, scrutinizing the postes restantes *expecting a letter until the plain telegram, opened with trembling fingers, that was waiting for you in Fez. A sudden break in your journey as a confused fugitive from yourself: you return immediately to Tangier, find momentary refuge at home, digest the crushing news, drown your resilient feelings of guilt and go up to the comforting shade of the citadel in search of hashish or majoon.*

From the moment you slump on your bed till the difficult, frequently delayed decision to get up painfully from the mess of topsy-turvy sheets, you lose all sense of time. No light filters through the half-closed shutter and when you look at your watch, it is almost eight o'clock. In the morning? The lights of the port and the nearby buildings dispel any doubts: it is dusk and your neighbors are gradually retiring to their rooms. What have you done during the day? A need to drink water, lots of water, to urinate, take a couple of aspirins. You will leave solving the riddle for later.

Twenty hours stretched out in bed, recreated gradually in the street taking deep breaths of the reviving breeze. Your head is still thick and aching but capable of reflection. Sitting on a terrace on the Avenida de España, the job of exhuming the incidents, encounters, visions, impulses, seizures of the longest night in your life: rescuing them carefully, like an archaeologist, from the depths into which they have subsided, dense strata of oblivion, shapeless masses, mists, opaqueness. Scrawling on the empty Gitanes packet the key words: pebbles, landmarks, signs that will lead you backward to the searing memory of what had happened.

Agile, light, delicate, perhaps momentary suspension of the universal imperative of gravity. You hover gently, no dizzy feeling, just above the ground, swift, tenuous, weightless, swaying or levitating in calm, wavering rhythm: a persistent dream ever since, strangely incorporated in the future into your usual modest repertoire. You are in Torrentbó: Father sitting in an armchair, probably dressed in white, with that natural, rather picturesque elegance that old age bestowed upon him during his final years. He's dead and you both know. However, you greet each other and exchange a few words. No pain on your part, no remorse. His presence is pleasing, gentle: he radiates a soothing impression of quiet, sweetness, peace. You say goodbye with mutual expressions of affection and you rise up again, garden, terrace, fountain of the frogs, somebody with a hoe over his shoulder (Alfredo?) smiles, waves from afar. A new decor, horse chestnut tree, wild plants, lemon tree and, in its shade, real Grandfather, in flesh and blood, his newspaper in his hands, looks at you for several seconds, he's old, very old, without interrupting his reading, there's nothing to say to you, absorbed in the news, world war has probably broken out.

Relapse into oblivion, spongy unreality, gradual distress, apprehension at the reunion that is being forged so tentatively, possible attempts to get up, piss, finish off the bottle of Sidi Harazm, peace that had vanished forever, anxiety, torture, tossing and turning in bed, black, everything black, your overburdened breast, head on fire, shooting pains, ominous premonitions, frustrated desire to escape, symptoms of panic, involuntary dampness, insistent palpitating of your heart, paralyzed limbs, imminence of the face you fear, the figure of Eulalia invoked by the excess of your own fear, already visible in the shadows, clearer and clearer, hair, skin, eyes, lips, cheeks, absolutely exact, shy, distant, silent, a bitter, reproachful gesture, image, presence, corporeality that overwhelms you, improvised, useless repentance, confused memory of pleas that went unheard, tardy declarations of love, an endless day in the dirty, stained bed, as if you were rooted there, spilling out everywhere, untrammeled, all you kept inside yourself, ghosts, mistakes, disloyalties, acts of cowardice, fears, a complete course of Freudian therapy for the price of a glass of majoon.

Fertile, germinative consideration of transmigration by the light of poetry: the easy flight of the soul from one body to another body, similar or identical to the one it sustained in life: moving from the hard times of this life to another that appears freer and more flexible, clothed with the respect for a belief that consecrates it and raises it to the heights of an ideal throne: sheltered by Islam's warm shadow, the crouching old man calls you silently: his hand is thin, stiff, emaciated: his jellaba's hood half-covers his face but allows you to see the lean face, skin stretched tightly over his bones, his curved nose and bloodless lips: looking at you as if you are transparent, he quietly repeats, perhaps to himself, fi sabili Allah and another traditional call to the faithful, with the resigned calm of that other moribund fellow, Alonso Quijano on the edge of his grave, when you tiptoed into his room as soon as you arrived from the airport: your father, the succession of incarnations of your father in the squares and alleys of Fez or Marrakesh, crouching down, dignified, begging, chance or methodically planned encounters generating the spark, the arc light that was never lit in life: itinerant ritual, maze evoking the sadness of a non-meeting that nevertheless recalls him to your memory and affectionately brings him to life.

· PART 2 ·

A T THE BEGINNING *of 1963, during your second visit to Cuba, a guest on this occasion of the Film Institute, you were invited by the poet Manuel Navarro Luna to accompany him to a meeting that was to be held in an education center for women conscripts on the outskirts of Havana. The old writer, whom you had met a year before on your visit to his native city, Manzanillo, was a convinced Communist, dedicated body and soul to the cause of the Revolution: he lived very modestly in a small hotel a few blocks from yours and was introduced to you by friends you had in common, who worked with him on the weekly magazine* Verde Olivo. *On his advice, the army magazine had published extracts from your report* Pueblo en marcha *and when lengthy sections of it appeared in the illustrated supplement to the daily* Revolución, *Navarro Luna warmly supported you in the polemic aroused by your phonetic transcription of popular Cuban speech. His great personal nobility and political integrity—the complete opposite of the revolutionary opportunism of so many other writers who had wretchedly compromised with the Batista dictatorship—together with his considerable devotion to Republican Spain, had swept aside the obstacles of his unconditional attachment to the USSR and, what was more serious for you, to the cultivation and defense of arthritic literary forms. At a time when the* arrivisme *of some of your first friends was beginning to show its true colors, his honest record, free of any ambition or desire for power, seemed a pleasant, comforting contrast. Several writers of your generation, like Heberto Padilla, shared your appreciation of the old poet whom they saw, not without reason, as the antimodel to a Nicolás Guillén, another lifelong Communist, but already complacent and proud of his privileges and official glory. Generous, selfless, exemplary, Navarro Luna embodied a moral strength not to be scorned in those agitated times of change and confusion.*

He picked you up at the Hotel Habana Libre along with an exiled Spanish Communist and the three of you went to the suburb where, he told you, he was going to preside over the closing stages of a political education course for several hundred girl volunteers. When you reached your destination it was already nighttime and the audience was waiting. One of the teachers of the course quickly told you about the day's activities: two lesbian girls caught en flagrante *in one of the school dormitories or showers had been submitted to public censure in an assembly and their final expulsion from the school had been unanimously agreed. Your companions supported the decision without a flicker of doubt and, feeling vaguely ill at ease with a stifled sense of disgust, you followed them to the platform erected in the school's main playground, from which Navarro Luna was to deliver his speech. You can remember the violent glare of the spotlights, the ritual greetings, the disciplined rhythm of the applause: your friend, the poet, had introduced you to those present with affectionate hyperbole, as "a young revolutionary intellectual from Spain" and the uniformed adolescents had stood up and clapped interminably in honor of that courageous, heroic representative of a people in struggle, a worthy descendent of the heroes of Guadalajara and Brunete, messenger from muted workers, avenging fist of the exploited who hand in hand with Navarro Luna and the school's spiritual director responded to their greetings with a gentle swaying of raised arms, repeated their slogans and calls with a fleeting, blurred smile, integrated into a kind of choral* sardana *or slave dance, you, I, that juan goytisolo suddenly ashamed of his role, of the unbridgeable abyss opened at a stroke between reality and words, overwhelmed by the tumultuous applause for the imposter who had usurped his name, that ghost imposed on his real self like a double, or an unwanted guest, as expressed by one of Cavafy's most beautiful poems: astonished and incredulous at the grotesque contrast between his hagiography and the opaque reality, totally alien to the puppet or robot whose voice had ceased to represent him, and on the contrary represented his oppressors: the pretender perched on the stage where the anomalous behavior of the accused girls had just been judged, the cowardly, silent legislator of a sentence directed in the end against himself, against his real unprotected crouching self: abandon the catacombs, come out, breathe, spit in the other's face, the double, the ghost, treacherous enemy of your intimate feelings, sad despoiler of your individual traits and coordinates, loathing, only loathing at his presence, strong desires to throw off the mask and be exposed to public scorn, to confront the destiny of the accused, anything but imitate the laughable, mechanical movements, the rhythmic shaking of raised arms, empty ritual, painful feeling of being rent asunder, deceit, schizophrenia, gagged.*

But the other, the ghost, stayed on the platform at the education center for militia women with their syncopated gestures and empty smiles, outwardly adapted to his contemptible fiction, a complete imposter, not one sign of cracking, waving and swaying to right and left like some rag doll, retrospectively the object of horror and hatred on the part of the spectator split in two and suddenly silent on the journey back to the hotel, impatient to be alone with himself, to settle accounts with the ventriloquist, rescue his voice before it was too late and the other, the intruder, imposed the correct tribal norms, stifled your surging rebellion, disguised the truth, changed you into a zombie.

Seminal value of an experience that, by putting you on guard against lies, would cut off the path to the precipice: things did not happen at the hectic pace of your narrative but more gently; yet what was felt in a confused way then would gradually become clear after a few months until its blinding evidence won out: fear had established a growing margin of alienation between you and your persona, and, as you can verify now, when describing the lasting consequences of the fissure, a sudden, overpowering desire for authenticity.

A CROSSING OF THE ways: few times in my life have I had the feeling I had that summer of walking on shifting ground from which my existence could branch off and take different routes. In spite of my absolute incompetence in mathematics and science, I had just passed the awesome state examination and, throughout what would be my penultimate holidays in Torrentbó, I contemplated the options opening up before me with a feverish mixture of excitement and apprehension. I knew that I was leaving forever my previous comfortable refuge—the family shell and its natural extension, school—and the instinctive fear of the leap into the void of my future independence often clouded my joyful anticipation of the latter. Indecision about the path I should take, awareness of the need to earn my keep because of family straits, tormented me through sleepless nights. As I struggled to get to sleep, I felt the desire to retreat, to shelter in the cheerful irresponsibility of childhood, hide my head under my wing, be protected by the maternal cloister. These brief, intermittent attacks lost their strength as summer progressed and the desired but dreaded date of my start at university approached. Gradually, the pleasing certainty of loosening family ties, of finally distancing myself from my father and the oppressive world of Pablo Alcover brushed aside those worries. The drive to flee from the past weighed more heavily than any uncertainty about the future. There were only a few days left before matriculation began and I was still hesitating about my choice of courses. I preferred the humanities, especially history and literature, but the ways in which they were taught, which I had already experienced at school, warned me to act cautiously. In contrast, my father's gentle pressure in the direction of profit-making studies and my elder brother's example suggested law as the right choice. After carefully considering the pros and the cons, I sat on the fence and enrolled in both departments. I thought that time and circumstances would provide an opportune solution to the problem.

There was a crucial factor behind my rather compliant decision to qualify as a lawyer: my stubborn obsession with travel, seeing the world, getting out of Spain, had led me to conceive the silly, inept idea of becoming a diplomat. At a time when the possession of a passport and the subsequent opportunity to leave the peninsula were jealously reserved for a privileged few, diplomacy appeared like a miraculous panacea, the open sesame that would one day allow me to live in another nation, different from mine, to know other customs and lands, in a word to visit those places and panoramas evoked in my conversations with Uncle Leopoldo or by the illustrated pages of my ever-loyal picture atlas. I thought any country was better than the one I had lived in till then and, unknowingly repeating Blanco White's experience a century and a half before, I sensed darkly that far from being a punishment for me, exile from my country would be a blessing. Although my present character and temperament are at the opposite extreme to the supple moderation required by diplomats, the underlying desire that dictated this choice was clear enough. I had proudly declared to all around me the irrevocable pattern of my future: I would become a kind of elegant, cultured Paul Morand, a brilliant polyglot, able to unify his personal literary inclinations with the pleasant tasks imposed by his career. The fact that I did not know any other languages beyond my impoverished Spanish did not even enter the arena of my preoccupations: I would study them. Armed with the conceit of my adolescence I felt ready to embrace a vast series of disciplines without sacrificing in any way my inveterate addiction to literature.

When I first entered the classrooms and courtyards of the old university building, I had no friends: the few companions I had been close to at school had enrolled in other departments and the handful who were studying law with me seemed either indifferent or alien. I had not found one familiar face in literature and arts lectures. This initial isolation favored my intention to concentrate entirely on my studies. My double matriculation, however, with its timetable clashes, presented me with a dilemma: as it was impossible to attend all the lectures, I decided to give priority to the law classes and restrict my commitment to the other courses as an "undeclared" student. This early choice had naturally been brought about by the routine, dull focus of the literature professors: this was my deepest, most vital interest and I feared, quite rightly, that a wretched time in the lecture theatres might make me hate what I was made for, the precious field of my future vocation and inclinations. I thought it was better to concentrate on boring, harmless subjects, with the prospect of one day entering, thanks to them, the Diplomatic School, rather than wasting valuable time on a counterproductive apprenticeship and throwing away my eventual talents as a writer. With the exception of Vicens Vives's courses and one or two other lecturers in areas remote from my interests, the arts faculty of the time could offer me no intellectual or moral sustenance. The civil war and its devastating aftermath had reduced university teaching to the lowest level: nine years after the end of the war, the majority of the chairs were still in the hands of mediocre, conformist teachers, chosen less for their knowledge or competence than by virtue of their faithfulness to the glorious principles of the Movement or the degree of their servility in the bending of their spines. The same desolate panorama, with the exceptions I shall later note, awaited students enrolled in law, but I personally didn't care. What I heard or might hear in classes flowed over me, I felt it was distant and alien. Having opted for a marriage of convenience instead of a passion that might be thwarted, I enjoyed the advantage of seeing things from the sidelines, with a generous margin of impassive detachment.

It is almost impossible for those who did not have the sad privilege of knowing Spanish universities at the end of the forties to imagine the soporific state of destitution in which they vegetated. After the hopes aroused by the Allied victory had vanished, student agitation reached its lowest ebb. The struggles to rebuild the University Student Federation were only a vague, distant memory: its members repeatedly fell into the hands of the police and this gradually destroyed the ranks of the organization until it was swept away altogether. When I ventured into the law faculty in 1948, nobody showed, not even privately, the slightest interest in politics except for the odd Don Juan supporter like Senillosa and a small band of rowdy Falangists who spoke openly about José Antonio and his supposedly betrayed revolution. The Opus Dei actively recruited supporters and followers: a few old acquaintances, including my Aunt Rosario's eldest son, had yielded to their assiduous attentions and then proceeded to eye fearfully those, like myself, who frankly rejected their proselytizing. A mere admission of religious agnosticism was enough to cause a furor: as I would later discover to my dismay, not one of my fellow students had had the courage to make one. Apparently unanimous attitudes of conformism in matters of religion, morals, and politics viewed any expression of dissidence as a challenge or as lunatic behavior worthy of punishment or contempt. The silent opponents whom I would detect later—including almost all those in the ranks of Catalan nationalism—shared sometimes, in other areas, the majority criteria: I can remember clearly the day when, because I had allowed myself a joke at the expense of the saccharine figure of Pope Pacelli, I only just avoided Albert Manent's hysterical kick at my innocent testicles. The politically and intellectually aware students of years previous to mine, people like Castellet, Marsal, Reventós, or Manuel Sacristán, had already finished their arts or law studies or were about to do so. Gil de Biedma was taking his first literary steps and was preparing to complete his studies in Madrid with a view to entering the diplomatic corps. Carlos Barral, not yet wrapped up in one of those showy cloaks that would later change him into the ideal protagonist of *Don Mendo's Revenge*, was already getting drunk and writing poetry. I would only hear of Gabriel and Juan Ferraté years later. My year and the ones that followed were probably the dullest and most mutilated in our wretched postwar period: the last embers of resistance had died out in the smoke and ash of a deceitful peace and the first sparks of youthful rebellion had yet to fly. The miserable experience of my school years was thus repeated at university: no teachers, no guides, often without the books I desperately needed—inaccessible because of censorship or my cruel ignorance of other languages—my intellectual and moral education was going to proceed by chance, falteringly, at the mercy of casual encounters, reading, conversations outside the lecture halls. Circumstances made me an autodidact and by myself I would forge a disorganized, capricious culture the effects of which would drag on into my thirties and from which I would not be free until the day when, definitively distanced from the atmosphere of Spain and Barcelona, I began my own revision of the values and norms that had ruled my life till then without the blinkers or prejudices inherent in all ideologies and systems.

WHEN RECENTLY, as a result of a public reading of *Makbara*, I walked once more through the classrooms, corridors, and inner galleries of the arts courtyard, my memory tried painfully to rescue from a confused magma a few details and snapshots to corroborate the presence in this milieu of that anxious, vulnerable, frenetic youth whose ironic condescension toward his peers, really aimed at hiding his profound timidity, led him to use and abuse a show of knowledge and paradox with pedantic satisfaction. Strangely I have no photograph of him, as if my present alienation from the period and my unconscious desire to throw off everything I did or thought then had induced me to destroy the proofs of our embarrassing identity. Well, the youth in whom I recognize myself only with difficulty was nevertheless me, and the image he projected in those years, perhaps retained by those whom I afterwards lost touch with, had followed a path separate from mine, as the gifts and powers of miracle workers are sometimes carried on from inertia long after the perplexed creator has lost faith in their existence.

Shoes: black. Suit: beige or light grey. A well-tailored overcoat and gloves the same color as the suit in the style of a future diplomat. The boy stationed under the courtyard arches, withdrawn and indifferent to the noise and bustle of his companions, is carrying a briefcase full of books in which course books and notes are mixed up with novels and plays printed in Buenos Aires. Since leaving school he has become a feverish reader. His favorite authors are still Unamuno and Wilde. The first taught him to ask questions that would nourish his naive philosophical anxieties; the second, the art of witty, disrespectful contradiction, the caustic timing of the *causeur*. Catholicism, morality, ecclesiastical hierarchy are the preferred targets of his lances. His irreverence causes a scandal and wins him some appreciation and a number of enemies. Significantly, it encourages his conceited propensity to stand out, to surpass the rest in originality and intelligence. He studies assiduously and is soon one of the top students. He has arrogantly revealed to his colleagues that he is writing novels and, in his spare time, begins to learn French.

Generally, he is bored by the teaching of the first-year topics in the law school, but will overcome the tedium with stubborn persistence. The university rector forces them to memorize with an undaunted smile twenty Latin definitions of natural justice and this youth submits unflinchingly to the loathsome test. Roman law appears more bearable inasmuch as it blends in with his reading at home: from the first Caesars to Justinian, its compilers emerge with a halo of long-standing familiarity. He is interested in political economy: his studies will help him to understand the relationships that exist between society and ideology, their mutual dependence and interweaving. Luis G. de Valdeavellano's classes surprise him with their clarity and rigor: the slanderers brand him as a Republican and the description, far from lowering him in his eyes, confers upon him the prestige inherent in the unusual. This is a *rara avis* in the university of the day.

The contacts and exchange of ideas with his companions are more encouraging. Bypassing untalented, boring grinds, he will soon discover links and affinities with three students as fond of reading as he is: the first of them, Juan Eugenio Morera, is an ex-seminarist who is striving to make up for the time wasted at a Jesuit school by taking on with ruthless self-discipline both the law and arts degrees; the second, Mariano Castells, offspring of a well-known Barcelona family whose brilliant, disorganized character, together with a passion for books only comparable to his own, seduces and attracts him. Although the third, Enrique Boada, does not reveal any great enthusiasm for his studies, the dandyism and ironic indifference he displays in class arouse his attention and interest. Thanks to Morera, who is older and so gains a degree of moral authority over Mariano and himself, the latter attend Lucas Beltrán's economics seminar for a few months where Keynes's and Schumpeter's theories are discussed in a heavy atmosphere of pipe smoke and American cigarettes: as participation in the discussions is unavoidable, our would-be diplomat and budding dilettante plays with the strange idea of focusing one of them on the untypical Wilde essay, *The Soul of Man under Socialism*. Lucas Beltrán cautiously sets out the different economic options in modern society and Marx's name will appear for the first time in our student's conversations without any of the insulting epithets that usually disfigure it. The publications of the Fondo de Cultura, introduced more or less clandestinely from Mexico, circulate by hand and the supposed brilliant contender for embassies acquires a good number of them in the name of his future studies. At the same time, Morera has put them in touch with an ambitious, mordant assistant lecturer who within a few years would scale the peaks of the university hierarchy: Fabian Estapé still lives with his parents in an old flat on the Paseo de San Juan, does not hide his atheism and hatred of the church, and supplements his meagre income as a lecturer by giving private lessons in political economy. The trio of friends agrees to join them and every week meets him in Mariano's grandmother's flat, where Balmes crosses over the Gran Vía. Through Estapé's influence our young man discovers Anatole France and devours at a stroke his *Complete*

Works published by Aguilar, the distribution of which had been forbidden by the censor. The economics classes often give way to religious or metaphysical discussions that confront Estapé and himself with Juan Eugenio Morera, who, in spite of having given up the novitiate, retains intact his faith in Christianity. Mariano hesitates, but finally opts for theories of agnosticism, much to Morera's annoyance. The varied diet of economics, law, history, and literature soon extends gradually to some philosophical works: Ortega, Croce, Jaspers, Bergson, Kierkegaard. The desire for knowledge, to accumulate the greatest erudition in the subject, nourishes a childish rivalry between Mariano and himself, in which intellectual progress will sometimes be confused with a desire to purchase more books, especially those that, being rare or inaccessible, convert their discovery into a sought-after, prestigious title of nobility. His small band—to which Enrique Boada does not belong because of his indolent individualism—tends to clam up spontaneously and greet any intrusion by strangers with reserve or distrust. The latter will be the target of their satire and, when they realize this, some companions who initially wished to ingratiate themselves will wisely opt to keep their distance. From time to time the trio and a few occasional guests celebrate a kind of assembly aimed at showing off their wisdom and learning to the outside world: our young man has prepared a long, pompous dissertation on French foreign policy, whether "from Talleyrand to Louis Philippe" or "from the Commune to Fashoda" and, with the same dauntless spirit that aimed the products of his wit at his cousins, he would now direct them pitilessly at his indulgent friends. Less fortunate than our student, an Argentinian outside the clan, the author of a huge tome on the Spanish spirit in the conquest of America, probably inspired by the ideas of Maeztú, Morente, and Menéndez Pidal—whom Mariano rapidly assigned to the thankless category of bore—conceived the unhappy idea of reading to them with great emphasis and enthusiasm the beginning and a few later chapters of his work. In his ecstasy he did not notice the exchanged glances, arching of eyebrows, grimaces, and chuckles of the genial trio until the deep, threatening silence after one of his pauses convinced him of the need to interrupt his reading and seek his audience's opinions: in turn, his implacable judges overwhelm him with sarcastic commentaries on the style, composition, opinions, and general aim of the book, leaving him sunk in a state of complete confusion and despondency. In a desperate attempt to break the siege, seeing a pack of cards on the table in the office where they are, the victim proposes a pause in the round of criticism: let's play a game of bank. The goat's always climbing up the bank, Mariano comments ironically. The Argentinian takes the blow courageously while our hero and his friends take delight in their cruel victory. Belief in their own superiority in their eyes legitimizes this harshness and bullying. The elitist philosophy, shot through with contempt for those judged to be on a lower level, gave them the right to adopt, for reasons of self-interest, a sycophantic, opportunistic attitude toward their teachers: private visits or consultations with professors on the pretext of broadening their studies, the organization of a celebratory lunch in the name of a group of "distinguished pupils." It is true that this example of *arrivisme* is ennobled by references to Machiavelli: Mariano and our man are at the time devoted admirers of *The Prince*. Such a cynical, cold strategy, together with the serious efforts devoted to their studies, will get its reward at the end of the year: when the exams arrive, Morera, Mariano, and himself will be awarded first-class passes in almost all their subjects.

The brief description of my homonym's first steps in the university thirty-five years ago creates in me an impression of amazement similar to that I imagine would be felt by a learned professor specializing in Calderón or the pre-Socratics if, as he walked along the corridors in the metro nearest to home, he were to come across a string of posters with a youthful portrait of himself advertising, all smiles and mustache, a natural, protein-filled shampoo or a snow-white, gentle, almost caressing shaving soap. Sleep-walking? Blindness? Nightmare? Instead call it incredulity tinged with sadness at the way this character totally contradicts your later reality. A nagging doubt about your identity after your childhood and the real existence of that absurd period would insidiously escort your steps to the main lecture hall where minutes later you were to begin your reading.

I S IT A FUNCTION *of involuntary memory to preserve the hidden impressions destroyed by the mechanics of remembering? Doesn't the Freudian hypothesis, attributing to the latter a cannibalistic, predatory action over the traces of a buried past, perhaps condemn your naive attempt at recovery, since the possible results may be opposed to the end you pursue? The slow sedimentation through the years, every stratum vegetating in fertile semi-oblivion, would in this case be subject to an organized raid, the structuring force of which would not compensate—quite the contrary—for the devastating manipulation: confronted by the harshness of the theory you have no choice but to accept the contagious suspicion: the task you so trustingly undertook, that sudden decision not to allow your life, experience, emotions, what you are and have been, to disappear with you has gradually been transformed into territory plagued with traps and snares forcing you to advance cautiously, to look backward, question the precision of your accounts, submit them to verification by other witnesses, have recourse to written documents that in some way correct or change their laborious reconstruction: like dreams recounted at the moment of waking so they do not fade from memory, change at once and lose their aroma, the fidelity of the impression you describe requires a prudent injection of disbelief: your changeable personality in those years, with its often antithetical features, tempts you to grant it a later coherence that, despite its teleological truth, will be a subtle form of betrayal.*

HAPPILY, I DO not think all the aspects and features of the youth I was are today distant or alien. My intense passion for books and firm twenty-year-old decision to doubt the norms and values of the social milieu in which I was brought up contained the seed of my later break with that milieu and a still confused reaching for new, more authentic forms of existence. Shut up in my room in Pablo Alcover, I often stayed awake until the early morning scrupulously reading through the French books in my mother's library or devouring hundreds of pages of Dostoyevski, Poe, Conrad, Pirandello, or Bernard Shaw. The choice of these authors was in my case, as with Mariano, a product of chance. Using the last penny at our disposal, we would search through the second-hand bookshops in calle Aribau looking for a possible bargain or a rare, fabulous copy. Books printed before the war, especially in the years of the Republic, were the continuous object of our searches: paperbacks published by Cenit, worm-eaten translations of D'Annunzio, Maeterlinck, or Andreyev. When the source of strange, extraordinary books seemed about to dry up, Mariano would take advantage of his family connections and enable me to penetrate the back rooms of two or three bookshops where prohibited books were kept. There, trembling with excitement, my friend and I scrutinized the shelves and heaps where these books were either lined or piled up, dazzled by the incredible plethora of authors and titles that we only knew from hearsay yet whose assimilation we sensed as indispensable to our correct intellectual development: Proust, Kafka, Malraux, Gide, Camus, Sartre. To meet my growing bookshop expenses, I had to have recourse to the pious strategy of convincing my father that they were legal reference works, vital to the success of my study. At home, I hid my purchases in different and often ingenious hiding places, fearing my sister would discover them and reproach me for possessing and reading works included on the index of forbidden books: at the time, I continued to maintain the fiction of a surface Catholicism and on Sundays, soon to be accompanied by Luis, I would walk around the district pretending to abide by the rule of attending Mass. The enforced furtive nature of my explorations—the enjoyable awareness of entering forbidden areas—infused my reading with a thrill of excitement and stimulation that can only really be understood by those who have tasted the same waters. The results of this precocious discovery would have a beneficial influence on my life: the idea of pleasure, associated in my inner self with notions of transgression and clandestine activity, would later open the way to the gradual, reticent, laborious acceptance of other more hidden, intimate impulses.

The relative tolerance of the Francoist authorities toward authors deemed "less dangerous" allowed them to turn a blind eye to the clandestine circulation of their works: although the performance of Lorca's dramas was prohibited, the Losada editions had begun to appear on discreet shelves in some bookshops; Ortega and Baroja were harshly censored in church circles but it was possible to read them. Other more hostile writers remained, on the other hand, on the regime's black lists and direct access to their writings was nigh impossible. During my first year at university, a companion fond of poetry had handed me typewritten copies of Alberti's poems: that kind of samizdat did not reproduce, as a reader today might imagine, the committed poetry of *Entre el clavel y la rosa* or some angry war poem, but innocent compositions like *Marinero en tierra* and *Sobre los ángeles*. The difficulty of approaching the work of intellectuals who had taken sides against Franco transformed the act of reading into an amazing adventure. Italo Calvino's paradoxical statement that repressive, authoritarian regimes are the only ones that take literature seriously by granting it subversive power that it unfortunately does not have and by trying naively to prevent it being read contains in my view a great deal of truth. The best readers of a work, yesterday in Spain, today in the USSR and Soviet bloc countries, have been, will be, the surreptitious ones: those who take a huge risk to get at the work and yet accept the challenge and gradually exorcise their fear. Compared to an experience of this order, the facilities enjoyed by readers in open societies inevitably lower the intensity of the lived feeling: it is in no way the same thing to creep furtively into a religious or pagan harem excited by the idea of a plot hedged with dangers as to choose without any kind of pressure from among the dozens of consenting wards in a brothel. At the cost of upsetting someone, I maintain and have always maintained that my most intense, fertile reads belong to my youth, either due to the vague sense of engaging in a criminal act, or the certain enjoyment of disturbing desecration. I am obviously not talking about the level or quality of the works but about the emotions that enriched my reading quite independently of the works themselves. While the purchase of books I wanted involved me in a series of sacrifices and hurdles—both from the prohibitive price at which they were sold and the difficulty in finding them—I collected them lovingly until I had a modest but worthy library. When, as a result of settling down in Paris, I could get all the books I wanted thanks to the position held by Monique Lange in Gallimard, there was a mysterious decline in the value I attached to knowing them and I renounced my collector's conceit, lost interest in owning them, and didn't hesitate to get rid of them or give them away with a detachment inconceivable only a few years before. This waning of my property instinct toward cultural goods—books, records, engravings, and artistic-style objects—from then on would become a lasting feature of my character. I haven't reached Genet's monastic asceticism but I find life easier and more comfortable without the showy cultural robes that surround the majority of writers I know. It is only the content of books that attracts me, they are an object for immediate consumption: once read they get in my way and I'm happy to get rid of them provided I can buy them again whenever I may need them.

In the Spain of my youth it was the exclusive privilege of a handful to purchase the works of Orwell or Bernanos, Vallejo or Neruda: as with today's refined drugs, whoever wanted to read them needed simultaneously money, connections, and patience. When one of us managed to lay hands on some precious volume, after it was read, it would circulate at once within our group of friends. Although the trio of Mariano, Morera, and myself did not allow intruders into its more private discussions, we sometimes met in a café on the Ronda de la Universidad to exchange opinions on books and authors with a dozen or so students. These gatherings were informal and any participant could speak. I remember the evening one of the members gave a summary of his recent reading of *Le deuxième sexe* and the rest, led by Morera, rushed in with rather pedestrian arguments against the then novel and bold exposition of feminist theories. Enrique Boada, although eyed suspiciously by Mariano, would come to these encounters and supported me in my arguments with the others over a totally hedonist conception of life: aesthetics, we claimed, was above, and not answerable to, ethics. The reading of Thomas De Quincey, discovered by Mariano, brought new, efficient, and sometimes unusual arguments to my passionate defense of Art for Art's sake. Although no one at that stage upheld the doctrine of the social value of literature—not one of us had heard of Lukács or Politzer's gloomy creed—our extremist positions collided head-on with Morera and his justification of moral values. At other times the gathering was the arena for strange incidents that enlivened the monotony of some discussions with an unexpected touch of color. One night a student in a higher year, whom I knew by sight from Jesuit school, read a very suggestive, well-written text on the presence of *duende* in Andalusian poetry. His contribution was welcomed and everybody congratulated him. However, a few days later I leafed through the latest Lorca volume to arrive from Buenos Aires with Mariano, and we discovered first to our amazement and then with a degree of perverse excitement that the passage we liked so much was right there. Wishing to avenge our gullibility and punish the deceit, we invited the guilty plagiarist to our next meeting and exposed him to public humiliation. The episode and the violence it generated among us put an end to our gatherings for a time. The approaching exams and consequent shortage of time I believe also led to the break.

The most serious literary discussions were held in Mariano's house. There, next to the beautiful, spacious, well-appointed library in his room, the books—the fruit of our *razzias*—were read, discussed, and commented on passionately and at length. My friend was not forced as I was to hide works judged to be immoral or anti-Catholic. His parents were extremely tolerant and, as I later discovered, his mother, although a strong supporter of the social order installed by the regime, shared our attitude toward religion. In her eyes, the latter fulfilled a useful, moderating function: it kept the lower classes in their place with the promise of wonderful rewards in the future. Because of that she accompanied her husband to Mass although deep down she felt the ceremony was hollow and without substance. She had the foresight and intelligence to grant her only son a broad measure of freedom trusting that he could use it sensibly to develop his understanding and culture in a society that she herself considered sterile and mediocre.

The front balconies of Mariano's house faced directly onto the Borne market: the area had lost its residential character decades ago but the traffic of commercial life gave it intense hustle and bustle night and day. His flat, stuffed with furniture and objets d'art that had been carefully preserved, was a stark contrast with the image of ruin and destitution in the house on Pablo Alcover. The presence of a woman, his mother, cruelly emphasized the gap left by the disappearance of ours. Mariano moved with natural modesty around his territory. Although his social position was superior to mine, he had the elegance not to make me feel this. It was in his house that I tasted for the first time since the war one of those Vienna rolls that my mother gave me for breakfast as a child: I was used to the heavy substance we still consumed at home and the difference made me ashamed. His grandfather was a famous art collector: he lived on the lower floors of my friend's house in a kind of museum that I visited more than once. Romanesque statues and carvings stood there side by side with numerous pictures by Catalan painters of the Quatre Gats period: one small drawing room was entirely decorated by Nonell murals. The cultural, artistic milieu where my friend was brought up favored the development of his sensitivity and had been a decisive factor in his early but determined resolution to be a writer.

Mariano had shared his secret with me from the beginning of our friendship and this mutual confidence had sealed a solemn pact between us: our law studies were but a means to gain time with our families, a kind of temporary screen to conceal our true vocation. We had just discovered *Metamorphosis* and *Nausea* and, in full existential, metaphysical rebellion, we perceived no other outlet for our doubts and anguish than through creation. We were both going to be great novelists, with the range and depth of those we so admired. To reach the level of our models, we needed total dedication to the enterprise, to channel all our energies into the completion of our future work. Intoxicated by our reading of De Quincey, Baudelaire, and Huysmans, we aspired to live by only one rule in life, the search for sensations and experiences favorable to literary and artistic genesis. Our schooling would be alcohol, drugs, and the most refined, exquisite vices. Cure the soul through the senses and the senses through the soul, advised Wilde. But while we repeated the formula like a magic spell, we remained entirely chaste and sober. Our defense of every vice and perversion, proclaimed from the rooftops, was only theoretical. Maldoror's cruel exploits, diametrically opposed to the insipid morality of Christianity, swept us along. We wanted to be pitiless, malign, extravagant, and adopt a morbid, scandalous life-style. However, apart from the ironic, contemptuous attitude we displayed to most students, we were very careful not to put our ideas into practice. Neither Mariano nor myself had ever stepped inside a brothel, let alone got drunk. Possessed by literary fever, we calmly hovered on the frontiers of our kingdom, in a delightful state of dreamy fervor.

As a result of this focus and consequent change in priorities, my zeal for study declined. The unbearable tedium of the second-year law topics depressed me and gradually I began to put them to one side. I didn't give them the final brush-off in order not to upset my father, but I ceased to be the model student I had been months before, both opportunistic and servile toward my teachers. Even the idea of entering the diplomatic corps lost its attraction: as time passed, and I became more convinced I would one day rival Gide and Baudelaire, I reached the healthy conclusion that that life was not for me. This change was not sudden and thanks to the knowledge gained and the prestige earned in my first year I was able to save face and keep out of any trouble. It had the advantage of giving me a year's breathing space: the time, on the pretext of continuing my legal studies, to complete the great literary work that would provide *a posteriori* justification.

My gradual movement away from the lecture halls had the unexpected effect of bringing me close to two students I had not previously been very friendly with on account of my devotion to my studies and my professor-worship: Enrique Boada whom I've already mentioned and Carlos Cortés. The former had followed my brilliant but short-lived career as a collector of first-class awards with indulgence and without comment: naturally endowed with aristocratic indolence, I readily accepted Mariano's criticisms when, perhaps jealous of my esteem for him, he branded him as capricious and unreliable. Boada's artistic tastes were much broader than mine: they ranged over music, dance, painting, and avant-garde events and activities. He accompanied his parents to the opera and occasionally succeeded in dragging me to the rare studio theatre performances tolerated by the censors. Just like Mariano and myself, he was confronting a problem of identity whose crises and sudden jolts would soon fill me with alarm. At that time, he was happy to stay awake at night listening to music and to go out at dawn driving fast through the city's deserted streets. Carlos Cortés only made the odd appearance in the arts faculty courtyard and I was introduced to him by a common friend before I totally rejected my dedication to my studies: he was an eccentric non-conformist dressed in a red bow tie that emphasized his bohemian looks, pleasantly different from the rest. He was a hardened reader like me and, to subsidize his addiction, he spent his time, like today's junkies, buying and selling literary works. He placed in my hands, for the first time, Blake's poetry in a prewar Catalan translation and encouraged me to read *Demian* and *Les caves du Vatican*. His passion for Gide and Hermann Hesse was contagious and as a result I wasn't satisfied until I had all their works. Cortés didn't come from a well-off family like the rest of my friends: his domestic straits and refusal to follow studies that were profitable forced him to live from day to day on the difficult, chancy book trade. He frequented the Barceloneta and Barrio Chino brothels, came drunk to the arts faculty, and displayed a gut aversion to the future lawmongers. In a rather provocative tone, he informed me that he was Jewish—his father's family belonged in fact to the *chueta* community of Majorca—and his contempt for social taboos and conventions made a deep impression on me. From the start he tried to initiate me into the mysteries of a life that Morera described as dissolute: those *leprous evenings*, as Cortés himself baptized them, devoted to alcohol and whores. I was totally unaware of Barcelona life outside the conventional bourgeois circles in which I moved, but cautious pusillanimous habits that I would take some time to get rid of made me resist and so waste what I now consider to be precious time. This fear—which I could not then articulate—of putting my senses to the test, together with the simple-minded idea of preserving my strength to execute the masterpiece with which I would amaze the world one day, killed off that first opportunity to match actions with words and cast aside the rigid corset of inner censorship that, despite my external display of liberated, experienced youth, oppressed and paralyzed me. Only two years later, in Madrid—and consequently safe from the inhibitions created by a close circle of eye witnesses—would I have the courage to confront the adult experience I stupidly rejected then: the sudden discovery of alcohol, brothels, red-light districts, bars open in the early hours, and alongside, in the cottony depths of the new, persistent reality, aspirin and bitter coffee to combat hangovers.

WITH TIME MY conversations with Mariano had centered on a single, almost obsessional topic: the creation of our work, of that future work the light from which would immediately project us to the pinnacles of fame, if not of immortality. We both declared we were engaged in the task and it was certainly true in my case: in that autumn of 1950 I had rekindled my old passion for writing novels and once more I was filling dozens of pages with scribble strongly influenced by the gods of the moment, Gide and Hermann Hesse. I wrote in my room in the afternoon and furtively hid the manuscript behind a pile of law books: from time to time my father would look eagle-eyed through the door to see if I was studying hard and the enthusiasm and concentration he discovered dispelled his doubts and soothed his mind. Civil law must be very interesting, mustn't it, boy? he mumbled before disappearing; and I would pretend to emerge from deep involvement with the minutiae and requirements of emphyteutic domain and affirm that indeed it was. My novel was advancing at a good rate, but the very facility with which I was writing, a product of unconscious, insidious imitation, at times filled me with anxiety. I knew that my Barcelona Spanish was impoverished and lacked precision and, forced to consult the dictionary continually, I fell into that rather stiff, bookish, stilted style that would to a greater or lesser degree affect the prose of my first novels. Neither was I convinced by the main theme: the moral, physical, and material decadence of a family as viewed through a refined, perverse adolescent was too transparent a result of my reading. However, fear of submitting myself to the criticism of others and confronting their negative opinions encouraged me to carry on to the end and avoid the temptation of discarding it halfway. Mariano was my only confidant and I often discussed the content of the book with him. Our rivalry had made us mutually demanding. My work had to be equal to those we most admired—*Les nourritures terrestres, Steppenwolf*—or be thrown into the wastepaper basket. Convinced as we were that one day we would achieve literary fame and glory, we could not endanger our objective by overhaste nor risk failure or mediocrity. Mariano was more radical than I and aspired to create a unique work that would be so absolutely perfect that to avoid its profanation by the gaze of others it would have to be eradicated once it was finished: a sublime act of destruction through love, he added, that a more responsible, conscious Creator than ours should have reserved for the universe rather than leaving us the wretched product he had cobbled together. As the months went by, my friend spoke with growing excitement about this work he had so severely, so implacably predestined to the flames. He composed by night, after drinking a few glasses to get in the mood: his writing then flowed automatically with no need for corrections or crossing out. Of course, I felt a great curiosity about the work; but Mariano was in no hurry to read to me from the closely written pages where he condensed his emotions, feelings, and ideas. There was probably a touch of coquettish apprehension in his reticence: a desire to keep my interest alive and at the same time a fear of disappointing me. One day when I confessed my lack of enthusiasm for my own novel—spoilt by awkward expressions, immature scenes, badly drawn characters, and influences that had not been at all assimilated—I succeeded in getting him to read a page of his: a text, written in the first person, which took on the voice of the *Maja Desnuda*, but I was appalled by the childish clumsiness of the writing. Mariano immediately broke off reading as if he had read my thoughts and did not ask my opinion. Neither did I dare to express mine and, although the episode seemed to fall into oblivion, as I later noticed, it opened a breach for the first time in our friendship. Mariano never mentioned his work to me again and ceased to be interested in the outline and development of mine. We went on talking about literature and the books that impressed us: however, the previous certainty about our exceptional, luminous talent vanished.

While our doubts about the value of what we were doing put an end to our frenetic duet, we began to feel the need to establish relations with other new writers, to exchange ideas with them and get to know their works. It was impossible to find anyone in our year who could meet our exacting standards so we decided to look around previous years. We knew from Estapé—whom we still saw in spite of our abandonment of the lecture halls—that Alberto Oliart had written a novel entitled *Gales* with which he hoped to win the Nadal prize. Estapé made out he had flipped through it and didn't spare us his sarcastic comments. He advised us to get to know Jaime Gil de Biedma, the author of a poem that earned the future rector's praises; the latter, playfully indiscreet, didn't hesitate to describe the amorous nature of the poem: read it slowly and you will understand, he said with a smile. But Gil de Biedma excused himself, invoking his end-of-course studies, and we could not associate him with our project. Fortunately, Luis Carandell and Mario Lacruz, two students in José Agustín's year whom I had met through him before my brother decided to take his law degree in Madrid, shared our interests and enthusiasms and were also looking for a platform from which to get themselves known. They welcomed the idea of meeting from time to time to read and discuss our work publicly; other people were also keen.

Someone suggested the desirability of also inviting writers who were successful or at least had some published work in order to give our meetings more prominence. Advised, I think, by Carandell and Estapé, we worked out the list of eventual participants and got in touch with them.

Until then, the only flesh-and-blood writers I had come across were Sebastián Juan Arbó and Ana María Matute. The former lived nearby in the Tres Torres district and used to work in the cafés: in the morning in the defunct Rhinegold and in the afternoon in another café that has disappeared from the corner of Aragón and Paseo de Gracia. Arbó was a pleasant, modest, middle-aged man whose rather awkward manners revealed his peasant background, an image that was completely out of line with my idea of a writer. I imagined the latter to be aristocratic and distant, haughty and slightly perverted, brilliant modern combinations of Des Esseintes and Dorian Gray. I often bumped into Arbó on the Sarriá underground and he was always kind and attentive toward me but his common ways, country accent, and the unfortunate story of his recent visit to the Mexico College in the University City of Paris with his naive fascination for the show of freedom displayed by French women students and the faunlike behavior of his fellow countryman, Palau Fabre, forced me to arrogantly dismiss him with severe contempt. I was convinced that the true writer's genius must be deduced not only from his work but from his dress and appearance and I wondered rather anxiously if I myself would one day achieve the exquisite dandy-cum-bohemian alloy that would unveil my inner greatness to the world. It is pointless to state that I am now truly repelled by this narcissistic, provincial belief in the glorious, unmistakable aura of the poet that is still common in Spain. When I wrote years later "a genius and façade right up to the grave: the greater the genius, the greater the façade: the greater the façade, the greater the genius," the Julianesque irony was not only aimed at the obstinate confusion of a great number of colleagues but at myself as a youthful would-be writer with pretensions. The continuous desire to perform, be in the limelight, play at being important, really converts the Hispanic literary tribe into a bunch of overdressed street performers: necklaces, cats, walking-stick handles, silvery slippers, admiral's hats, learned poses, old sea-dogs' beards, and cultivators of amphibious prose. If I compare the mimicry, showiness, and gauche manners of the baritones and tenors of the day with the simplicity, modesty, and reserve of Genet and other writers whom I had the opportunity to meet or know simply by sight, the contrast fills me with shame and strengthens my decision to keep myself on the edge of the dominant exhibitionism: I shall be that withdrawn, furtive Arab in Paris, dedicated to the tenacious exercise of his unspeakable manias. I must add in self-defense that, in spite of my ideas then about an artist's manner and appearance, I issued the invitation to

Arbó: but he declined it, alleging overwork and scant liking for nocturnal activity, and perhaps he mistrusted the young amateur who disguised his condescension with the opportunist's obsequious manner.

My relationship with Ana María Matute was different right from the start. I also knew her from the Sarriá metro and two of her brothers had studied with me in the Jesuit college: I can remember them clearly, dressed as acolytes, in shiny red silk cloaks, edged in imitation mink. Ana María was at that time a very young, beautiful woman: she had already published a novel and was writing others that, according to gossip, posed serious problems for the censor. I maintained silent admiration for her, not daring to speak to her, until a mutual friend introduced us. Her warm, sweet voice, her openness and modest ways, immediately won my sympathy and affection. When I explained to her our plans for a literary circle, she gave her generous support: she knew and appreciated Mario Lacruz and promised to come to our discussions.

The initial nucleus that launched the Turia gathering soon counted on new patrons: the most enthusiastic of these was undoubtedly a theatrical author and director of some renown, full of plans for cultural developments and with more experience than we in organizational matters. It would be impossible for me to state now who introduced him to us and how he won our confidence. The dramatist—a lean, nervous man, in his forties—was pleasant company and showed us friendship and sympathy. He was branded as a homosexual in theatrical circles but Carandell and Lacruz were convinced that it was merely an artistic pose: the innocent pygmalionism of someone anxious to bring about the spiritual development of the young and in turn be enriched by their refreshing, exuberant company. In any case, our new friend revealed genuine interest in our first hesitant steps in the world of adult writing; he read, censored, corrected, and encouraged us; he returned the pages that we timidly submitted to his scrutiny with comments and notes that were often critical, I seem to recall, of our intellectualism and lack of tenderness. With general agreement, we had decided to adorn our gathering of budding and almost unknown authors with the prestigious, classical name of Mediterranean, which we all liked. We had invitation cards printed for the inaugural session, but the illustration that should have figured on them was a source of problems: our new friend suggested an athlete by Phidias while Mario Lacruz and Carandell insisted on it being a Venus, symbol of fertility. After a series of erudite discussions, the latter got their way and the card with the engraving of Venus was posted to a hundred friends, writers, or simply lovers of literature.

I do not propose to trace the ephemeral history of our circle nor to describe the presence there of people as different as Barral, Oliart, Díaz Plaja, and Salvador Espriu. We paid an unusual homage to André Gide on the occasion of his death and there was a competition for short stories, read by their authors, which I entered with two short texts and which was won on a show-of-hands vote by Ana María Matute. The latter's story and my tale, *"El ladrón,"* would be published months later in a literary magazine subsidized by a devotee of the circle, a sailor-poet who wrote gloomy poetry on the human condition in the solitary refuge of his boat, which apparently was moored along the quayside of the Seine. This first entry into print, rather than flattering my vanity, depressed me: suddenly faced by the weakness and poverty of my creative powers, I realized that I was very far from the imaginative genius I aspired to and that I naively believed I had within me as a result of my conversations with Mariano.

During those weeks—February, March 1951—the dramatist had tightened his links with us: out of curiosity not without other motives— the desire to put to the test the purity of his intentions toward the group—my brother José Agustín and myself spent a weekend with him in a pension in Llafranc. But, either through cautiousness or lack of desire to confess his position, our friend kept up his guard, avoiding the verbal traps José Agustín cunningly set for him. His role as the open, refined educator, a kind of chaste Tiresias, admirer of noble, youthful beauty, had begun to establish credit with us all when an incident occurred that not only destroyed the image but also precipitated the end of our brand-new literary circle.

One night, Mariano turned up at home in a state of great excitement. He had gone out by himself for a walk with the dramatist in the Mont-juich gardens: they had a friendly conversation on life and literature until his companion, with the mistaken belief that he had cleared the ground by quoting Plato and referring to Gide, tried to Mariano's horror and surprise to put words into action. Mariano's innocence in the matter and his desire to be admired as an expert in the field of art and literature had of course played an important role in the unfortunate slip: my friend needed someone to believe wholeheartedly in the genius of the work he was planning and, disillusioned with me because of my cold reaction, he thought he had found a substitute in the person of our mentor. The scene could have been comic had it not been for Mariano's rage: he was abso-lutely incensed by the act and demanded that the whole group ostracize the guilty party. Although I thought his reaction was exaggerated and tried to underplay the event's importance, the news spread. The circle's other patrons joined in Mariano's furious attacks: as I had already seen from what happened in my family, the insulting term of queer continued to be the *monstrum horrendum, informe, ingens*, a stigma or reproach that allowed no excuses or pity. Luis Carandell was given the task of telling the reprobate of his expulsion without it ever occurring to the latter to rebel or protest. Society's sacrificial lamb, he bowed his head like Grandfather and respected the oppressive, iniquitous law: having internalized the discourse of condemnation, there was no other way out but silence, shame, and humiliation.

Although my sexual inclination was in no way resolved at this time, I was disgusted by the prophylactic measures of my friends. Enrique Boada felt as upset as I did, and we agreed, behind the backs of the others, to make an embarrassed visit to the outcast, assuring him of our cowardly esteem and friendship. But the following gathering took place without him in an atmosphere rarified by rumors about what had happened. Given the lack of an organizer capable of coordinating our activities and the studied movement away by some members, Lacruz, Carandell, Mariano, and myself decided to make a clean break with the public announcement at the end of our fifth or sixth meeting of the definitive close to our literary gatherings.

MY DECEITFUL BEHAVIOR in the contemptible episode I have just related was of course the reflection of an embarrassing uncertainty about myself. At twenty years of age, my identity, not only as far as my character and moral standards were concerned but also the pleasures and phantoms that would later shape my life, remained shrouded in a mist that I could not clear away. I had noticed with anxiety and surprise from adolescence that, unlike my friends and companions, I was not at all aroused by being close to women physically or emotionally. The neighborhood girls I passed in the street did not make my heart beat more quickly nor was I filled with a desire to go out with them: no falling in love, no sudden passion but alienation and introspection while in sharp contrast to me José Agustín went from flirtation to flirtation and Luis, with remarkable precocity, began to get telephone calls from his admirers and friends. This indifference to the opposite sex extended equally to my own: the close friendships I maintained with some friends did not involve any elements of ambiguity. My male friendships were always straightforward and have continued to be so to the extent that they have not gone beyond the limits of my social class and the aseptic milieu of my culture. My coolness and indifference toward the girls and boys my age and, in general, to all the men and women integrated in the daily texture of my life did not, however, exclude the insistent pursuit of my instincts. As in previous years I continued to masturbate with monotonous regularity. The mental images that assaulted me at such critical moments invariably introduced ingredients of force and even violence: I remember the day when a gypsy savagely beat his mule in front of our house and that scene, far from arousing feelings of mercy, excited me so much that I came in the middle of the street. The external paraphernalia of exuberant, exotic, overwhelming virility—the photographs of Sikhs in military training, of two strongmen locked in the sinuous, oiled embrace of Turkish wrestling—similarly provoked and stimulated my fantasies. But these sudden, repeated sensations did not mesh with the rest of my daily experience: they remained isolated and beyond assimilation, totally outside the events of my real life. As I still had not gone beyond the frontiers of the bourgeois world and urban space in which I lived, my mental representations and the figures in my dreams had no possibility of taking on real shape: they were merely persistent shadows, condemned in the circumstances to wither in a hidden, latent

state. In my maturity, I have often thought of the absolute lack of connection in those years between my libido and the objective world and I
have reached the conclusion that if I had then lived in a heterogeneous or
less closed environment—or, even better, under the favorable cover of
*sotadism**—things would have been different. But, immersed in a limbo or
a void worthy of a bell jar, the lashes that sometimes pained me did not
provide any lead or key to an eventual way out: the pure civilian territory
entirely occupied by my peers excluded *a priori* any possible temptation.
Since nobody around me attracted me physically, I didn't even pose the
question of whether I was homosexual or not. Consequently, I experienced
a feeling of anxiety and astonishment the day Mariano—months before
the incident with the dramatist—confided that someone I had met by
chance days before had gone to him scandalmongering that I was a pansy.
The accuser—the representative of a famous Argentinian publishing
house—earned a living selling books as a door-to-door salesman: I had
ordered some books from him and, if my memory does not deceive me, he
asked me pointedly when he delivered them why I was interested in
Wilde and André Gide. Incredulous and angry I persuaded Mariano to
invite him to his house and to rebuff his slander with some energy. My
friend did just that, while I listened to their conversation hidden behind a
half-closed door to the sitting room. The book-trader—from a well-off
family who would be arrested months later for his involvement in an
armed robbery—had to confess that he had no proof, but insisted on the
assumptions he based on my literary tastes. Before bidding farewell he
mentioned various acquaintances who were also homosexuals and fans of
Gide according to him. Although soon forgotten, the incident nevertheless left me with a bitter taste. The idea of being taken for a member of
that guild, an object of universal contempt and hatred, filled me with
anguish and fear. My father's pathological horror, daily exacerbated by
enforced coexistence with Grandfather, had left a deep impression on me.
All my friends, with one or two exceptions, professed equally virulent
disgust toward "perverts." Eager to escape possible suspicion, I began to
show a simulated interest in the girlfriends of Mariano and Juan Eugenio
Morera. But these attempts to forge a "normal" image for myself
immediately struck the impenetrable obstacle of my reserve and distance
from girls. Since there was no ground for common understanding—a love
of reading, personal likes—their company bored me and I soon left them.
In the months after the end of the Turia gatherings, my previous warmth
toward Mariano went cold. While he seemed to consider the period of his
literary ambitions closed and was preparing to engage in stormy intrigue
and adventures with women as I would have the opportunity to testify a

---

* See "Sir Richard Burton, peregrino y sexólogo," *Crónicas sarracinas*, 170–71.

year later in Madrid, I had sought refuge in writing and tried unsuccessfully to rewrite my novel. Among the people we saw during our failed cultural initiative, there was a poet and art critic from Santander whom Enrique Boada and I visited in his home. Fernando Gutiérrez was a man in his forties, simple, warm, and honest: he welcomed us straightaway with open arms and from that first encounter his house was a real home to me for just over a year. His wife and daughters were friendly toward me and my life with them became a regular habit. The gloom, decay, and old age that dominated Pablo Alcover suffocated me: forced to hide from my father the fact that I had abandoned my studies, I wrote in hiding, in a state of anxiety and oppression that clearly influenced the predictable collapse of the novel. I needed to escape, to flee from that intolerable climate and begin my work from a new base. Fernando Gutiérrez understood this and gave me invaluable support. After piously promising my father that he would help me review my law subjects, he managed to get me away from home regularly without arousing his fears. Established in his flat on calle Bailén, packed with books and paintings, I helped him correct his translations, sought his advice on the difficulties and snares of my novel, and enjoyed the comforts and advantages of family life, away from home but as if I were at home. I possessed an instinctive fear of stepping out of my sterile, anesthetized world into other territories where I felt in an uncertain, intuitive way that life existed; a fear of leaping into the void and discovering what I really was kept me wrapped in a chrysalis for a year—no temptations, no desires whatsoever. Neither the sudden explosion of the tram strike that shook Barcelona out of its stupor nor the showy, shocking celebration of the Eucharistic Congress, with its cohort of grotesque ceremonies, succeeded in taking me out of my soft shell. My exclusive interest was the novel. Fernando Gutiérrez had soon noticed the defects and gaps in my Spanish and encouraged me to overcome them. Although through my own shortcomings he could not then share his love for the poetry of our classics, he did manage to extend and improve the content of my reading, limited at that time to French books and stodgy translations from Buenos Aires. His patience and generosity toward me led him to support my entry for the Prize for Young Literature created by the publisher Janés, for which he was secretary. In spite of the many corrections, my novel was clearly clumsy and immature: the shadows of Gide and Hermann Hesse were visibly present and situations and characters suffered from melodrama and lack of realism. Nevertheless, the affectionate, prejudiced vote of my friend and his absolute confidence in the value of my work persuaded the publisher to award me the prize, incredible in my eyes, of a check for ten thousand pesetas. Fortunately, *El mundo de los espejos* was never published: Janés himself, when he received me, had very tactfully let me know that his prize was only a stimulus to continue along the path to become a real writer one day. In the company of Fernando Gutiérrez and his family, I feasted my sudden riches on oysters and champagne. His wife, who maintained intense passionate relationships with his friends, also encouraged me to continue my apprenticeship with them and even dreamt of seeing me marry one of her daughters. One of her letters had fallen into my father's hands and its excited tone made him mistakenly alarmed about the nature of her feelings. I disillusioned him immediately, but with the not-totally-erroneous idea that my friendship with Fernando Gutiérrez was visibly taking me away from my law studies to bring me close to literature, he began to make frequent lengthy visits difficult. The fiction of my legal studies poisoned my daily life and was each day more difficult to sustain. I didn't know how to tackle the dilemma I faced when chance decided for me. My father's miraculous business with one of these half-Nazi half-professional swindler characters who inevitably crossed his path had taken a disturbing turn during 1950 until it became an unmitigated catastrophe threatening to ruin us. José Agustín had carried through the necessary deals in Madrid, avoiding the firm's bankruptcy with money from the sale of one of Grandfather's properties, but, when he was forced to join the army after finishing his legal studies, salvaging whatever from the shipwreck fell to me. That blow had finally sunk my father and the atmosphere in Pablo Alcover could not have been gloomier. After bidding farewell to Fernando Gutiérrez and the few friends I still saw, lighthearted and greatly relieved in spite of the gravity of the circumstances, I took the plane to Madrid.

F ACES APPEARED ONE *morning nobody knew from where: ghosts from beyond the city wall, perhaps from the executioner's wall where they had been shot to pieces: righteously anonymous, their symbiosis in a common grave, a forgotten bed of hollyhocks: with us once more, despite that great clear-out, the seed of some deep, unbearable nightmare: an empty gesture to rub your eyes, wake up all at once, smile at a life that remains unchanged, at the civilian horizon of peace won through arms: still coming across them, rough, dark, frowning, with cold determination: an image aroused of times of whispered exchanges, a nervous start at the ring of the bell, a furtive, withered hand drawing a lace curtain, steps muffled by the carpet in the passage, prayers muttered under the breath, fear, lots of fear: they're advancing in tight-knit groups from the crowded side streets, worn-out shoes, threadbare clothes, external signs of poverty unseemingly displayed: a beslippered, middle-aged woman giving out leaflets to the curious: hoarse, incomprehensible cries from a small, lean individual wearing glasses: dozens, hundreds spring up from the urban asphalt at the bottom of the Ramblas like mushrooms after a shower, chanting slogans next to the smashed glass from the trams, general transport strike, a city completely paralyzed: the authorities rendered powerless, overtaken by the breadth of the protest, the sudden collective fiesta atmosphere, removal of the fear that kept lips sealed, the passersby's timid smiles, amorphous camaraderie, clumsy relearning of words and gestures that had been eliminated. Fleeting images, scraps of sentences, Father's anxious conversations, Eulalia's sighs in the kitchen, waiting expectantly, the crushing official response, the resonant voice on the radio, bold type in all the newspapers, foreign agents, revolutionary groups, hostile elements, actions skilfully coordinated from abroad, the traditional enemies of our values, dark conspiracy, hatred, ancient anti-Spanish hatred.*

Gradual preparation of the ground: machinery carefully arranged in the weeks preceding the great event: a general cleanup of the city, erection of crosses, podia, Eucharistic emblems, proliferation of shields marked with the symbol, setting up of loudspeakers on the main roads in the center: obsessive propaganda over the radio, entire editions of newspapers devoted to the event, Pastor Angelicus's ubiquitous photograph, expectation raised to the point of paroxysm: first motley experience of mass tourism: enthusiastic pilgrimages, flags, banners, oriflammes, greetings written in Latin: priests, nuns, monks, prelates, chaplains, deacons, curates,

In Cuba Grandfather Antonio had married the daughter of rich settlers of Anglo-Menorcan origin, Catalina Taltavull y Victory ... (8)

... the wedding photo: unusual portrait of the couple who twelve years later would procreate you ... (27)

... on the tennis court, radiant, confident, spontaneous ... (27)

... your father fixes the serene beauty and expression of the eternally mysterious youthful woman ... (27)

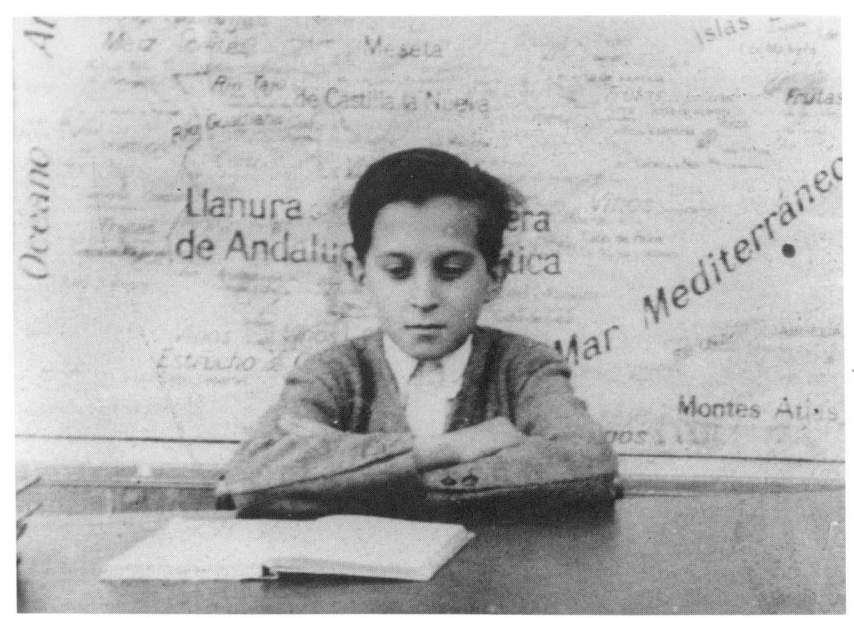

I soon memorized the size, population, capital, main cities, legal status, and
natural riches of every country in the world … (75)

Marta, a woman, ready to get married; José Agustín,
a university student, and about to leave home … (85)

Luis and I, still tied to school, but ready also to take
flight, as it sadly felt, to flee from that house that was
falling down around us ... (85)

Blurred images of the Torrentbó terrace, its eucalyptus trees,
balustrade ... (27)

... the strange, unexpected aura of her smile: an open,
warm, generous smile, tinged with melancholy ... (178)

Raimundo seems happy to see you with a friend ... (156)

... the contact with the soldiers and prisoners would allow you a glimpse of areas and hidden corners of Spanish reality that you could have penetrated in no other way ... (186)

... thin, honed down to the fragile birdlike profile he acquired in those years ... (169)

... two strongmen locked in the serious, oiled embrace of Turkish
wrestling ... (116)

protonotaries, bishops in residence and in partibus *dressed up in their corresponding clothes, habits, ankle-length suits, birettas, bonnets, chasubles, mitres, rain capes: far-sighted construction of walls to hide the wretchedness of the areas close to the processional route: peremptory expulsion of hundreds of slumdwellers, rapid removal of prostitutes and undesirables: enormous nighttime purges of our traditionally welcoming, hospitable city today held in check by an emotion impossible to put into words while it awaits the arrival of the Nuncio and his impressive retinue of military, civilian, and religious leaders: ever-present, hateful voices of an aggressive, dominating state Church that would pursue you for days, wherever you went, with tenacious persistence: to return home after an investigative wander through the devastated shacks and find your father kneeling opposite the radio set that is broadcasting at that moment the solemn blessing of the Pope.*

Those who expected their liberating fleet to disembark in forty-five, just after the Allied victory and the four-sided Potsdam agreements, were probably not the same ones who came to welcome them on that luminous morning along the breakwater: men, women, children, the elderly, drawn by curiosity, a novelty soon to become routine: the Sixth Fleet's aircraft carriers and vessels anchored on the horizon on their first friendship visit: smaller boats brought the sailors on leave to the quayside of Peace: tall, strong, cheerful, friendly, dressed like in the films, they waved to the pleasure-boat travelers, gave cigarettes to the boys, willingly gave themselves over to the touts and pimps, went off with the boldest early risers amongst the prostitutes: admired on all sides they went up the Ramblas surprised by the gleeful disposition of the women, the incredibly cheap prices, the broken English of guides and waiters, the atmosphere of expectation, as if there were a fiesta in all the lower part of the city: society was changing, politics were changing, the world was changing, and the Americans were there, in their immaculate uniforms and hats, just like in Gene Kelly's musical comedy, walking across the Plaza de Cataluña, through the pigeons, happy, arm in arm: street photographers and amateur snapshooters captured the scene from Singin' in the Rain *in the sun, without the tap dancing, although it was being played, as someone gloomily remarked, after a delay of seven bastard years.*

DURING THE TIME I lived under the friendly shadow of Fernando Gutiérrez and his family, my links with my university friends loosened. In some cases, as with Morera and Mariano, the branching out was mutual; in others, it was due to outside circumstances that unexpectedly broke off our relationship: Enrique Boada had suffered a crisis of conscience—the first of what was later to be a rapid succession of them—and, for a period of a year, he took refuge in the diocesan seminary in calle Balmes. I visited him there two or three times in his ridiculous disguise as a novitiate, just before he set his habits on one side, obviously disenchanted with the boredom and routine of his experience. After completing his military service on a RIF air base, he entered the White Fathers community and disappeared for a time in the mirages and illusions of Algeria. Although it happened after my journey to Madrid, the break with Cortés was even more sudden: I knew of his hatred for the regime and his Catalan nationalist sympathies, but I was totally taken aback the day I found out that he had been imprisoned. Apparently he had been caught in a police roundup of a clandestine organization of the socialist movement then led by Pallach and he remained under arrest, awaiting trial, in the military fortress of Montjuich.

I left Barcelona certain that I was beginning a new stage in my life: the city where I was born and had grown up was hardly visible in outline, already lost in the mist, and I was moving away, as a poet wrote, "without grief or nostalgia." Madrid was still not the free land where, sleeping or waking, I stubbornly sought asylum; but the degree of movement it allowed me, without the ties or restrictions imposed by proximity to my father nor my overwhelming distress at the family scene in Pablo Alcover, seemed broad enough to make a paradise out of the capital that was still hungry, provincial, mediocre, and savagely punished by war. For the first time, I didn't have to tell anyone about what I was or was not doing. Although I had promised my father that I would continue studying to be a lawyer and would matriculate in the new Faculty of Political Sciences, I did not intend to waste my time on subjects I hated and I freely used my time to explore a world that, because of timidity or inhibitions, I had not even approached, without neglecting my plans and ambitions as a writer. My duties concerning my father's unsuccessful business venture were lighter than I supposed. My first cousin, Juan Berchmans Vallet, my Aunt

María's elder son, had been given a post as notary in the capital two or three years before and, with a true family spirit and affection that I would have occasion to experience later on, he gave me valuable directions to steer through the legal labyrinth of the case to which we were committed to try to rescue what could still be rescued. My cousin Juan was a traditionalist, Catholic father of a large family, and had a virtue unheard of in the Spain of those times: respect for the ideas of others. Although he knew that mine and my brothers' were a thousand miles from his own beliefs, he courageously intervened first during the imprisonment of Luis and later in the campaign unleashed against me by the regime as a result of what happened during the presentation in Milan of *Campos de Níjar*, to stem the torrent of insults poured out by the press and to reestablish the truth.

When José Agustín was in Madrid finishing his law degree, he had stayed in the university residence hall, Our Lady of Guadalupe, then situated on calle Donoso Cortés, in the Argüelles district. This hall was originally created for young Latin American students pursuing their studies in Spain but some Spaniards from the provinces also stayed there. The political characteristics of an authoritarian government like Franco's had naturally attracted a handful of intellectuals and university students who were sympathetic toward them; some even enjoyed official scholarships and set themselves up as defenders of nebulous Falangist ideals: poets like Ernesto Cardenal and Pablo Antonio Cuadra worshipped the unblemished figure of José Antonio, before undergoing religious conversion as the first did to revolutionary ideals and yielding to the spell of charismatic leaders like Castro and Guevara. Others, like fellow Nicaraguan Mejía Sánchez and the Colombian Eduardo Cote, prudently stayed outside politics. When I arrived in Madrid, future poets or novelists like José Angel Valente and Julio Ramón Ribeyro had left the college or were about to do so, but two enthusiastic lovers of literary life still lodged there: Hernando Valencia Goelkel and Rafael Gutiérrez Girardot.

In the rush to organize the journey, my family had forgotten to reserve a room: when I appeared, they were all let. But Argüelles was then a residential student area and there was no problem in finding a sublet room. I settled down in one, hardly two blocks away from the college, in a family lodging-house, where they served both breakfast and lunch. Although I knew no one when I moved into the area, José Agustín's numerous friends immediately appeared on all sides. Besides, winning the Janés literary prize gave me a little fame and the poets and writers who gravitated around the Guadalupe wanted to get in touch with me and cultivate my friendship. Thanks to Eduardo Cote and Hernando Valencia I discovered the North American novel, alas, through very poor Argentinian translations: from Dos Passos to Hemingway, Madrid was just one moveable feast. It was the year of the publication of *The Old Man and the Sea* and Hernando Valencia was preparing a critical study of the work. I can remember that it was Hernando who showed me the first copy of the novel *Other Voices, Other Rooms,* by the then very youthful Truman Capote, which I read at one sitting as enthusiastically as he had. However, the author I found most fruitful during those months was William Faulkner. I was engulfed by his novels, captured by a tension and fascination that were new to me and, paralyzed by the sumptuous violence of the universe that closed around me, I stopped writing for the moment. I was helped along by this pause in my obsessive addiction to writing: freed from the burden of having to scribble futilely on sheet after sheet, I could at last devote myself to simpler, more pleasant activities. The Argüelles bars and cafés were the assiduous haunt of my new friends and, with a rapidity that surprised me, they initiated me into the attractions of leisure, lounging, and alcohol.

As I write these lines I can picture mentally every small detail of the tiny bar where we used to meet: the owner, Honorio, jovial, bald, friendly, preparing coffee or washing spoons, cups, and plates, always chatting to his customers; the vaguely academic barmaid, with her glasses and apron, who shared the confidences and worries of the Latin Americans who frequented the place, one of whom she would finally marry; the line of tables and benches parallel to the bar at which students, youths, or scholarship-holders and the less young but unemployed drank, smoked, discussed, played dominoes or cards throughout the day; at the back the gloomy lavatory to which the beer-drinkers regularly retired and where for the first time in my life I was sick from pure inebriation. Honorio's regulars were older and more experienced than I: on the whole they were lifelong drinkers who had generally neglected their studies and vegetated in Madrid thanks to opportune help from their governments or the monthly checks from their families. Some of them owned real individual stashes of wine or museums of alcohol catalogued under "literatures" according to their peculiar terminology: English, Russian, or French depending on whether it was gin, vodka, or cognac. Their cheerful lack of occupation and abundance of money made relations easy with girls and women in the area: their standard of living, much higher than the contemporary Spaniard's, turned them into real potentates and they peacefully enjoyed life untroubled by conscience. Their world, manners, behavior, accent, idiomatic expressions were new to me. I was accepted into their midst as the younger brother of José Agustín and their immediate friendliness helped me overcome my natural shyness.

The first day I stepped into Honorio's bar I met a couple of Colombians whose strangeness and fondness for drink attracted my attention. One of them, Lucho P.B., was a strapping man almost in his thirties, dark-skinned, with a face that seemed to have been carved in a violent fit of vision, endowed with extraordinary strength, vitality, and magnetism; he was finishing his medical studies but used to spend most of his time in the local bars. The other one was related on his father's side to the populist leader Jorge Eliecer Gaitán, murdered in Bogotá a few years before; young Pedro Antonio Gaitán looked more like a flamenco singer or a temporarily unemployed tango dancer whose company had gone bankrupt. With a lively gift of the gab he combined the odd check from his disappointed family with efficient, elegant recourse to the art of borrowing: as I later discovered, he was not following any studies and strove to prolong his stay in Spain with every kind of argument or excuse. Pedro Antonio had boundless admiration for Lucho: he followed him like a shadow, sang his praises, encouraged his alcoholic leanings, and when he succeeded in getting him drunk, would chastise him till he was beside himself and then let Lucho's insults rain down on him.

The group of Colombians addicted to Honorio's bar also included three students who more or less successfully alternated their attendance at lectures with a hectic nightlife that swept beyond the familiar boundaries of Argüelles and reached the bars in the center and the San Marcos brothels: Ramón, Herman, Jorge Eliecer would turn up at dusk when their two fellow countrymen had already drunk a lively mix of rum, beer, and cognac and were enmeshed in one of their interminable arguments. Pedro Antonio—with that drooping mop of black hair which, like a monk's cowl in a hygrometer, forecast an impending storm—would run off when it was time to pay, and his financial irresponsibility would provoke a thunderous downpour of insults from his irritable although faithful benefactor. At other times Lucho, possessed with the dark aura of a giant gladiator, responded to the curiosity or doubt of some passerby with one of his wonderful shows of strength. He theatrically wrapped a handkerchief around his left hand, seized an uncorked bottle full of water by the neck, and with his other hand dealt it a confident crisp blow, shattering the bottom of the bottle. The group of friends was then possessed by a powerful external force and suddenly swept out of the bar.

Barely two weeks after my arrival in Madrid, I was already part of that select band of drinkers. Conscious of dealing with a novice, my new companions took every care in my education: the airs I gave myself as a serious, shy, wilful young man with a promising career as a writer before him were soon scattered in that happy den where fortune or misfortune had guided me. I began to mix wine, manzanilla, and cognac: I remember clearly my innocent surprise at the heavy blanket cast over my mind and the clumsiness of my movements as I got up to urinate. Honorio's bar became my canteen and my support system immediately: after lunch, I settled down there with some novel recommended by Cote or Hernando

Valencia and read and waited for the noisy arrival of my friends. At night
I followed them to the bars or cafés in the area or I went on a bar-crawl
with them to the farthest dives of Carretas or the drinking houses on
Echegaray.

The promiscuity, dirt, and harshness of the areas through which we
flitted naturally affected my moral sensibility; but the fascination and
stimulus they exercised over me were more powerful than my feelings of
pity or condemnation. At the age of twenty-one I thus discovered what
would then be a constant in my life. My dislike and even horror of urban
areas or zones that are open, clean, symmetrical, and despairingly empty,
with their beautiful, well-planned streets, fenced-off spaces, rapid traffic,
and dreamlike existence: inhabitants entrenched in their houses, gardens,
fences, external signs of unshared wealth, frigidity, egoism, anesthetized
vitality. My passion, on the other hand, for street chaos, the brutal
transparency of social relations, the confusion of public and private, the
insidious flood of merchandise, precarious lives, improvised, packed
tightly in a merciless struggle for survival, fertile barter, a mysterious
magnetic pull. A bipolarity that would be intensified with the passing of
time to the extreme of dividing up the urban landscape and my feelings
for it into two opposed, irreconcilable camps: an irreversible hatred for the
monuments and symbols of an ever-cynical, cruel history, for those severe,
threatening, official districts whose false grandeur and solemnity hide the
original sin of their construction at the expense of humiliations, sufferings, and blood; an attraction toward those areas where life is spontaneous,
dark, dense, and proliferating, in which the creative act can take root and
nourish its juices. My subsequent obsessive movements whether in Paris,
Istanbul, New York, or Marrakesh—the instinctive seer's guesses guiding
my steps toward territories neither sterilized nor subject to rigorous
planning or control—perhaps originated thirty years ago during my
hazardous forays through Madrid with my group of Colombian friends.
The picaresque movement of beggars, aggressively displaying their poverty and servile respect for an authority that was no less terrible and
suffocating for being distant or discreet, distinguished that postwar
capital—no longer heroic but in thrall—which, with its sores and violent
convulsions, would be my entry to the present metropolitan centers
threatened by the subtle, avenging infiltration of the formerly colonized,
the marginalized, and the victims.

My nightly excursions with Lucho, Pedro Antonio, and his compatriots
went on pleasantly for several weeks: I experienced the problems and
inconveniences of hangovers, thick heads the morning after, the confused
impression of unreality. My brand-new incarnation as a drinker appeared
from under the skin of my old life and made me realize how unstable and
false that was. As on other occasions during those years of apprenticeship,

I could identify surprising discontinuities in my biography: the existence of breaks or ruptures in habits and norms of behavior that I thought had deep roots. The curious, extroverted young man who had put his writing aside and expectantly savored the friendly immediacy of his companions in Honorio's bar seemed at first glance to be setting out on a carefree, untroubled phase in life when an inopportune event upset his hopes and brought him back to earth.

On one of my now daily alcoholic evenings, I accompanied Lucho and his friends through the different bars in the area; whether because I had drunk more than usual that day, or because Lucho insisted on putting my resistance to the test, what is sure is that we were both left at 2:00 A.M. in a café on Gaztambide near the college, having left our fellow adventurers behind on the curbside like lost possessions swept from a carriage by a furious wind. Slumped over the table next to the last round of empty glasses we exchanged the usual drunkards' confidences and I think, although I am unsure of the murky chloroformed images filtered by memory, we embraced and I caressed him under the waiter's impassive gaze. I don't know how we managed to leave the place given our state nor how I dragged Lucho to the bedroom in my *pensión* where he collapsed on one of the beds as soon as we arrived and his violent snoring prevented me from sleeping on the other one. When we got up the day after, neither of us remembered anything: we went down to Honorio's bar for a coffee and said a cheerful goodbye. However, some hours later, Lucho appeared in the *pensión* with a worried look on his face. He told me in an even tone, unreproachfully, that he had been seen the night before in a local bar as drunk as a newt and an unspecified friend had been acting in a *strange* way toward him. Although Lucho didn't spell out what this strangeness consisted of, he asked me to go out with him and, rather anxiously, I followed him to the café where we had both collapsed the night before. My friend exchanged a few quiet words with the waiter and left again with me. That fellow says that my companion touched me up, the whole works, Lucho commented laconically. His words terrified me; but Lucho interrupted the conversation: he insisted on inviting me to dinner and without mentioning the incident or my behavior, he embraced me as usual when we said good night.

That moral setback sank me into a state of humiliation and disarray that is difficult to express: what I had darkly and instinctively felt since I ceased to be a child had happened with an alarming sense of timing. I felt naked, vulnerable, defenseless, exposed without reason or guilt to insult and condemnation. What most upset and offended me was that the episode happened without any intervention of my will: simply and inevitably, it was an absurd punishment or cruel trick of destiny. Someone lurking within me and taking advantage of my temporary incapacity had become involved in improper behavior that I myself, when in control of my faculties and lucidity, condemned without qualification. But who was that malevolent, mocking intruder who, with alcoholic courage, identified me with pariahs, as an object of general repulsion, and was within an ace of discrediting me with my friends? My fear and horror for this undesirable Mr. Hyde, of whose stealthy reality I was suddenly aware, forced me to rekindle my vigilance toward myself: to avoid in the future, if I wanted to restore my damaged image, whatever circumstances might favor his reappearance. But the evil was done and, overwhelmed with gratuitous remorse, I nevertheless rebelled with all my might against the verdict of my distant, elusive tribunal.

In the light of my later experience it would be very convenient to endow what happened with some prophetic sense and establish a perfect chain of causes and effects from then on. But that is not my aim: I intend to narrate events as I perceived them when they happened. My helplessness and inability to interpret things exactly encouraged the vague, derisory hope I could disregard the truth. One way or another, the episode had its impact: with ill-concealed envy, Pedro Antonio referred to it maliciously. Forced to confront this disaster in my biography, I redoubled my efforts to bury it in oblivion. Fortunately, Lucho did not show any resentment: curiously, he had increased his display of friendship toward me. With a delicacy that was hardly in harmony with his brusque, direct manner, he never mentioned the matter nor allowed anyone else to in front of him. Perhaps enjoying his secret power over me, taking me affectionately by the arm, he insisted on my joining his group of friends in their customary forays in the carefree quarters of the city.

On one of these evenings, seven or eight of us settled down in the private room of a bar with two prostitutes. One, called Mely, was slim and well proportioned, with her hair dyed blonde; the other one, Fernandita, looked robust and healthy and acted like a peasant. Wine flowed freely, unleashing nostalgia and tongues, and my friends came dangerously near to an out-and-out declaration of their deep patriotic feelings: from "When you have departed, the shadows will consume me" to "Look they are looking at us looking at each other" the chorus of Colombian songs uttered in alcoholic tones resounded more and more enthusiastically in the private room while Lucho, embracing the two women, made them take turns sitting on his knee, proudly displayed his muscles, drank mouth to mouth with them from the same glass and observed me with his dark, metallic, inscrutable eyes as hard as mica. I interpreted this as a silent message and, changing my seat, I settled down next to Mely. I kissed and embraced her clumsily with an audacity I didn't think I was capable of— sustained of course by alcohol and Lucho's watchful presence. She looked at me with eyes I imagine were beautiful and light and, more experienced than I, her lips separated mine and her cool, slippery tongue entered my mouth like a dart. We went on kissing for a long time, sucking each other, savoring that new, warm intimacy. Meanwhile Lucho had taken Fernandita's breasts but I noticed that he was following my progress out of the corner of his eye. His implicit approval and my desire to eradicate all memory of my past behavior encouraged me to copy his example: I leaned over Mely's breasts now freed from the black bra and caressed, kissed, and nibbled her nipples. I don't know if it was she or her friend who decided it was time to go. There was a *meublé* next door, she said, and we could conclude our respective activities there more discreetly. We paid the waiter and went into the street. I remember the drunken Colombians' songs, Mely embracing me, and Fernandita, Lucho, the sharp, dry wind, the numbing wait for the nightwatchman to open the front door. Then the night in the company of Mely, her ritual stripping, the black lace garters tied round her waist, the generous crop of pubic hair, her friendly help in achieving an erection, the disturbing touch of her nails, the syncopated, panting coming together; and my light sleep, hearing her measured breathing, as if shaken by the wind, my feeling of relief at washing away the stain, that I was the same as everybody else, I could look Lucho and his friends in the face without blushing.

Comforted by this first experience, I continued to frequent the bars and whorehouses of Echegaray and San Marcos. My inhibitions and frigidity toward "decent" girls and women had gradually given way with those whose time and services were paid for. Although since my demonstration to Lucho I no longer felt the need to justify anything, I continued my visits to the cheapest, busiest brothels, directed by some inner affinity with that harsh, sordid, irregular universe, which in my eyes had a coherence and suggestiveness that reduced the people and places in my family, school, and university by contrast to the size of a decrepit, dusty window in a bourgeois store, crammed with fans, dolls, and junk; the brutal, unadorned image of a ruined, crumbling society where the ordinary people of the capital survived with a struggle was then revealed, I intuitively felt, in those bawdy houses, combining hospice, public auction, marketplace, and hideout and seeming to await the brush of a Goya to startle us with their mocking familiarity. During that harsh winter of fifty-three, full of events and new developments, I was unexpectedly visited by Mariano in the *pensión* where I was staying. I was surprised by the way he had changed in a few months: his youthful features looked as if they had gone flabby and he spoke in confident, rounded tones entirely new to him. I was told how he had problems with his family because of the girl he was living with: she was a dark, very beautiful Andalusian girl called Argelia whom he introduced me to one night in Barcelona just before my departure. Argelia had a flat on the other side of the Retiro Park and they had decided to take refuge there for a while waiting for the storm to die down. There were spare rooms in the flat: if I was interested, he could let me have one where I could live and write in peace and quiet. Although the offer did not appeal, since I would leave behind my fiery, sparkling band of friends, I finally accepted. The meagre funds I was getting from home were rapidly disappearing on my nightly jaunts and I now had no money to pay my lodgings. On the other hand, he added to tempt me, he and his girlfriend would have to go to Barcelona on the slightest pretext: in their absence, I would be in charge of the flat and would enjoy total freedom.

Perhaps to avoid the boredom of living alone with Argelia, Mariano tried to rekindle our old discussions on literature. However, his rich, exuberant passion for the novel seemed to have waned. His points of reference hadn't changed in two years, from which I deduced he had given up reading as well as writing. Like many other youngsters smitten by a love of literature and repeatedly scorned, he had signed an individual peace treaty with literature out of exhaustion. While even I was temporarily setting to one side my plans for novels, the only virtue of his well-meaning advice was to annoy me. The timeworn discussion of Hesse or Lafcadio's gratuitous act was a muted repetition, like a scratched recording of our university arguments. I tried to communicate my recent admiration for the North American novelists of the lost generation to him, but Mariano, browsing through the mediocre translation of a Hemingway novel, proclaimed contemptuously it was the work of a village idiot.

Taking advantage of his generous hospitality, I invited my gang of friends, much to Argelia's delight. My memories of that evening are fairly confused with music, dancing, singing, and alcohol on tap. Lucho had assiduously flirted with our hostess—clearly very happy to arouse Mariano's jealousy—and ended up drunk, unable to stand up. I went with him to my room and helped him to lie on the bed. Just as I was about to leave, I heard his hoarse voice pronounce my name and invite me to stretch out beside him. Even today, after thirty years, I cannot decipher the real meaning of his words: was he suggesting real intimacy between us or else, as I then perhaps mistakenly judged, was it a final test he was putting me through to clear up the truth about my *strange* behavior? If this were the case, if his drunkenness were exaggerated or put on, couldn't he be setting a trap only later to show me up in front of the others? The magnetic attraction he held for me in my alcoholic stupor did not work that night when I had only drunk a few drops: Mr. Hyde did not reappear. With a prudent small-mindedness that later I wouldn't hesitate to reproach myself for, I acted as if I hadn't heard him and tiptoed out of the bedroom, pleased with myself, but my heart was beating loudly. My stay in Argelia's home didn't last long: the possible legal consequences of my father's ridiculous business venture were almost resolved and my presence in Madrid was no longer indispensable. I held on as best I could for a few weeks to bid my leisurely farewells to Cote, Hernando Valencia, Ernesto Mejía Sánchez, and the group of Lucho's friends. The thought of returning to Barcelona, to the decline and distress of the world of Pablo Alcover, depressed me. But I wanted to rewrite the novel in the light of my new experiences and knew that for that reason I should leave Madrid.

AWARENESS OF THE *dangers and snares of the enterprise: futile attempt to erect a bridge over the discontinuity of your biography, to grant coherence after the event to a mere accumulation of ruins: looking for the underground channel that nourishes the chronological succession of events in some way without being sure whether it is an archaeologist's dig or a dazzling work of engineering: not just the arbitrary omission of memories judged to be unimportant but the embroidering and assembly of the ones chosen: a deceitful precision of detail, unconscious anachronisms, presumptuously clear outlines: looks and appearance of the first woman you went to bed with, means of transport used to go to the capital: images evoked but impossible to verify, lack of trust in your rescue work, worrying absence of proof: the impression you're building with precarious materials, transmuting uncertain reality into the faked structure of a book: clearing out what remains of your past on the treacherous subterfuge that you are saving it from the viscous density of oblivion: the initial impulse to tell all, to accept metaphorically the painful goring of the bull, dissolves and loses shape when submitted to the insidious laws of written and oral narrative: to convert life into style would be to have the ingenuity or pretensions of an alchemist: your arduous, uninterrupted struggle with writing has yet to endow you with the secret of the philosopher's stone.*

I N MY ABSENCE, things had subtly changed: Luis had finished his secondary schooling and had started on his law degree with no more conviction than I had and had begun to mix with a group of students who were intellectually aware and interested in politics; José Agustín, after completing his military service in Mahón, was working and writing a book of poetry, *The Return*, his hopes set on the Adonais prize; Marta had a rather evasive, mysterious boyfriend: his surname, of unclear origins, displeased my father, obsessed as ever by genealogies; he referred to him as "a nameless being" and didn't hide his fears about possible Jewish forebears.

But changes were not restricted to my family: they extended similarly to the cultural, university circles in which I moved. My elder brother, after getting a job as an adviser to a private water company, had reestablished contact with the writers and intellectuals gathered around the *Laye* magazine: Sacristán, Castellet, Barral, Gabriel, and Juan Ferrater. This publication theoretically depended on the Falange Propaganda Office: consequently it was not subject to censorship. Thanks to this and taking advantage of the personal friendship that linked some of its members with the man nominally responsible for the publication, our friends had infiltrated the editorial board until they had changed it into something entirely different: a space for discussion where, with the necessary precautions, one could criticize more and more clearly the stagnation, poverty, and oppression of contemporary Spanish cultural life. Studies or essays on poetic language and the narrative techniques of the North American novel rubbed shoulders with brief, incisive, shattering notes on the protégés and clowns canonized by the official press. The ferocity of some reviews added to the obvious nonconformism promoted by the editors soon aroused suspicions and created obstacles. When José Agustín and I approached the nucleus that animated *Laye*, the magazine was going through a period of conflict. Pressure from the media and people criticized in its pages to get it suspended was intensifying daily. Months later a journalist sadly famous for his attacks on writers in exile and morbid detection of "reds" would write in a Falange daily a note entitled "The crows won't peck our eyes out," which, as an official denunciation of the small flock of black sheep, achieved final closure, after a violent tussle between the editorial board and the man responsible for the Propaganda Secretariat who was indirectly implicated in his accusations. My only article in the magazine—a criticism of Guido Piovene's novels—appeared in 1954 in the very last issue. As it was impossible to explain the reasons for the closure or even mention the fact, the editors used their wiles to put on the front cover a strip of mourning black with the piquant quotation from Garcilaso, "Suffering that I cannot name."

But I am anticipating events. In the summer of fifty-three, the major intellectual novelty for me was the double discovery of politics and narrative objectivism as defended by Castellet. The impact of the works of Sartre and Claude Edmonde Magny in relation to the novelistic technique of Dos Passos, Hemingway, and Dashiell Hammett—evident in Castellet's essays as collected in *La hora del lector* and their direct offspring, my short articles in *Problemas de la novela*—confronted us simultaneously with the concept, or rather dilemma, of "commitment," which was apparently insurmountable. I was writing, with the incorrigible haste of my youth, the definitive version of *Juegos de manos*: although I had included in it the milieus and experiences of my stay in Madrid, the novel still revealed the influence of Gide and other French writers. The unpleasant aftertaste of intellectualism and unsuccessful attempts at poetic writing for which I would reproach myself over a period of time nevertheless prevented me from falling into the morass of some works that I then took as models. On the other hand my first theoretical steps under the umbrella of Lukács and Sartre would lead to thoughts that, rather than reflecting the fruit of my experience as a reader and writer, would reveal the same painfully undigested reading as the majority of my innovative colleagues of that era. Like all-consuming energetic boa-constrictors we gulped down the ceremonial oxen of recently discovered Marxist aesthetics and remained quiet, passive, bloated, belching over the enormous, stolid prey until they were finally swallowed. Although the results of such gymnastics were of little relevance for a foreign reader with direct access to the sources where we anxiously drank in our ideas and doctrines, the latter fulfilled the function in our closed, provincial society of spreading the good news about what was happening on the other side of Franco's protective wall. From today's point of view, what then happened to my friends and me seems inevitable. Our intellectual orphanhood and the cultural desert we inhabited encouraged us to make the mistakes of those who have nothing to cling to and yet strive to take their first steps. Terrified by the void we suddenly discovered around us we embraced a body of clear, coherent doctrine that allowed us to rapidly forge a theory explaining our backwardness: imported bit by bit from France or Germany, the defense first of "behaviorism" and then of "critical realism" would be the tribute we paid to the intellectual wastes of the postwar years in our well-meaning desire to eliminate them. As T.S. Eliot says in a quotation picked out from José Angel Valente's recent illuminating book, "to theorise you need tremendous ingenuity; not to theorise requires tremendous honesty." Cast fatally into the ranks of the ingenuous, our task of knocking down the opened doors required in Spain the application of elementary, commonsense criteria. The need for an honesty beyond simplistic dogmatism and opportunistic, Manichaean attitudes would only be clear to us many years later when the practice of politics and the mocking persistence of concrete reality would force some of us to open our eyes.

The old idea of going to Paris took firmer root as I got on with the novel: to prepare for my first timid attempt to escape, I threw myself into studying and speaking French. In the Turia discussions I had met a youth my age with a British name and French origins: in his house on nearby calle Ganduxer he used to welcome his compatriots or Frenchified Catalans with whom it was possible to talk and improve my accent and vocabulary. There I heard for the first time Brassens's repertory and numerous of Piaf's creations with that excitement that "the unexpected imposes on the imagination."* In my usual hurry to achieve what I thought to be desirable at a particular moment, I wasn't satisfied till I understood the words of the songs. After assimilating the slang in Sartre's novels and stories I felt ready to tackle the plan I had nurtured from adolescence. Such a state of mind and mental disposition may explain the fact that my first novel, magnificently translated afterwards into French by Maurice Edgar Coindreau, read much better in this language than in the original defective Spanish: when I had to revise it some years ago to be included in some pompous Complete Works the continuous difficulties I met in revising the text convinced me that the only satisfactory way to erase them would be to retranslate the novel scrupulously from the language in which it was unconsciously conceived. My physical stay in Spain, apart from two excursions to Paris, would last until fifty-six. However, my intellectual life, and not only my fantasies, began to develop outside the country. I abandoned the translations imported from Buenos Aires and read the work of Proust, Stendhal, and Laclos, as well as authors from other quarters, only in French. This filter would distance me for some years from poetry and novels written in my own language, with consequences not difficult to calculate. But literature is and will be the kingdom of the unexpected: my passion for that world, lived like a real leap into the void, would cast me one day into a mysterious enjoyment of Spanish by virtue of the same strange logic through which I would find that my identity was aggressively affirmed in sex.

---

* Jaime Gil de Biedma, "Elegy and Memory of the French *Chanson*."

I T WAS NOT only intellectual factors that intervened in my nascent interest in politics—understood already as a critique of the conservative, clerical, authoritarian system imposed on Spain by the victory of the military insurgents of 1936. Scorn for my social class, the decadence and precarious state of which I saw reflected in the decline of my own family, had grown as I bitterly witnessed the robbery and lack of scruples in that collection of virtuous bourgeois Catholics behind the swindling of my father. It immediately became a moral imperative for me to put an end to that hypocritical society, a real cradle for the worst instincts of theft and plunder. When someone placed in my hands a Marxist primer bound in hardback with the title of Ignacio Agustí's novel, *Mariona Rebull*, in order to confuse any possible inquisitive eyes, to my excitement I discovered that the implacable portrait it sketched of merciless competition and barbaric exploitation by the captains of industry of the time coincided exactly with my own personal observations. Thus my precocious, burgeoning anticlericalism was joined by hatred for the bourgeoisie that supported the Church: a bourgeoisie that I then thought was condemned to die shortly, a victim of its own crimes, contradictions, and abuses.

On the other hand my short but fruitful stay in Madrid had corrected and broadened my narrow, limited perspectives. The territory where I usually lived, centered on home and university, was a miniature reproduction of a compact, well-structured world to which aliens and the marginal had no access. The poverty and helplessness that dominated the areas on the outskirts of Barcelona were totally unreal to me: fleeting, almost dreamlike images of wooden and tin shacks, snotty-nosed, barefoot children, pregnant women, overcrowding, squalor, heaps of excrement, glimpsed from the window of the train that took us to Torrentbó. Strict sanitary control kept these inhabitants far from the places I frequented: their intrusive, vaguely threatening presence was upsetting and, conscious of this, they humbly sought to be invisible. On my return I could see these things in a different light: less restrained by shyness, I wanted to repeat the experience of my explorations in new places and contexts. If the slum areas in the suburbs seemed difficult to reach, the mixed, colorful, bubbling districts to be seen in the lower reaches of the Ramblas or from the sixty-four tram on the final stretch to the beaches and the old skylift in the port filled me with less panic. My plans to poke my nose into the dense, effervescent reality of the Barceloneta and the Barrio Chino and to discover there an intellectual vital energy not offered by the insipid areas where imagination and sexuality did not thrive were first tentatively realized on my own, but were then helped after my return from Paris by the release of my friend Carlos Cortés from the Montjuich fortress. He was the best person to show me into a milieu that none of my previous friends even wished to penetrate. While in jail with common criminals, he had deepened his knowledge of that world by getting to know its customs and slang. I was very excited by his first-hand accounts of a hermetic universe very close to the one I would later find in Genet: his description of the queers going to Mass all made up with their combs and mantillas, of the blind girl led there by her mother on visiting day to suck the prisoners' pricks for a handful of coins, have not faded from my memory. Ignorant of all that extended beyond the sterilizing walls of my education, I didn't even know the terms he used: pimp, grass, fix, bugger, fence. My friend had put together a glossary of underworld phrases, which he generously lent me years afterwards and which I used openly while writing *La resaca*. Alone or with Carlos, I carefully explored the bars and dives on the back streets between Conde de Asalto and Atarazanas: the Criolla had disappeared after being frequented by the author of *Journal du voleur*, but other haunts exuding filth and dirt still justified the reputation of that Barcelona opposed forever to the homogeneous, paternalist, limp ideal of its petty bourgeoisie and the magnetic attraction the city held for writers like Genet or Bataille. Cigarette girls, blackmarketeers, cripples, dope peddlers, vile, ill-lit bars, adverts for permanganate baths, contraceptive shops, grotesque sights from the Bodega Bohemia, rooms let by the hour, six-peseta brothels, the entire Hispanic court of miracles imposed a brutal reality that burst the bubble around me with one blast. The public whorehouses of Robadors and Tapias, the opulent, sometimes obese shapes of the women queuing on the benches, their legs wide apart, half-naked, preoccupied, in a posture of innocent bestiality, attracted me not only because of a consciously perverse Baudelairean aesthetic but because of their tangible, disturbing promiscuity. As I said, after my time in Madrid, I had lost all reserve or fear with prostitutes: entrusting the hidden part of my body to lips, mouths, hands capable of providing me with more enjoyment than my solitary manipulations also in reality justified my repeated visits. To complete the picture of my adventures I must add that at this time the need to clarify my position after the wretched episode with Lucho encouraged me to overcome my anxiety and worries and accept the offer of going to bed with known homosexuals from some bar in the area. But my clumsiness and frigidity with them, just the same as I would have experienced, I imagine, with a fussy, well-off girl, convinced me it was useless to persist in that direction; with a

mixture of disappointment and relief—a relief slightly tinged with sadness—I strengthened myself for a time in the soothing, analgesic idea of
an evident if errant "normality."

My fervor for slum areas, which urged me on for years, was incomprehensible and even shocking to most of my friends. Monique has always
been right to reproach me for my immediate acceptance of impoverished
places and situations that would be unbearable for her without an explicit
Christian or Marxist will to change them. The charge is true to a certain
extent and I will return to it at another time. But this provisional, selfish
adaptation to a reality experienced by others as unjust and oppressive,
partly originating in my unquenchable curiosity for what is different,
alien, and beyond assimilation—curiosity with both political and literary
meaning—nevertheless had other elements of personal authenticity
beyond any would-be love of the picturesque or the "low life." In 1955
when Jaime Gil de Biedma recorded in the pages of his *Diario* one of our
sprees in the company of a drunken, gypsylike, sinister bootblack or ex-
legionnaire, emphasizing my "excessive *mauditisme,*" he leaves out an
essential fact: my sexuality—except on very few occasions on the female
side—was never bourgeois or polite. As I told him on one occasion when
we sat chatting in the early hours in a car opposite our front door, I was
never attracted by writers, intellectuals, or, simply, well-brought-up
people wearing ties. My halogenous fantasies were then developing along
lines that did not exist in Spain: lacking the physical, cultural model of
bodily form that would come naturally to me years later, I sometimes
chased, under the influence of alcohol, after a sad, degraded shadow, with
predictable frustration, bitterness, and failure. This half-baked relationship through hash and the bottle never got beyond posturing. But even at
these times, which were depressing and humiliating for me, I didn't try to
deceive myself by hypocritically confusing the levels. The motive for my
streetwalking was not just to satisfy in some way or another my desire for
sex. The urban milieu into which I sank and its creative phantasmagoria
sharpened my perception of things, opened up new, juicy bits of reality.

That summer I spent the time left by the hasty writing of my novel in
fruitful wanderings through the Distrito Quinto and the bars in the port.
My manuscript was almost ready and in September I typed it out. The
granting of a passport—previously rejected brutally just as with the
heroine in Menotti's *The Consul*—had been just a matter of patience for
some time: while I corrected the typed copies of *Juegos de manos* I completed the forms and complied with all the necessary formalities. When I
finally received it, I deposited the novel at the offices of the Destino
publishing house before the time limit expired for the Nadal prize. My
father was resigned to the idea of my trip to Paris: he prepared a letter of
introduction for distant relatives, put me on guard against the dangers

and temptations of the city. The French are very immoral, my son; you must have a temper of steel to resist them. With a tiny offering from Grandfather—his only source of income, after the financial disaster, was now his pension from local government—and the profit from the resale of my books—the forbidden novels printed in Argentina—I went to Paris in October, to await there, at a distance, the favorable or unfavorable result of my first incursion into literature.

F
OR YEARS CROSSING *the frontier by train would be an*
oppressive rather than an exciting experience for you: the
dull yet persistent impression of going through no-man's-land, and of being under
close watch, strengthened as most passengers abandoned the train, you left Fig-
ueras, plainclothes inspectors severely studied passports, the landscape became sad
and empty, walls were in ruins, buildings near to Port Bou assumed a gaunt,
threatening air, the station itself became a broken-down, inhospitable place, with a
strictly barracklike atmosphere: traces of a recent past were still to be seen: barbed-
wire fences, sentry boxes, watchtowers, protective cordon sanitaire, *fear of infil-*
trations by the maquis, omnipresent police: grey caps, braid, three-cornered hats,
sinister offices, corridors with benches where you must wait: perhaps the room where
on the 26 September 1940 a group of fugitives, countryless men and women, stayed
for hours and hours begging and crying before the impassive officer who, seated at
his desk, made routine invocations of the text of the decree that prevented their
admission into the country, of his duty to take them under escort to the frontier
where administrative internment in a camp awaited them, to hand them over to
those they were escaping from: all that he, the man with the traits of a Jewish
intellectual, vaguely Trotskyist because of his glasses, a member of the group, had
foreseen for years: better to halt the game there, take advantage of the truce at
night, absorb the dose of morphine carefully kept for the eventuality: although you
knew nothing of him and nobody then cared for the exile's tomb, a trace of the old
horror—like that insidious whiff in the well-aired room of the dead man after
they have taken out shoes, ties, hats, that miraculous syrup against coughing with
which he tried to cure himself, all the pathetic faded details that identified him—
still lingered, you now think, on the dark station in that apparently deserted,
barren town where you impatiently awaited, suitcase in hand, your departure from
Spain.

WITH MY FATHER's card in my pocket I came out of the underground station in search of that Beauséjour boulevard where my relations from the Gil Moreno de Mora family had lived since their childhood: a beautiful villa like so many in the district, draped in a mossy haze, horse-chestnut yellows, closed lace curtains, stuffily silent and discreetly senile. The ring of the bell, almost mute as if contaminated by the rampant anemia, caused a brief flurry on the top floor: minutes later, one of my aunts, old, tiny, and dressed in black, came to the door and, after enquiring who it was, escorted me along a carpeted staircase to their rooms with white, ghostly, covered furniture. She had just come from a visit to her sister, a nun in a local convent where she carried out her daily worship, and asked after my father, his delicate health, poor Julia, my plans and studies and the reason for my trip. She had carefully noted down in pencil my name and my brothers' and sister's, at her age she forgot everything if she didn't write it down at once in her little exercise book; perhaps, as I later suspected, she wanted to have us there one by one in her rosaries and prayers so rich in indulgences and other spiritual benefits. This was my one and only visit to their house and the residential district where they lived. Fifteen years later, in their eighties and one of them ill with cancer, my aunts sent one of their nephews to Italy to ask the famous, charismatic Father Pius whether they would be safer in Paris or Spain in the case of a Chinese Communist invasion: the oracle's reply favored the desire of the family to move to the peninsula where they perished, I think, just after their arrival, relieved and happy to have escaped the cruelty and horrors of the Asiatic hordes.

Apart from these anachronistic relatives and two French girls who had studied in Spain, the only person I knew when I arrived was a schoolfriend of José Agustín, who had also been expelled by the Jesuits, and with whose family we had kept in contact after one of his sisters married my uncle Josep Calsamiglia. Alberto Blancafort was learning musical composition, aspired to be the leader of an orchestra, and lived with a Swedish girl in some attic or small hotel in the Latin Quarter. Thanks to him, I assimilated the work of a group of composers whom I have listened to ever since: he played Erik Satie's *Gnosiennes* and *Gymnopédies* on the piano, and eagerly reread the partituras of Milhaud, Poulenc, and Béla Bartók. Alberto mixed with a group of Catalan musicians, artists, and writers who had lived in Paris for years, and I soon got to know some of them.

Guessing that my scarce funds would not allow me to keep on paying for the hotel room where I was staying, he immediately offered to find me somewhere to lodge. He said he knew an old spinster in the septième arrondissement who rented rooms cheaply to students: he himself had lived in one of them before moving in with his girlfriend and he could introduce me.

Mlle De Vitto's flat was on the ground floor of a silent cul-de-sac off the rue de Varenne: the owner or, more correctly, the tenant was a tall, straight, mustachioed woman, untidily dressed, with a strange, rather warlike air, especially with the extravagant hat that made her look like a transvestite *bersagliere* or an officer in the Garibaldi volunteers. In fact, she had been a soloist or singer in a distant era of fame and splendor that she remembered nostalgically in contrast to her present straits. Faded diplomas, old printed invitations to one of her recitals, the blurred photo of a memorable soirée in honor of those wounded at the front, presided over by Clemenceau or Pershing according to her successive, embroidered versions, hung on the dusty wallpaper or rested on the shelves, consoles, mantelpieces crowded with figurines, jugs, and bric-a-brac. Several cats moved around that melancholy scene with svelte indolence, sometimes perched on their mistress's shoulder, sovereignly inured to her slobbering caresses, with bristling, emblematic power radiating outward as if from an ancient magical print or engraving of witchcraft. Mlle De Vitto was not satisfied with her modest role of subletter: the guests she took in had to share her musical tastes, have refined artistic sensibilities, and listen devotedly to her repertory of past triumphs. She tried to disguise her boardinghouse to outside acquaintances by inventing classes in opera singing and tonic sol-fa: she would often clear her throat before softly humming the first bars of an aria or lightly running her fingers across the piano keyboard. Art, the great Art to which men and women used to dedicate their lives, was about to perish. *Regardez autour de vous, mes pauvres amis, il n'y a rien, mais absolument rien.* Alberto and I nodded in agreement while she, enthralled by the evocation of her own magnificence, condescended to talk to us, in suddenly hoarse tones and with a nervous twitch in her cheeks that revealed her impatience and greed, about the price of the room. Settled in her house, accepting the rules of the game of a daily conversation with her either by myself or with another lodger, a delicate, ethereal Uruguayan pianist, I awaited Alberto's visit to go to one of the places in Saint-Germain or the Latin Quarter where he used to meet his friends. Just after my arrival, my friend gave me the address of the now-defunct Foyer Sainte-Geneviève, near the Panthéon, where I could have lunch for the same price as in the university restaurants without having to show the student-card that I didn't possess. When we were queuing up there one day, trays in hand, he introduced me to the Catalan poet Palau Fabre, who had been in exile for years, and his friends, the actor Sacha Pitoëff and his Argentinian wife. Palau Fabre, whose bitter rebellion against the bourgeoisie and nationalist intransigence reminded me of Great-uncle Ramón Vives, had broken ties with his well-off family and preferred an austere but free existence in Paris to tolerating a regime like Franco's that, apart from the many reasons that made it hateful to me, was vigorously oppressing his culture and language. His moral attitude, reflected in the bare simplicity of his daily life, filled me with admiration. The violence of his poetry, marked with the inimitable stamp of Rimbaud, helped me to understand the drama and frustration of that remote, rebellious relative who was ignored and hated by his own family circle. Palau Fabre had met Artaud before he was interned and enthused about his work. I remember he once took me to his tiny attic on the Ile-Saint-Louis and recited some of his texts to me. As I was not yet suffering the sterility of my Marxist phase—Karl Marx, *éternel voleur d'énergies*, Rimbaud would have written a century later—I was moved by his reading. Palau Fabre was an original character, a kind of sniper within a cultural panorama that was fatally being politicized. When I decided in 1956 to make Paris my definitive place of residence, Artaud, Bataille, Breton meant nothing or next to nothing to that young Spaniard imbued with Marxism, the supporter of Sartre's thesis on commitment. My friendship with him could have given me the opportunity to penetrate the work of some authors that I only discovered eight years later, when I was freed from my ideological blinkers; but our short-lived relationship, cut short by my return to Spain, spoiled that unique opportunity to hew out the path that would lead me to achieve a responsible, personal form of writing.

Alberto's other friends used to rendezvous in the Dupont on the boulevard Saint-Michel, or in the Mabillon or Old Navy in Saint-Germain-des-Prés. The latter gave shelter at dusk to a group of rather self-deluding writers and artists whose grandiose work, repeatedly advertised in the café, would never take shape: an Italian poet with the serene beauty of a Botticelli painting; a dramatist, author of a piece to be performed in La Huchette; an operatic Basque, would-be Luis Mariano, self-styled lover of the daughter of an important publisher for whose sake he would on one occasion try to open his veins while sobbing hysterically. The undeniable star in the Mabillon constellation was *el Campesino*: the former Republican general seated on one of the benches at the back, surrounded by a small faithful band, possibly Argentinians or Chileans, relived the heroic moments of the civil war, and reenacted with a fine flurry of waves and gestures the scene of his dramatic break with Stalin. Later, after eating a sandwich or sausage and chips, Alberto Blancafort would sometimes accompany me to a bar on the rue des Canettes where the grotesque survivors of the existentialist fauna had taken refuge: there a solemn, hieratic girl, systematically dressed in black, with her face painted like a mask, declared that she lived in a damp cave with mice and called on the most daring to try her one night in a cemetery. The Pouilly was filled to the brim with *voyeurs*, drug addicts, and drunks. Customers' disputes would often come to blows and the arrival of the *panier à salade* put everybody to flight. The bohemian life of the cafés offered a provincial like me a string of surprises: I met my first flesh-and-blood Communist on the terrace at the Old Navy where he spent the afternoon engrossed in his reading of *L'Humanité*, admiringly translating for his companions and then underlining in pencil the speeches or commentaries of some leading French or Soviet comrade, as if to mark out the main lines of thought and the need to come back to them at a quieter moment. The desire to taste the forbidden fruit led me one night to accompany a Norwegian journalist friend of Albert's to a Communist meeting chaired, I remember, by Auguste Lecoeur, shortly before his expulsion from the Party: the showy display of flags and the broadcasting of hymns—so similar to the patriotic Falangist performances of my childhood—the strident slogans, the disciplined rhythm of the applause at once doused my enthusiasm: I would experience a similar reaction in Cuba during the great revolutionary celebrations—also the fruit of my precocious experience of the art of manipulating the masses under an opposing symbol. My antipathy toward this kind of meeting, strengthened over time and with the loss of my political innocence, thus had an early manifestation independent of the vicissitudes of my ideology or affiliations. If the friends or acquaintances I had during those years when I was a fellow traveler of the Party had forced me to participate in such acts and ritual assemblies, I am sure that my rather reserved collaboration with them would not have lasted long: the victory parades that I observed with my father and brother from the balconies of the ABDECA office would cure me of demagogy for posterity, and inspired me with a healthy distrust of the sincerity of the people's fervent applause.

Inevitably, in my circumstances, I was dazzled by Paris and limited my tourist roving to the areas with historic and artistic sights. My anxiety to be up-to-date, to see, to read, to experience all that was impossible in Spain made me go from the second-hand bookshops in the Latin Quarter and on the quaysides of the Seine to the tiny cinema on the rue de Messine where I gulped down, in cycle after cycle, the films of Pudovkin and Eisenstein, pre-war French films, a choice sample of Italian neorealists. I discovered all at once Beckett and the Impressionists, Genet and Prévert, Schönberg and Ionesco's first works. I had never felt so happy as during those weeks when, with my stomach sometimes empty and my head full of plans, I walked for hours to tame the city. An intense desire to adapt myself to France, to be submerged in its culture and language, impelled me to polish my pronunciation and to erase the stigma of foreign extraction. If I compare my present careless, opaque French—largely the result of the defensive instinct of my Spanish against the prolonged daily assault from other languages—with the French I used to show off then in my conversations with the natives, I can only draw the sad conclusion that that was the shining peak of my life as a French speaker, and that I have gone backward like a crab rather than advancing. The twenty-year-old's zeal to master the vocabulary and accent of others would be repeated again at different intervals and moments in my life. The auditory enjoyment inherent in the first stages, the sudden power of novelty, perhaps explain this strange whim: the fact that the uncodified, changeable dialect of Arabic today stimulates my appetite to dominate it while the languages learned previously wither in the attic of routine familiarity. At distinct stages in my existence I would be impregnated with French and American English, only to dedicate myself later in my forties to a tardy assault on Arabic. Spanish was reduced almost entirely to an instrument of literary toil and inversely would attain a unique status: to be my opponent in intricate unarmed combat, the sensual ferocity of which would give way after *Don Julián* to a happy love affair.

After a few weeks the money I had brought from Spain began to decrease at an alarming pace. In order to extend my stay in Paris until January, I decided to restrict my daily diet to lunch at the Foyer Sainte Geneviève. At night, if I didn't manage an invitation to a roll from some friend or acquaintance, I went to bed fasting or found frugal satisfaction in biscuits. A contemporary photograph shows me as skinny, emaciated, wrapped up in my expensive overcoat on the day two Colombians from the Guadalupe College landed in Paris and invited me to a banquet that I reckoned Rabelaisian. Several of Alberto's friends collected paper, rags, and lost property for a junk merchant on the rue Saint-Jacques: the work wasn't excessive and it paid for a day's food, but a mixture of tenacious snobbery, sloth, and weakness kept me from that exploitation of the student world some considered manna. Forced to choose, I preferred to tighten my belt another notch and go to bed with the cautious, parsimonious forethought of someone who has learned to keep a chunk of bread dipped in mustard from lunchtime in his pocket.

My slow physical decline was worrying Mlle de Vitto: she thought she knew why I was skin and bones and tried to worm my financial situation out of me in order to cushion my eventual disappearance from her list of "pupils." Perhaps I was expecting a check from my family? Did I hope to be awarded some scholarship? When she gave me my post, she stood over me with one of her cats on her shoulder tacitly inviting me to open my correspondence. As I did not give in to her blackmail and locked myself in my room to read it, she waited for me to come out to ask if there was a pleasant surprise or if it was really good news. Dismayed and somewhat annoyed by evasive answers, Mlle De Vitto cleared her throat as she reminded me I must pay the rent before the end of the month if I wanted to carry on my so-called lessons with her.

In early December I had received Castellet's letter: he told me he was to spend a fortnight in Paris and wanted me to help him find a room. I passed on his message to Mlle De Vitto and she was so worried by the dreadful state of my finances and also the dramatic desertion by another of her guests that she received the news like a blessing. She wanted to find out about that *signor* Castelletto: his family background, education, artistic inclinations, whether he had means. My replies seemed to satisfy her and his arrival was anxiously awaited. I can remember how the visit from one of the Old Navy dreamers, would-be leader of the surgery team at the Neuilly American Hospital, had dazzled my hostess, who was convinced for some hours she had met a great authority from the medical world whose wealth and influence gave him the natural role of adviser and patron to me. After the portentous Galen vanished, Castellet would briefly be the man of her dreams. When he finally came, Mlle de Vitto welcomed him with open arms: my friend's serious, distinguished manner surpassed all her expectations. With his help I was able to pay off the rent I owed and wait for the award of the Nadal prize while acting as his guide and critic through the world of books, films, and plays. Castellet knew a Catalan art critic who lent me an old radio set on Twelfth Night. For a while we searched in vain for the wave with the Barcelona station that was broadcasting live the result of the voting: we found it only to learn that my novel, the favorite according to bets laid by people at the dinner, said the commentator, had just been eliminated in the penultimate vote. Minutes later the award would be given to an unknown woman whom no one would hear of again a few months after her book's publication.

DAYS BEFORE MY return, Luis and José Agustín wrote to me about what had happened: as soon as the voting started, the rumor spread among those present that my work was "leftist" and had "prerevolutionary overtones," a fact that was enough to explain its disqualification. At home they all followed the drama of the prize on the radio: Eulalia "was beside herself and in tears" and lost her temper with the winner; Father and Grandfather were reconciled for a moment and greeted the news with despair and despondency.

Back in Barcelona, hopeful and impatient, I rushed to see the publishers at Destino who were quick to remind me of the limits and restrictions of reality: they said they were interested in the work, but in present circumstances it was difficult to publish. As their relationships with the then all-powerful general director of the press were going through a delicate phase, the mere act of presenting it to the censors would, they added, not only be useless but counterproductive. If I could rely on some serious patron, it would be better to have recourse to his services: once it was approved by Juan Aparicio or the minister himself, they would include it in their collection.

As I had no friend or supporter with influence in the ministry, I went and saw Dionisio Ridruejo, whom I did not know personally but whose reputation for honesty and independence of judgment converted him *a priori* into an ideal intermediary. Although he had been on the margins of the system for some years, Ridruejo had not yet made a definitive break and maintained a series of connections with his former comrades in arms. At the time he was directing a private radio station in Madrid, where he gave me a friendly welcome when I arrived in his office with the manuscript of the novel. He promised to read it in order to have an informed opinion and to be able to defend it before a minister as soon as he had the opportunity. A few weeks later, after telling me some of his strictly literary criticisms of the novel, Ridruejo informed me with a smile of his conversation with Arias Salgado. The Minister for Information and Tourism—famous for his theory that, because of his provident leadership, Spain was the country in the world with the fewest souls condemned to the eternal tortures of hell—had explained to my go-between his most noteworthy criteria on the matter: namely, that a novel was only worthy of publication "if husband and wife, joined in legitimate matrimony, could read it to each other without mutually blushing and especially, he had emphasized, *without being aroused.*" I don't know if the joint reading of *Juegos de manos* made the ministerial couple blush or filled them with desire or whether, absorbed in his numerous good works, Arias Salgado had the leisure or curiosity to read it; the truth is that, despite Ridruejo's good offices, the novel remained stagnating at the ministry for several months and it would probably have slumbered there until the final destruction of the regime if there hadn't been a new, more direct intervention in the meanwhile.

On the advice of Fernando Gutiérrez, I had explained the problem to José Manuel Lara. Thanks to his well-known sympathies for the person and work of Franco, the Planeta publisher was in a better position than Ridruejo to defend my book successfully: he had been told by Gutiérrez that I was preparing another book and he felt obliged to intervene and get me out of the jam in return for my promise to let him see the manuscript of *Duelo en el paraíso* first. I promised, and to my great relief my novel was soon authorized with a few cuts that were fortunately unimportant. I returned to Destino with the *nihil obstat* of the censor and signed the contract for publication during the summer of fifty-four, although for planning reasons, it only appeared at the beginning of the following year.

Apart from writing the novel pledged to Planeta, my reentry into Barcelona life was achieved between my discovery of the floating dive on the Varader and my presence at Castellet's literary seminars. After the closure of *Laye* and the failure of our attempts to create a new magazine, the original nucleus of founders broke up: Sacristán went to finish his studies in Germany; Gabriel Ferrater was traveling through Europe; Barral, about to get married, was meeting to a large extent the requirements of his industrial surname. Benefiting from his friendship with the director of the Institute for Hispanic Studies in Barcelona, Castellet organized a course on criticism and the novel that brought together a group of young students who had entered university after my premature departure: my brother Luis, Joaquín Jordá, Salvador Giner, Jordi Malaquer, Nissa Torrents, Octavio Pellissa, Sergio Beser, and others whose names I don't recall gathered in one of the rooms in the old flat on Calle Valencia to discuss critical realism, commitment, and Marxism. While I was away in Paris, the circles in which I had moved had suddenly been politicized. Octavio Pellissa, from a family that belonged or had belonged to the Party in Republican times, did not restrain her Communist ideas even in public. Through Castellet or one of his friends, magazines like *Europe* and *La nouvelle critique* began to circulate secretly. Terms such as surplus value, objective conditions, correct line, formal freedoms, democratic centralism thus gradually entered our vocabulary. Equipped with a solid array of arguments, we submitted daily reality to the restructuring process of the brand-new doctrine. The songs of Yves Montand, Léo Ferré,

Atahualpa Yupanqui were often listened to communally with liturgical solemnity and all aroused our enthusiasm. With the zeal of the converted, I took advantage of some short holidays to spread my newly acquired ideas among the farmers and peasants in Torrentbó: I was horrified by my playboy privileges and informed them that the revolutionary struggle had begun that would soon put an end to their serfdom and exploitation. Alfredo and his friends must, I imagine, have listened with condescending skepticism to my halting speeches and my naive voluntarism that had little in common with the other elements of their daily experience. From the start my sentimental adherence to Marxism, although largely dictated by my desire to atone for the original sin of my class and my family's odious past, met with difficulties and insoluble obstacles. I remember very clearly the day someone slipped me a packet of back issues of the clandestine Spanish CP's cultural magazine: with the nervous delight of someone about to taste the forbidden fruit, I eagerly began to read but was straightaway flung into profound consternation by the contents. It was the time of the cold war and the thaw after Stalin's death had not yet begun. Violent language, bristling with invective and insults, stigmatized not only the behavior and ideas of authors known for their Francoist sympathies but also some of the foreign writers and intellectuals that I most admired: Gide, Camus, Malraux, Sartre himself were pinpointed as hyenas and jackals, agents of the Pentagon, faithful lackeys of the bourgeoisie. This stream of unfounded accusations, tied together like a bunch of cherries, evoked the dogmatism and poverty of the salvocs against freethinkers, Masons, and Jews in Father Ripaldo's catechism and other such manuals. A sensation of déjà vu made me break off my reading with a feeling of bitter disappointment. But, convinced that it was an error capable of treatment and determined not to allow the trees to prevent me from seeing the forest, I just made a comment to Castellet and my friends—as surprised and upset as I was—on my total disagreement with the magazine's editorials and the absurd accumulation of insults. Consciousness of the need for a radical change in Spanish society both politically and socially, and of our moral duty to participate in the process, kept our illusions intact.

Parallel to the literary seminar in the institute, we got together periodically in a place called the Bar Club a few blocks away. The discussions and conversations there were predominantly political. Commentaries on the international situation—the last lashes of McCarthyism, Guatemala, the defeat of the French in Indochina—took up most of the sessions. Octavio Pellissa seized the opportunity to underline the manifest moral and material superiority of the socialist regimes: racked by its internal contradictions and struggles, faced by the unbreakable strength and solidarity of China and the Soviet Union, the capitalist world would finally collapse by itself. One day, very excited, we were visited by a mysterious person who had come from Peking: the guest in question, whose name was not revealed to us for obvious security reasons, described a few events and anecdotes from his journey without recourse to flights of propaganda. Although we were disappointed by his coldness, we listened devotedly, unaware that this anonymous man, Julio Cerón, was the diplomat and future founder of the *felipes*, the Popular Liberation Front. I saw him again ten years later, after he left prison, when he was confined to a town in Murcia where I went to meet him, I remember, in the company of Ricardo Bofill.

Through common friends, our group had entered into contact with two young writers based in Madrid: Rafael Sánchez Ferlosio and Carmen Martín Gaite. The former had published a remarkable novel, *Industrias y andanzas de Alfanhuí*, which overwhelmed me: at twenty or so he had a style rich in shades of meaning and suggestion and without any apparent difficulty had reached a density of expression that I would only forge as a goal after painful struggles and conflicts at the time of writing *Don Julián*. Ferlosio and his wife had just come back from a trip to Italy and willingly accepted my invitation to rest in Torrentbó. That was the first of a series of reciprocal visits over the space of two years. While I dedicated my energies to the novel pledged to Lara—on whose advance I was relying to return to Paris—Ferlosio entrusted me with the manuscript of a rather Kafkaesque work of his that he too wanted to submit to Planeta. *El fontanero*—this was the novel's title—was probably just a stage on the path that was to lead from *Alfanhuí* to the marvellous adventure of *El Jarama*; but even taking into account the fact that it was a minor work, its irony, rigor, and sharpness stood out against the barren Spanish landscape of the time. Months afterwards, when Ferlosio had shelved his idea of publishing it, we both exchanged confidences on our respective interviews with the publisher. In the case of *Duelo en el paraíso*, he warned me in his very Sevillian accent that children weren't a commercial subject but advised me to present it for a prize and generously undertook to publish it. The conversation with Ferlosio, as related by the latter, was more colorful and spicy: Lara greeted him with "You write well, extremely well; almost too well!" and, after giving good advice on the theme of novelistic ingenuity, assured him that one day he might become a worthy rival of Pombo Angulo—if he followed it.

My contact with Ferlosio, which was then broken off by my self-exile in Paris, was of great significance and value to me at the time: in pleasant contrast to the self-sufficiency, vanity, and exhibitionism of the majority of his colleagues, he was proof that a serious writer need not take himself seriously. An eccentric loner, full of ironic humor, he professed absolute contempt for the theatrical emphasis and lofty solemnity of the fashionable clowns. Always sincere and unconditional in his literary opinions, he did not hesitate to attack currently accepted ideas: I can remember very clearly the day he heard me and Castellet cite *La colmena* as a paradigm of an objective novel and he suddenly exploded to say that Cela was a tyrannical author who didn't even allow his characters the right to breathe. His analysis was not hypothetical and inappropriate like ours: *El Jarama* was already underway and he knew very well what he was saying. For me, above all, Ferlosio incarnated the creator who is resolved to live literature like a prison sentence or a benefaction, not as a way to make a fortune. His later silence—so like that which would in turn affect Genet—would confirm his conception of writing as an extremely volatile, serious act—beautiful and unexpected like falling in love—the experience of which forces whoever lives it to be quiet if the gift suddenly abandons him and he does not wish to fall into the unpardonable, common crime of wordmania. In opposition to the verbal pollution of ordinary publishing, the moral courage to shut one's trap and swallow one's own words is and will be moving evidence of personal faithfulness to an existence that is enjoyed and suffered by the writer like slow, gentle self-consumption: a new, torn Prometheus who can no longer offer the harrying, persistent eagle the bait of his miraculously recreated liver.

THE PLACE WAS one of those privileged scenarios, like the central square in Marrakesh or the Small Market in Tangier, that immediately appeal to the imagination and are mysteriously transmuted into the written word: a rectangular pontoon about fifty meters wide, with a hut with a sloping roof, reached by a small bridge. To walk there from the tram terminal in Barceloneta the visitor had to cover more than a kilometer past the quays and port paraphernalia by the breakwater: a journey undertaken mostly by fishermen, mussel gatherers, or owners of the boats being careened or repaired. When the weather allowed, the Varadero's customers would sit in the open at the tables the owner had set out near the coils of ropes, fishing lines, and bilge-heads. From there, while they drank a coffee and brandy or a beer, they observed the general movement of the boats, lighters, tugboats, swallows, and fishing vessels; the jetties and docks of the maritime station; the rusty towers of the cable car; the seagulls' swooping flight, at times still as if suspended in the air, about to dive down upon their victim. The pontoon swayed gently when the police launch or the Americans with their outboard motors sailed by and the thick mooring ropes would creak painfully in an almost animal-like whimper. Present in the mind's eye, like actors in a live show, the regulars will always be the same: Alonso the boss, tubby, small, with blue, melancholy eyes, usually half-opened, an angelic air, and a eunuch's tone of voice; Amadeus, with his cheerful smile and beret to one side, a great drinker, fond of humming habaneras; Miss Rosi, well into her forties, fat, a furious smoker of Bisontes, with her bag on the table, "just like a whore" she would say mischievously to herself. Mussel gatherers and sailors play a game of cards, joke and swear at each other, watching the shipwrights at their daily tasks out of the corner of one eye. Moving in between them, weighed down with buckets of water or ready to patch up the cracks in a boat's hull with pitch and oakum, one man walking unshod, wearing just torn shorts, commands your attention.

From your first visit to the Varadero, he has attracted you. Raimundo is of average height, athletic build, with muscular legs and arms, unkempt dark brown hair standing on end, hairy-chested, a wild mustache. His face is tough but energetic: his sparkling dark eyes, the whole of his character and physique, radiate powerful animal magnetism. Along with these physical features—which for the first and only time you will appreciate in one of your fellow countrymen—the laborer in Alonso's service enjoys others that you will eventually learn to discern in the natives of that Sotadic Zone described by Sir Richard Burton, the frontiers of which extend from Tangier to Pakistan: a degree of coarseness in appearance not without charm; instinctive warmth and availability; a proud rejection of the ways and means that open the doors to social climbing in the industrialized countries. Although apparently not belonging to a foreign or alien community like Parisian immigrants from the Sotadic Zone, Raimundo nevertheless represents absolute marginality: he cannot read or write, has no normal family or fixed abode, his past seems cast in a shadow that you will not penetrate despite your efforts: he married or moved in with a woman who had his daughter; he lived for a time in Fernando Poo; he was a sailor and stoker on a merchant ship; for an obscure reason, he spent some time in prison. His explanations change according to the circumstances, as if obeying the artistic imperatives and requirements of the narrative; now he is a widower, now he isn't; the mother-in-law who falsely accused him of incest with his own young daughter will later be transformed into his own mother; the deed that sent him to jail changes color, texture, skin with a chameleonlike versatility. Although he was born on the Costa Brava, his surname isn't Catalan and sounds gypsyish. His ancestral distrust of *el payo* would in this case explain his defensive attitude to life, his tenacious, deep-rooted individualism. Whatever its origins, the fact is he lives alone, sleeps on some sacks in a cubbyhole on his floating palace, never has visitors or leaves the port area; he has lost or has been robbed of his identity papers. When you spot his coercive, magnetic violence you do not even think of resisting and, for the first time in your life, you take on your uncertain addiction with an unblemished feeling of happiness. The social, cultural abyss existing between you fulfills, will fulfill in the future, that differentiating role, fascinating closeness to what is alien and unknown usually corresponding to the complementary dissimilarity between the two sexes. Your friend's world, a thousand miles from the one you have inhabited till then, becomes a kind of drug for you: you will be chained to it for months. Raimundo's wild appearance, the broken-down palafitte that is his home and lair, justify your daily visits to the Varadero from the other end of the city: the gleaming smile on the sunburnt face when he spies you in the distance and the rough, embarrassed gestures with which he greets your modest presents will be your reward. Although he doesn't suspect the real nature of your feelings, he feels visibly flattered by your interest and, as you are pleased to discover, tries in turn to keep it alive: exoticism has a mutual impact and if he embodies for you the elemental and the forbidden, your upbringing and involuntary snobbishness also captivate him. At nightfall, when he finishes his labors and the bar lights are reflected and sway in the dark, oily glow of the waters, you both drink beer and cognac in one corner beneath the owner's impenetrable, Buddha gaze. The strange couple you make doesn't attract anyone's attention there. The Varadero's regulars have already become used to your presence: Miss Rosi flirts till very late with the mussel catchers and the fishermen and one day when she is offended by a cutting remark and threatens to depart, suddenly standing on a show of dignity, Alonso interrupts, hoarse with emotion, to assure her that there "she is appreciated, loved, respected, admired, and well-regarded"—a phrase divulged by you in the Bar Club that will become the usual farewell formula of the members of the group when months later they write to you in Paris. The night visitors to the floating bar usually come by taxi: owners of boats being careened, couples, the bourgeois in flight from domesticity. In Madrid you learned to take your alcohol or quell it with hash bought in the port. Raimundo's tongue loosens as the number of drinks increases and, somewhat tight, you say good-bye on the gangway when it is closing time. The long walk back along the jetty toward the San Sebastián Baths and the Barceloneta tram-stop helps to clear your head and clean up your appearance in the like-lihood that your father is awake waiting for you to come home, awake in his gloomy bedroom on Pablo Alcover.

One night when you pretended to be more drunk than you really were you walk back along the quay and climb up to the bolt-hole where your friend sleeps: your desires to lie next to him, to feel the heat of his body close to you, were stronger than your shyness and physical inhibitions. But the liberating gesture you expect from him—and he is genuinely surprised by your reappearance—will not materialize: the intimacy you secretly long for was anyway unthinkable for him. The aggressive, showy virility of your friend is not, as you will later discover with the sons of the Sotadic Zone, a sign of complicity aimed primarily at sex: Raimundo doesn't even sense that your attraction to him is mainly physical. He just covers you affectionately with his only blanket and after making sure you are comfortable, he stretches out to sleep about a meter from you on his wretched, inhospitable mat. While he snores loudly, you meditate lucidly on the fact that you are experiencing an impossible, nameless passion; that the lack of correspondence between your impulses and the type of body that invites them condemns and will condemn you, you then think, to cruel, inexorable solitude. A gesture or initiative from you seems sacrilegious. What would your friend's reaction be? Don't you run the risk of a harsh, humiliating rejection? The subtle tissue of the uncertain bond that links you can, you know, be shattered by one rash slip. The repulsion aroused by the vile term "queer," the weighty family stolidity you carry around, suggests resignation and prudence. The happiness you foresee in spite of everything has been decreed out of bounds: it is better to leave things as they are and prolong your emotions with impunity in cowardly, anonymous discretion.

The almost holy terror you felt during puberty at the photo of the two strapping lads locked in embrace, almost union, as they wrestled, overwhelms you again in your sleepless night at the Varadero with that pervasive force that, although haphazard and suppressed, will shoot to the surface one day and sweep away the defenses and barriers by virtue of the inescapable law that, as Ibn Hazm beautifully says, "destroys the toughest, unleashes the most consistent, demolishes the sturdiest, dislocates the stoutest, settles in the recesses of the heart and makes the forbidden legitimate." What most impresses you as you remember the episode in Marrakesh, from a vantage point of those thirty years, is the incredible loyalty of your mental apparatus to a particular spatial framework as well as to qualities, features, and parts of the human body that, beyond parentheses, haziness, and oblivion, independent of your love and its adjacent feelings, will nevertheless be for you, in the words of the Arab-Andalusian poet, "culmination of your desires and peak of your delights." You now view that impotence with Raimundo as the necessary tribute to your birth in an unsuitable cultural and social environment. The deflection that would later mark you out would take place far away and in opposition to the initial boundaries of your life when, settled in Paris and happy in your relationship with Monique, you would again suffer the attacks and pursuit of that ancient, disturbing image: the successive reincarnations of the template spied in other brash, instinctive, hospitable bodies the invasion of whose intimacy you would welcome as you joyfully vindicated the figure of the mythical Don Julián.

The failure of your nocturnal approach does not interrupt your friendship: during 1954 Raimundo will be the brightly burning, radiating center around which your existence gravitates. You visit him daily, by yourself or with your friends: Carlos Cortés, the regulars at Castellet's gatherings, will spend many an afternoon with you at the Varadero, cradled by the creaking of the mooring ropes and the intermittent lapping of the water disturbed by some passing launch. While you drink, you talk about literature or conjecture about the imminent, irreversible fall of the regime, you furtively spy on his movements, the easy rhythms of his daily tasks: the complicity that exists between you is a closely guarded secret and nobody but you will grasp his cryptic allusions and jokes. Sometimes, he goes with you at dusk to the bars and cafés in the Barceloneta: the world later drawn by you in *Fiestas* suddenly assumes, as a result of his presence, a brutal, wounding reality. Your friend's contagious, physical energy draws around him a motley retinue of hags, gypsies, drunks, and beggars. He is the indisputable king of that court of miracles seduced equally by his magnetism and eternal vitality.

Before and after your second visit to Paris, you will visit the brothels and whorehouses of the Barrio Chino with Raimundo, introduce him to one of the prostitutes who go out with you, and you, all three, walk along hand in hand, with the obese, painted woman in between, until it is goodbye time on the sordid steps to some *meublé*. Imperceptibly, as with Lucho, your friend had gradually been changing into a literary character independent of the real model with whom you struggle daily. This change in status implies a tacit distancing from the latter, the end of your previous subordination to his overwhelming, oppressive personality. The day when for some reason he fell out with Alonso, you left the scene of the Varadero with him and followed him to the places where he briefly worked as bath attendant, fisherman, and lifeguard. His rough, marginal existence—unprotected, plain, no property—moves you and is appealing; but the spring of his liminal power over you has broken. After a year Raimundo has become living evidence of the truth written in your novel: someone to show to friends as additional proof of authenticity. When Monique first visits Barcelona you will include on the program for her stay a compulsory visit to the port: Raimundo seems happy to see you with a friend and the three of you are photographed against the backcloth of his former workplace. Later on you carefully examine the photos and notice on his face the signs of sudden ageing and tiredness, the traces of the illness that is destroying him. But you were absorbed in Monique, her immediate warmth, and did not pay the necessary attention, you didn't pick up the ominous signs of his approaching end. With that cruel indifference inherent in the loss or decrease in physical interest in people we once desired, you live the moments of your amorous happiness far from Raimundo and his host of pariahs. Ten days after the event when you find out about his death, his terrible, lonely, drunken agony in the taverns and bars in the port, only then will you shed a few useless, belated tears. Your letter telling Monique what happened, just before you finished military service in 1956, reveals real grief and a crushing sense of guilt and remorse: your retrospective shame at having changed your friend into a fictional hero only to abandon him to his horrible fate; a sharply painful awareness of your selfish, privileged position. The distressed reference to his calloused hands, converted into tools, is not accompanied however by any mention of the past splendor of his body and the way it intoxicated you: splendor and intoxication that, now relived in memory, redeem the harsh wretchedness of his fate, eliminate your versatility and, just as in the times when you went to the Varadero to catch a glimpse of him, confer on his welcoming smile, darkened by his fierce mustache, a warm, consoling impression of everlasting life.

S LOW COGNITION AND *apprenticeship of your body undertaken
with that delay so essential for you in everything profound:
vertigo, immersion, whirlpool, the secret vortex of which is within you: silent
descent to the abyss, animal pull: desire for annihilation, mysteries of joy and
pain, harsh, exciting Stations of the Cross: gradual, step-by-step appropriation of
the mental scatology you had foreseen: martial images of force and subjection, limbs
cruelly tied, bright sheet lightning, refined happiness: suffering, beatitude, rapture
close to the poet's mystical experience that confer on the search for the germinal
nucleus of power a discreet halo of sanctity.*

*Sudden discovery: you are only shell, not knowing the fiery reality at the center:
cautiously sounding out the core from which bubbles the magma of filth, incinerated
matter: orgiastic crater of slippery, seminal lava: plethora, unquenched thirst,
essential density: mere indication of what is hidden, of the burning pressure
sheltered in the chasm: deepening your knowledge of it, polishing, purifying,
establishing the hidden laws of an intimate, personal vulcanology: enigmatic
relating of the causal, inductive image, the persistent probing of glorious suffering
and sudden, syncopated bliss: cliff, precipice of jaws opened up within you, yet
hardened and resistant to awareness of its illuminating clarity. In an after-dinner
conversation, at the time when Monique and you frequented the rue Saint-Benoît,
the discussion had turned to the sexual peculiarities analyzed in a book by Stekel
or another similar author specializing in such matters: the story of a devotee of a
brothel who always went there with a case filled with twenty-three kilos of chains:
some of your guests smiled or made facile jokes about the individual when
Marguerite Duras interrupted you with that intense, serious voice that seduced and
seduces those around her.*

I find it admirable, *she said*, to have such a perfect awareness of oneself to
determine the exact weight of the chains, to arrive precisely at this figure of
twenty-three and not twenty-two or twenty-four, for knowledge to the mil-
ligram requires a long, painful novitiate that only the purest people have the
courage to confront.

Iᴺ ᴛʜᴇ ᴍᴏɴᴛʜs before my next trip to Paris, my friendship with Luis became closer: the secretive, reserved adolescent I used to come across at home had been transformed since he had entered the university into a serious, questioning, intelligent youth as passionate as I was about literature and politics. Our daily exchange of ideas and opinions, respective discoveries in the field of literature, laid the basis for a relationship that, with time, would be fruitful and indispensable to us both. Luis also wrote with a surprising maturity that he acquired suddenly: from the publication of his first story in a Barcelona magazine, any sensitive reader would realize that here was a real author. Our narrative routes, with two or three years' difference in the decade of the fifties, display in their contrasts and similarities the artist's broad margin of freedom in relation to his conditioning and origins: the existence of an active, corrective will opposed to the inertia and fatalism of necessity.

In a well-known passage Freud,* the author of *Moses and Monotheism*, formulates a hypothesis according to which, when a child discovers that his parents are normal human beings, he creates a "family novel" in order to compensate in some way in his imagination for his cruel disappointment as he enters life: he invents at will a family that is out of the ordinary in its virtues and its defects, where he can shelter from the unhappy discovery and thus deaden the shock produced by the depressing intrusion of reality. This "family novel" constructed in unpleasant, inhospitable circumstances would be the germ of all fictions later developed by the writer: the acorn bearing the tree of his future work. If literature, as Pavese said, is "a defence against the offenses of life," the neurotic child's first defensive act would shape the whole of his novelistic constellation: a kind of secret code to his affliction and his temptation to struggle with the pain until it is eventually cured.

Although not all neurotic children become writers and not all writers' fiction is the fruit of precocious, compensatory fantasy, there is not the slightest doubt, as Marthe Robert has pointed out in writing about Flaubert, that the initial impulse that generates, fertilizes, and structures the work of some creators comes from a *Familienroman* conceived in an

---

* This and the two following paragraphs come from my essay, "A Family Reading of *Antagonía*," published in *Quimera*, 32.

effort to overcome a disappointment or protect oneself from an attack. The literary vocation, both mine and my brothers', brought out of a social and educational milieu that was *a priori* not very favorable to the cultivation of literature perhaps cannot be explained without the existence of an anguished need to recover from early traumas and disappointment. The primitive "family novel" we forged could merely have remained latent at the obligatory stage of self-delusion: that was my first, irresistible temptation in childhood and adolescence, which I could only get through by writing dozens and dozens of trashy novels with a kind of obsessive persistence. My decision at the age of twenty to be a writer and make a tardy offering to literature was to a certain degree the result of arduous, complex negotiation: the carefully delineated deal between my distressing awareness of reality and the balancing counterweight of my mythomania. A slow, difficult process that, from *Juegos de manos* to *Señas de identidad*, was gradually to purge me of the latter as I moved toward a style stripped of all "novelistic" trappings: the painful conquest of my own voice, the destruction of the *Familienroman* on the altar of personal honesty and subjective authenticity.

That a similar stimulus and initial situation—the gradual decline of our family's social status, rejection of the father figure, the sudden, brutal disappearance of our mother—have had such a different influence on myself and my younger brother should give some hasty and often dogmatic adepts of psychoanalysis a cause for reflection. Starting from identical roots and parameters—hatred for our class's traditional values, distance from the Catalan language on our mother's side, patriotic and religious indifference, search for a lay substitute for Catholicism in the ideology that stiffened the clandestine struggle against Franco, a precocious conception of literature as the only sure value—the path we have subsequently followed has marked dissimilarities: if it would be easy to prove the existence of numerous common keys to works like *Duelo en el paraíso, Fin de fiesta*, and *Las afueras* or even draw parallels between the odd chapter of *Señas de identidad* and sections of *Recuento*, still the direction taken by both of us in the last fifteen years will be radically opposed: while the world of my childhood slowly abandoned my writing and was replaced by other mental scenes, myths, and ghosts, Luis's creative work has remained anchored there. In my case the break was not only internal but physical, with the family milieu of my early years, with my birthplace, with Catalonia where I had always lived as a foreigner, with Franco's oppressed and oppressing Spain, in order to forge my work and source of energy. In opposition to all this, immersed in a French, Arabic, or North American environment without ever being totally integrated in any of them, I was morally and physically stateless but fatally united to the language in which I expressed my first feeling of "difference" and through which I could be saved. My brother's work expresses faithfulness to truth, an unshakable will to leave a record of the past, to temper his sudden disillusion and destructive impulses with a deep, fertile sense of creative pity. Since *Antagonía* can be read, at least at some levels, as a lucid chronicle of the largely Castilianized or independent bourgeoisie of Barcelona, of its contradictions, crimes, nostalgia, real unhappiness, impossible dreams; or the cultural, historical landscape of Catalonia whether the Empordà or Tarragona, the old quarter of Barcelona or the genial madness of the Sagrada Familia, nobody before had recreated all of this with so much talent, power, understanding, and objectivity.

This early awareness of our vocation as well as a premonition of our respective theatres of action is already clear from the few letters from Luis that I have saved from our spasmodic correspondence. While his narrative tastes centered on Conrad at the time, mine reflected the influence of Faulkner and his young followers in the South. During the autumn of 1954, when I finished writing *Duelo en el paraíso*, my brother had not yet joined the clandestine CP, but his group of friends began to enter its orbit. The nights I didn't go to the Varadero I went out with them, exploring the alleys by the Arco del Teatro and the promiscuous side street next to Escudillers. The desire to exhaust the limits and possibilities of nightlife, the generous, regular consumption of liters of Coke with rum or gin were part of our vital rejection of Francoist and bourgeois forms of life. Whether on their own initiative or contaminated by my influence, Luis's companions had also discovered the delights of the underbelly of the city and for several years—until the *gauche divine* appeared with its elegant haunts in the hills at the beginning of the sixties—the idea of night and alcohol would be almost exclusively associated for us with visits to a series of very mixed, sordid establishments between the Ramblas and the Paralelo. Our favorite places for some time would be the Pastís—with its progressive clientele drawn by the Piaf in the background and the Marsellais exoticism of the couple who ran it—and the nearby Cádiz bar—packed with prostitutes and North American blacks—whose lively descent into the lowlife evoked Hollywood images of Hamburg, Singapore, or Tampico. Later on, when we were fed up with the Gambrinus, Bodega Bohemia, and other axes of the Fifth District, we moved our quarters to the Andalusian Tavern and other bars near the Cosmos hotel where I would soon stay with Monique.

About this time a short and rather old story of mine appeared in the *Destino* magazine and the editor gave the illustrations over to a distant cousin of ours. María Antonia Gil was a niece of the pious Catholic lady I had greeted on my father's orders in her mansion in the Bois de Boulogne: I had probably met her years before when her mother died; but her telephone call telling me of the arrangement with the magazine took me by surprise: not only was I unaware of her artistic abilities but in the rigid Barcelona stratification of the time, in which her rich, aristocratic family was horizontally layered above ours, such a form of communication was outside the usual channels. Since her parents died María Antonia had been sharing the family flat in calle Balmes with her two sisters, and she invited me to dine there, to the great satisfaction of my father, who was flattered by my new, unexpected link to the most prestigious branch of his family. Luis's future wife was on my side immediately; clearly depressed by the traditional, conservative circles in which she moved, she readily accepted my invitation to go out for a few drinks at night and cheerfully joined the pilgrims in their worship of the Barrio Chino.

Our nightly topography wove a kind of cobweb from the bars and brothels of the Barceloneta to the cafés and bawdy houses of calle Tapias. With María Antonia, Cortés, and Luis's friends we followed the usual route, stopping off to visit different places like stations on a profane, happy Way of the Cross. When the Planeta prize was awarded to Ana María Matute that year, I had met at a public ceremony Ignacio Aldecoa and a girl of my age, Josefina Dalmau, the author of a novel that remained unpublished, for some reason or other. Both enjoyed the nightly visit with me to the Varadero and when he went back to Madrid she soon became a friend and was gradually integrated into the group. The oscillation from literature to alcohol, from enthusiasm for the lowlife to political commitment, reflected very clearly, at least in my case, the action of the conflicting, heterogeneous currents influencing our lives. Crawling through the dirtiest, most wretched areas in the city, rubbing shoulders with criminals and prostitutes, smoking hash, were transformed into a kind of militancy. The instinctive, gut aversion to the world from which I came found an opportune outlet in those places, which were the opposite side of the coin. Such an attitude, shared by the small bourgeois nucleus of our incipient class of progressives, seemed far from orthodox from a Marxist perspective. Manuel Sacristán's return from Germany, with his impeccable doctrinal baggage and his geometric reasoning, would soon call into question that confused, unsettling example of decadence and depravity.

W HEN I RETURNED to Paris in January of fifty-five I
was not feeling my way as on my first visit but
instead had a very precise plan of action: while my objective in living
outside Spain was still in force—and consequently I had to resolve
somehow the requirement of a modus vivendi compatible with writing—
the idea of establishing regular contact with left-wing intellectual circles
in France, in order to harness their moral and material support for our
nascent struggle against Francoism—often nurtured in the Bar Club get-
togethers with Castellet and his friends—infused my deferred, obsessive
trip with an urgency and interest that were not entirely selfish. Once I had
solved my lodging problem in a bourgeois edifice on the rue de L'Uni-
versité next to the Gallimard publishing house, I looked for ways of
making links with some of the magazines and journals that for months
had been satisfying our political and cultural appetite, furiously stimulated by the diet forced on us by the indefatigable Juan Aparicio's censorship department. Someone, I think it was Palau Fabre, had told me
about Elena de la Souchère, whose solitary zeal was then responsible for
the few reports and news items about Spain in the left-wing press, and I
went to meet her in the *France-Observateur* offices, on the top floor of the
building that would later be occupied by *L'Humanité*. At that time Elena
was a pale, lean, angular woman in her forties with sober but elegant,
clear-cut features, wearing a tight, severely tailored suit with shirt and tie.
She spoke in correct Spanish, with well-rolled *r*'s, as if she were on the
defensive against the twang of so many French or francophile speakers. As
I learned immediately, she lived very modestly in a small hotel in the area,
belonged to no party, and opposed Stalinism and Franco with equal gut
conviction. Her sources of information on the peninsula were haphazard:
so she welcomed my proposal to keep her informed about the changes and
events I thought were being hatched. She asked me to write an article on
the consequences of censorship for Maurice Nadeau's magazine,*
encouraged me to publish reports under a pseudonym in *Les Temps
Modernes*, and, eager to broadcast my points of view as a young intellectual
from the inside, she invited me to set them out before Claude Bourdet, don
Julio Álvarez del Vayo, and the Yugoslav ambassador. This generous,

---

* "La littérature espagnole en vase clos" appeared months later in *Les Lettres Nouvelles* with only
my initials as by-line.

disinterested support of hers for the Republican cause—motivated beyond a doubt by her family background—would nevertheless conflict from the start, as usually happens in Spain, with the reserve, distrust, and lack of understanding of its immediate beneficiaries. No one to my knowledge— with our left officially in power—has yet recognized Elena de la Souchère for her years of selfless journalistic labors in support of democracy or has thought to invite her to the country to pay her a much-deserved homage. Gratitude has never been a Spanish virtue and backbiting, silence, and oblivion are our usual reward for any action undertaken without desire for self-promotion. My experience of the political struggle against Franco has shown me those who were in some way involved in it and those who stepped in and reaped the benefits were generally not the same people: on the one hand, the Ceróns, Amats, and Porqueras; on the other, the old technocrats now sitting in government offices and antechambers. While some showed their faces when it was dangerous or inconvenient to speak up and sometimes paid a very high price for acting or telling the unsavory truth, others waited patiently in silence for the time to move their pawns forward from comfortable, profitable positions. Acting as she did outside the parties, an independent person like Elena aroused fear and hostility from left and right: closely watched by the Spanish police, as I would later substantiate myself, my Communist companions spread the most absurd fairy tales about her. I can clearly remember the day when one of them, a very close friend at the time, informed me in all seriousness that he knew on good authority that she was working for the CIA. Such an obviously false accusation was the first of many confidentially whispered in my ear in the years when I was a loyal, disciplined fellow traveler. With a worrying, confusing regularity one of the "cadres" or lesser intellectuals with whom I was in contact would utter the same or similar denunciations against Pallach, Miguel Sánchez Mazas, and Trotskyist militants. The left-wing French writers I met didn't get any better treatment in private; but, with the pragmatism evident in the double-talk of their ethics, the ones who placed the deadly labels in their intimidation exercises asked me to ask the help of those they were discrediting and obtain their signatures in support of some press campaign in the despised bourgeois news media against Francoist repression or in favor of an amnesty for the political prisoners in Burgos or Carabanchel. When the break occurred between Claudín and Semprún and their comrades in the Party leadership, the same charges rained down on them and indirectly on me and I was reminded of that simple, good-hearted, gentle friend who "revealed" to me with an ineffable smile Elena's secret connections with North American espionage: an ignoble, angelic image, difficult to remove ever since.

The obsession of Communist parties and revolutionary groups with labelling those who differ from them as "lackeys of imperialism" or "agents of the Pentagon" does not date back, as I thought for a time, to the particular historical conditions in which the Marxist and non-Marxist working-class movements were shaped and structured before the victory of the Bolshevik revolution: it is a response to a series of social and psychological factors that, as I would be shown by a reading of Blanco White, have their roots through the centuries in notions of orthodoxy, absolutism, and infallibility—the fruits of Saint Paul rather than Marx— firmly anchored in human nature. "Individuals organized professionally in an orthodox body will resist and sanction with every means any attempt to dissolve the vital principle behind their union. And as a consistent political body, an orthodox Church will easily realize that nothing binds groups of humans together better than their opposition to the rest. . . . Hence the fact that condemnation of the latter is the real essence of orthodoxy."* A rigidly hierarchical party will thus have recourse, as Blanco prophesies, to the simple expedient of marking out those who are not in communion with them with some vile or sectarian label, to bewilder and exhaust them, forcing them to ignore the real reasons for their disagreement and to nervously and rather guiltily refute their presumed identification in deed or word with the worst, most implacable enemy. The future designation as "intellectual bourgeois agents," "shameless pseudoleftists," and "minor agents of capitalism" bestowed by the great Cuban leader in 1971 on Sartre and a group of writers politically aligned with him would again confirm the deep-rootedness of the old custom, but I was not then surprised or upset. My involvement in the political world in my first years of hardened self-exile had revealed the abuses of such a mechanism ad nauseam and I was, you might say, inoculated against such terror.

The interest aroused by my approaches to journalists and politicians hostile to Franco had given me the naive conviction not only that our intellectual struggle was on the right track but also that, as I heard my Communist friends repeat, the demise of the regime was at hand. In the heyday of wishful thinking, I sent a coded letter to the members of the Bar Club, bringing them up-to-date with my contacts and activities; but the code was transparent as I deduced from the anxious reply they sent me. Whatever the truth of that, Elena de la Souchère's first notes and articles on the cultural opposition to Francoism, partly put together with facts and details I had supplied her with, filled me with optimistic satisfaction. The belief that we were not alone, that our guerrilla war against the censors was sympathetically supported abroad, encouraged me to redouble my efforts. During my stay in Paris, the censored text of *Juegos*

---

* See my edition of the *Obra inglesa de Blanco White* (Buenos Aires, 1972), 256–63.

de manos had come out and Castellet's review of the novel, underlining its non-conformist, critical tone, guaranteed that it would find readers skilled at reading between the lines. For the same reasons, less literary than political, Elena de la Souchère and Palau Fabre made friendly overtures to different publishers with a view to eventual translation.

Busy with my anti-Francoist activities, my initial provincial absorption into French culture waned slightly. The idea of being naturalized French, changing nation and language, gradually lost interest for me, sacrificed to my new plan to carry beyond our frontiers my friends' modest daily struggle for an open, untrammeled culture. My casual acquaintance, I'm not sure how or when, with a couple of very young intellectuals contributed to my timid, inexperienced detachment from the official clichés of Paris and its great names: Guy Debord and his companion at the time, Michèle Bernstein, lived in a hotel on the rue Racine adjacent to the boulevard Saint-Michel and published a journal called *Potlatch*, organ of their tiny Situationist International. Bitter, implacable enemies of the whole literary establishment—enveloped in internecine quarrels and ferocious splits that at times humorously mimicked Breton's terrorist language and the Stalinist trials—they possessed an all-embracing curiosity and an acute, demystifying vision of things. Their admiration for the *Palais idéal du facteur Cheval* and delight in visiting places and settings as far as possible from the tourist routes and famous monuments and vistas matched my developing taste and provided an intellectual justification that it lacked. In their healthy, consistent contempt for everything bourgeois and well-off, Debord and his friend used to visit the Arab cafés that were then located in the rue Mouffetard and the back streets of Maubert-Mutualité next to the Seine and one day they took me by bus from the Gare de L'Est to the proletarian suburb of Aubervilliers and a dive frequented by old Spanish Republican exiles, whose walls and owner I think were filmed by Carné and Prévert in their beautiful film on the poor children in the district. The subtle dovetailing of their tastes and mine, strengthened with the passage of time, conferred a baptismal, initiating value on that first tour with them around districts I would soon assiduously trawl on my own: that compact, aged, broken-down Paris, shot through by canals, viaducts, railways, and rusty underground arches, which, from Belleville to Barbès, is crowded in a perspective like an illustration of an "Industrial Landscape" from an old, dog-eared children's picture encyclopedia. The harmonious, elegant, cosmopolitan metropolis that dazzled me on my first visit—the famous second home of all artists, so lauded by the "lost generation" and their Latin American followers— would gradually lose its primitive attraction at the expense of a bastard halogenous urban environment, polluted and fertilized by the clash and interweaving of so many different cultures and societies. When it was already dark I crossed the rue d'Aubervilliers with Debord and his companion and walked along the giant meccanolike boulevard de la Chapelle, far from thinking that one day the mere idea of crossing the Seine to meet someone in the intellectual districts of the Left Bank where I then lived would seem to me as remote and unappealing, say, as going on safari in Kenya: my almost animal longing for the Sentier and its continuous creative improvisation would later not allow me any other excursions except to those luxuriant, teeming areas where I truly found my feet, guided by my initiator's prophetic instincts.

SHELLS, PEEL, SLOUGHS *cast off along your road to a future, defunct career as an official intellectual: dedicated to what? to promoting a blissful tomorrow or petty self-interest? an ambiguity preserved for years and then observed, from the barrier, on the smiling faces of the heralds of a progressive society: an ethical squint, profitable dividends, the application of bastardly means to the realization of noble ends: ability to split yourself in two as if you were someone else and to ruthlessly examine the insidious, larval simony: to be successful, like so many others, in cultivating the tragedies of history, ennobling your person in the shade of an attractive, rallying cause: the mythical civil war, famous million deaths, distant, vanished heroism: your presence at the slow, infectious, step-by-step climb upwards: a journey plagued by color blindness, sudden attacks of silence, opportune losses of sight, mystification: calculations, strategies, advantages happily cut off in time in an obstinate war against yourself: rhythmic gestures, hollow smiles, the swaying raised arms of the double or robot who, perched on a stage of moth-eaten fame, would later epitomize in your eyes the abject pettiness of the impostor.*

I RETURNED TO SPAIN proud and happy with my mission, as if bathed in the pleasant but illusory power of the late afternoon sun. The certainty that I had built the first bridge between our group and the European intelligentsia, that I had laid the bases for close, fruitful cooperation, gave my escape to Paris, I thought, a collective transcendence, and I was thus in a way transformed into a kind of ambassador. My closeness to the non-Communist French left—clustered around Sartre and *France-Observateur*—started from the assumption that our commitment would develop outside the parties, in an open, pluralist discourse. As I soon realized, such a position was on the naive side and did not take into account present circumstances or the ponderous inertia of reality. When someone breaks with a coherent, compact set of beliefs that can be as much religious and metaphysical as social, political, and moral, their first almost irresistible temptation is to seek refuge in a system with intrinsically similar characteristics, although on the surface they are opposed in conflict. As a result of a series of reflexes and habits rooted in his internal makeup, the deserter from a church will often be very attracted by the language, structure, and hierarchical model of the rival church. Suckled as a babe in a belief in a unique all-embracing key to explain the world, in a closed, self-sufficient frame of references, in infallible, dogmatic truth, he will abandon the ranks of the doctrine thus inculcated only to embrace with equal fervor and absence of critical spirit the system of the irreducible but symmetrical adversary of his first official credo. In a country like Spain where debate and the free contest of ideas had disappeared with the civil war and its ferocious settling of accounts, the political common-ground inherent in democracy was difficult to implant and lacked the magnetic power to attract the new generation of intellectuals and university students. Decimated by Francoist repression, the Socialist and Republican left vegetated in the land of pious hopes and had no practical contact with the evolution of the country. In the eyes of a youth tempted by action and radicalism, groups like Reventós's and Pallach's suffered from a weak reformism. In such a climate, the Communist party with its well-disciplined, iron structure, splendid ideological cohesion, and heroic resistance to police raids and persecution seemed to many to be the only viable alternative. The political fluctuations and doctrinal squabbles of the members of the Bar Club were unfortunately real: enemies of the authoritarian national Catholicism of the regime for ethical and ideological reasons, nevertheless we did not have our own program and strategy beyond these feelings of rebellion and disaffection. Sympathy for Sartre's revised interpretation of Marxism was not translated into concrete actions: totally cut off from the working class and its struggles, we still did not belong to the ennobling Gramscian category of organic intellectuals. On his return from Germany, Sacristán was to find fertile ground: a group of youths with beliefs close to his own who wanted to turn them into joint action with all the forces present in the revolutionary process.

In the months following my second trip to Paris, Luis, Joaquín Jordá, Pellissa, and other members of Castellet's literary seminar contacted Sacristán and formed the first Communist Party cell in Barcelona University with him as the leader. Although I was not informed personally of this collective adherence—my "bohemian" life and inveterate taste for the Barrio Chino no doubt aroused the fear and hostility of their conscientious mentor—I soon learned what was happening through my daily contact with Luis. I remember very clearly the day Sacristán and the other members of the group came separately to our house to hold one of their cell meetings, and when they were all there, the former hinted with a smile that my presence was not required. These meetings in Pablo Alcover upset my father and aroused his suspicions. The stiff, rather Prussian good humor of Sacristán, the mystery surrounding conversations officially dedicated to matters related to the university, inspired a hazy but accurate presentiment that there was a snake in the grass. Several times, on those afternoons, he popped into the room where I was working on the manuscript of *Fiestas* to communicate his anxieties to me: I can see him now, thin, honed down to the fragile birdlike profile he acquired in those years, clutching at his grimy dressing-gown and ever-present rosary beads. What did I think about those meetings? What were they discussing for hours and hours with that strange, bespectacled professor? My soothing replies did not succeed in allaying his suspicions. Politics only brings unhappiness, my son, he would say suddenly, interrupting the conversation: remember the Republic and the suffering it brought me and Mother. And again, as he left my room, I could hear him wandering along the dark passage, whispering to Eulalia, curtly asking Grandfather for the daily newspaper, only to return to the subject for the nth time: if they are talking, as they claim, about topics in their course, why did they close the dining room door and break off their conversations when he went in to look for the yogurt spoon or ask if they needed anything? Soon afterwards the cell-members stopped meeting in our house, no doubt realizing the risk of a possible indiscretion on his part.

From this time to his death, my father would live in a state of anxious preoccupation about our political ideas. Although my brothers and I avoided all discussion of the subject, his hunch that things weren't going as they should, that we secretly professed harmful, obnoxious doctrines, never gave him a day's peace. Neither our formal, external respect for Catholic dogma nor the pious lies with which we wrapped everything related to our ideas and private life succeeded in sweeping away his dark, persistent foreboding. With an absentminded innocence, which at the time made us laugh, he would butt in to comment on international political events from principles based on homespun pedestrian common-sense, exempt from the irreproachable, rigorous dialectic that then sustained our own: the friendship between the Chinese and the Russians, he maintained, was not going to last long; as early as the time of Genghis Khan the latter had fought against the yellow peril, and sooner or later they would become aware of this, for, however Communist they might be, all in all they were still Europeans. While we listened to him with haughty condescension, we were far from believing that a few years later facts would prove him right and, in spite of our supposedly scientific laws and peremptory arguments, the break forecast by him would happen and the official bard, Yevtushenko, would publish a poem in *Pravda* evoking the heroic knights of Muscovy hated because of their blue eyes and white complexions by the threatening swarm of Asiatic hordes, and we were heartbroken when we read it. Today, when I look back and recall our blindness to historical, ethnic, and geographical realities and conditions captured by an eccentric bourgeois like our father, such petulance makes me smile: to submit the rich complexities of the world to a single-voiced reading, to exclude from the analysis of reality dreams, feelings, defects, secret drives of human beings seems not only a monstrous reduction of the latter but also incredibly puerile. The head-shrinkers with their single official ideology, in leaving out of their projections and analyses man's irrational elements, were unwittingly contaminating all their schemas with delirious irrationality: what they threw out of the door slipped back in again through the window and penetrated to their marrow; hardly had they built the protective, sanitary wall of the ideal city where the new man would reside than they would see arise there the cruelties, misery, madness, and extravagances of the old barbarian against which they initially fought.

My father's premonitions about the risks of the new and for him odious ideas we defended would be sadly confirmed before his death by a campaign in the regime's news media against my "anti-Spanish" activities in France and, especially, by the predictable arrest of Luis. Immersed in a conservative milieu both in the family and society where our ideas and behavior caused a scandal, he would be singularly ill-equipped to support us publicly against the avalanche of insults, judgments, and condemnations that rained down on us, having to do it as he did in the teeth of his dearest and deepest convictions. His well-intentioned letter to Franco, written during Luis's imprisonment—recalling his life and beliefs as a right-wing Catholic, his widowhood, and the unhappiness caused by the war, the traditional religious system in which he had brought us up—the revelation of which by José Agustín would make me blush with shame, now seems to me, after some years, both moving and pathetic to the extent it reflects his loneliness and the painful conflict of his ideas and feelings. At the time our mutual lack of comprehension—not imputable only to him—prevented me from pitying the isolation in which he lived and the corrosive harshness of his fate. His recourse to that other tyrannical, castrating Father whose ubiquitous, all-embracing presence extended over us and eclipsed his own, reveals crudely and sharply the correlation of strength between the two and the weak, vicarious nature of his parental authority: the impotence, senility, frustration of a nominal progenitor obedient to the one who really ruled and shaped our lives from the pinnacles of absolute power. From then on my hatred for the Other, the recipient of the humiliating letter, would be transformed into a real mania: compulsive desires to stamp on, almost crush, like a furious, energetic, punctilious post office worker, the pile of letters with his grotesque effigy reproduced to infinity on the stamps; hopes of being present some day, as would happen fifteen years later and in North America, at the death rattle of a cruel, sordid, and prolonged death agony.

The reasons, or rather the doubts, that prevented me from following Luis's example and asking for Party membership, would be difficult to specify. I was intellectually mature enough; at the same time as other Barcelona friends I had read Dionys Mascolo's article in the special issue of *Les Temps Modernes* on the left, and his lucid, persuasive argument that the need to extract the minimum common denominator from all the nonconformist, rebellious positions and attitudes must inevitably lead to the assumption of the "universal need for Communism" had made a strong impression on me. Both Castellet and myself felt tempted to take the step and Jaime Gil de Biedma later reached the point of asking to join only to be turned down for the same intolerant criteria that caused Cernuda's persecution in wartime. In my case, my inhibition probably fed on some anti-Soviet reading in my adolescence about the Moscow trials and a frequently unfortunate experience with Communist militants who defended socialist realism to the death. Fleeing as I was from a world where I felt alien and marginal, I was unconsciously afraid of being interned in another where these feelings of difference and disagreement could be reproduced. But the chance, and perhaps decisive, reason would be, at least externally, a meeting set up for me and Castellet with the person who was to act as our Virgilian guide into the heart of the organization. The contact chosen by the CP turned out to be Juan José

Mira, a writer barely in his forties, who had won, if I remember correctly, the first Planeta Prize with a detective novel. Mira sublet, I think, one of those dismal, oppressive flats on the Ensanche, furnished on purpose, one would say, to imbue visitors with an insidious feeling of unease and give them repeated nightmares. He welcomed us in his dressing-gown, jovially, and after a brief exchange of pleasantries, he went straight to the point. He was aware, he said, that we were well disposed toward the Party and had been charged to meet with us on a regular basis in order to clear up our problems and uncertainties. After such an alarming prologue he opened a cupboard stuffed with clandestine journals, which, being negligently arranged, suddenly fell noisily on the carpet. He looked through the scattered publications and gave each of us a copy of *Mundo obrero*. He pointed out an extensive, solid speech by Bulganin, illustrated with his photo, and asked us to read and think about it at our leisure, so that we could discuss its "political and philosophical" content with him at a later meeting. But unhappily for our guide there never was another meeting: we had hardly left the flat in a sleepwalker's daze than the astounded catechumens threw the bemedalled marshal's stodgy prose into the nearest drain and disappeared from sight forever. Soon afterwards, the mighty Bulganin would fall into "the dustbin of history" and from then on neither of us—nor probably Mira himself—would hear of him again.

As one might have expected, even before the change wrought by Sacristán's arrival, the Bar Club political discussions and my French contacts attracted the attention of the police. Just before my new trip to Paris and Monique's first stay in Barcelona, I received a telephone call from an inspector of the Social Political Brigade, famous at the time for his unswerving persecution of Communists. Antonio Juan Creix and his brother Vicente played a leading role in the regime's repressive apparatus and their harsh, suspicious nature made them rightly feared by the different "families" of the clandestine opposition. He said that he wanted to discuss a personal matter with me and, although the point of his call was perfectly clear, I feigned surprise and with rather rash, provocative cheerfulness I made a date for the following day in the Pastís. When I arrived at the appointed time, he was already waiting for me and, from the owner's tight-lipped, impassive gaze, I deduced that he had questioned her about me. Antonio Creix was a sturdily built man of average height; he wore a Bogart-style raincoat, and had one of those mustaches so characteristic of his profession, as painted carefully and artistically by Arroyo in his recent, polemical picture. Our conversation, spelled out in a letter sent to Monique via an intermediary, centered at once on my meetings with Elena de la Souchère: somebody from Paris had informed him of our interviews and my visits to the editorial board of *France-Observateur*. Creix handled his information with ease and self-confidence, pleased to demonstrate that no movement, even abroad, had escaped the police's eagle eye. As I saw, he was especially interested in tracking down the sources where my friend obtained her information: did I know that my relationship with her could cause me unpleasant consequences? Was I aware that she was planning a visit to Spain? Although I protested my innocence and pretended I had only spoken to her about literature, he insisted that I must inform them if she came to see me in Barcelona, even perhaps under a false identity. His aim was not to arrest her nor to harm her in any way, he added, but to talk to her, show her the real country that she did not know, and make her realize that her articles suffered from serious prejudices and a total lack of rigor. On the subject of the anti-Spaniards who obsessed him, Creix expressed absolute contempt for the Catalan, bourgeois opposition while his hatred for Communists revealed an obvious sickly fascination: his ashen face would suddenly light up when he spoke about them and take on a more human expression. Later on he changed the subject and chatted about the literary, cultural world, of how exposed we writers with some weakness or defect—he didn't specify which—were to blackmail, to being changed into enemy agents without realizing it. While we walked up the Ramblas, he asked me to sign a copy of *Duelo en el paraíso*; he then bid goodbye with a pleasant but curt warning that our exchanges could be quite different if I went back to my old ways.

That first police warning bell would be followed by others that fortunately weren't serious either. As a result of an organized foot-stamping by our group in the Calderón Theatre at a Luca de Tena play in which a cruel, heartless Communist slumped to the ground after being executed shouting "Death to Spain!" to the applause of a bourgeois audience fond of that kind of creation, Luis, Castellet, and a dozen friends who turned up spontaneously in the police station to accompany one of the protestors arrested by a plainclothes inspector would be rounded up later in their homes and released hours afterwards, having made statements about the events. As I had been forewarned by Creix, I didn't follow the rest out of the theatre although, as I soon discovered from Castellet, he interrogated him during his questioning about my nocturnal habits and sexual inclinations. My recurrent, distressing nightmares of persecution related to Spain date back to this time: a mental scenario of denunciations, secret hiding places, harassment, frenetic flights from the police resulting from some dark, vaguely dishonorable crime, a scenario that would not disappear when I uprooted myself from the country nor even after Franco's death. The sequence with the Reverend Charles Lutwidge Dodgson at the Police Headquarters in my novel *Paisajes después de la batalla* is the faithful transcription of one of its versions in which sex and politics, exhibitionism and revolutionary militancy are subject to sarcastic attack by a chorus of inspectors whose dress, features, and manner recall those who, with the sensitive intuitions of bloodhounds, fanfared *avant la lettre* the perverse likelihood of my *defects* and *weaknesses*.

T HE CHAIN OF events that would unexpectedly favor my plans to leave Spain—at least that Spain in the grip of an arbitrary, anachronistic, sterilizing regime that I hated with all my heart—began to come together throughout the summer of 1955, in a period of personal frustration and political doubts when I devoted my free time and efforts to writing *Fiestas* astride the Bar Club and the Varadero. Soon after the publication of one of my first books, I received a short note from the North American Hispanist John B. Rust in which, after expressing his appreciation of these, he offered to negotiate the possible translation of *Juegos de manos* with one of the New York publishing houses open to European narrative; he added that he had handed my novels to his friend Maurice Edgard Coindreau during the latter's visit to Sweet Briar and that the French translator completely shared his point of view. I was filled with surprise by the reference to Coindreau's praise: although I knew his excellent versions of the great North American novelists—Dos Passos, Hemingway, Faulkner, Steinbeck, and Caldwell—I did not know he read Spanish and had been interested in our literature from his youth. Rust had previously sent me a questionnaire about my tastes and the influences on my novels and my replies included a group of authors, starting with Faulkner, that I had often read in Coindreau's translations. Some days later I received a letter from the latter whose generous, magnanimous praise of my work filled me with elation. In his support for the judgments advanced by Rust, Coindreau not only overwhelmed me with sincere and copious praise but offered to translate my novels and suggest them to Gallimard. To a raw provincial writer like me, dazzled by the novelists he translated and the prestige of the publishing house for which he was assessor, the letter seemed like a wonderful dream, too beautiful to be real. It was a singularly propitious stroke of luck that my enthusiasm at the time for Faulkner and young Southern narrators like Carson McCullers, Capote, or Goyen coincided with Coindreau's likes and interests. He still taught French literature in the Princeton Romance Languages Department, but traveled to Europe every year, and he suggested it would be convenient to meet in Paris where he would be staying for a few days at the beginning of October so he could introduce me to his publisher.

In our correspondence during those months, which unfortunately I haven't preserved, Coindreau showed his delight at discovering in the novels of a young writer brought up under Francoism the impact of an author like Faulkner whose work he had defended from the start against the hostility and lack of understanding of the majority of his colleagues. His prologues and studies of him had cleared a path for a pioneering set of disciples and then a pack of imitators to follow in his footsteps and throw themselves into mapping out imaginary geographical landscapes directly or indirectly inspired by his at once realistic and fantastic vision of the decrepit society of the South. Today, when despite my continuing admiration for Faulkner I haven't read him for twenty years, I feel that it is fortunate his influence on me was only a brief, if intense infection activated particularly by the work of Capote and McCullers, before I discovered the much closer reality of the committed art of Pavese and Vittorini. As shown by the example of Latin America in the last twenty years, the powerful fascination exercised by his universe has not only had positive effects: if, on the one hand, it has allowed the creation of novelistic worlds as seductive and attractive as that of García Márquez, the immediate, devastating success of the latter has given rise, on the other, to the fortunate but doubtful formula of "magical realism," a luxuriant plantation of epigones, grandchildren or descendents of the author of *The Wild Palms* who have transplanted or tried to transplant the hallucinating world of Yoknapatawpha—seen through the multicolored lantern of Macondo with its levitations, witches, wise grandmas, miraculous girls, downpours of blood, and galleons moored in a silk-tree wood—not only to the heart of the *selva* or the Indies but also to lands as parsimonious and unfriendly to that kind of portent and marvel as León and Galicia. Nothing so easy and tempting as to transpose into a language often as opaque as Spanish Faulkner's long, heavy sentences stripped of all prosody, rhythm, and suppleness: if we add to that an area as well-defined as that county on the lower banks of the Mississippi complete with ordinance surveys, a transfer of the Macondo reincarnation, we can capture with hindsight the grandiose extent of its influence and, willy-nilly, the ravages of contamination. But Coindreau couldn't guess then what the first swallows of Faulknerism would herald in a long exhausting summer, the end of which is still not in sight. He had spotted, with his most delicate literary scent, before anyone else, the seminal value of a work that, through him, was going to change the direction of our narrative fiction. That first meeting of ours in the Pont Royal hotel would also be the beginning of a close, fruitful collaboration that would extend from his versions of *Juegos de manos* and *Duelo en el paraíso* to *Señas de identidad*. I discovered then that Coindreau's initiation into the art of translating had been Valle-Inclán's *Divinas palabras* and that only the accidents of his university career in the United States had deflected him from our language and made him discover at its source the work of the "lost generation." His return, after more than thirty years, to the love of his youth would not be limited to translating five of my novels but would extend to those of authors like Sánchez Ferlosio and Marsé, who would penetrate the French literary world thanks to his influence and prestige.

After I arrived in Paris at the beginning of October I went to Gallimard, the publishers, where I had an appointment with Coindreau. I asked for him at the receptionist's desk in the entrance lobby: the receptionist informed me that he had just left and that he expected me in his hotel in the afternoon, but that the secretary from the translation service wanted to see me. I waited nervously and soon a young woman appeared on the linoleum-covered stairs; she was sunburnt, had very short hair, and I can remember her smile very precisely. Monique Lange told me in rudimentary Spanish that her boss Dionys Mascolo wanted to talk to me and asked me whether I spoke French. *Je le baragouine un peu*, I replied with false modesty. I followed her through a labyrinth of stairs and corridors to the spacious office looking out over a beautiful interior garden where her boss was waiting for me. Mascolo welcomed me with a simple show of affection: Coindreau had written to him recommending my books and, he said, he wanted to take advantage of my visit to inform me of the usual clauses in the contract. However, the dialogue veered off at once toward Spain, where my interlocutor had just been on holiday with Marguerite Duras, Vittorini, and a small group of friends. Their attention had been caught by the country's development even under a system as authoritarian as Franco's; but unfortunately their ignorance of Spanish and lack of contact with intellectuals in the country prevented them from penetrating to the heart of things as they would have liked. What did I think of the situation? Could I see, as they had, some hopes of change? For a good hour I set before Mascolo my violent anti-Francoist feelings: with the naive optimism I then cultivated, I explained to him that the new generation of intellectuals and university students was opposed to the dictatorship and was adopting more and more open, radical positions. In spite of our isolation and the fear provoked by the harsh repression of the postwar period, the young generation was beginning to open its eyes and was planning actions in support of its demands in harmony with the clandestine trade union opposition. Attributing to our tiny group's experience an impact it never had, I forecast that the country would very soon enter a phase of revolutionary agitation. Mascolo soaked up my words with rapture on his face and when our conversation ended, expressed a desire to see me again. Monique, who had remained in a discreet middle ground, asked me whether I would be free to have dinner with her the following day: I've also invited Jean Genet, she added straightaway to persuade me. I accepted and wrote down her address, that number 33, rue Poissonnière, that would soon become my refuge and haunt: the "permanent" abode that has for almost thirty years appeared on my official documents.

As Monique revealed later, Mascolo exclaimed after I left his office: "This is the Spaniard we have been waiting for." After that, infatuated with him and influenced by his ideas and opinions, she interpreted this comment as an order. With her typical lack of self-confidence she put forward Genet's name and its power of persuasion to ward off a possible rejection. My political vehemence and Belmonte-like appearance impressed her: after I leave, she asks the receptionist whether she thinks I'm interested in women. Geneviève says yes. Monique isn't so sure: my gaze reveals no personal emotion beyond my hatred for Franco's system and existence. Anyway, she decides, my coming conversation with Genet will clear up any doubts.

On the night of the dinner, the eighth of October, I leave the Bonne Nouvelle underground, immediately locate the Rex cinema opposite the old offices of *L'Observateur* where I met Elena de la Souchère months before, look for the adjacent building, not in the boulevard but in the street, take the lift to the third floor, walk to the second door on the left, and ring the bell. Monique comes to welcome me and introduces me to her guests: a fair-haired, bearded young Englishman named Peter and, bald, slight, beardless, wearing corduroy trousers and a leather jacket, Genet. I am intimidated by his presence and my intrusion among these strangers but, happily, Genet only seems interested in Peter, with whom Monique is having a passing relationship after her divorce. He asks him about his likes and dislikes, slyly makes fun of him, tries to make him confess that he has at some time felt repressed or secret attraction for a male friend or companion. He denies this, which amuses and excites Genet, leaning on the couch next to Monique. Suddenly he turns to me and asks point-blank:

"What about you? Are you a queer?"

In my confusion, I reply that I have had homosexual experiences—something that until then I had never revealed in public—and it helps me to clear things up with Monique, toward whom I already instinctively feel warmth, but my boldness—I suppose I blushed when I answered—makes no impression on him at all.

"Experiences! Everybody has had experiences! You talk like an Anglo-Saxon pederast! I meant dreams, desires, fantasies."

Genet doesn't speak to me again that night and, with a mixture of disappointment and relief, I understand I have not passed the test. I let him ironically court Peter while, during the dinner and afterwards, I devote myself entirely to Monique.

When I try to recall my first images of her these always hinge on the strange, unexpected aura of her smile: an open, warm, generous smile, tinged with melancholy, which is exclusively hers and is impossible to forget once it has been noticed and internalized. Throughout my life I have not come across another endowed with such expressive intensity: relaxing, warm, moving, and yet imbued with a mysterious fragility. Even at the harshest moments of our troubled and sometimes painful coexistence, the mere evocation of her smile has been enough to instantly sweep away bouts of sulking, break down ideas of moving apart or splitting up, recreate the disturbing emotion that overcame me the day I really discovered her and found out I was the fortunate recipient, making me relax and unwind, bewildered, intoxicated by pure happiness.

From that night on, despite Genet's interference and his overbearing personality, a reciprocal feeling was established between us, the nature of which is difficult to capture. Monique in some way broke down the cautious, prickly, defensive barrier that comes between women and me, with the exception of a certain kind of prostitute. Although my affection is not yet physical, her body does not leave me unmoved nor does it inspire fear. The unmentioned but obvious relationship with Peter does not favor our coming together, it will however make me understand that my arrival has brought a small change to her life and scale of priorities: when it's time for me to go, in a conspiratorial gesture aimed at me, she bids farewell to him rather abruptly, as if telling me that the way is clear. When I realize what has happened, I am in the street with Peter, too late for the underground or bus and without the means to permit the luxury of a taxi. We have no alternative but to walk back to the Left Bank together and we silently walk the long distance; I'm still agitated by the memory and novelties of the evening while, by my side, he seems absorbed by the bitter, gloomy thoughts of a displaced gallant.

During the next few days Coindreau and I resolve some of the problems and difficulties posed by the translation and sign the contracts drawn up by Mascolo, which Monique has typed out. My long-standing, persistent goal of settling in Paris is now within reach but I have to return to Spain to fulfill several months of military service or be dubbed a deserter and be forced to cut all my ties with my brothers and friends and reject the country, if not definitively, at least for several years. Convinced of my usefulness as a link between our group and the European intellectuals we take as our model, unenthusiastic about selfishly deserting the struggle we are engaged in, I prefer to sacrifice myself for a time and return free from burdens and obligations. Monique, to whom I explain my problems of conscience, supports my decision and, although our connection is still hesitant, promises to come and see me in Spain. I see her daily, alone or with one of her friends: Mascolo, Marguerite Duras, Florence Malraux, Odette Laigle. In her initial flush to introduce herself and seduce me she spread out her radiant, showy visiting cards like a fan: not only is she an intimate friend of Genet but also someone as unapproachable as Faulkner writes to her affectionately and is her daughter's godfather. Her close friendships, in fact, range over a list of writers I have read and admired: she wishes to know if *je suis ambitieux*—I understood *un vicieux* and, comically, I hurriedly soothe her—whether I am worried, like many of her colleagues, more about the desire to make a career than by writing as such. Her moral vigilance in a matter she judges to be fundamental— from her privileged vantage point she has been able to witness ad nauseam the vanity, stratagems, envy, and wretchedness of the ever-grotesque literary tribe—will be a tremendous help, during our first years together, in curing my initial propensity to snobbery and the obscene flattery of fame: a long, difficult battle with myself in which her rigor and the simultaneous example of Genet will prevent me from becoming one of those smug, dropsical self-sufficient barrels who, with telegenic ubiquity, exhibit themselves daily on the peninsular Parnassus.

Gradually, as an already tender but delicate and uncertain relationship strengthens, she reveals details and mysteries in her biography: her Jewish origins, childhood in Indochina, conversion to Catholicism and immediate loss of faith, discovery of Indian poverty, return to Paris, friendship with Genet, impact of the journeys to Spain, joining the Communist Party. Her humor, frankness, and natural emotion sweep aside my restraint and afford me a warm immediacy I am ready to reciprocate. Used to the narrow, trivial, tight-lipped behavior of Spanish middle-class women of the time, her straightforward language, her total lack of embarrassment and fear of the ridiculous, surprise and attract me. After she finishes at the office we go out for a walk, I show her my favorite spots by the Mouff', the canals and cafés in Aubervilliers discovered by Guy Debord. Encouraged by her spontaneity and candor, I confide in turn my inhibitions and hang-ups with women. Till now I've only been able to fuck whores, I tell her. We all dream about being whores to the man we're interested in, she replies.

In order not to force things, Monique tactfully prolongs the ambiguity of our bond. Although we kiss and act as if we are lovers in public, we aren't yet, and she organizes the day so we say our farewells in a public spot. We have tacitly agreed to postpone the experience for a few weeks, until she comes and visits me during her end-of-year holidays. As she later tells me, this leap into the unknown, strongly discouraged by some of her friends, seems like a real act of madness; but, determined to win the bet, she comes to see me on the agreed date, even at the risk of failing and biting the dust. When we say goodbye on the twenty-third in the Gare d'Austerlitz we both feel confused and excited: our relationship is precarious and fragile; any unlucky or chance event could still destroy it, wipe it out.

During the weeks after my departure, mainly spent in Torrentbó, I correct the *Fiestas* manuscript and read the books by Genet, Leiris, Violette Leduc, Elio Vittorini that she sent me; I listen time and again to the records we listened to together in Paris. My letters contain weighty Sartrian reflections upon Genet's committed attitude toward the FLN rebellion in Algeria in opposition to the silent, indifferent complicity of the "mandarins." I am ashamed and worried by my social status as a "young gentleman"—emphasized by time spent with Alfredo and the peasants: I am objectively *une ordure*, I write to her; I belong unwillingly to the camp of *les ordures*. What can I do to avoid this? Even if I were to enlist in the Communist Party like her, my position would not change since the economic structures in the country would still be the same and unjust class differences could only be abolished by a hypothetical revolution. If I showed a real interest in their fate, didn't this imply the risk of stifling them with my paternalism and thus contributing to their acceptance, however provisional, of their state?

When, after a month and a half of letters and telephone calls, she disembarks in Barcelona, I wait for her at the end of the platform in the old station for trains from France: Monique walks toward me laden with suitcases, smiling with the sensitive, receptive expression I anxiously expect from her. I booked a double room in the Cosmos hotel whose position in the middle of Escudillers and vaguely suggestive *meublé* appearance appeal to me: Gil de Biedma strongly recommended the "nuptial bedchamber" where he once spent a glorious night; but it is let and we move into another more modest room. Luis, María Antonia, and several friends come to meet her and celebrate the occasion. We have lunch in the Amaya, drink, and go for a walk round the port: when we return to the Cosmos at night we are slightly tipsy. We both explore our nakedness tentatively: her skin is firm, soft, welcoming and my much-feared frigidity melts away at her touch. Happy and excited I penetrate her time and again, get lost between her breasts, belly, and lap. Joined to her body, I unhurriedly find the necessary gestures and movements, I share with her the beautiful, leisurely intimacy. The telephone rings and we leave it on the hook: we live isolated in our fiery bubble, disconnected from the outside world.

For five or six years, the relationship begun among the loud colors of the Cosmos bordello will experience its ups and downs and quiet interludes, but will not fade away: Monique will also be, at the sexual level, the omnivorous center of my life. We will love each other, fall out, deceive each other, and then have reconciliations like any couple in Paris, Italy, Barcelona, Andalusia: we try each of the four beds in a solemn, anachronistic hotel in Cartagena; make love naked on the burning sand dunes on the Guardamar beach spied on by a local lad. The sumptuous, baroque scenes of virility, all-consuming passion, violence, do not disappear entirely from my dreams, but remain silenced, vegetating in a kind of back room, as I discover later to my distress; when the opportunity arises they will reappear and dominate me.

Exhausted but happy, we dine out very late on elvers and red wine. To justify my absence from home, I explained to my father that I was going to Calafell for a few days and, from this date, the term *calafell* acquires for Monique and myself the Proustian dimension of *faire catleya*. During the day I show her the Varadero and Barceloneta taverns that I had toured with Raimundo; at night, we go to see the blacks dancing in the Cádiz and drink manzanilla in the Andalusian Inn. María Antonia and Luis usually come with us, and during one of these soirées we meet up in the last bar with Gil de Biedma and a stranger, Jaime Salinas, who has been exiled since the war and is walking on Spanish soil for the first time. Monique then declares an irresistible passion for gays and dykes: the ones she meets in Barcelona with their heavy makeup, hysterical agitation, titters, and to-ing and fro-ing confirm for her Genet's age-old opinion that the Spanish variety are undoubtedly the most comic, saddest, sauciest, and grimmest in the world. On that and subsequent stays, the port, the Ramblas, the Barrio Chino, and the pompous, counterpaned nuptial couch in the Cosmos will be our exclusive, absorbing haunts. Our only incursions into the well-off bourgeois districts in the hills will be to Pablo Alcover and the Barrals' flat, where we had a date with Castellet on one of their literary Tuesdays.

My father is disconcerted by the Frenchwoman who inopportunely crosses his path, however much she shows off in his honor the very limited and at times mistaken repertory of polite formulas she memorized in his language in far-off schooldays. Eulalia belies my fears, likes her immediately, and looks after her during and after lunch with gushing emotion. Grandfather stays in his corner leafing through the newspaper or scratching his scalp. The ghostly, ageing, decrepit scene in the house impresses Monique: after a few hours there, she tells me, she feels as oppressed as I do and has the same desire to escape.

The meeting in the just-married Barrals' flat, though enlivened by Ferrater's shining presence, suffered from that mundane literary itch *d'être à la page* illustrative, for a Parisian woman used to Genet, of our incurable provincialism, but it did later enable the publisher not only to introduce in Spain some of the names revealed by Monique but also to establish, thanks to her, the basis for a fruitful and stimulating close relationship with Gallimard that will climax in the future Formentor Conversations and the creation of the innovative but ephemeral International Prize for Literature.

When Monique says goodbye, our life is about to alter. I must turn up some days later at the Mataró barracks to fulfill a sergeant's apprenticeship in the so-called University Militia, but we agree that after that's finished we'll meet in Paris and spend a few months together in daily contact to see if the experience suits us. In the meantime, our correspondence, her telephone calls and visits will, we hope, keep alive the warmth of a relationship that, without either of us suspecting it at the time, is going to have a lasting, definitive influence on our destiny, character, and ideas.

THE RECORD OF the months after your first meeting in Barcelona is minutely detailed in the correspondence you maintained and its reconstruction poses no difficulty. The majority of your letters are from Mataró from January to July in fifty-six, and the continuous flow is only interrupted by her brief, infrequent visits. Rereading them, almost thirty years later, one often sees praiseworthy frankness and openness alongside some character traits you would struggle against afterwards: the adolescent tendency to embellish or magnify all that happens to you, which, had it not been soon lopped off, would have swept you into incurable mythomania; the vanity of the well-heeled young leftist, which, paradoxically, you would cast off thanks to an excessive if healthy creative pride: the fact experienced day in and day out that, as your addiction to literature intensified, you weren't modest enough to feel flattered by the fame and honors that sustain that activity; that the giddy adventure of writing discovered in *Don Julián* finally constituted something alien and even opposed to worldly glory: a new expression or unexplored territory of your sexuality.

Your dialogue at a distance reveals the cautious pleasure of those walking to an amorous encounter between dunes and shifting sands. The plans you forge for the future are fragile and transitory: on your return to Paris, you book in alone to a small hotel on the rue de Verneuil and you spend the weekends together. Each of you preserves your freedom and neither aspires to exclusive possession of the other. While you remain separate you must "cheerfully" accept minor infidelities. When Monique tells you the details of the adventures she had on some of her trips, both before and after getting married, you write to her that you have never loved her so much or felt so proud of her independent, fearless qualities. You list your mediocre ambidextrous *calafells* and encourage her to relate hers in turn. Her parallel story with a friend in common and the unexpected, painful problem it throws up force you to deepen your thoughts on the subject: the word "whore," used with moral connotations, repels you. Everybody, female and male, has changing fantasies and desires about the other sex, independently of their emotional ties. The notion of deceit, you tell her, is reactionary and confused; you don't feel betrayed by the fact she has been with another man; real betrayal would have stemmed from any attempt to hide it like a bourgeois wife. This does not prevent, logically enough, a tingling jealousy; but it is a bearable unease that is

even pleasantly melancholic. Taking into account your hatred for traditional female passivity and frigidity, you are impressed and excited by her
Don Juan qualities. Sometimes you tell her about your dreams of fucking
her and don't leave out, on occasion, the presence of some Algerians you
went drinking with in Mouff and their sudden, disturbing promiscuity.
You have entered the Mataró barracks at the beginning of the year and
your description of the tedium and brutalizing absurdity of life there
takes up a large part of the letters:

> This morning, Mass. A terrific ceremony: the priest flutters about the altar to
> the sound of drums and cornets like a prima donna. On the other side of the
> yard, surrounded by armed guards, the prisoners attend the service bare-
> headed, and prostrate themselves on bended knee during the Consecration.
> The priest, childish and angelic like a doll, preaches the sacrifice and resig-
> nation appropriate to Lent. Rather moving. I was looking at the prisoners—
> some have been inside for years—the priest, host, noisy military band, the
> officer's gleaming sword. Everything beautiful and well-ordered: morality,
> religion, God, etc. How I remembered, loved, and missed Genet!
> The Thursday procession was really beautiful! Helmet, machine gun, one,
> two, slowly keeping in step behind the God-child to the rhythm of the band.
> In front of us, the First Communion girls with their candles and little white
> wings and priests, priests, still more priests while we sweat blinded by the sun
> and its reflection in the bayonets, one, two, one, two, and I am stupefied,
> exhausted, with the distressing impression I am an ape.*

To tell the truth, your life is not always as harsh and depressing as you
paint it. Even in a system as rigid and hierarchical as the army and under
the diffuse but real oppression of the dictatorship, typically Spanish
disorder, arbitrariness, and incongruities palliate what in other latitudes
could have been inflexible Prussian regimentation, opening up gaps and
breathing spaces, pleasant like holes in Gruyère, in a life at first sight
constrained, stifling, and airless. The daily routine and discipline of a
Francoist barracks—imagined with anguish and horror by the French
friends you write to—contain a series of whimsical imponderables,
improvisations, and fantasies that only those who know the Spanish
character and its weak points can assimilate unsurprised. Monique has
been telephoning you regularly since you arrived with the twenty-sixth
Badajoz Infantry Regiment and these calls from a Frenchwoman not only
give you the enviable status of a deserving, tough Hispanic conquistador
but also create a palpable atmosphere of expectation and lust among the

---

* Neither of the two letters quoted, which I have translated from the French, carry a date
although this can be deduced from the text: the procession mentioned in the second relates to
the festival of Corpus Christi.

officers: while one lieutenant tries to gain your esteem with a view to an eventual trip with your "fiancée" and some French girlfriend, followed by a cheerful, carefree spree by all four, another suggests the possibility of obtaining through her one of those Parisian magazines that today would fall from the hands of any eight-year-old, so insipid are they, but which then aroused in repressed, frustrated soldiers an excitement difficult to imagine. Discreetly courted by your superiors, you use the situation to get out of the most painful duties in your life as a sergeant—processions, reviews, marches—by invoking the exotic need to stay by the telephone in case of a call from Paris. Francoism was also like this and had little in common with the iron, monolithic, totalitarian regime that exiles and Republican sympathizers used to describe and evoke from afar: despite your religious agnosticism and well-known disaffection from the regime, the long-distance telephone calls from an invisible, suggestive French fiancée conferred on you a special, privileged halo within the regiment.

Neither would the experience of those months in Mataró be purely negative: the contact with the soldiers and prisoners would allow you a glimpse of areas and hidden corners of Spanish reality that you could have penetrated in no other way. In one of the stories in *Para vivir aquí* you capture your fleeting vision of the unjust, irrational world of prison: the assortment of pathetic or eccentric individuals brought together by an accident of fortune in the barrack cells. You can remember the poor peasant who deserted when he received a letter from his father demanding he join in the reaping; the Lombrosian deserter whose sorties out always ended up in the whorehouses on calle Robadors; the queer detained there for the sole crime of being one, and whom the officers in their drunken parties would order out of the cell to sing and dance in front of them dressed and made up like a woman; the lad who dictated a letter to you with only this address, "To Pepe who sells melons on the Side of the Road," and you never persuaded him that without more exact details the letter would never arrive; finally the day a small, stunted recluse wrapped himself up in his friend's soft, clean sheet, masturbated, and ejaculated over it, provoking the wrath of the others and a noisy attempt at lynching.

Your indignation at the abuses and outrages of the system, restrained within the barracks, is poured out in every line on the pages of your correspondence. But the events of February 1956—the first open political crisis within the regime—and subsequent police measures—the arrest of Ridruejo, Pradera, Múgica, Miguel Sánchez Mazas—force you to take extreme precautions. Thanks to some friends who travel, like Jaime Salinas, and are willing emissaries, you inform Monique regularly of all that is happening: you tell her how blacklists of oppositionists are circulating in Barcelona, those who must be neutralized if necessary, and your name appears there as "the C.P.'s intellectual link with abroad." Although these are only alarmist rumors, you and your colleagues take them seriously and for some days you break off all contact and meetings. "In such circumstances," you write, "I honestly don't know what awaits me: I cannot even make plans: will I complete my military service without any problems? Will they grant me a visa?" Fortunately things go no further and, after Ruiz Giménez's dismissal, life returns to its normal channels. However, foreseeing future obstacles, you establish alternative methods of communication through intermediaries while awaiting her next trip.

Monique's frequent calls and visits to Barcelona have repercussions on the hypocritical, evasive but irritating relationship you maintain with your father. The would-be trips to Calafell and prolonged absences from home and barracks reveal the kind of bond that offends his Catholic principles. While María Antonia's family background and religious upbringing put her beyond suspicion despite the frequency of her meetings with Luis—to such an extent that years later he will point out to you that both needed great strength of character "not to fall into temptation"—he has no doubts about your clandestine affair with a Frenchwoman. But, as you are quick to notice, if Monique is "the divorced Jewess" with whom you are living in sin, your cohabitation seems to have taken a weight from his mind and does not arouse the same reproaches as it would have in your brothers: his secret, unavowed apprehension that you were homosexual, incubated and latent since the episode with Grandfather, might have robbed him of hours of sleep, and even with her matrimonial separation and "Jewish blood," Monique seems a lesser evil to him. His easygoing views about her and confidences to Luis and José Agustín make his ambiguity transparent. When his younger sister meets Monique's mother by chance in Puerto Alcudia, her very favorable opinion of her and her bourgeois position alleviate his fears that you are in the hands of someone on the make and lead him to accept the accomplished fact: although without the blessing of the Church, your partner is "normal." His death, eight years later, will protect him from confronting a truth much harder to handle than his brutal discovery of your Communist sympathies: the development and flowering in one of his sons, despite his precautions and defenses, of that monstrous seed of disorder, aberration, and deviance from the maternal side that was the obsession of his life, although he had laughingly, in vain, tried to exorcise it.

A HIGHLY FORTUNATE COINCIDENCE *of lasting consequences for you determined that the company to which you were sent as a sergeant was mainly made up of Murcians and Andalusians. Until then, circumstances had imposed on you a reluctant distancing from them: fleeing the injustice and greed of their land, they came to the industrial regions in the north of Spain hoping to find work and a roof over their heads, only normally to meet exploitation very much like that from which they were fleeing. Overcrowded, next to the gypsies in the slum belt surrounding Barcelona, they were marginalized and discriminated against by the indigenous population, marked out with the insulting label of* xarnegos. *The wretched conditions in which they camped out and the continued persistence of their migration had often led you to wonder about their situation in their native provinces; however, apart from the odd chance encounter on one of your forays into the slum areas, you never had an opportunity to mix with them or consider their problems. The negative opinion held by your social milieu, including the nationalist sectors, was based on their ignorance, laziness, and excessive birthrate when it was not preoccupied with their supposed enthusiasm to join the Civil Guard and other repressive branches of the army and the police. As Albert Manent's friend had said at the university, "without those Andalusian guards they send us from Madrid, Catalonia would be free."*

Your company's soldiers came from the most forgotten areas of the steppes of Spain. Their social and cultural defenselessness, the jokes that the others sometimes played on them, very naturally predisposed you in their favor: you remember as if it were today the time when two of them went out for a walk, as they used to in their villages and as men still do in the whole of North Africa, with their little fingers entwined, and the laughter and sarcastic comments their innocent gesture gave rise to. Transplanted into the city directly from their farms and villages, some seemed frightened by the traffic and the bustle, crossed the road clumsily, and gazed in amazement at the much freer, casual ways of the local boys and girls. Catalonia was their El Dorado and the majority cherished plans of settling down there. Almost all had a friend or a relative in Somorrostro, Pueblo Seco, Casa Antúnez, or La Verneda; but knowledge of the situation their fellow countrymen struggled with daily did not discourage them. As they would gradually reveal to you in your conversations with them, the poverty of the Barcelona hovels implied an escape from an even harsher, more inhuman poverty that apparently gave no sign of softening.

This discovery inspired you with the desire to travel to their land. The recruits with whom you would break regulations when you had the chance by going out for a drink together would talk to you with real feeling about their villages:

Mazarrón, Aguilas, Totana, Pulpí, Huercal Overa, Garrucha, Lubrín, Níjar, Carboneras ... The story of their life there, its beauty and backwardness moved you. Although your obsession after leaving the army was to depart from Spain as soon as possible, Monique wanted holidays in the sun: impressed by the stories of your friends, you suggested a trip by bus through the coastal towns of Murcia and Almería; she was delighted with the idea. When, free at last of your military duties, you welcomed her as before on the station platform, your space to be happy would no longer be the Barrio Chino or the Ramblas or the shiny, soft bed in the Cosmos. Impatient, excited, wanting to drink, make love in new settings, you caught the train to Valencia, on the way to Guardamar, Cartagena, and the distant beaches of the luminous, longed-for south.

Purifying bath, brilliance of epiphany: fleeting images imbricate, visual maelstrom, expansive bliss: a prolonged operation to thread in a veiled order, the torrential flow of still photos: violently dislocated strata, bare, clean stretches of whitish land, erosion refining down ochre stones subject to slow, millennial torture: thirsty tracks, scattered oleanders, stunted vegetation, the ubiquitous sun: a light that seems to vibrate and thicken while the bus wearily clings to the leaden tar on the road: flattened hovels, shining firmament, repressed, ephemeral attempts at greenery: pervasive sensation of beauty and wretchedness, cruel, unshod, ragged existence, heartless mineral splendor: the exhausted tranquillity of mountains with tight rumps, sharp, broken backs, and heads embellished by a painter's capricious palette: skin rash, pink sores, sinuous scars, whitish gashes: desolation, severity, magnificence, corrosive pain, diaphanous splendor: an instinctive, spontaneous affection for the sumptuous, orphaned landscape, sharp realization of the enjoyment of your identification, blinding recognition of your spatial frame: affinity, immediacy, harmony with an almost African land that endows the journey with the initiating aura of a second, deferred nativity.

As bitter as crab apple: that's how the boy defines his own region, the boy who, lying on the sand next to you, vaguely flourishes his arm toward the harsh, burnt countryside, the beach blurred by the mist, the plain, white town sunk in the lethargic depths of the siesta: ravaged, bloodless land, abandoned mines, ruined chimneys, blackish profusion of slag: evidence of past euphoria aggravating the unwelcoming impression of poverty: horizontal lives, yawning caves, calcareous desolation, ancestral stubbornness: women in mourning, prematurely worn out, laden with pitchers next to the freshet: sleepwalking peasants, strings of mules, sad, silent men peacefully sheltering under a sunshade: no change nor likelihood of change: solitude, repetition, monotony, desire to escape, to throw the dust off the soles of their shoes: emigration to Madrid, Barcelona, France, wherever: the price of a bus ticket and a suitcase with their only inheritance: their brutal life-sentence and also their hope.

A drowsy, decrepit, colonial city: police dressed in drill and wearing white tropical hats: horse-drawn carriages sway indolently: the marketplace bustles promiscuously: the Hotel Simón with its ancient rooms.

Discovery of rhythms, smells, voices, sweet apprenticeship in idleness: tentative exploration of the urban scene, horror and fascination intermingle, inner civil war, insoluble contradiction: plurality, alternating current: creative, spermal spark, product of a simultaneous collision: an exercise in ecstatic contemplation of a world that in another way wounds your defenseless moral sensibility.

The harsh, guttural or singsong accent of the south, through which your love for your language will perhaps mysteriously be filtered: territory conquered inch by inch, listening to the dull tones of resignation and poverty, gradual dual apprehension of a possible belonging and of the uncertain, chance nature of the doubtful identity granted to you.

Your indifference to Spain—that incomplete, fragmentary entity, which is sometimes obtuse and pigheaded, at other times brutal and tyrannical—in whose negligent bosom you have grown, will suffer the impact of the brief, fruitful trip through the region of Almería: to your youthful tiredness with the pobre, brut, trist, dissortat *native town beautifully evoked by Espriu, and to the dreams of escaping to some place in the north where the people are* neta i noble, culta, rica, lliure, desvetllada i feliç *will be counterposed henceforth to the image of a radiant, captive landscape whose power of attraction will divert your compass and draw it toward the tormented configuration of its tracks, hills, and steppes: your first holidays with Monique, on the eve of your journey to Paris, will thus be cause for an unforeseen, fertile combination: source and subject of nostalgia, compensatory vision of a frustrated homeland, glimpse, hint, forerunner of a world that is still fantastic but already present in your mind, silent, near, lying in wait for you.*

REALMS OF STRIFE

· I ·

The Stealer of Strength

WHEN I MOVED temporarily into Monique's flat on the rue Poissonnière, I was again toying with the idea turned over so often with Castellet and Elena de la Souchère of creating a forum for both the opposition in exile and within Spain to discuss political and literary trends in European culture. My first thought on that 15 September 1956, which would be the start of decades away from Barcelona and Spain, was to suggest to Mascolo the setting up of a committee of French anti-Fascist intellectuals supportive of such an enterprise. Shortly after my arrival, Monique and I were invited to dinner on the rue Saint-Benoît with a group of writers Mascolo had informed of the plan: not only his companion Marguerite Duras and members of the clan but also authors like Edgar Morin and Roland Barthes, whose *Mythologies* I had read avidly in Garrucha weeks before in regular installments in *Les Lettres Nouvelles*. However, to my great consternation, the conversation over dinner centered on the possible success of an assassination attempt on Franco's life. Apparently such a liquidation was feasible in a bullring: one of the guests had been to a bullfight presided over by the dictator and was emphatic he would be an easy target. The police did not suspect tourists: a foreign-looking crack marksman could sit in a nearby box without alarming anyone, shoot and then melt into the crowd, taking advantage of the first moments of confusion. The then secretary to Sartre, Jean Cau, warmed equally to the idea: weeks later, in the course of a political discussion on the rue Poissonnière, he confidently, almost arrogantly, declared that he was capable of organizing single-handedly within a few months the outbreak of revolution in Spain. My idea of a committee did not prosper, despite that first rush of enthusiasm in our after-supper discussions on the rue Saint-Benoît nourished by a generous intake of alcohol. History was in a hurry, the world was entering an eventful era, and the political compass of Mascolo and his friends would immediately swing toward new poles of attraction. The internal crisis of the Soviet system in Poland and Hungary, Nasser's nationalization of the Suez Canal, and the NLF offensive in Algeria hogged the newspaper headlines, and the modest, minor cause of Spain was suddenly of no interest. Mascolo went to Warsaw and returned in a state of great political and emotional excitement, in love with a young Polish lady who lived with him for a while a few months later. Monique and I accompanied them on a long weekend trip to Chartres and Chinon. When we visited him on his return, Wyborowa vodka had replaced dry sherry, and instead of the background flamenco music that followed his holidays in Spain, we now listened to a mournful, almost whining chorus of Slav or Baltic melodies across the staircase landing.

The Budapest rebellion crushed by Soviet tanks shook meanwhile the firmness of our convictions. Monique was still a member of the French CP and I still saw in Paris some of Luis's comrades, members of the Barcelona university group. The spectacle of thousands of demonstrators storming the local office of *L'Humanité* shocked and upset both of us. The police cordoned off the area, and when I went down to the street to see what was happening, one of Reventós and Pallach's comrades-in-arms, the trade unionist Ramón Porqueras, was shouting anti-Soviet slogans. His vehement tone filled me with dismay: the Hungarian events confused me. If, on the one hand, Mascolo, Marguerite Duras, and generally the French writers I knew denounced Russian imperialism and spoke of a second Kronstadt, on the other, my Spanish friends maintained unperturbed that it was a bourgeois uprising and fruit of intricate counterrevolutionary plotting. Octavio Pellissa or one of his comrades went to the press conference given by one of the first refugees from Budapest. He was an obese, decadent individual, laden with rings, complete with French accent learned in childhood from governesses or nurses, the total opposite of those heroic militiamen in the dramatic photographs of the pages of *Paris Match*: a reactionary bastard, they said, whose wealth had been expropriated by the new society and who, not content with saving his ugly skin, dared to criticize from Paris the magnificent conquests of the people. Monique was more exposed than I to the indignation that abounded in intellectual circles, and her faith in the Party evaporated:* I remember accompanying her, as her partner, to a district branch meeting in the side road leading to the Bonne Nouvelle church, next to the steps later filmed by Louis Malle in *Zazie dans le métro*. The agreed agenda items avoided all mention of events in Hungary and, rather than an assembly of revolutionaries, I had the impression I was attending a meeting of the parish council or of Catholic Action devoted to planning or completing routine duties. My reference to Khrushchev's report, published by the bourgeois but not the Communist press, led to an embarrassing silence: although a number of those present were certainly familiar with the report, it had not received the blessing of the leadership and did not officially exist. Mon-

---

* Her friends Claude Roy, Roger Vailland, and J-F Rolland deserted the ranks of the CP at that time.

ique yielded to the friendly pressure of branch companions and renewed her Party card, but she ceased to participate in activities and gradually distanced herself from the organization.

In the first hectic weeks of my stay in Paris I also met up with Spanish exiles and visitors from the Peninsula who were mostly within the orbit of the Spanish CP: Tuñón de Lara, Antonio Soriano, owner of the Spanish bookshop on the rue de Seine, Eduardo Haro Tecglen, Ricardo Muñoz Suay, Alfonso Sastre and Eva Forest, and Juan Antonio Bardem. A few days after my arrival, Mascolo took me to the office of Maurice Nadeau, editor of *Les Lettres Nouvelles*, so I could tell him about my idea for a Spanish magazine aimed at breaking the tight grip of the censor. This was the first of a series of related initiatives that usually ended, after interminable futile discussions, vetoes, expulsions, and confrontations, with the project being shelved and forgotten, but only after provoking in those involved feelings of anger and hurt pride that were difficult to heal. Although Nadeau generously approved the plan, he did not have the means to finance it and advised us to negotiate with Albert Beguin and Paul Flamand. After my visit to the former, we accompanied Mascolo and Muñoz Suay to the latter's office. Flamand, at the time the editor of le Seuil, gave us a courteous welcome. As I was setting out in general terms the political and literary range of the project, I realized that my argument, or rather the scheme's viability, was not convincing the man opposite me. The enterprise as presented to him was political philanthropy pure and simple and of no interest to a responsible publisher. After a pointless wait of some weeks, I put the fantastic concept to one side and decided to wait for that hypothetical moment to resurrect it when favorable developments within the Peninsula would naturally put the spotlight on Spain.

Around this time—October 1956—I met Eduardo Haro Tecglen in the Deux Magots café. He was a journalist on the Madrid daily *Informaciones* and the author, as I would later discover, of an amusing analysis of Spanish censorship and of the most original theories on the subject of the current minister of the department, Rafael Arias Salgado, which had just appeared unsigned in the magazine *Esprit*. With the knowing, mysterious air of one at the center or in the holy of holies of the organization, Muñoz Suay led me to understand that Haro was "one of us"—the password or magic phrase that in years or months to come Party members would whisper in my ear, suggesting a flattering complicity. One of the first to be endowed with that halo of concealed, almost sibylline prestige was, to my surprise, Enrique Llovet, the Spanish general consul. Before we were introduced, I remember Muñoz Suay and Bardem telling me that "you could talk freely" with him. With their go-ahead, I set before Llovet the idea of the magazine; but his affable caution discouraged me. A few months later, when I had already abandoned the scheme, he invited Monique and me to his home for dinner, on the eve of our planned trip to Almería.* His wife, the daughter of Ricardo Baeza, the writer and translator of Oscar Wilde, defended much more liberal positions than his own and, against the old Trojan-horse Leninist practice of infiltrating the enemy, she was in favor of a public break with the Régime to bring his ambiguous diplomatic role to an abrupt, sensational end. A kind of euphoria we all shared lulled us into believing that Franco's days in power were numbered. In the space of a year, the Party had extended the radius of its clandestine activity into the different branches of the country's cultural life, gaining positions and influence there never again to be reached; but the phenomenon was limited, as facts would soon prove, to a very narrow segment of the intelligentsia and had not spread, as we then believed, to the historic protagonists of the revolution, the proletariat and the peasantry. The momentary rapprochement of the Party to a handful of civil servants and members of the Spanish ruling class was and would be interpreted not just as individual breaks whose centrifugal strength was cast within the framework of the relentless pressure of an unchanging social order, but as a general indication that the inner disintegration of Francoism had reached the centers of power, now convinced of its imminent demise and the advent of a new society in which the Party would naturally play a leading, rallying role. The later, almost Pauline conversions of some children of ministers of the Régime or aristocrats like the Duchess of Medina Sidonia would for years bolster the hopeful but mistaken image of the country as a "volcano on the point of erupting." I don't doubt that this revolutionary subjectivism or voluntarism was necessary to maintain the structure and morale of an organization constantly under attack in its long and often disheartening trek across the desert. Nevertheless, the unwarranted belief in a discourse developed for propaganda or tactical reasons became over time a kind of mirage or self-deception, as I learned to my cost in 1964, during the internal Party crisis that climaxed in the expulsion of my friends Semprún and Claudín. This mystification, of which we were all victims to a greater or lesser extent, was difficult to diagnose in the early stages. Within our small circle the feeling that great changes were in the offing was strengthened daily with new examples and experiences. In one of the consulate offices on the boulevard Malesherbes, Llovet had introduced me to a colleague of his, the vice-consul Rafael Lorente. A generous, impulsive extrovert, endowed

---

* On Tuesday, 12 February 1957, according to Monique's diary, to which I shall be referring whenever I mention a date.

at times with that likable, youthful, irresponsible extravagance that is so common in Spain, Rafael displayed great interest in getting to know me. He made several visits that autumn to the rue Poissonnière to tell me his personal anxieties and political worries: unlike my Spanish friends he was sure that Communism would not survive Budapest and was trying to organize people like me into a new party that we would jokingly baptize "the party of caring snobs." One night he came to ask me a favor: he wanted to be introduced to la Pasionaria, to converse and have a drink with her. Although I said I didn't know her and was totally unaware whether she secretly resided in France or the Soviet Union, I saw he only half believed me. Then under the influence of the cognac or calvados I was pouring him, he told me of his plan to land in Fernando Poo with a handful of friends and proclaim the Republic: if we could withstand the onslaught of Franco's navy for a few days, we could bring together there both the politicians and government in exile and win diplomatic recognition from socialist-bloc countries. Although we never spoke of the subject again nor mentioned his meeting alone with la Pasionaria, I continued to see him for several months until, after receiving another posting, he decided to abandon his career and, infected by my enthusiasm for Almería, settle down in the coastal village of Aguas Amargas and devote himself to the cultivation of his land.

However, Rafael Lorente was a pleasant, unusual exception in the group of Spaniards surrounding me, all of us steeped in crude, vulgar Marxism, almost always through Politzer's dogmatic simplifications, and a linear conception of history based on so-called scientific observations. Alfonso Sastre was obsessed by the idea of compromise and hesitated even at that time about asking to join the Party, but he did not vacillate for long: on his return to Madrid, after his son's birth, he entered the organization and was soon catapulted onto its central committee. Antonio Soriano and Tuñón de Lara, with their long but discreet records as militants, did not talk about their political connections and remained tolerant and open. The future publicist and popularizer of history had just published a book on Spain written jointly with a Hispanist, Dominique Aubier, whom my French friends carefully avoided. She would later be known in my adoptive province as the "Dame de Carboneras," and would wear an Indian sari and ride on the back of a camel deep in a cabbalistic reading of Cervantes. She already displayed an exuberant passion for Spain, translated the chroniclers of the Indies and, as I had the opportunity to discover, welcomed visitors to her flat on the rue de Seine in a bullfighter's hat—the cool fount of her stylistic inspiration, she would add. Tuñón and Soriano tolerated the torrent of overpowering rhetoric as best they could, but I was less patient than they and resolved at once to avoid her: once apprised of my plan for a magazine, she had wanted to participate, decide

on the content, on who should and should not contribute. Her interference alarmed more than one friend and was probably crucial in my loss
of heart and subsequent decision to throw in the towel.

My stubborn loyalty to the idea of a magazine bore fruit many years
later, by which time I had already abandoned en route many an illusion
and flourish. Although my early sociability faded with time and the idea
of teamwork no longer appealed, I still associated myself with the *Cuadernos de Ruedo Ibérico* enterprise and lent my voice from the start to the
Libre scheme, knowing that it would never bring me any satisfaction nor
really suit my character. As in other areas of my life, I would achieve the
objective I had anxiously sought at a moment when it had lost its previous attraction and my interests and taste were heading in a new
direction. I would make moves at the wrong time and even against the
tide of history, and changes and new developments would catch me
without appetite rather than unawares—like the absurd, untimely corpse
of Franco, whose death I had ceased to believe in.

What most impresses me as I review, pen in hand, and with the hindsight
of thirty years, my first months in France are the different political
positions or, more precisely, the varying degrees of political maturity and
experience of the Parisian or Spanish friends who appear in these pages:
while the latter as Party members or sympathizers lapped up their daily
copy of *L'Humanité* and accepted its theses and explanations of the radiant
society of the future, the former had already passed through this phase,
spoke scornfully or with distaste of the USSR and pursued a complex,
sophisticated political line which, although in my view unrealistic and
even ridiculous, was nevertheless much more lucid and honest than the
color-blindness and moral deafness at which my compatriots and I
excelled or would excel. Apart from a few isolated exceptions like Soriano
and Muñoz Suay, everybody judged harshly my friendship with those
"renegades" and expelled members. My close relationship with the contingent on the rue Saint-Benoît, Roger Stéphane—whom I would soon
meet through Monique—and Elena de la Souchère, aroused the reservations and criticisms of my comrades until the need to resort to the
bourgeois media, like *France-Observateur* or *L'Express*, to spread or support
their new policy of "national reconciliation" or the campaign for amnesty
for Franco's political prisoners led them to revise their position and use
my connections and influences to further their own interests and aims.
But in the period covered by my narrative—including the reverberations
from Khrushchev's report and the invasion of Hungary—the "irresponsibility," "contradictions," "double game," and "anarchist spirit" of left-

wing French writers had attracted like a magnet the criticisms and withering observations of my fellow countrymen. What was behind that morbid preoccupation with human rights in Poland and Hungary? Didn't they notice perchance that the tiny, inevitable imperfections within the new societies of the popular democracies were small potatoes in relation to the social injustices and inequalities in the so-called bourgeois democracies and their lack of broadly based freedoms? By criticizing the USSR, were they not falling into a clumsy, diversionary maneuver directly or indirectly manipulated by the agents of imperialism? The genuine fickleness of the intelligentsia of the Paris Left Bank, their inclination, rightly satirized by Genet, to change causes, if not political allegiance, as they swayed to the breeze of *France-Soir* headlines, often opened the way, it is true, to such attacks and sarcasm: months later, one of the writers I entered into contact with as a result of the committee for solidarity with Spain abandoned that project entirely, and, to my great surprise, led a futile, esoteric call to support the Dalai Lama and Buddhist monks in Tibet following the Chinese invasion. However, together with these unconscious comic tics and traits of the *animaux malades de la pétition*, as one of their friends affectionately dubbed them, Mascolo and his colleagues' generosity and desire for justice—opposed both to the Right and the Party, to the moralizing of Camus and to Sartre's fellow traveling— were soon evident in a concrete, risky, and practical form—in sharp and healthy contrast to the Party's ambiguity and caution—if not in relation to Spain, at least in respect to the Algerian war. Among the devotees of Marguerite Duras's flat on the rue Saint-Benoît—Robert Antelme, Louis-René des Forêts, Blanchot, Edgar Morin, etc.—appeared Madeleine Alleins, the wife of a famous doctor and passionate defender of third-world causes: a founding member of one of the clandestine support groups for the NLF like the renowned Jeanson network, the future novelist hid money, propaganda, weapons, and even members of the Algerian resistance in the homes of her trusted friends. A few weeks after my arrival, she came to our place at the suggestion of Mascolo and asked if we would look after the organization's funds for a short period. Monique accepted unhesitatingly and, a few days later, Madeleine reappeared with a big suitcase, which we placed on the top shelf of a pantry next to the front door. For almost a year, our contact dropped in from time to time to collect the amounts of money she needed, the totals of which she spelled out in coded telephone calls to Monique at Gallimard. At such times, I would open the suitcase stuffed with five-thousand-franc notes of the period, put the right quantity in an envelope, and give it to our friend when the doorbell rang punctually. Living as I was on very little money— my only source of income came from the reader's notes I began to write for publishers—I would often lament with Monique, also dazzled by the spectacle of that prodigious Ali Baba's cave, the fact that the treasure belonged to the NLF fighters and had not been mistakenly entrusted to us by an agent of Franco, Trujillo, or Somoza, so we could cheerily spread it around traveling the world in the footsteps of Phileas Fogg.

My first contact with North Africa, through the process of decolonization, was intensified throughout the Algerian war and its hateful repercussions in the metropolis: racial discrimination, persecution of North African immigrants, curfew, murders, and *ratonnades*. Just over three years later, Monique would be one of the first to sign the "manifesto of 121," which encouraged recruits to the expeditionary force to desert and which led to a conviction for her and a dozen writer-friends for "attacking the morale of the army" and "inciting soldiers to disobey the orders of their officers": "Anyone would think I'd been streetwalking in front of a barracks!" she exclaimed in amusement when she received notification from the court. While recalling later the vicissitudes of this period and my subsequent Arab affinities, she would laugh and comment that, although she in no way regretted her signature nor the subsequent complications—summonses, telephone threats, trials—if she could relive that time, she would fight for "my" Algerians with slightly less zeal and enthusiasm.

But I must get back to the strict chronology of my narrative. In January 1957, on our return from a brief, exciting trip to Italy, the French edition of *Juegos de manos* appeared with a well-documented, enlightening introduction by Coindreau. The novelty value of a novel from Francoist Spain after fifteen years' opaque silence aroused immediate, disproportionate interest in critics from *L'Humanité* to *Le Figaro*. Left-wing newspapers and weeklies emphasized, logically enough, the novel's rebellious, nonconformist tone, my implicit but undoubted hostility to official values. In spite of its great defects, limitations, and influences, the book fulfilled an expectation and was welcomed with unstinting enthusiasm: not one of my adult works from *Señas de identidad* to the present would win in any way such wide-scale approval, which clearly indicates the time-serving imponderables of that journalistic pseudocriticism, subject in Paris as elsewhere to a combination of prejudice, fashion, self-interest, and backslapping that distorts its function and changes it into a hollow charade swinging from ecstatic praise to the heaping on of ridicule. If the furor around the novel uncovered me in no uncertain way to the Francoist authorities, it granted me in passing a degree of immunity: to the extent that the Régime aspired to European respectability, it would not do to persecute an author who had built a reputation for himself as a result of cultural activities and works that would not be considered criminal in any democratic country.

On my arrival in Paris, Monique and I had agreed that after three or four months I would return to Spain for a period: just enough time to bring myself up-to-date with the situation in intellectual and university circles and to visit, without the haste of my previous trip, the villages to the south of Garrucha. On 14 February I boarded the train in Austerlitz station pleased with myself and naively proud of my book's success. If the external vision of things predisposed me to optimism and even euphoria, the relentless, implacable flow of facts at once brought me back to reality. After my happy, stimulating stay on the rue Poissonnière, the return to Pablo Alcover dampened my spirits: decrepit people and things, cold, stingy light, my father's anxious questions, Grandfather's silence, Eulalia's pathetic smile, diffuse oppression, painful memories, anguish, anxiety, remorse. The depression that was insidiously overpowering me in the family hearth filled with skeletons from the past was deepened by an event that occurred on the eve of my arrival: Octavio Pellissa's arrest. His capture endangered the university group organized by Sacristán, and Luis, who was directly threatened, was being extremely cautious. I remember that just after my return someone rang our doorbell very early in the morning, when we were both asleep in our bedroom at the front of the house. Eulalia peeped into the garden and came and informed us, with that worried look brought on by our new acquaintances, that a man was asking after us. We were startled by the news but, belying our apprehension, the visitor turned out to be, not the feared police inspector, but an old friend of mine from Paris, the art critic Arnau Puig, sent from there by the CP leadership to find out the cause and extent of the raid in which Pellissa had been arrested. That rather rash and amateur mission to enable my brother to put him in contact with the "cadres" of the organization rightly alarmed Luis: the elementary lack of caution at a time when he was possibly being watched was not at all in keeping with the need for the meticulous rigor of clandestine activity. Although Octavio bravely resisted the "interrogations" and was the only Communist student to be caught, the police clean-up operation extended on the following days to every area of opposition, from monarchists and Catalan nationalists to the socialists of Pallach and Joan Reventós.

In the midst of that oppressive atmosphere, which was both uncertain and threatening, we tried to lead a normal existence: we dined out with friends who were less compromised than we were, visited the bars of Escudillers and the Ramblas and returned home in the early morning. But the earlier excitement of my forays into the red-light districts had disappeared: my cheerfulness was forced, I was bored by the nightly sessions with whores and queers in La Venta and El Cádiz: we wearily complied with the empty, tedious ritual. Monique telephoned me daily and our long conversations in French mysteriously disturbed my father. His instinctive, but well-placed, fear of our suspicious carryings-on kept him awake until we were back: as we tiptoed across the passageway, we heard him stirring medicine or yogurt with his spoon, then look for his light switch and without fail ask us the time. Under the pressure of circumstances I abandoned the planned trip to Almería: in case of danger or a new police roundup, I would be unable to help or get information from that remote and isolated province. Monique, for her part, began to be worried by the politicizing of my novel in Paris and, finally persuaded that I would be more useful outside than in, I decided to cut short my visit and rushed back to Paris.

To avoid being exposed at the first police passport control between Massanet and Gerona to the needless danger of inspectors consulting with central police headquarters, I thought of the idea, which now seems childish and ridiculous, of catching the train in Figueras. Jaime Gil de Biedma, whom I sometimes accompanied on his most cautious nocturnal ventures on the Ramblas,* offered to drive me there, and I remember how en route, in the late afternoon sun of 2 March, he brushed against the wheel of a cart he was overtaking and we almost skidded and crashed, either as a result of his jittery nerves at that journey-cum-escape or his absorption in our weighty conversation on Gramscian compromise. After apologizing to the muleteer, we continued the drive to Figueras and said our goodbyes when the train arrived. The passport check proceeded without incident in the down-at-the-heels station of Port Bou: the inspectors stamped mine without comment and minutes later I was on French soil.

The frontier syndrome, which developed on my first journeys outside Spain, gradually diminished with the frequency of trips, as I learned to control my fears, but vanished completely only upon the death of the dictator. In years subsequent to the present stage of my narrative, when I crossed the frontier in potentially riskier circumstances, I did so with greater sangfroid, a mixture of casual indifference, fatalism, and irrational faith in my lucky stars that amazed those around me. The cheeky bravado of such an attitude aroused admiration, as I had noticed in the university militia camp where I spent the first months of my military service, on the day I decided to slope off, come what may, and not go through with the drills or exercises I most detested. However, in neither case was it in fact these qualities, but something more modest: my personal inability to accept the likelihood of punishment, my superstitious faith in a separate destiny. Sustained by both, I acted without considering the risks. To talk

---

* See his *Diario del artista seriamenta enfermo*, Barcelona, 1974.

then of courage would not reflect the reality of the feelings with which I confronted my journeys in 1960 and '61; nevertheless, if at decisive moments I acted with a calm of which I am proud, my dreams were finally penetrated by the threat implicit in everything related to Spain. The ambiguous nature of my future relationship with Spain could perhaps be explained by the country's early association with a nebulous idea of danger, with a place where one could be arrested for no reason. While my European colleagues walked the world in a state of innocent tranquillity, conscious of exercising an inalienable right, I did so for years in a state of suppressed terror, with the persistent but fortunately mistaken foreboding that, like Luis, I was walking into the lions' den and sacrificing myself to a cannibalistic saturnine deity that implacably devoured its more lucid children. My early experiences at home reinforced the impression of fatally belonging to a nation eternally at war with itself that relentlessly trans-mitted its savage settling of accounts from one generation to another. Until I was well into my forties, Spain would symbolize for me not a welcoming, benign land receptive or at least indifferent to my labors on behalf of its language and culture, but a hostile arena of rejection threatening punishment from unexpected quarters. It is difficult to erase the scars left by dictatorships and totalitarian régimes. The treatment is long and uncertain: ten years after Franco's death, it is quite revealing in respect to myself that I still feel more at ease in Paris, Marrakesh, New York, or Istanbul than in the cities and places that formed the backdrop, for good or for evil, to the fears and fantasies of my childhood and youth.

On my brief visits to Spain in February and August 1957 I explained to my few journalist friends on the official press Gallimard's publishing plans, namely, our efforts to promote in France the most outstanding novels recently printed in the Peninsula. The list of works under contract included a good dozen authors representative of different postwar narra-tive trends—Cela, Delibes, Ana María Matute, Sánchez Ferlosio, Fer-nández Santos, etc.—but this initiative would be predictably met in Madrid with suspicion and mistrust, although less Cain-like countries than ours would have greeted it with praise. Some writers who were not selected and enjoyed posts of responsibility in the official ranks of the Régime began to communicate their anger and pique through the Movement's press. The translation of a proscribed work, *La otra cara* by José Corrales Egea, served as a pretext for the launching of a campaign of slander led by Aparicio, still the General Director of Press, and his col-league from *Pueblo*, Emilio Romero. The departure of the former in 1958 may have opened up new areas of cultural freedom, with the appearance of magazines like *Acento* and the timid, drip-feed surfacing of the name of some banned writer, but it did not substantially change the situation.* The attacks in *Pueblo* and *Arriba* intensified, coinciding with the publication of my manifesto, or statement, by *Ínsula* magazine, "Toward a National Popular Literature": perhaps Emilio Romero was offended by the fact that not a single creation of his own genius figured in the collection I was mounting and so launched an offensive, through his acolytes, against "the rival to Blasco Ibáñez based in France" whose sinister "customs-officer" role prevented, in his view, contact with the real glories of our contemporary literature.

The *Ínsula* manifesto, a product of an insatiable reading of Gramsci and not of my own still modest narrative experience, led to a ripple in the quiet waters through which the magazine used to steer, because of my rather unfocused and unfair criticisms of Ortega and my obvious, if rather confused, threading of openly Marxist theses. What surprises me most when I reread it today is not the revisiting of stale formulas repeated with wearisome insistence by professional "progressives," but the chasm separating the ideas and slogans set out there and my literary personality and novelistic production: none of the work of my youth—*Juegos de manos, Duelo en el paraíso, Fiestas, El circo*—had fortunately anything in common with the waffly schema for national popular literature that I propounded, nor did the sensationalist strident promotion of my fiction in Europe and North America harmonize with the somewhat Barresian Gramscianism that it flaunted. Guillermo de Torre, in his acid response to the pamphlet, would rightly underline the weakness of its premise and, without fighting shy of *ad hominem* arguments, its flagrant lack of coherence. The *enfant terrible* of the Barcelona bourgeoisie that my New York publisher, in his raucous publicity material, compared to the then fashionable Françoise Sagan did not suit the helmet and armor of the provincial ideologue who assailed the lack of transcendence in decadent, dehumanized experimental literature. Criticism scored a direct hit when it brought to light the duality of my position or, rather, the gap between mask and reality: while my work revealed the influence of Gide, Malraux, Faulkner, and the young southern novelists, my manifesto implicitly rejected those authors and defended principles and norms at the other end of the spectrum. Although in my wounded pride I would not admit to the shortcomings and contradictions denounced by my adversary, I did from then on strive to align my writing with the more or less Marxist declarations I was parading about: after failing with *La resaca*, my attempt at a social novel, I followed in the footsteps of Rocco Scotellaro, Vittorini, and Pavese, trying

---

* Aparicio temporarily suspended the publication of *Ínsula* and *Índice*, despite the carefulness of the former and the notorious ambiguity of the latter.

out, with greater or lesser success, the literary mode of social documentary and short story, from *Campos de Níjar* to *Pueblo en marcha*. With his usual clumsiness, Julián Marías had indirectly attributed my article to an international conspiracy against Ortega and had evoked in this respect the specter of "Maoist communes" and, together with the spontaneous reactions of other opponents, allowed me nevertheless to interpret the polemic as the fruit of a counterattack from the right and thus sidestep the indispensable debate with myself. That Corrales Egea, Juan Nuño, and other Marxists came to my defense spared me the need to reflect on the dichotomy of my behavior and hidden moral schizophrenia: numerous intellectuals from the Spanish-speaking world still commonly have the attitude that they can chase success and take advantage of the benefits of bourgeois democracies, win scholarships, and teach in North American universities, and at the same time adopt extremist Jacobin, dogmatic positions in the field of politics and theory.

As far as I am concerned, the mismatch between life and writing was not resolved till some years later, when hand-to-hand combat with the latter, the exploration of new areas of expression and conquest of subjective authenticity, gradually integrated the former in a universe of text: the world conceived as a book ceaselessly written and rewritten, rebelliousness, struggle, excitement fused in life and script as I was consumed by the delights, white heat, torments of the composition of *Don Julián*.

Seven months later I embarked with Monique on the visit to Almería, postponed because of Octavio Pellissa's arrest; we left her daughter in the Valencian village of Beniarjó and paid a return visit to our friends in the pensión Zamora in Garrucha. In a small four-horsepower Renault we drove round the villages and communities of the area: Huércal Overa, Cuevas de Almanzora, Mojácar, Palomares, and Villaricos. Monique was deeply impressed by the forlorn poverty we saw: she did not share the personal motivation nor secret affinities which drew me to that land, and she was horrified by the idea of vacationing, sunbathing, enjoying life with the reptilian indifference of a Swedish blonde in a landscape that was luminous and beautiful while harsh and poverty stricken. That was the starting point for our frequent discussions of the subject: Monique would reproach me from then on for my aesthetic fascination for places, regions, and landscapes where living conditions inevitably offended anyone with a minimum of social awareness. I was more hardened than she to the spectacle of poverty and strangely attracted by human qualities and features that have been inexorably swept away by the leveling commercialization of progress: my attitude was indeed ambiguous. The feelings of immediacy and emotional warmth that I discovered in Almería provoked a painful, bitter, insoluble conflict within me. Moral anguish based on the reality of my experience would then emerge: it was not the superficial by-product of my class guilt or reading of Marx, but the fruit of thoughts that encompassed sympathy and solidarity alike. My desire to denounce the reality was tempered by love and prospective nostalgia for what I was denouncing: the struggle to eradicate the iniquitous situation that pre-dominated in Almería did not exclude the real, if uncomfortable, con-viction that the necessary social and economic transformation would sweep away in its path those ingredients of openness, close-knit living, and spontaneity that were the seed of my commitment. I did not allow myself to be paralyzed by this conflict but returned to the province alone, determined to write an eyewitness account. In the future this southern aesthetic would color my interventions in the area and reflect in its light the hidden turmoil or civil war between the realities of beauty and underdevelopment: as I would point out in one of my first exercises in lucidity, we intellectuals who are not single-minded but are made up of variegated, antithetical features struggle for a world that we will perhaps find uninhabitable.

Rather than continue to Sorbas and Carboneras as we had initially planned, we turned off toward Granada and Málaga in pursuit of greater comfort and pleasure. I returned to Almería without Monique in August 1958 and in March 1959 and explored the disturbing region of Níjar on foot, by truck, and by bus, and when I had finished the manuscript of the book in Paris—fusing in one journey for reasons of narrative practicality the incidents, events, and encounters of the different visits—I returned to scrutinize the whole area by car, in order to photograph the places described in the account with the film director Vicente Aranda. My later journeys to the region were in difficult circumstances that did not favor my aims: if, on the one hand, Luis's arrest, the Milan affair, and the furor aroused by the press around our wretched name exposed my apparent freedom of movement as an illusion, on the other hand, the appearance of *Campos de Níjar*, in spite of the censor's *nihil obstat*, had provoked the angry reaction of the town mayor and the provincial government authorities. While in 1959 I managed to penetrate incognito the cave district of La Chanca, on the pretext of looking for the relative of a friend exiled in Grenoble, without raising the suspicions of the inhabitants or attracting police interest, a year later my presence did not go undetected and I was forced to take a number of precautions: in the company of Vicente Aranda, I first visited Almería with Simone de Beauvoir and Nelson Algren and then with the filmmaker Claude Sautet, without daring to pursue my surveys of Níjar or La Chanca. My fear of compro-mising my informants was not at all imaginary, as I would later be able to prove at the bullrunning in Albacete. However, stripped of its purpose and attractions, my stay in Almería became meaningless. Like the locals, I was imprisoned in a diffuse atmosphere of policed freedom and felt caught with them in the net. It is difficult to express the bitterness and gloom with which I would decide not to return, thus depriving myself of the warmth and sense of belonging that by instinct, and in compensation, I would search out and find in North Africa.

The writing of *Campos de Níjar* closes a chapter of my narrative in relation to Spain. It is written extremely carefully in order to avoid the attention of the censor, and the book's technique, structure, and focus can all be explained by reference to censorship: the use of ellipsis, association of ideas, implicit deductions that may seem obscure to readers used to freedom of expression but not at all to those long manacled by the censor's iron grip, who acquire, as Blanco White intelligently pointed out, "the skill of the mute at communicating with signs." An experienced student in the art of speaking to the voiceless, I took up the challenge of writing a work full of hidden messages and winks and nudges to the alert reader, without the stalwart functionaries of the Information and Tourism Ministry—information for images to please the tourists—being able to latch onto anything in particular to justify cutting even a paragraph. Although this was a victory of which I was then proud, subsequent thoughts persuaded me that it was a double-edged sword or, in other words, a Pyrrhic victory. To escape the traps and snares of the censor, I had turned myself into one. Forced to obey the rules of the game, to act within the limited field of what was possible, I had paid hateful tribute to the guardians of the Régime. As the defenders of this strategy rightly pointed out, the frontier between the banned and tolerated was not fixed and established forever: the mood of the times, persistence of writers, circumstantial changes allowed small advances, the freeing-up of space that had been closed off for a long time, a series of partial if comforting successes. Nevertheless, such an exercise involved the writer in a painful self-mutilation, the devastating effects of which would be later revealed: a continuing imposed respect for dominant norms, fear of one's own ideas, insidious conformism, exhaustion, and sterility. When adapting to the censor's rules, an author cannot be sure of emerging unharmed, of not displaying forevermore the melancholy scars and traces they leave. The idea of marking out the boundaries—of letting the censor get on with his work while I got on with mine, not worrying about his existence—slowly gained ground. Five years' practice in doing what was possible had forced me to swallow too many snakes and, as my friend Fernando Claudín would say in circumstances fairly similar to the ones I describe, everything has a limit, even the consumption of snakes. This liberating decision was obviously going to unleash unbridled attacks on my work and character:

after the salvo of accusations and insults orchestrated by the General Director of the Press, Don Adolfo Muñoz Alonso, they would ban in Spain everything I wrote up to the death of the dictator.

The absurd power that oppressive governments of right and left endow upon literature—a totally undeserved honor—by preventing its dissemination and putting all manner of obstacles in its way, arouses a curious reflex-thought in opponent practitioners of the art: the belief that a poem, novel, or theatrical work, through the mere fact of its being banned or possibly being banned, has a direct impact on reality and enjoys the miraculous virtue of molding it in its own image; an obviously inept supposition, since the influence of the literary text on the reader's mind is fortuitous and develops slowly over a long period. However, a Party comrade, filled with enthusiasm by *Campos de Níjar*, had tried to convince me on the eve of one of my visits that the account would, and these were more or less his words, "awaken the consciousness of the popular masses in the province"; with unbounded optimism and excitement concerning my powers of enlightenment, he urged me to visit the bookshops and cultural centers in Almería, introduce myself to the clerks or managers, and fruitfully discuss the work's social content. Although I did not share his illusions, I decided to follow his advice, and, once in the city, I went into the bookshop that seemed to have the best-stocked window. In muffled tones, because of the timidity that always overtakes me when I refer to my work, I asked the clerk if she had a copy of *Campos de Níjar*. Her reply, as she raised her eyebrows in an astonished, friendly look, immediately shattered my dream castles. "I'm sorry," she said, "Campos where?"

Apart from my trips to Almería, two political-cultural events in which I participated in one way or another stand out as interesting in the course of that troubled and at times bitter year of 1959: the homage to Machado in Collioure and the Peaceful National Strike of 18 June, which, according to its organizers, ought to have marked the beginning of the end for Franco's dictatorship.

In a pamphlet commemorating the Machado gathering, Claude Couffon generously attributes the initiative to me: "It was the idea of Juan Goytisolo, who at the time lived in Paris, where after the success of M.E. Coindreau's translation of his novel *Juegos de manos*, he was busy bringing Gallimard's Spanish department up-to-date. Machado was God and model of national angst for all the resistance poets of the interior. Goytisolo told me of his plan: to set up an honorary committee and bring together the two Spains in Collioure."* To tell the truth, the suggestion came not from

---

* *L'Espagne au coeur, Souvenirs à propos d'une Anthologie*, Paris, 1982.

me, but from my Party comrades: Pellissa's friend and mentor, Benigno Cáceres—a small, bespectacled man, strikingly ugly but endowed with real charm and a charismatic personality—had persuaded me of the timeliness and importance of commemorating the twentieth anniversary of the poet's death by gathering anti-Francoist writers and intellectuals of every tendency around his tomb to render homage to his political and literary stature. I became the spokesman for the idea and with the help of Couffon, Elena de la Souchère, and other friends organized the committee of distinguished names that would back the event: after visiting Bataillon at the Collège de France, I collected, among many others, the signatures of Marcelle Auclair, Cassou, Mauriac, Sarrailh, Queneau, Sartre, Beauvoir, and Tzara while my Party comrades obtained Picasso's and Aragon's. In that first fruitful harvest of famous names—an activity I would excel in for a number of years—I experienced only one refusal and partial failure: the director of the Institut Hispanique on the rue Gay-Lussac, whom I had invited to join the committee, demanded first to see the list of members and suddenly went red with rage: what the devil did Sartre and Simone de Beauvoir have to do with Machado and Spain? Albert Camus, to whom Elena de la Souchère wrote a note beginning *Cher Maître*, informed me through his secretary that he was overwhelmed by the title and that, although he supported the celebration of the poet, did not want to be part of a committee whose makeup he disliked.

On 20 February our contingent of more than a hundred people caught the night train at the Gare d'Austerlitz. On our arrival in Collioure, we met up opposite the Quintana Hotel with our friends from Madrid, Barcelona, Geneva, and elsewhere: Blas de Otero, Gil de Biedma, José Ángel Valente, Costafreda, Barral, Castellet, Caballero Bonald, Senillosa, my brother José Agustín . . . The cortège made its way to the poet's tomb, covered in flowers for the occasion, and Don Pablo de Azcárate read out a few words in the tense, emotional silence. After a crowded meal, plied with toasts and references to Machado and Spain, the small throng dispersed. There were embraces, pious wishes, souvenir photos, and farewells. Then, the return journey, in a second-class compartment, with Benigno, Isidoro Balaguer, Octavio Pellissa, discussing for hours art, politics, and literature. I can remember Benigno's passion for the latter and also his gut rejection of Cernuda's homosexuality and Arrabal's first plays. Half Pygmalion and half Tiresias, always surrounded by young militants, Benigno was in many ways a different kind of Communist, and he maintained a lively, attractive personal relationship with me right up to his illness and death.

At the end of May I went to Spain with Monique for the first literary conversations at Formentor, and when they were over I stopped in Torrentbó for a few days with Maurice E. Coindreau before returning to Paris on 9 June. In Barcelona I saw the preparations for the strike organized by the Party, with the often symbolic support of other anti-Francoist organizations: there was an atmosphere of euphoria in opposition circles, and I left with the impression that big changes were on the horizon. In the working-class districts and even on some areas of the Ensanche, strike slogans and the Protest "P" were everywhere: as it was impossible to erase them daily, the police changed the words into a Miró-style scrawl, thus converting Barcelona into an extraordinary capital of abstract graffiti. One manifesto signed by all the opposition—with the notable exception of Llopis's Socialist Party—sent through the mail, stuck on the fronts of buildings, scattered through the streets at night by brave drivers, called for a protest against the Régime's corruption and economic policies, amnesty for those in prison and in exile, the removal of Franco, and free elections. Luis and his friends had actively intervened, with differing means, in that display of propaganda: while some students threw handfuls of leaflets from the top of the El Águila department stores, others, led by Ricardo Bofill, repeated the exploit from the heights of Columbus's statue at the end of the Ramblas. Simultaneously, intellectuals, writers, and establishment personalities who could in no way be tarred with the Communist brush—such as Menéndez Pidal, Marañón, Azorín, and even General Kindelán, head of the Francoist air force during the war—supported the amnesty petition in a letter sent to the Justice Minister and which circulated clandestinely. Although the press and other news media kept a total silence, Radio España Independiente broadcast la Pasionaria's fiery calls from Moscow. Faced with this proliferation of hostile acts, the dictatorship finally set in motion its vast arsenal of weapons of dissuasion: brought to Madrid on the pretext of a routine discussion, the diplomat Julio Cerón, leader of the Popular Liberation Front (FLP), was arrested as he left his airplane in Barajas; a vast preventive raid on intellectual and working-class circles made inroads into the ranks of the Party, FLP, and MSC; the newspapers broke their silence, reacted hysterically to the danger, denouncing the "attempt at communist revolution," and dug out memories and photographs of 1936 that exemplified the crimes and atrocities of the "reds."

The prevailing climate of confrontation finally attracted the attention of the French press. Although from my first day in Paris I had warned my friends on *L'Express* and *France-Observateur* of what was on the way, their response had been lukewarm: nothing ever happened in Spain, for the moment it was best to wait. I was thus completely taken aback when, on the eve of the strike day, Florence Malraux phoned me to see if I would be interested in going to Spain as a correspondent for *L'Express*. I agreed immediately, rushed to collect my ticket from the travel agents, and caught the first plane to Barcelona. I stayed there and in Madrid for scarcely three days, after which I flew back to Paris as dejected as a bullfighter after an unlucky afternoon,* to write the report headlined "P for Protest." It was published with a by-line that read: "*L'Express*'s clandestine reporter in Spain has lived through the 'great day of protest' of the resistance to Franco and signed with the pseudonym of Thomas Lenoir in order to envelop the author in a cloud of ink." I had been eyewitness to the strike's failure—shops and businesses open, public transport chockablock, factories apparently working normally—and strove to go back to its source and provide a rationale. I will not relate now my nosy prowl round the streets near ENASA and España Industrial but will merely reprint a few paragraphs from the article which, although of necessity a piece of superficial journalism, hinted at deeper causes and may interest some readers today.

The two camps eye each other warily and a foreign observer like myself experiences a singular feeling of suspense on the days leading to the strike. Two contestants: one, the Régime, makes great show of its strength and its cards. Daily newspapers, radio, official media continuously proclaim the first; the second are fear, the army, and the police. But the people around me, all from the opposition, stress the courage and bravery of their side. Had I lived exclusively with them, the date of the 18th would have seemed a decisive watershed: all clandestine movements communicate this feverish excitement, as if the inner awareness of their weakness pushed their leaders to live in a frenzy of expectation...

The appearance of Barcelona and Madrid, their streets patrolled by the police, the ever more strident tone of the government dailies have a paradoxical calming effect on the strike promoters. The show of strength displayed by the Régime is the mold where they think they see the cast of their own power. Isolated, not knowing each other, broken up in a variety of small groups, they have only one mirror in which to glimpse their reflection: the device arranged against them. Personally, I can discern here a second error common to all clandestine movements: that they measure their imaginary strength against the real forces their adversary is methodically organizing...

The opposition leaders I managed to meet in Madrid all agreed on the failure of the strike. These were their explanations: in previous years, the strike movements in Barcelona, Madrid, Asturias, and the Basque country scored partial victories because they came spontaneously from the rank and file: on this occasion, the order came from above and the day was set by the general staffs of the political groups not in line with the situation in Spain, but as a date they could all agree on. .... The idea of a national strike was amazingly optimistic. The political illiteracy dominating the Peninsula means that the masses respond only to concrete proposals (the boycott of streetcars,

---

* That is how it would be described by Kindelán and Girbau, who were waiting in the airport for the report of another traveler, the emissary of the University Socialist Grouping.

for example) with limited objectives (a reduction in the cost of transport). . . . Fear of layoffs and unemployment—in the period of deep crisis Spain is passing through—has clipped the movement's wings. . . . But above all, beyond tactical reasoning, is the reality of a country that after twenty years of Francoism no longer has the taste for politics. If, paraphrasing Valéry, Fascism is the art of preventing people from doing what interests them, Franco, much more than Hitler, is master of the art.

I am agreeably surprised by the lucidity of this report when read a quarter of a century later, unlike other of my texts of the time, laden with the undigested deadweight of dogma. It was written straight off, without consulting my friends, free of any ideological filter or correctives, and naturally provoked angry exchanges with Party comrades, who branded it as both pessimistic and shortsighted. A few weeks after its publication, I was called by Octavio Pellissa to a meeting with two members of the leadership in a café on the place de la République. Those charged with discussing my conclusions and teaching me a friendly lesson turned out to be Jesús Izcaray and Fernando Claudín, whom I met for the first time. I remember that when we debated the problem of whether the strike could be considered a failure or not, I was impressed by the way he received my comments, a million miles from the confidence of a bringer of truths flaunted by his companion: in a rigorously organized hierarchy, like all those inspired by the Leninist model, the "correct" version of the facts always percolates from the top downwards and never in reverse or from the periphery: as Claudín would reveal to me years later, my comments and arguments really hit the mark inasmuch as he had been able to see the limitations in his work when he traveled secretly to Madrid to prepare the strike. Strangely, I had gone to Pilar and Eduardo Haro Tecglen's flat not knowing that it had served as a hideout for Claudín days before, and this clarified in retrospect the feigned bewilderment of my hosts when I asked them for news of what had happened, totally unaware that the police might have followed me. The Régime's cat-and-mouse game with the opposition fortunately had its lapses: thanks to these, we rodents could run out of danger when the cat was off hunting and momentarily sidestep the mousetrap or piece of cheese that it set out for us from its position of serene omnipotence.

Some three or four years after the date of the events I am now relating, an old Party militant, whose wife typed out my manuscripts, entrusted me with a copy of the record of secret police observations kept by the Valencian Regional Brigade of Social Investigation, which the defense lawyer of one of the recently arrested Communists on trial had got access to and secretly microfilmed in one of the courtrooms. It is an extra-ordinary, juicily significant document in the taste it gives of the methods, organization, language, and even sometimes surprisingly perceptive cultural references of an adversary who was ubiquitous, implacable, and all-embracing, but unknown and abstract beyond flourishes of power and sudden lunges, a comprehensive portrait of the unequal, quixotic, doomed-to-failure struggle of the clandestine opposition groups whose slightest muffled cry was spied on day and night by a hidden but ever-present network of informers, eavesdroppers, lookouts, and guards whose constant diligence showed up as derisively pathetic the opposition's careful efforts to maintain invisibility. The immediate, almost intimate relations between persecuted and persecutors, crossing and losing each other in bars, cafés, avenues, and on curbs, trace in filigree the image of the cat-and-mouse game I suggested before and bestow a general emblematic importance on that document, which is narrated in an impersonal, objectivized style according to the strictest canons of behaviorist fiction. When I tried to describe in *Señas de identidad* the disproportionate struggle between the police and the friends of my alter ego, Mendiola, the best way I found was to insert the secret police account into the novel itself: a real document integrated into the literary text in the same way that an artist sometimes makes his canvas from materials or substances such as sea-weed, shells, bits of rope, and ironware—rather than imitating the external world—and then paints them. The life and vicissitudes of the characters would thus acquire a degree of representativeness in the national context that went beyond the situations and plot reproduced in the book: the epitome of my personal and family history, of that of my friends and acquaintances, and, beyond them, of all the student, intellectual, and worker anti-Francoist militants who fell sooner or later in the police net during years of patient toil and vain hopes, the weaving and unweaving of Penelope's cloth, cobwebs remade and continuously stamped on or swept away by a remote deity at once stubborn and malign.

The persecution, trailing, vigilance, and arrests described in the fourth chapter of the novel faithfully translate my experience in those years. November 1958: the imprisoning of the leaders of the University Socialist Grouping, including Francisco Bustelo, Juan Manuel Kindelán, and the diplomat Vicente Girbau. June 1959: the arrest, trial, and later sentencing of Julio Cerón and the other visible heads of the FLP. The patient siege laid to Communist intellectuals and students in Barcelona became more and more obvious, and any slip or mistake in the Party security machine could automatically unleash the reflex action of the police. From March 1958 there was a worrying increase in the frequency and regularity of Luis's visits to Paris, either alone or with María Antonia. Monique's diary shows he was there in May, October, and at Christmas, when he stayed temporarily with us. I could see that an ugly, strange toilet bag made of fiber or imitation lizard skin, not at all in keeping with his taste or personality, was the hiding place for his messages and postal reports to the Party leadership. From his conversations with Pellissa I deduced that he had seen Carrillo and stepped up his activity and the level of his contacts. I also remember him arriving on the rue Poissonnière on 13 December 1959, on the eve of the journey which, together with Solé Tura, Isidoro Balaguer, and other acquaintances of mine, was to take him to the ill-omened Prague congress while, with Monique and Florence Malraux, I went to visit Genet and Abdallah in Amsterdam and enjoyed with them the spectacle of canals, bridges, museums, fading dusks, barges slow and majestic like alligators, in a precarious state of ecstasy and delight.

A few weeks later, on 7 February, from Barcelona, Barral called Monique in her office at Gallimard: Luis had suddenly fallen ill in what looked like the outbreak of an epidemic and the infection was serious. The news, which I had been dreading, depressed me not only because of the misfortune my brother was suffering at that very moment but also because of the family context in which it took place: that gloomy, spectral, decrepit universe of the Pablo Alcover residence, with the elderly trio— my father, Eulalia, and Grandfather—shattered by the catastrophe that had befallen them; my feelings of guilt and remorse at living so far from them, protected from the vision of their anguished, devastating orphanhood. The two images pursued and harrassed me, and I rushed to find Pellissa, and through him the Party, to discover what had happened and get some direction. As Pellissa would tell me hours later, the leadership was not aware of the arrests and for the moment could not take any measures or advise anything until trustworthy reports arrived. Thrown back on my own resources, I worked out a plan of action with Monique and our French friends: to inform the newspapers and weeklies that we had access to of the police operation against a dissident writer like Luis, whose novel *Las afueras* was about to be published in French by le Seuil, and to set in motion, as with the homage to Machado, the collection of well-known signatures, this time in protest. I instinctively knew that only an outcry, better still, a scandal of international dimensions, could save Luis and those, like Isidoro Balaguer and the painter Joaquín Palazuelos, caught with him, from a long stay in prison. From home and from Monique's office at Gallimard we telephoned or got in contact with a great number of writers and artists, getting their approval for a statement in which they expressed their concern about my brother's arrest and demanded he be allowed to exercise his rights to a defense as recognized in the United Nations Charter. Picasso, Sartre, Paz, Mauriac, Senghor, Genet, Peter Brook, Gabriel Marcel, Marguerite Duras, Butor, Robbe-Grillet, Queneau, Claude Simon, Nathalie Sarraute, and other figures signed the letter that was published a few days later in *Le Monde*. In Italy, through Vittorini, we got the support of Pasolini, Moravia, Carlo Levi, and twenty or so famous names. In Mexico, Max Aub, Carlos Fuentes, and the members of the 1959 Spanish Movement organized meetings and the collection of signatures. Thanks to my friends in Caracas and the magazine *Marcha*, I also got condemnations from many writers in Venezuela and Latin America.

Realizing the prejudice and suspicious nature of the bourgeois media at the slightest whiff of Communism, I tried to separate out the presentation of the case of Luis and his friends from their participation in the Prague congress. Jacques Grignon Dumoulin, a *Le Monde* journalist specializing in Spanish affairs, wrote an article in which, following my suggestions and at my insistence, he described and interpreted the arrests as a warning from the authorities to intellectuals judged to be "lukewarm and hostile to the Régime"; such an abrupt measure, he added, led one to believe that, despite its evolution in the field of diplomacy, the Francoist government had "not lost internally a single drop of its intolerance." Other similar commentaries appeared in *L'Express* and *France-Observateur*, giving fresh impetus to the collection of signatures and displays of solidarity.

The news I had of Luis through José Agustín was not encouraging. After being transferred from police headquarters to the Model Prison in Barcelona, he was sent within a few weeks to Carabanchel, which made regular visits difficult. At home the atmosphere was oppressive, and father gave his *sui generis* version of the facts to whomever would listen to him, insisting on our history as a right-wing family and our strict religious upbringing: the target of poisonous reproaches from one or another of my aunts, he defended himself as best he could and protested our innocence. One day he phoned me in Paris: he had received a visit from a police inspector, a real gentleman, as polite as you could wish for, who had given him comforting news of Luis; it was not a serious matter and could be resolved, he told him, but from the outside I was politicizing things with signatures and articles that could only harm Luis and make his problems worse. In trembling tones my father begged me to stop the French press from talking about Luis, and he put forward the defensive arguments that, as I would discover much later, he used in a petition sent to the authorities. Although I did not then possess my present experience of dictatorships, forever caught in the dilemma of silencing dissidence by coercion yet presenting a façade of respectability to the outside world, it was my intuition that silence was the best accomplice of oppressive systems and that only a repeated denunciation of their abuses could finally put an end to them—an intuition that was strengthened by this incident. If the police had dispatched one of their functionaries to our house to get father to put pressure on me to be quiet, this was an indication that my activity was upsetting them and should consequently be pursued. That demonstration *a contrariis* of the effects of mobilization abroad for the release of Luis was further reinforced when the press silence on the subject was broken and the daily *Pueblo*, organ of the so-called Vertical Unions edited by Emilio Romero, revealed its annoyance in two editorials, "The French Fashions of Young Spanish Writers" (29 February 1960) and "Distortion" (15 March 1960).

The anonymous author of these articles was surprised by the strange devotion of the French press to the fledgling author of *Las afueras* and denounced the vogue for Spanish literature that was translated not as a measure of its value but as "evidence of opposition to present-day Spain"; then, with an obvious allusion to me, he continued: "there is even a customs post, which is very difficult to avoid, that hands out licenses, and the customs official bears the same surname as the young writer recently canonized." Two weeks later, in response to a brief note in *L'Express* inspired by me, although I was not responsible for the sensationalist illustration, the *Pueblo* editorialist took up the cudgels again, justifying the newspaper's interest in our surname to the extent, he said, that it enjoyed "favorable treatment from some foreign press, not so much for the literary activities with which their authors cause a stir in the bookshops as for their political activities, which are more likely to give them a stir in the police stations." On 24 March I replied in the French weekly * to the accusations of Emilio Romero's daily, with a defense of the realism of the Spanish novel, a defense that in hindsight does not seem entirely off-track.

A few days later, taking advantage of the right to reply recognized in the press law passed by the Régime, José Agustín and I sent two notes to *Pueblo*'s editor, while forty-odd colleagues from Madrid and Barcelona in an open letter, which would be published only outside the country, protested against the style of political denunciation used in the paper's attacks, expressed their human and professional solidarity with me, demanded the publication of my reply, and described my literary activity at Gallimard as "truly favorable for the publication of our literature abroad." After several weeks' silence, the spokesman of the Vertical Unions devoted a double page to the affair, including our letters and a fresh extensive onslaught on my political position and cultural activities ("The Young Wave and Other

---

* "*Pueblo* and literature." The text, also published in Mexico with the rather provocative headline "Spanish novelists' realism irritates Francisco Franco's inquisitors," says among other things: "In a society in which social relationships are deeply unreal, realism is a necessity. From morning till night the Spanish intellectual thinks he is living in a dream world. Everything around him contributes to uprooting him from the time in which he is alive, until he finally feels like an inhabitant of another planet, dropped by mistake into his country. This uprooting creates a vacuum that must be filled, and which each individual fills in his own manner. For writers in Spain, reality is the only escape."

Matters," 22 April 1960): the editorialist's clichés and personal attacks—
I don't know if it was Romero himself—anticipated those that would
be used in massive doses a year later by the press, radio, and television.
Four days after the publication of this unusual controversy, aired by
Romero in a pamphlet translated into French to teach *L'Express* a lesson
at the expense of union funds, I traveled with Monique to Spain, where
the second literary get-together at Formentor was about to be celebrated in somewhat Kafkaesque circumstances.

Contrary to what one might at first think, judging from the verbal
acrimony of the attacks on me, my alleged dossier as a resistance fighter
against Francoism can lay claim to neither torture nor arrest. If we discard
the time I was interrogated by the Albacete civil guard during the
bullrunning in Elche de la Sierra, my only stay in a police station, in
August 1958, was apolitical, fortuitous, and far from heroic: I was caught
with Jaime Gil de Biedma and a friend of his in a police clean-up raid on
the Barrio Chino, and we spent a sleepless night in a badly lit dingy room,
with a selection of individuals—drunks, pimps, hustlers, and even a
handsome blond youth accused of the outrageous crime of "going with
French women"—while we waited for the van to take us to headquarters
on the Vía Layetana, to be classified indelibly as louts and set free a few
hours later—obviously without anyone realizing who we were or trying to
exploit the incident—thanks to the successful intervention of Jaime's
father. It was scarcely an exemplary episode, and if I aspired to an official
hagiography or a preening self-portrait, I should put it carefully aside
rather than shine an inopportune spotlight on it at a point in my narrative
when my public acts lend or could lend themselves easily and unin-
tentionally to idolizing eulogy!

Nevertheless, when we landed in Barcelona airport on Sunday, 26 April
and handed our passports to the police, the officer in charge of the control
disappeared with mine into an office, probably to consult with his
superiors. Monique, who was right behind me in the line, bravely stuck
her head round the half-opened door and smiled at the inspector who was
phoning headquarters, my passport in his hand. Is something the matter?
she asked innocently. No, nothing was the matter, and my passport was
returned to me without explanation or apology. As we commented on the
episode while waiting in the transit lounge for our connecting flight to
Palma, the functionary picked out by Monique came up to us and, as if
apologizing for being caught in the act, said that he followed my work
very closely and would like to welcome me: after politely asking permission to sit at our table, he ordered drinks from the waiter, asked after

Luis and the polemic with *Pueblo*, and debated novels and literature with me until the loudspeakers summoned us to the departure gate, where we met up in a cheerful, excited mood with the other writers and publishers who were also leaving for Formentor.

During the literary discussions and group sessions devoted to the future international prize, we circulated a petition on behalf of Luis, which was signed by all those in attendance. The presence of well-known writers and personalities gave me a temporary immunity that I could use and did use quite unashamedly. With a political instinct and judgment that now amaze me—maturity or mere exhaustion would later make me clumsier and cruder—I adapted my tactics to the space for maneuver allowed by the circumstances, without resorting to rash acts or false moves. Lacking, as I do, any Christian propensity to self-sacrifice, I surrounded myself with defensive walls and parapets. The best way to avoid the misfortune that befell Luis was to present the enemy with the dilemma of having to resort to drastic measures harmful to its image or having to tolerate pinpricks without loss of composure, and to do so in such a way that the balance would logically swing toward the latter. Although I harbor not the slightest doubt that the supporters of a hard line within the Régime wished to teach me a good lesson, I did not give them the opportunity, for the negative factors such action would bring outweighed any possible advantages.

Back in Barcelona after the congress, we spent a night in our old haunt at the Cosmos after a nostalgic walk along the Ramblas. Then, like some unhappy guilty prodigal son, I paid a visit to the house on Pablo Alcover. Luis's enforced absence had clearly precipitated the degeneration of people and things, and the picture presented by the aged trio filled me with both anguish and consternation. Father spoke obsessively about a supposed Communist trap set for Luis, Grandfather said nothing, and Eulalia inscrutably stroked the suede coat and presents we brought her from Paris. Before leaving for Majorca, Monique and I had agreed that when she resumed work at Gallimard I would stay on for a few weeks in Spain in order to visit Luis in jail, finish off the inquiries we had planned on his behalf, and travel to Andalusia with Simone de Beauvoir. On 8 May I bid her farewell at the airport and, after a stressful, restless night at home, beset by most disturbing nightmares, as I mention in a later letter, I traveled to Madrid, where I had agreed to meet up with Florence Malraux three days later. I can remember my visit to Carabanchel: the line of prisoners' relatives, where I came across the poet Gabriel Celaya's wife, carrying a parcel of food for one of his brothers, and saw the mother of Luis and Javier Solana, two future Socialist leaders; the conversation with my brother through two iron grilles; he looked calm, if sickly, as a result of the hunger strike he had participated in; my feeling of impotence and emptiness when the bell rang and we were obliged to break off the exchange.

On 13 May I collected Florence at Barajas and stayed with her in an old-fashioned but comfortable suite in the Hotel Victoria, the balconies of which looked out on the plaza del Ángel. The daughter of the writer, who was at the time Minister of Culture in General De Gaulle's government, had met Luis in Formentor the previous year and with a show of generous affection toward Monique and ourselves that I shall never forget, she agreed to my idea of coming to Madrid to ask her country's embassy to intervene on my brother's behalf. Florence's stay was hectic and short: my memories of it are limited to a variegated succession of snapshots and minor details. For twenty-four hours we rushed in the rain from the Prado to the mansion on the calle Serrano where she was received by the ambassador just before a dismal dinner with a group of friends. The diplomat promised to make a discreet approach to the Ministry for Foreign Affairs, and his words inspired in us a cautious but wary optimism. On the day of her departure she briefly met Simone de Beauvoir and Nelson Algren, and I accompanied her to Barajas in an emotional state of gratitude difficult to express.

We were to leave Madrid two days later to allow the recent arrivals quick visits to monuments and places of interest in the city. Forgetting Sartre and Castor's horror of shellfish I took the latter and her companion to dinner in the Hogar Gallego, where the vision of pink carapaces and retractable lobster limbs, crabs, and prawns took her to an isolated corner far from the aquariums and baskets where the owner proudly exhibited his exquisite delicacies. Either that evening or the following one I also organized a small dinner with my Party comrades. As everyone wanted to meet de Beauvoir and the number of possible guests was rising alarmingly, my colleagues adopted the heroic but misguided decision to leave their wives behind in order not to overwhelm her with the uncomfortable pressures of a formal banquet. What a crass, unforgivable mistake!: we had hardly sat down in our private room in a restaurant next to the Plaza Mayor when one of those present mentioned his wife's tremendous interest in *Le Deuxième Sexe*. What! He was married and had come by himself? Castor looked at me and asked if they were all married. I said they were with one or two exceptions. "But for heaven's sake," she exclaimed, "you call yourselves antifascists and then leave your wives at home as if they were your servants. That's really incredible!" Neither the embarrassed excuses or explanations of the diners nor their later instructive descriptions and analyses of the situation in Spain managed to dispel entirely the bad effect of their well-intentioned macho behavior. With the professional, Cartesian, relentless plainspokenness that characterized her, the writer told me afterwards that although my friends had made a favorable impression at the political level, their immaturity regarding the position of women and relations between the sexes confirmed her fears that the struggle against the residues of patriarchal society would be particularly difficult and arduous for us.

It is not my intention to narrate the twists and turns of the journey that took the three of us and Vicente Aranda to Granada, Almería, Almuñécar, and Málaga for eight to ten days. Simone de Beauvoir describes them briefly in the last volume of her memoirs and with greater humor and powers of imagination—sometimes bordering on the whimsical and the absurd. Nelson Algren drew a series of portraits or vignettes of the journey to be published months afterwards by a North American magazine. Without wishing to draw any conclusions, I will just make one simple observation: the passion minutely described in *Les Mandarins* seemed to be water under the bridge and while accompanying Algren out of a kind of friendly fidelity, Castor was living mentally with the author of *L'Être et le Néant*, to whom she continuously referred when she saw or heard something interesting, adding the inevitable comment, "Oh, I must tell Sartre about that!"

After saying goodbye in Málaga—and while they went on to Sevilla—I went back to Madrid with Aranda. The parents of my sister-in-law's brother, Luis Carandell, had offered me hospitality in their flat on the calle Libertad and it was there on 28 May that I was surprised by the good news of my brother's release just as I was getting ready to visit him in Carabanchel. I can't remember exactly whether my cousin, the notary Juan Berchmans Vallet, went and collected Luis at the prison door or whether my brother and I met up with him later to thank him for his constant, valuable help. But I have not forgotten that long mutual exchange of information in our room at the Carandells' nor the visit and congratulations of Señora Solana, whose son was still in jail. To avoid showing openly that they had given in to the protest campaign centered around the figure of Luis, the authorities also released the less-committed participants in the Prague congress, including Isidoro Balaguer, while others arrested with him on the same charge spent months and even years behind bars, in a convincing illustration of the rule according to which silence has been, is, and will be the greatest accomplice of the abuses and crimes of dictatorships. I retain only one of the stories and anecdotes recounted at the time to us by our Madrid friends: that of the novelist who stretched back in his armchair at the Café Gijón, after reading aloud one of the reports or lead articles about my brother, and stigmatized, in the hollow resonant tones of an ex-bureaucrat or retired officer, anti-patriotic behavior in "those times rent with polemical tensions" and, infected by the virulent affirmations of the editorial writer, he endorsed them with all the power of his hoarse authority: "It is quite plain his activities verged on those of a common criminal."

After accompanying Luis to Barcelona and his jubilant reunion with the family and María Antonia, I returned to Paris on 8 June.

The euphoria created by our modest victory had strengthened my determination to continue the struggle and increased my confidence in the possibility of an imminent radical change in Spanish society, along the lines of the "democratic, antifeudal, anticapitalist transformation" at the heart of the Party's program. A fortnight after my return to Paris, Monique and I were back in Spain with Carole, Florence Malraux, the filmmaker Claude Sautet, and other friends: ensconced in the family mansion at Torrentbó, we were visited by Luis and María Antonia, Ricardo Bofill, Castellet, Barral, Gil de Biedma, and other writers and intellectuals who would soon make up the so-called *gauche divine*; we would often meet up with them in Barcelona and, after dinner in the Amaya or the Barceloneta areas, we tramped around Escudillers and the Barrio Chino, visited El Cádiz and La Venta, perhaps hoping for my catastrophist perspectives to be confirmed in the dirt and poverty of that setting. Unaware of the lung infection he had contracted in prison, Luis seemed possessed by a violent desire to live and make up for lost time; my malingering crisis with Monique and the tension of those last months had equally intensified my capacity for late-night drinking and other diversions. The drinking habit, which all three brothers suffered at one stage or another in our lives, was violently at odds with the fanatical anti-alcoholism my father had inculcated in us from childhood. In my case, it revealed a feeling of growing exasperation at my own contradictions and personal inability to develop or resolve them. The dichotomy between bourgeois lifestyle and Communist ideas, love and sexual urges—the sudden, devastating lashes of which I suffered on occasion on those nighttime forays—could only be overcome, I thought, in a wave of revolutionary action when it would lose all its raison d'être. As I waited for the earthquake and the flowering of the new morality from the ruins, I tolerated with increasing difficulty the stubborn blindness of reality to the omens of cataclysm. In these years my letters to Monique, both from Spain and Cuba, reflect an irrepressible impatience with a development that—as a result of what had happened on the island since the fall of Batista—seemed just around the corner. What an illusion! The slow but deep transformation of Spanish society which began at that time would catch me and many others totally unawares. I can remember my last visit to Almería in September 1960 with Aranda and Sautet and our chance encounter with a group of French actors and filmmakers dazzled by the beauty of the landscape and its future possibilities: the newcomers spoke of hotel complexes, film studios, installations worthy of a new Cinecittà or mini-Hollywood. Was that the change you had bet on? Could material well-being and progress be disassociated from the conquest of freedom and justice? Apprehensive, anxious, in inner turmoil, you left that land— so poor yet coveted, exhausted, but appealing, rich in attributes and nonetheless abandoned—and only returned sixteen years later, when transformed into a completely different being: anonymous like any other foreigner, stealthily visiting the countryside you had dreamed of, hoping to come across familiar faces or friends, and only hearing, as in the fable, the dogs' accusing bark.

The discovery of Luis's illness and his symbolic withdrawal to Viladrau, the drawbacks and stress of the last trips to Spain had dashed your plans to spend Christmas at home. As you were going to Italy two months later for the launching of one of your books, you decided to postpone your visit for a few weeks and fly to Barcelona from there. On 11 February 1961 you were in Rome and after a number of days promoting your book and meeting writer-friends, you went to Milan, where Feltrinelli was organizing a cultural soirée at the Teatrino del Corso. His literary adviser, Valerio Riva, had supported your idea of illustrating the theme of *La resaca*—the plot of which was set in the Barcelona shantytowns inhabited by gypsies and Andalusians—by showing a documentary about emigration, filmed without permission with a 16-mm camera by two acquaintances studying with Ricardo Bofill at the Geneva School of Architecture. Following your guidelines, the filmmakers, Paolo Brunatto and Jacinto Esteva Grewe, had been to numerous villages and districts of Murcia, Almería, and Granada, photographed half-depopulated rural areas and then interviewed in Switzerland some immigrants from those areas; other sequences showed the shacks and caves that then made up a good slice of the industrial belt of your city. The film, *Notes sur l'émigration*, was rather amateurish and fell prey to historical and social simplification, but Riva agreed with you that it contained scenes and images of interest and deserved to be shown. To round off the soirée, the publishers had programmed a recital of Spanish songs, with a more or less political content, that had been popular in Italian anti-Fascist circles ever since the time of the civil war.

On 18 February, after Riva's brief introduction and a few words from you on the novel, the film was shown in the small crowded room. It had hardly started when you heard two muffled explosions and the room was suddenly filled with smoke. There were moments of panic, those present ran to the exit, and a voice started shouting, "Someone's been hit." In a flash, and everything happened amazingly quickly, two nurses miraculously appeared from nowhere with their support equipment and stretcher, and took the would-be victim outside wrapped in a blanket.

Although it was a ridiculous scene, no one thought to stop them or to follow them out to the ambulance. While you recovered from the shock and the spectators returned to their seats certain it was a Fascist provocation, Brunatto and Esteva Grewe emerged angrily from the projection room: taking advantage of the confusion, someone had removed the rolls of film and quickly run off. The setting off of firecrackers and appearance of the stretcher-bearers then became perfectly clear: the men responsible for the theft had completed their mission with professional skill and efficiency. The following day the Italian press related what had happened in banner headlines and put the crime down to Milanese Fascists, closely linked to their Spanish counterparts: a police investigation of the former would lead on 3 March to the arrest of four individuals, a former blackshirt and three members of the parachute brigade well-known for their involvement in extreme right-wing circles of the city. You were able only years later to establish the real identity of the intruders, which was, however, hinted at by the fact that the stolen copy was shown soon afterwards in Spain. Anxious to avoid any diplomatic repercussions, the local authorities were quick to bury the matter; the interrogation of those arrested bore no fruit and they were soon released.

The incident and, especially, the reactions in the Italian press made you immediately fear possible reverberations in Spain. Your worries, communicated by telephone to Monique and a couple of friends in Barcelona, were quickly confirmed. On 22 February the whole range of Peninsular media published an EFE agency dispatch about the episode, insidiously linking it to an FAI terrorist attack on the Spanish consulate in Geneva and the celebration of "an act of anti-Spanish propaganda" chaired by Waldo Frank and Álvarez del Vayo in the Barbizon-Plaza Theater in New York. While some newspapers wrote about this triple attack in fairly subdued tones, *Arriba*, the Movement's official organ, gave it front-page prominence: "CNT-FAI, Álvarez del Vayo, Waldo Frank, Goytisolo: a new model of Molotov cocktail against Spain" and the *Pueblo* headline splashed over three columns: "J.G. tries to screen a lying, insulting documentary on Spain; a group of spectators protest and throw smoke bombs." The EFE statement underlined the Communist character of the Milan "mass-meeting," indirectly attributed to you authorship of the incriminating documentary, pretended that the firecrackers had been thrown by honest, upright Italian patriots. "The Communist press"—it concluded—"has been upset by the incident, rails against the disappearance of the film during the melee, to the point of stating that it was all a provocation by agents from the Spanish consulate." At about the same time, a lead article in *El Español*, probably written by its editor, Juan Aparicio, came out against your vile campaign of "defamation" in Europe and an ineffable report from the Rome correspondent of *El Diario de*

Barcelona, "J.G.'s Latest Pirouette," accused you of publicly intervening, "with cool and collected tactics, not to challenge Spain's régime politically but to slander your own Fatherland"; after dubbing you "the gangster of the photo or film camera," the writer lambasted the "sour cocktail of Soviet-style words, images, and songs, which insulted Spain on the pretext of introducing a book by a Spaniard living it up abroad and paraded around by the Communist Parties."

But that astonishing flood of slurs and attacks in print was only the beginning. On 28 February, José Agustín telephoned you and said that the film stolen in Milan had been shown the night before on Spanish television, together with a thunderous reply from José Antonio Torreblanca that described you as an impostor, mercenary, with other charming epithets. In fact, as you discovered straightaway, it was a cut and doctored version of the film with a sound track and commentary that in places differed from the original. As the copy that had been shown seriously distorted the content and intentions of the film, you dispatched registered letters to EFE and those in charge of television, invoking the right to correct the impression given. But your protests, this time, remained unpublished. Spanish television's showing of Esteva Grewe and Brunatto's film was to unleash a strident pack of hunting dogs after a silenced prey. Rereading today the press clippings you have preserved,* and from which you composed the soliloquy of Voices in your first adult novel, is enough to bring on a laughing fit; a quarter of a century ago you had mixed feelings of devastation, sadness, and incredulity. Sometimes the accumulation of denigrating terms and absurd accusations is so exaggerated that it borders on the grotesque and seems like a caricature or parody ("That series of acts of aggression against the Iberian Peninsula is dominated by the participation of that 'fellow traveler' and young gigolo, J.G., who has set up in Paris"); at other times the emphatic style, rather familiar to your journalist's ear, recalls its deliberate insertion or parody in the body of *Señas de identidad* ("Resident more years in France than in Spain, with habits that are more French than Spanish, even as far as his mistress goes ... he gives them what they ask for. Turning out scenes of poor suburbs is exceedingly easy. A few extras, dressed up as policemen, can 'beat up a worker,' strip a little boy, cover him in coal dust and sit him on a heap of manure—this is within the reach of any unscrupulous hack. But whoever does this reveals such a moral stature that it is better not to mention him, although it would only require two substantives and a preposition"). The top prize in this wretched contest should perhaps go to Manuel Aznar, the editor of *La Vanguardia*, for his lead article on 16 March 1961 "Feltrinelli, or the Festival of Insults," a real monument to

---

* The fullest collection of clippings is in the archive of my papers at Boston University.

demagogy, hypocrisy, and grandiloquence that, unable to appear in the eventual edition of "An Individual History of Infamy," also received its just reward by being included in your book. However, it is a long list of examples, and you will break off here so as not to take advantage of your readers.

You would then discover that spite nestling within the heart, "the terrible Spaniard's eternal bile" so beautifully evoked by Cernuda. The insults that then poured out and their impact on your family—your father's visits and worried letters to newspaper editors, quixotically intent on saving the family's good name—will leave a bitter aftertaste in the mouth but on the rebound will grant you a kind of immunity, by transforming you into the prickly writer you are today, insensitive and hardened to the never-ending succession of insults and vicious taunts. To tell the truth, your reaction to what happened in Milan symbolically prefigured your relationship with the secular customs of the tribe: everything that came later—ostracizing, scandal-mongering, and vindictive jibes—would have the tired look of _déjà vu_. What had been singled out decades or centuries before by other sharpshooters and dissidents was duly proved in your case: those who attack in Spain one day from the right attack later from the left while waiting for the opportunity to repeat the attack from the right—and the victims are always the same. This showed you early on—and it would be a discovery of prime importance— that your people will praise or reward only dead writers or works. Those who preserve their lives are a source of concern and arouse that indirect form of praise lurking behind the treacherous form of an insult. The disgust and horror you would provoke in the future only echoed, sometimes literally, expressions and turns of phrase coined years ago and which have no impact on you; reading them inside out, following the Poet's gloomy advice, as higher forms of praise, you would derive a sense of pride from them. Your apprenticeship in the customs and laws of the tribe would be completed only years later; but the lesson you received then would be a warning or threat whose imprint will never fade.

While the Francoist press boasted of the honesty of its news service by offering your countrymen on Spanish television a film documentary "aimed at deceiving the naive"—but being very careful not to explain how your so-called creation had reached them—there was no reply to the questions formulated by the Italian newspapers. There was no doubt that the Spanish authorities had intervened in the affair; the riddle would have remained shrouded in mist had not the blustering indiscretions of one of the protagonists later and unknowingly furnished you with the key. In the autumn of 1965, during your first fertile and contagious stay in Tangier, Eduardo Haro Tecglen, who had moved to the city when appointed editor of the now defunct daily _España_, revealed to you that in the course of a dinner attended by the general consul in Tetuan, the latter had glorified his peculiar involvement in the affair to the rest of the guests; according to his account, the perpetrators of the aggression against the gathering in the Teatrino del Corso entrusted him with the copy of the film and, following instructions from Madrid, he ensured it reached the right destination by way of the diplomatic pouch. Such praiseworthy behavior had won him the warm congratulations of his superiors, and the former Spanish vice-consul in Milan still trembled with excitement as he recalled the amusing, action-packed episodes of this James Bondish thriller...

Although this man's sad role in a police plot whose ramifications helped to embitter the final years of your father's life would justify the pillorying of his name, the bullet with which he suddenly ended his days in Argentina moves you to have mercy. A faithful servant to a system of which he was both creation and instrument, he finally and tragically set himself up as his own implacable judge. The holy terror suicide inspires within you demands respect; grant him silence, and leave him in peace.

The aim of that violent campaign seemed obvious: by presenting the Milan anti-Francoist cultural event as a gathering of "reds" and linking my participation in it to terrorist activities backed by "international Marxism," the authorities wanted to scare me and force me into voluntary exile. My ambiguous dissident status, eyewitness accounts of trips to the Peninsula, pro-Communist sympathies, and connections with the French press had finally riled the high priests of the Régime, who were confronted with the dilemma of arresting me or of continuing to tolerate behavior whose example could spread and contaminate other writers and artists. I was the victim of a flood of insults and veiled threats with which they tried to shut me out, turn me into a remote, innocuous outlaw. I was sure of this and adopted a poker-player's tactic: misleading my opponent with a false show of strength, to persuade him that I was setting a trap by returning in order to be arrested. During Luis's imprisonment the previous year I had traveled to Spain swathed in a protective band of well-known personalities, but this time I decided to go back quite openly, with the feigned lack of care or awareness of someone cheerfully stepping into the lions' den. Seeing that my demands for the truth to be published remained unanswered, I had recourse once again to the good, selfless offices of my cousin, the notary Juan Berchmans Vallet: with his customary calm and common sense he advised me on a trustworthy lawyer, completely outside politics, who under his guidance would accuse the all-powerful General Director of the Press of slander. It seemed an absurd undertaking, and the possibility of bringing the case before the courts was clearly very slim indeed; however, the manner of my attack drew my enemy's attention from my main aim: to return with impunity to Spain. On 21 April, a week before Monique's visit to the Formentor literary conversations, I went by plane to Madrid, where I was met at Barajas airport by my cousin. I cleared the police entry procedures without incident. That same night, Juan Berchmans Vallet had set up a meeting with my lawyer to plan a successful strategy on the eve of my scheduled visit to the Ministry. I can remember very clearly arriving there in the morning and the vast mural in the entrance hall with the images of the archangel's annunciation to Mary. If, as Umberto Eco pointed out in his day, the amount of information transmitted by a communicative unit depends on its degree of probability and, the less this is, the greater will be the unit's informative content, the Francoist Ministry of Information could not knowingly have chosen a better symbol: the chubby, blond, salutiferous envoy of the Lord transmitting the improbable communicative unit to the blushing Virgin and, consequently, the most substantial information about the unexpected benefits of the visit of a dove whose plump white sheen keeps the pious spectator of the fresco in an understandable state of confusion between the Holy Ghost invoked by the opulent Mahalia Jackson and the colorful advertisement for Avecrem will not fade from my memory and will surface in the pages of *Don Julián*.

The General Director of the Press, the philosopher and professor Don Adolfo Muñoz Alonso—who in those blessed times would gloriously represent Spain in all the international congresses on thought and knowledge: a profound, illuminating contribution, whose lasting effects deserve some day to be calmly glossed—received us with unaccustomed speed. Gesturing affably, he was an unctuous man, sure of possessing the Truth and conscious of his importance. On his table he had a voluminous dossier of foreign-press articles devoted, he said, to my political activities. He added that he was aware of everything: my attitude of continuous hostility to the Régime and the values it embodied could not be more patent or open. Acting as I did outside the framework of legality, I should not be surprised by the violent reactions of condemnation aroused by my wretched behavior. He understood, he made clear, young people's political preoccupations; but these should be directed along the available channels. He turned to one of his secretaries—a bespectacled young man busily going to and fro from his office—and introduced me to the writer Jaime Capmany, an example to be followed: He also has his worries but expresses them responsibly and constructively, rather than trading as you do on the fair name of Spain. If, he concluded, you are upset by the harsh, biting tone of some replies and attacks in the press, it is your fault: to keep silent on insults to the Fatherland would be to display a lack of courage and to reward immorality. He listened in silence as my lawyer, my cousin Juan Berchmans, and I set out our views. It was a complex, serious matter, he finally replied, and required time for reflection. After an exchange of opinions as to the legality or illegality of my actions, he told us to return to his office on the following day.

At the appointed time we went back to the ministry, and Professor Muñoz Alonso gave me a welcoming smile: "Last night," he told me, "you were very much in my prayers." I must confess that I blushed maidenlike at that confidence, as unexpected as the amorous approach of some heavenly creature. I stared at the wall, carpet, or ceiling, incapable of articulating a response. The professor's angelic sophistry had suddenly lifted me to a confused limbo of unreality where I gently hovered throughout the laborious interview. The text of my letter, drawn up with the help of my cousin and the lawyer, did not belie my hostility to Francoism as our distinguished thinker intended after consulting his pillow; it simply established the bare truth of the facts. After exchanges in which I made no pertinent intervention from the perch of my sudden nirvana, the General Director of the Press agreed to a brief note of clarification to the effect that my involvement "in the cultural event celebrated in Milan" was purely literary and I had not assumed in the course of the same any "insulting, indecent, or contemptuous attitude toward the Spanish régime." This comment would be published in *Arriba* and *La Vanguardia* and, in return, I would withdraw my slander charge against the Ministry of Information. We parted amicably and, as agreed, my letter appeared immediately in the two newspapers. As for Professor Muñoz Alonso, absorbed in his many-sided official tasks and distilled Augustinian perceptions, I am unsure whether he had time to think of me and devote any prayers to me as he generously promised when we said goodbye. He became the flaming torch of Hispanic thought and died fifteen years later from exhaustion or sadness, when his Benefactor went into decline and made a definitive exit.

I continued my travels through Spain despite my transformation into that character in Chamisso stripped of all shadow—an unattached citizen, condemned to silence, held in moral quarantine, watched over meticulously, if discreetly, by the authorities. I would be forced to prolong for some time my leprous or ghostly eyewitness presence out of fear of a leap into the void—cutting the umbilical cord that tied me to the tribe, feelings of solidarity and patriotism soon to be alien to me—how was I going to act in support of others if, as I would gradually discover, I had hardly any sympathy toward myself, toward the official character I embodied? In May 1961 I participated in the Formentor literary gatherings, although my name does not appear in any of the reports, while Jaime Salinas, then the secretary to the international jury that awarded the prize to Beckett and Borges, would be visited by two inspectors with a keen interest in the words and deeds of Feltrinelli and my humble self; for the penultimate time until Franco's death, Monique and I went on holiday to Torrentbó in July, accompanied by Florence Malraux and our friends from Barcelona; between the seventh and twenty-eighth of September I traveled to Albacete with Aranda and Ricardo Bofill, captivated by the dark splendor of the Yeste mountains and the fascinating brutality of the bullfighting festivals of the area; in April 1962, on my return from my exciting stay in Cuba, I attended, like the Commendatore's statue, the international Formentor meetings—under attack from some newspapers as a "hotbed of communists"—and the Barcelona Publishers' Congress—during which, with exemplary irony and boldness, a small Portuguese publisher would denounce the ravages of censorship in our unhappy Peninsula: there I learned, from the foreign press and radio, of the slow but irresistible spread of the Asturian miners' strike to neighboring regions and the first contagious outbreaks in the city's industrial belt.

I returned to Paris on 12 May, but ten days later I was back in Spain. The breadth of the strike movement and the challenge it posed to the Régime suddenly rekindled my illusions that the final struggle was at hand. Sent by *France-Observateur* to report on events, I visited working-class districts in Madrid and Barcelona, though I was unable to reach Asturias as initially planned because of Interior Minister Camilo Alonso Vega's proclamation of a state of emergency in the province. I had few contacts with the political leaders of the strike: caution was the order of the day and most of them slept away from home. Even so, I can remember López Salinas taking me to a terrace on the Castellana where Federico Sánchez was waiting for us, totally at ease in his role as the carefree bourgeois with time on his hands: his incredible rash calm at a moment when he was the man in Spain most wanted by the police impressed me inasmuch as it perfectly matched his legendary reputation as an elusive, mocking Scarlet Pimpernel. The political climate of the period is described fairly accurately in my report "A travers l'Espagne en grève," which was published on 31 May 1962 with a note that "the writer must remain anonymous since he is still in Spain." I reproduced some paragraphs word for word in *Señas de identidad*—the visit to the cemetery of Francoist martyrs in Paracuellos del Jarama. Others, read with hindsight, reflect the ambiguity and contradictions between the bare depiction of the facts and the corrective "ideologized" interpretation:

Although it is true that the strike began spontaneously and for strictly trade-union reasons, the movement's development immediately revealed the existence of a political coordination and focus. . . . If, as the failure of the Day of National Reconciliation on 5 May 1958 and the Peaceful National Strike of 18 June 1959 testify, the Communist Party lacks the necessary strength to initiate a strike of its own, it has now shown that it wields enough influence to channel the protest of the masses, thanks to discipline and experience acquired over twenty years of clandestine activity. . . . Confronted by the orderly calm of the strikers, the government alternates between policies of force and appeasement, with a lack of decision that reveals the profound crisis in its institutions and structures. . . . With an eye on foreign powers, it strives to benefit from the situation by portraying the present movement as proof of that "democratization" necessary for Francoist Spain's entry into the Common Market. It is easy to foresee that Spanish diplomacy will develop this line during the months to come. The plan to legalize purely trade-union strikes is already a first step on this path. . . . A train has just set off and Ridruejo is advising the bourgeoisie to get on board before it is too late.* The supporters of a liberal government run the risk of being overtaken by events if they do not assume their proper responsibilities at once.

But to this reasonable statement, which I can support today, I appended conclusions that only revealed my impatience and gut hostility to the painfully protracted if predictable Europeanist solution:

Gradually abandoned by its supporters, the State seems more isolated than ever. In any case—as is confirmed by the attitude of the youth—its days are numbered. . . . The Régime has entered a stage of disintegration and, after slumbering for twenty-three years, the country is on the eve of enormous changes.

Nevertheless, after some significant concessions from the employers, the impact and drift of which would become clear only years later, the social unrest declined. I was disappointed and, after holidaying with Monique and her daughter in Capri—where we met up with Semprún and his wife, guests of Mario Alicatta, then the editor of *L'Unità*—I returned to Spain on 11 September to complete my research into the May '36 events in Yeste and be present at the fierce, compensatory bullrunning ceremony. Along with Ricardo Bofill and Vicente Aranda, I visited the dam and the shores of the reservoir that caused the tragedy, I followed the forest paths and byways where the peasants were massacred, I climbed the stockades and crossed squares and alleys where one of the beasts would drag me twenty years later, I chatted at length to a local about what had happened there before and after the war, I dallied till late at night around the stalls and sideshows of the fair until I finally came across a pair of civil guards

* A reference to a well-known interview with the poet that had appeared the week before in *Le Figaro*.

stationed in an alley next to the inn, waiting for us to arrive. The nighttime interrogation—Why had we gone there? Why was I interested in talking to the fellow with the criminal record so well-known for his opposition to the Régime? Who had introduced him to me, and in what circumstances?—took place in a doorway, almost in pitch-dark, as if they were trying to intimidate us. Although it did not go any further and we were allowed to leave after showing them our papers, the incident did have its repercussions: the intrusion of some "well-heeled reds" from Barcelona was noted with fear and hostility in the village. As I recently discovered when I returned to the fiestas in Elche de la Sierra, my casual conversation with the victimized socialist had been spied upon by two pillars of society—a veterinary surgeon and a chemist who have since died—who not only spread their story around the café but stretched their patriotic refinement to the point of denouncing me to the civil guards. Only one guest at the inn—an emaciated, bald-headed, middle-aged individual of ascetic Castilian mien—dared smile at us and begin a friendly conversation with me about that latest piece of village gossip. After carefully sounding out my ideas, he pointed at Bofill's red car, I remember, and asked if my friend was of moneyed stock. "Well," I said, "he's a member of the bourgeoisie." "National or monopolist?" The national bourgeoisie, I assured him. From that identificatory tag, as clearly as if he had shown his Party card, I soon guessed that the place where he told me he had lived with a really smart painter from Paris was prison and that the artist's name was Pepe Ortega. "How do you know?" he exclaimed in amazement. "The way you talk is your visiting card," I replied. This militant—one of those people who looked as if he were called Ramiro, Prudencio, or Casto—had a toy stall at the fairground, and there we bid him farewell when we left the village, just as he was broadcasting the merits of a pretty articulated doll over his homemade loudspeaker from his perch in his modest stand.

That incident frustrated my attempt to continue on-the-spot research and brought to a definitive close my wanderings through the southeast of Spain, to which I had tardily discovered a sense of affinity or belonging and whose poverty and oppression I intended to highlight. From then on, when I returned to Spain I would do so reluctantly and under compulsion, in a gradual state of disaffection from a country on the road to progress but morally and politically stagnant, perkily healthy but stubbornly mute. Like many Spaniards my age, I had prepared myself for something that never happened and for a time experienced a strong sense of being cheated. The actual prospects were as obvious as they were unpleasant: the Régime would last as long as the hateful figure of its creator. The year after this gloomy conclusion, I would seek out consolation in Cuba in the shape of the flame of a miraculous revolution promising justice and freedom. A *fuite en avant* from Spain and myself that finally led to a change in my writing: a change of skin, an end to posturing, gradual purification, a purging of a surly, inhospitable identity.

In 1962, where your narrative is lurching in fits and starts, your political activism intensified and spread from the strictly Spanish field to new, more exciting revolutionary challenges. It coincided with a period of literary fame that bore no relation to the real merits and stature of your work—the undoubted fruit of your convenient and profitable position as a fellow traveler—and was at the same time, as you will subsequently try to show, the unhappiest period in your life. The unresolved problems of your sexual identity, the precarious nature of your links to Monique, the stifled, corrosive impression of being sucked down by your contradictions, further and further from any way out, had gradually led you to neurosis and alcohol, brief interludes of euphoric excitement, spiraling cycles of depression and suicidal obsessions. Your enthusiasm for the Cuban epic followed not only from your welcoming there a kind of settling of accounts with the execrable past of your ancestors but also from its value as a prophetic new dawn of the social revolution that was to transform your life Rimbaud-style. The victorious struggle of a handful of men over the supposed inertia of Hispanic peoples and their traditional fatalism constituted in your eyes irrefutable proof that things could change radically in your country, providing imagination and daring were combined with strength of will and spirit of sacrifice.

Although it was the most spectacular, the example of Cuba was not unique: in the heart of Paris, where you were living, the Algerian people daily showed that the cause of justice and dignity could triumph over brute force. Curfews, arrests, covered-up murders, torture, threats, outrages had not succeeded in daunting the tens of thousands of immigrants who arose miraculously at midnight from the métro stations of Saint-Michel, Opéra, or Concorde, in a calm, serious, clear-minded provocation. Excited, full of indignant loathing for the *white skins*, you were present when they were rounded up and arrested, when they were driven by truncheon into the prison vans without offering the slightest resistance or when lined up in compact battalions on the place de l'Étoile, which *tout à coup était devenue jaune*, they stood firm, like ghostly sleepwalkers, marked out by the crude brushstrokes of the gyrating police spotlights. Your feelings of immediacy and intense involvement were not only a response to your natural sympathy for the underdogs or to political motives. They were also inextricably intertwined with a hidden, intimate detail—you were dazzled by the physical beauty of the immigrants. As their faces gradually matched those that appeared fleetingly but clearly in your innermost dreams and fantasies, that feeling turned to passion: close by, though still forbidden, the masculine world that rushed blindingly into your life was awaiting the opportune moment to strike and throw you headlong.

A peculiar mixture of anguish and personal dissatisfaction, frustrated revolutionary desire and solidarity with a human and cultural landscape that would soon fascinate you, impregnates the pages of the books and articles you wrote at this time. While you then strove to sift things through and separate out the critical vision from the reality of your mental scenario and libido, your essay "Spain and Europe" painfully reflects the tensions, turmoil, sublimated instincts, and opposing demands with which you were then struggling. The dark, opaque, censored shadows on the surface of the text finally contaminated it with insidious irrationality, and through the fallacious warp of Marxist ideology there emerged in places the thread of a somnambulist revolutionary fantasy. Straddling the outside world and subjective authenticity, your critique was at the very least confused and incoherent. The lack of an unsullied relationship with yourself was thus inevitably translated into a sullied relationship with the world and everybody else.

The article was written, if you remember correctly, at the request of Simone de Beauvoir or some other member of the editorial board of *Les Temps Modernes*, and was intended as a response to an essay by Enrique Ruiz García that had appeared a few months before: after carefully weighing the pros and cons of Spain's entry into the Common Market, he concluded that it would imply historical progress for the nation and in the long term there was no alternative but to take up the challenge. Although his analysis did not conceal the problems that this eventuality would pose to the different layers of Spanish society from a liberal, democratizing perspective, it clashed head-on with the Party's political conceptions, which were trapped in the ostensible dilemma of the perverse status quo of Francoism or the antifeudal, antimonopolist democratic revolution required by the growing pauperization of the masses. You aligned yourself externally with the positions of your friends, and your text sketched in broad outline the history of the failures of Europeanizing Spanish liberalism only to draw the somewhat paradoxical conclusion that, in the light of recent anticolonial and anti-imperialist experience, Europe represented the dead past and the third world, a luxuriant, brilliant future:

> For more than a century and a half, the progressive Spanish intelligentsia tried to suppress the Pyrenees and the barriers that cut us off from Europe, and the conservatism of our ruling classes ruined their efforts. Now, when the old gravediggers are proposing union, we must not fall in the trap that this is a

hidden concession, nor be lulled by their hollow rhetoric. Our response should be quite simple: "Too late." . . . Today we should turn our gaze toward Cuba and the peoples of America, Asia, and Africa who are fighting for their freedom and independence. Europe now symbolizes, historically, the past, stagnation. It is now perhaps time to Africanize, as Unamuno would say, and turn the stale irony of that phrase "Africa begins at the Pyrenees" into the slogan for our banner.

If the facts entirely justified your expression of solidarity with the world exploited and oppressed by the "civilized nations," it was a real aberration to identify Spain with that world, and it clearly revealed your unfortunate propensity at the time to convert your impatience into a law of history and take your desires for reality. The deep crisis you were experiencing, still hidden under the disguise of political compromise and revolutionary ecstasy was, however, transparent in a few lines whose painful sincerity stood out from the gray prosaic magma of your confused feelings and ideas: "The reader must pray understand that to write in Spain is to weep and that there is no worse punishment than to face our reality without blinders or excuses. The intellectual in Spain is the victim of a profound neurosis. Larra's despair pursues him like a specter, and how can you escape it if every day is gray? Forgive us then our homicidal instincts. It is difficult to live and always keep calm."

In a fragile, morbid, turbulent mood you went to Sicily with Monique for a few weeks' rest and were caught there by the October crisis—the Khrushchev-Kennedy confrontation over the missiles—that put the world on the brink of war. Your moral conviction that the Castroite revolution embodied the values of justice and freedom which you defended drove you to abruptly break off the holiday and return to Paris. A few hours later you sped to the Cuban embassy to offer your services to the Revolution, ready to fly to Havana on the first plane to break the blockade. At a time when the future could not be more uncertain and foreign guests and sympathizers were rushing to abandon the island (including a Communist poet with a worldwide reputation), your decision seemed adventurist, if not rash. Nevertheless, you reached it without fear or hesitation. For the first and only time in your life, you took the risk of losing it on behalf of a worthy cause: you would reach the besieged Cuba after an interminable journey with stops, delays, searches, and friskings in various airports, in a clumsy old jalopy closely inspected by American fighter planes. You landed in Rancho Boyeros and, dressed in a uniform provided by Carlos Franqui, spent the night on an airbase bristling with useless Soviet artillery; later, with a number of Army officers and chiefs, you followed the "clean-up" operations in Escambray. In retrospect, you still warm to that ingenuous reaction which you do not disown: it was so similar to the feeling that led poets and writers of the stature of Cernuda, Spender, and Auden to place themselves at the disposition of the Spanish Republic at the very moment the ideals that sustained it were yielding to the double-flanked attack of Fascism and Stalinism. However, the apocalyptic vision of life and unconscious desire to solve your problems in a suicidal act of self-immolation seem now overly dramatic and exaggerated—you fell into a pathetic fallacy that is now upsetting and embarrassing. Although sincere, your gesture was excessive and theatrically avoided the debate with yourself and with your own reality. Your stay in Cuba, justified by your work as a scriptwriter for the Cuban Film Institute, ICAIC, was rich in political and personal experiences but did not on this occasion fulfill your enthusiastic expectations: the gradual degeneration of the revolutionary process, the anxieties of the writers and intellectuals you met, the first rats bearing the message of the plague that would years later ravage any kind of nonconformism and unseemly behavior—these were too visible for you not to see them. Full of doubts as to the viability and desirability of the Cuban model for Spanish society, you went back to Europe to confront a harsh but pertinent response to the vagaries of your third-world proposals.

Francisco Fernández Santos's article "Spain, Europe, and the Third World," written for the *Tribuna Socialista*, rebutted the conclusions in your article and laid bare its defects, distortions, and illogicalities. Santos argued that the Europe we faced was many-sided and ambiguous: a left-wing intellectual's opinion on Europe's colonial policy toward the third world was one thing, and the question of the structural impact of the entry of Spain in general, and of the Francoist régime in particular, was something of quite a different order.

> But, isn't Spain African enough in the worst sense of the word? . . . How can anyone seriously think that a policy based on Africanization (supposing that one can be formulated at all coherently, which I doubt) would not be greeted with wry amazement by the Spanish people? Can one predicate as a goal for that people precisely that which they are trying to get away from? . . . I think it quite clear that in today's world, oppressed as they are by the feudal-capitalist dictatorship, the popular masses of Spain have no other solution, no other more real or practical pole of attraction than Europe. Europe's advanced capitalist countries appear in the eyes of the Spanish like a nearby, tangible, tempting reality to which ever greater numbers have access. In such conditions . . . a real move toward Europe is *in practice* a revolutionary project.

Your opponent's well-constructed arguments and sharp tone wounded your vanity and self-pride. Hurriedly, you wrote a riposte in which you drew out and clarified some of the confused points in the previous essay, while insisting that alongside the concrete European solution, which was undoubtedly popular and seductive for a majority of Spaniards, others did exist, which, as in the case of Cuba, had imposed the dialectical surprise of a new reality, despite their difficult, minority character. In fact, you felt very uncomfortable defending yourself against Fernández Santos's criticisms, since you were forced to take up in public Jacobin positions that you were gradually ceasing to believe in under the twin experience and influence of the Cuban police-state bureaucracy and the evident flourishing of your own bourgeoisie. To understand your sudden volte-face months later, one would have to realize that it had been gestating ever since your second visit to Havana, and it was only the wretched polemic which enmeshed you that forced you to keep it hidden and display a circumstantial radicalism to the gallery.

Fernández Santos put his finger on it when he defined your attitude as the typical "pseudorebellious or revolutionary escapism" of a bourgeois with a bad conscience; but he was less accurate when he noted signs of moral opportunism and political careerism. The controversy began as a straightforward conflict of ideas and finished very Hispanically in an acerbic exchange of personal invective and contemptuous animosity. If the *genus irritabile vatum* you exhibited soon disappeared, along with your attachment to the literary world, the lesson you learned then both exorcised and initiated you. An essay containing practical proposals had to be clear and could not be contaminated by compensatory fantasies or filtered through your libido. Henceforth, though you would express opinions and ideas in your articles, the irrational component at the heart of literature—that purely poetic truth that loses all meaning and may even seem an aberration once transposed to the sphere of reality—would nevermore pour over into the empirical world or treacherously transgress its Maldororian boundaries.

As a result of a dinner at Gisèle Halimi's house with Jorge Semprún and Teresa de Azcárate, Monique and I began to see a lot of the mythical, elusive "Federico Sánchez." Until then, my dealings with him had been limited to my almost always silent participation in the cultural seminars held in the studio of the sculptor Baltasar Lobo. With the distant, superior tone of seriousness endowed by his position, Sánchez would interject succinctly in the discussions or conversations, as if he had an urgent appointment at the other end of town and was internally appalled by that dreadful waste of time and words: sideways glances at his watch, professional condescension toward the creaking Hispanic verbal diarrhea, a forced smile as he got up and brought to an end the archaic Leninist dialogue. Although no one had told me about the Semprún identity of Federico Sánchez, I soon put two and two together. Monique shared my fascination for this character and his Janus-like face: unlike those leaden, stodgy comrades in exile, whose never-ending nostalgia for Spain sounded over the years like an old unbearable scratched record, Jorge was cultured, seductive, and brilliantly fluent; he moved like a fish in water through the French intellectual world and matched his bravery as a man of action with a hidden passion for literature. As I soon discovered, he was writing *Le Long Voyage* in bursts, but jealously guarded the secret of that activity alien and, in truth, opposed to the responsibilities and funereal solemnity of a "cadre." It was only months later, during my second stay in Cuba, that Monique managed to loosen his tongue about his mysterious manuscript: she did not give up till he lent it to her. It was a splendid novel, she wrote to me at once in Havana, full of enthusiasm. Behind the trappings of an ideologue and urban Robin Hood, Jorge suddenly appeared as an important ambitious writer: two or three months later, the international Formentor jury would reward his book, while the paparazzi hurried to spread the sensational news that the prize had gone to public enemy number one of Franco's police.

Jorge's companion in the CP leadership, Fernando Claudín, in spite of his long stay in the USSR and a curious, and at first sight disturbing, physiognomy that I hesitate to describe as Russian or Soviet, came over at a personal level as someone sincere and open, interested in artistic and cultural problems and at a Patagonian or Australian distance from the monolithic narrow-mindedness that was such a distinguishing feature of his coreligionists. He and his wife Carmen would often come to have dinner with the Semprúns on the rue Poissonnière: used to the harsh rigors and caution of clandestine life on the Paris industrial belt, they were stimulated and attracted by the free, disorderly bohemian atmosphere that they encountered at our place. For the first time in my life, I had dealings with Communists—what's more, Party leaders—with whom I felt naturally at ease; I did not experience that unpleasant sensation of conversing or laughing with the representative of an iron-cast assemblage that, like all religious sects in possession of the truth, endows its membership with a sacramental hue and transforms their faces at times into rigid, unfathomable masks. Consequently, when they both told me that they were going to take over responsibility for the Party's cultural magazine and asked me to join the editorial board, I unreservedly accepted their invitation: despite my reptilian inability to digest doctrinal oxen and their ephemeral external manifestations, the open, antidogmatic line defended by my friends was entirely at one with my taste and temperament. Claudín's long essay on the plastic arts would be proof of the new path taken by *Realidad*: in the eyes of a Western reader, this essay merely established arguments and facts that were now beyond dispute, but they constituted a truly subversive manifesto in the Soviet bloc and its territorial and ideological dependencies; moreover, the essay had appeared in the official journal of a sister party and was, to boot, the work of a member of the executive committee. Claudín's heterodox theses had an immediate and dramatic impact on the closed, self-sufficient world of dogma: Alfredo Guevara, the director of the Cuban ICAIC, was then in the thick of a bitter polemic with the figureheads of the old Popular Socialist Party on the issue of his showing of "bourgeois" and "decadent" films, and he had the essay reprinted *pro domo* in Cuba as an opportune ideological shelter. Rumblings of scandalized sour protest began to rise from the ranks of the Spanish party and, although silenced for the moment by the rank and file's sacred respect for authority and hierarchy, they would soon be exploited by Carrillo and his faithful in the political and doctrinal destruction of his colleague on the day their differences came out into the open.

Our friendship with the Semprúns and the Claudíns strengthened throughout 1963: the prolonged, cruel death agony of Monique's mother at a time when my relationship with her was at its lowest ebb; our impotence in the face of the parody of a trial accorded to Julián Grimau and his legal murder, when Monique and I ran at midnight to the Secours Populaire building where Jorge, Carrillo, and other leaders and well-known members of the CP waited in vain for a miraculous papal intervention to suspend the sentence; the pleasure and happiness when Jorge's novel won the prize—all this had brought me politically and humanly closer to both Semprún and Claudín, despite my frequent depressions and anguished internal crises. Their sure and subtle vision of Spain and the democratic possibilities opened up by the rapid evolution of our society had an obvious influence on my own views as I rejected my theoretical daydreams and illusions that were on the edge of reality. At the end of December I began to write an article in which, from less subjective, hobbled, rickety premises, I posed once more the problem of Spain's relationship with Europe. It was a decisive question for me, not only for reasons of a strictly political order but also because of its personal and literary resonances. Although I had believed in the possibility of a violent, radical change in Spanish society, I had put my pen at the disposition of such an objective in a sometimes elementary and didactic manner. My nationalist, patriotic attitude in those years derived from the mistaken conviction that a Spanish revolution was a desirable alternative and close at hand: but my fervor evaporated when I saw clearly that the country was becoming modern and bourgeois under the Franco régime and that the latter would last as long as Franco. As I concluded years later when analyzing this change, the Spain that took wing around 1960, owing to the favorable European conjuncture and the peaceful invasion by millions of tourists, could no longer fan the amorous flame of its intellectuals nor the burning mysticism of commitment: "This in no way means," I wrote, "that the latter cease to take any reasonable or practical interest in their country's destiny: what I mean is that their passion, when it exists, is directed toward other climes."* Comparing the situation in Spain in the sixties with that of Britain at the beginning of the nineteenth century— when political freedoms had been gained, religious conflicts resolved, and the country was thrust into a savage industrial revolution that destroyed both the physical and moral landscape, the national problem ceased to inspire writers and artists—I noted that if the latter still intervened in English social and political life their hearts beat for other causes, as happened even in July 1936, when the Spanish civil war began. The caboose of Europe, our country was losing the dramatic contrasts and features of its picturesque backwardness without yet acquiring the moral and material advantages of the richer nations. The struggle for political and trade-union freedoms, the elimination of social injustice, the abolition of censorship was to continue; but such goals were hard pressed to provoke the depth of feeling created, for example, by the cause of Palestine or Vietnam. The image of Spain already was, and would continue to become, closer to the image of other European countries, and just as no left-wing French intellectual could be stirred by France, nor Dutch or English intellectuals by Holland or England, thus our attachment to a Spain that was neither fantastic nor revolutionary lost its raison d'être. It was necessary to bury the hatchet of anachronistic nationalism and adapt to reality. This metamorphosis affected the writer's strategy and the very nature of his discourse: there was a different mental target. When renouncing the values underlying my previous "committed" literature, I did so naturally aware that I belonged not to a weak or persecuted culture but to one that was vast, rich, and dynamic, as Spanish culture is in the dual compass of Spain and South America. The act of casting off oppressive, sterile identity markers opened the way to a plural literary space that had no frontiers; banned by Francoism, my books could seek refuge in Mexico or Buenos Aires. From now on, the language and only the language would be my real country.

Enlivened by my new certainties, I tried to set them out in a clear, concise, and convincing manner. Thanks to its repression of the working class, maintenance of old production relations in the agricultural sector, and surrender of Falangist rhetoric to the interests of the monopolies, the Régime had laid the basis for modern capitalist accumulation: though, on the one hand, the success of the stabilization plan offered the bourgeoisie

---

* Interview with Julio Ortega reprinted years later in *Disidencias*, Barcelona, 1977.

unanticipated prospects and gave it a confidence and security it previously lacked, on the other hand, massive emigration to Europe and a spectacular increase in demand within the domestic labor market placed the Spanish working class in an advantageous situation; in this framework its program of demands was more like that of French or Italian workers toward their countries' employing class than that of the peninsular proletariat ten years earlier, which confronted defenseless the harsh monolithic state supported by a frightened and constrained bourgeoisie. The two-way traffic of tourists and migrant workers was to sweep aside traditional mentalities tied to traditional modes of production. Through both, the Spanish people discovered the economic values of "advanced" societies and mimetically adapted their behavior and aspirations to Calvinist principles of modernity. Only Republicans in exile and especially, although I never mentioned the fact, the Communist Party, maintained the relevance of an analysis that was progressively less connected to reality: Francoism would collapse not through the revolutionary struggle of the masses but as the victim of a social dynamic that would empty it of any substance and convert it into a useless, hollow shell:

> The fact that the path of evolution is not the one predicted in 1951, 1956, or 1961 is insufficient reason to reject it or act as if it did not exist. Analyses and programs must fit the facts, and not vice versa. There is no doubt that the change requires extremely painful rethinking on moral, political, social, economic, and even aesthetic fronts, but we must have the intelligence and courage to accept the challenge.
>
> The seductive and somewhat romantic vision of the heroic Spain of '36 has been replaced by a reality that is ambiguous, trivial, and unpleasant. A train has taken off after twenty years of immobility and, caught unawares, the parties and intellectuals of the left have been left on the platform. But it is futile to deny the reality of the train or to pull the rear carriage by rope in the opposite direction. The problem is, on the contrary, how to board the moving train and accelerate its speed as fast as possible.*

My article was ready in January 1964 and I showed a draft to Semprún and Claudín: I remember that they both expressed their disagreements and differences, suggested small changes and clarifications, argued with me over particular points and questions of emphasis. This exchange of opinions had a very marginal effect on the final version; contrary to what was said later, it was in no way crucial. Although I had taken the article to

---

* The perception of structural change within Spain is quite transparent at the time in the *Carta de España* by Jaime Gil de Biedma, which is in *El pie de la letra*, as well as in José Ángel Valente's beautiful and incisive poems, like "Melancolía del destierro" and "Ramblas de julio, 1964."

L'Express at the beginning of the year, the text was only printed three months later: the editor-in-chief had sought a significant date for publication and had reached the conclusion that 1 April would be the most suitable, the twenty-fifth anniversary of Franco's victory. The length of the essay and its reflective character, detached from the details of day-to-day events, meant that there could be such a delay without any loss of immediacy. In the period between my handing it over and its publication, the theoretical and strategic disagreements between Semprún and Claudín and their companions in the Party leadership, already revealed in a "cadre" training course held near Arras in the summer of 1963, provoked a series of discussions between them and the Carrillo-led majority. I was totally on the periphery of all this, and my two friends did not break the silence imposed by their secret character; nevertheless, from laconic allusions to the existence of problems, I sensed they were worried and anxious. As I later discovered, a first round of conversations with executive committee members resident in France had not brought agreement. Forced to formulate their criticisms as plainly and simply as possible, Claudín and Semprún agreed to a request to present them in writing and argue them through weeks later with their colleagues in the presence of la Pasionaria. The meetings of the *Realidad* editorial board were temporarily suspended and Claudín dedicated all his usual calm and energy to explaining and defending his positions. At the end of March they were both traveling to Prague, and at a dinner for the three couples on the rue Poissonnière they said their farewells like actors well-versed in their roles and the unhappy conclusion of the drama: in fine fettle with a touch of melancholy resignation. Spanish readers would find out years later, upon the publication of the *Autobiografía de Federico Sánchez*, what happened in that decisive plenary. While the harsh and bloody confrontation was waged, I was in Paris, a million miles away from the gathering storm. On 2 April my article "On ne meurt plus à Madrid" came out in *L'Express*, with a striking intro on the "decisive change" in Spain over recent years. Two or three days afterwards, I was visited by a writer-friend newly arrived from Madrid who had just been told in very hostile terms of the content of my essay. Although he had not yet read it, he informed me he was worried about my possible revisionist and bourgeoisified positions. Rather upset by his warning, I told him to look at the essay before issuing a condemnation, since I doubted it was as negative as it had been described to him. I added that I had shown it to Semprún and Claudín and that apart from a few minor differences and reservations they had not felt it to be defeatist or out-of-focus. My colleague promised to read it carefully and discuss the content with me before returning to Spain. There was no such conversation, but a telephone call from Gregorio López Raimundo, whom I knew only by sight, to tell me he urgently wanted to see me. I agreed to

meet him that afternoon at home, intrigued by his visit and the speed
with which it had been arranged, and we had hardly exchanged polite
greetings when he asked if it were true that I had shown the *L'Express*
article to his two colleagues. I said I had, but only on a personal or
friendly level, as I might have done with any other Party acquaintance,
like Sastre or Teresa de Azcárate. I was insistent that they had formulated
some objections which I had not always taken into consideration and,
consequently, responsibility for the text was mine alone. López Raimundo
made no secret that this was a serious matter: he said it was part of a much
wider assault on the political line of the Party. It was his duty to inform
his companions in the leadership of the content of our interview: he or one
of his colleagues would call me later to discuss the problem.

On their return from Prague, my two friends described the broad
outlines of the plenary meeting in the old castle of the kings of Bohemia
and their expulsion from the executive committee. I related to them my
interview with López Raimundo and his interest in their possible link
with my article in *L'Express*, but they did not pay too much attention to
the matter given the circumstances in which they found themselves,
subject to that character assassination or process of discredit and moral
death that corresponds to revisionism within the purest Stalinist tradition. Their previous experience of Party methods of eliminating, even
physically, Trotskyists and dissidents, conferred upon them the cheerful
bravura of those on death row for whom all is lost except their self-respect.
My concern over the business with *L'Express* was, however, justified. A
fresh phone call, this time from Juan Gómez, warned me of his impending
visit. Teresa de Azcárate's husband, at the time the Party's leading expert
on economic questions, angrily asked me if I had really told López Raimundo that his wife knew of the article. I made it clear I had not: López
Raimundo, suffering from slight deafness, had misheard me. Slightly
calmer, Juan Gómez went to the heart of the matter: whether or not the
two dissidents had helped me write it, the article was full of serious errors,
it directly attacked the Party, and it was to be refuted in the pages of
Realidad. The task of composing the reply had fallen to him and, as he
solemnly hinted, it was going to be very tough-minded. As the French
version of the article had suffered a number of cuts and contained a few
mistakes, I handed him the Spanish original, recently published in
Mexico. Juan Gómez politely said goodbye, but not before he had suggested that it would be helpful if I met Carrillo in order to clarify fully
my role in what he obviously judged to be a burgeoning, well-orche-
strated conspiracy.

But Moscow, Rome, or Santiago had pronounced without considering
my testimony or protests. On 19 April the CP leadership called a meeting
in a hall belonging to the Communist council of Stains, where Carrillo,

who had no legal status in France, spoke for the first time in public; he denounced a sinister plot against the Party, in a speech full of cryptic allusions and veiled attacks on the two absent comrades, of which the only clue visible to the uninformed membership led straight to me: the revisionists and capitulators hidden away in the ranks of the Party could henceforth, if they so wished, communicate through the pages of *L'Express* but not through *Realidad*! As Semprún and Claudín told me—several present at the meeting informed them of the drift of the speech—Carrillo had decided to air the polemic within the leadership before the rank and file, and used my article as a weapon against them, accusing them of disgraceful responsibility. Unable or unwilling still to mention their names, he centered his attacks on my article, thus converting it into a butt for all censors, a punching ball upon which blows would rain for weeks and months.

Though not entirely surprised by such behavior, I was upset by the cynicism, contempt for truth, and lack of respect for people that it revealed—attitudes so similar to those that prospered in the beleaguered camp of the Régime. They trampled with abandon on the elementary rules of democracy and free discussion; the struggle of ideas was transformed into a petty-minded interrogation, the aim of which was to destroy the enemy or present him as the devil. As Francesc Vicens later informed me—he was a member of the editorial board of *Realidad*—the board's next meeting was convened behind the backs of the three lepers and, without condescending to explain such striking absenteeism, Juan Gómez announced that the editorial in the third issue would be devoted to attacking my ill-starred article. Vicens and others present intervened to suggest that since I was part of the committee, I should be invited to debate the question with the rest of them. Their proposal did not pass, although backed by a majority, and those who supported the measure were dismissed from *Realidad* without a second thought. However, the show had only just begun and, while the crisis between the Carrillo leadership and the expelled comrades developed and deepened, my astonishment grew apace. One fine day I discovered that my ideas were being "discussed" at all cell meetings, as an hors d'oeuvre to a meatier, more treacherous attack on my friends' positions. As the two Catalan Communist Party members, labor lawyer August Gil and former architecture student Javier Martín Malo, explained in a long interview published by the weekly magazine *Mundo* on 3 April 1978, both were summoned at the end of May 1964 to a clandestine meeting of the Barcelona committee to which they belonged: there, the messenger from the Paris leadership, Josep Serradell, alias "Román," brought them up-to-date on Claudín and Semprún's expulsion from the executive committee and their suspension from the central committee for their "right-wing,"

"defeatist," "anti-Leninist," and "social democratic" stances: "As the only
definitive proof, Román read us an article by Goytisolo in which he more
or less said that Spanish capitalism was in a growth phase and that, in that
context of economic development, all illusions about the collapse of
Francoism were pure utopianism. ... What is incredible is that J.G. was
not even a Communist militant, but a personal friend of Claudín and
Semprún. However, he made out that they had used him to publicize
their theses." A corollary of this conspiratorial paranoia, so rooted in
clandestine organizations, would be Román's secret report, the content
and code of which Vicens deciphered for me when he brought his archive
to Spain: aware of my presence in Catalonia—my last holidays in Torrentbó just before my father's death—Serradell warned the membership of
this fact and advised them "to keep an eye" on me. The repetitions of
history are sometimes grotesque, and drama turns to farce: after the
Régime's written attacks and police vigilance, I found the similar situations and attitudes that I was now experiencing particularly enlightening
and exemplary.

One cannot today read Juan Gómez's long-awaited reply without
blushing on his behalf: the leading Party authority on economics
manipulated and doctored the data with the wiles of a puppeteer to
demonstrate that, behind the appearance of progress, Spain was still
lagging behind the rest of Europe, the Régime was in an irremediable
state of decay, and it would be "finally" swept away by a sharpening of the
class struggle. Unfortunately his delirious fantasies of victories and cat-
astrophes were not unique: they impregnated all the Communist Party
commentaries and declarations. Coinciding with my article in L'Express, a
Treball editorial ("Twenty-five Peaceful Years?") described the situation
in these terms: "While the working class and people reach this anniversary confident of a not-too-distant future of freedom—the process of the
liquidation of the Franco régime has never been so clear as over the past
year—the dictatorship celebrates its quarter of a century of victory with
the sound of funeral rather than victory marches." In that rarefied, self-
satisfied world, to have recourse to the language of facts was like speaking
to a brick wall; Semprún and Claudín's daring in doing just that constituted a crime of lèse-optimism and the consequences were quite predictable.

If those months were painful for me, they were even more so for my
expelled friends, especially for Claudín and his family. While Jorge had a
series of cards in his favor—legal residence in France and a promising
literary career—Fernando was out in the cold, with no documents, money,
or work. Slandered, placed in moral quarantine, the object of intense
pressure to leave France and accept the "generous offer" of retirement or
eternal rest in the Eastern bloc—from the attempt to evict him from his

tiny flat in La Courneuve and leave him in the street to physical intimidation that forced him to temporarily leave home and live in a Parisian *chambre de bonne* in hiding from both the French police and his own comrades—Claudín resisted those trials without losing his sangfroid, patience, or sense of humor. Years later, when surveying Blanco White's pages on the inquisitorial methods of the Church—its stratagems, tricks, and ploys to cow or eliminate heretics—I was shaken by the parallel between his historical sketch and the recent chronicle of my friends. The use of *ad hominem* arguments, the desire to deprive the enemy of all rights, the absolute contempt for ethical norms and justice that I then discovered filled me henceforth with a healthy skepticism for the would-be democratic ideals of an organization that did not flinch from the use of force or slander against its own members. The future society envisaged by the Party's public face could only with difficulty spring from such an array of blows below the belt, grudges, lack of scruples, thirst for power, spy-itis, and irrationality. I have not been surprised or saddened by events in Spain since the blessed legalization of the CP—that grotesque tableau of schisms, splits, expulsions, accusations which would end, *risum teneatis*, in the buffeting and fall through the trapdoor of Carrillo himself, in a burlesque atmosphere of farcical exaggeration complete with hairpulling and insults worthy of street urchins or fishwives. After the anathematizing of Claudín and Semprún, whenever I heard righteous, well-meaning criticisms of my movement away from "real socialism" and its rose-tinted promises of happiness, I would keep my ironic amusement to myself. Accusations of bourgeois individualism would bounce off a hide toughened by experience. Without bitterness or rancor, and at the cost of a few feathers and a few scratches, I had earned this privilege with the sweat of my brow: the right to smile inwardly.

The systematic denigration over those months was water off a duck's back. After the downpour that followed the inglorious Milan episode, I was aware of both the harshness of my country and the splendor of my own isolation. There was no sense in replying to Juan Gómez's editorial and getting entangled in a fresh polemic. An internal struggle of the left, in its precarious besieged state, could benefit only the supporters of the Régime: in a mood of exceptional levity and relief, I resolved to abandon my fumbling apprenticeship as a politician and leave the subject until the hypothetical day of Franco's death.

You lived for eleven years physically and morally cut off from your country, outside its historical development, the master of a vast void: your name disappeared from the newspapers and your work—printed in Paris,

Mexico, or Buenos Aires—was strictly banned. This ostracism never-theless favored your decision to be yourself, to defend your truth and scale of values against the norms and rituals of the tribe: to put a halt to the insistent pressure of the stealer of strength. From now on, you would express political opinions on Santo Domingo, Czechoslovakia, or Pales-tine, but not on Spain. You were no longer enthralled by its predictable evolution under Francoism. You occasionally crossed through on your way to Oran, Oujda, or Tangier; a fleeting impression of a hotel, an inn, a stopping place; a blot on the map. Disaffection, indifference, distance, which at extreme moments would nourish your dream of becoming Maltese, of attaining by whatever means the sought-after papers of a stateless citizen: far from your own sleeping-beauty society, the great country of mutes deafened by their long, noisy silence. An obstinate, neurotic denial of your land, an instinctive desire to run away if your neighbors loudly expressed themselves in your tongue, inexplicable unease when you bumped into fellow countrymen who addressed not you but your tiresome double: you shamefully deny your identity and respond to the intruder in a strange abrupt language. The violent rejection of a world, which, with significant ambivalence, you compensate for by a growing passion for its history and culture: you ravenously devour the classics, reread Asín and Américo Castro, are dazzled by and appropriate Blanco White. The unforgettable experience of translating yourself as you translate him, without in the end knowing if he really existed or was a distant incarnation of yourself. You realize that his struggle and moral trajectory were the same because the oppressive régime with which he struggled stretched down to the one you knew. Like him, you transformed punishment into a state of grace. You lightly assume to your own advantage the burden imposed by your destiny: an airborne species, a carnation in the wind open to other climates and stimuli. Seminal stays in North Africa, journeys to the Sahara, carefree wandering through Istan-bul, slow river descent to dark Nubian splendors. An apprenticeship in the novelties and hazards of the role of the visiting professor: fertile proximity to the university world, fascination for the melting pot of New York. You share out your life between Paris, Manhattan, and Tangier without the pain of nostalgia for the Peninsula.

An illusory impression, as reality saw fit to demonstrate.

In September 1975 you had flown to the United States, to give one of your usual courses in Pittsburgh, where you heard the news of the trial, sentencing, and execution of the Basque militants. The image of the moribund dictator delivering his grotesque speech reminded you of the drama of Inés de Castro that you had seen in the cinema as a child: her corpse solemnly reinstated on the throne, dressed in the attributes of authority, she too received the silent homage of her courtiers, who were bewitched by the symbol of motionless power that inertia seemed to perpetuate beyond death. Violently repelled by the spectacle, wishing to see the drama filed away forever with its whole troupe of heroes and extras in the library of your classics, you understood that your indifference was a fiction and that the old feeling of shame for everything that the official Spain of the time stood for would stay with you to the grave. Isolated in the stone, metal, and cement landscape of the Golden Triangle, for several weeks you hung on the television news, a prey to the anger and impotence that you had thought gone forever. From Monique's telephone call telling you the news—later denied—of his death until it was over, you remembered your Spanish childhood and youth as if you had been present at the death agony of someone who was really the monstrous head of your family. The certainty of at last being orphaned by the man whose shadow had hovered over you ever since the devastating blast of the civil war rekindled the imperious desire to write about him, to clarify once and for all the nature of that relationship beyond and above the one tying you to a merely putative father. On the night of 20 November you prepared the draft of the text you read days later in the Library of Congress in Washington, as your puny if invigorating revenge on that unvenerable institution that had so much contributed to keeping him in power in your lifetime: a text that, while avoiding direct mention of his name (*In memoriam F.F.B.* 1892–1975), claimed the vile reality of his paternity and would be (though you were unaware of it at the time) the seed or kernel of this incursion into the minefield of autobiography.

· II ·

The Slippers of Empedocles

MY NAME APPEARED after Cervantes in the list of most-translated Spanish writers published under the auspices of UNESCO in an annual survey of world literary activity relating to 1963. Rather than being flattered by this fact, I was filled first with anxiety and then with despair. What had I done to deserve it? Success so at odds with my feeble, unsubstantial work could only be the result of a combination of circumstances and misconceptions that in one way or another converged on my person. Had the opportunist, much-abused identification of my name with the cause of Spanish democracy and my minor position of privilege in the world of journalism and publishing perhaps created an easily exportable image of the young committed writer that faithfully fitted the clichés and stereotypes of our country? The phenomenon entirely omitted specific literary factors: it developed exclusively from the world of publishing. As one of my critics wrote at the time—expressing, in truth, my own feelings of unease—wasn't I "an amazingly distended balloon" that would be duly deflated "till it reached its rightful size"?

An amazingly distended balloon, like the *hot air* man that Larra describes in such masterly fashion in one of his essays: the likeness of the portrait astounded me. But distended by whom and how? A well-oiled chain of cause and effect had turned me in the space of five years into one of the official standard-bearers of progressive causes in the Hispanic world, welcomed both by the party propaganda machines and an intelligentsia anchored to the myths of Romantic Spain and its unhappy civil war. While the Slovak, Ukrainian, Norwegian, or Finnish versions of my work piled up on the shelves of my library, the rue Poissonnière was an obligatory meeting place for all involved in projects or cultural encounters concerning the Peninsula. My friendship with the editors of *L'Express, France-Observateur*, and *Les Temps Modernes* allowed me a small patch of political and literary influence that I unashamedly cultivated for a time. A mixture of Marxist sectarianism, desire to be in the spotlight, and petty feelings of rivalry led me to act rather ingloriously, like those social climbers in the world of the press and publishing whose Shakespearian passions and Machiavellian ruses I would have occasion to experience many years later. Perhaps, like a handful of writers whom I now detest, I had built a precocious, flamboyant literary career on the back of the historical misfortunes of my own people? In such circumstances the exalting of the work of a patriotic author fighting against the abuses of a hateful régime is the same as defending the cause of justice, and vice versa. It is, of course, a simplistic and deceptive equation, but extremely beneficial for the poet or novelist who unscrupulously adopts it. One can criticize an individual who publishes his writing, but not a people in struggle and even less a whole continent. The amazingly distended balloon, voice of the anger, dreams, and hopes of two hundred million beings, would float miraculously above good and evil.

Smug pride, narcissistic complacency, the conceit of a peacock? The arrogance existed and it was palpable: imbalance between being and image, external persona and the ego lurking behind, the approachable worldly novelist and his insomniac, depressive support, the "normal" husband and the one gradually taken over by violent, sumptuous, martial nocturnal fantasies. A delicate if persistent feeling of precarious uncertainty—just like the one we experienced when we dreamed, for example, of dancing with the carefree agility of a Fred Astaire only to remember in semiconsciousness our real country-yokel awkwardness—increased the distance and alienation I felt from myself. The *other's* vanity, his political enthusiasms, worldly ways, moral opportunism, pettiness, and pride oppressed me and were difficult to live with. My political zeal began to weaken as I established that outside the realm of theory Marxist ideals were gathering rust and looking not just miserable, but tarnished and dishonorable as well. Didn't my participation in meetings, projects, discussions, and congresses constitute an enormous waste of time and an exhausting squandering of energies? Did the dinners and engagements with writers, journalists, and publishing people really suit Monique's character and mine, our growing desire to retreat and to be near each other? Had we set out on a course that did not agree with us and demanded an effort that was not matched by the satisfaction obtained in return? These and other questions posed over two or three years pointed me in the direction of a decision, and finally bore fruit: it was necessary to puncture once and for all the distended balloon and reduce it to fairer, more human proportions.

The decision to wage war on my image was firmly taken, but the skirmishes in the battle extended over years and results were late in coming. Even now I have not succeeded in entirely erasing it from the minds of people who met me then and, in spite of my efforts at eviction, small echoes or traces remain within myself. Of all the struggles I have fought against personal inclinations that I abhor, this has perhaps been the most unpleasant and harshest. How could I free myself from this young double, at first sight so blessed by fortune but whose ideas, tastes, and ambitions had ceased to be mine and even repelled me? The patient labor of separating myself out from him has not always been crowned with success. The bursting of the balloon required a series of rejections and transformations that turned my life upside down. To do this, I had to sabotage my modest, but envied, position in the world of publishing in exchange for another doubtful, risky, difficult life in literature; I had to find an economic alternative to my income as a writer; defend lost or unpopular causes against those that were profitable or fashionable; live in isolation and cultivate enemies; stop conceiving of the vocation as a career and the novelist or poet as spokesman for the national interest. Only time and its inevitable cortège of mishaps and mistakes would allow me to assemble a few analects on which I would try to model my behavior: a minor victory but one that would in the future clarify with nodular precision my past confused relationships with myself and with everybody else.

F ROM A CERTAIN *age, one learns to strip oneself of all that is
secondary or incidental in order to bind oneself to the areas
of experience which apportion greater pleasure and emotion: writing, sex, and love
will henceforth be the deepest and most authentic configurations of your territory:
all else is a poor substitute that an elemental principle of purely selfish economy
advises you to do without and which you will do without entirely: as you will see
from your own example, whoever aspires to become a public figure sacrifices his most
intimate truth to an image, an external profile: literary favor is a chance and
subtle matter and it usually takes vengeance on those who rush in search of
recognition by distancing itself and then abandoning them: from your publishing
watchtower you will witness over the years numerous examples of literary and
moral erosion: that process of self-advertisement by the writer who, because of
unfaithfulness to the most genuine sources of his being, finally loses, unawares, his
pristine state of grace.*

A FEW WEEKS AFTER my arrival in Paris, Mascolo asked me to help him clear the backlog of work by reading and selecting from the manuscripts in Spanish that were gathering dust in his office at Gallimard. Although it was badly paid work, it had the incentive for me of strengthening my relationship with Monique and her colleagues, while putting me in contact with writers I admired or had heard of when I was at university. The effect of that friendly proximity on a provincial greenhorn like myself was both stimulating and damaging. If, on the one hand, it brought me close to the work of the novelists, poets, essayists, or dramatists whom I often saw in the entrance hall to Gallimard, on the other, it flattered my youthful pride to move among them, to accept their condescending and undeserved familiarity. An interloper in the *sancta sanctorum* of the Parisian intelligentsia, I, like many others, would have yielded to the glamour of literary society—that universe so long-windedly described by Proust's novelistic genius—if it had not been in my case opportunely counterbalanced by my political militancy and Monique's healthy rigor. My association with her and Mascolo's crowd drew me into a very well defined group whose trenchant attitudes to Stalinism and writers designated as right-wing discouraged me from any personal excursion outside those carefully traced boundaries. Although their intransigence did not reach the extremes of Debord and his minuscule Situationist International, it did, however, rival that of Breton and his followers. In the peremptory style so typical of Rive Gauche circles, the mere enunciation of their ideas and positions automatically implied the ridiculing and rejection of those of their opponent. While Camus symbolized in their eyes hollow, abstract moralizing, Aragon embodied the image of the perfect, total *salaud*. Even Sartre, with whom they nevertheless shared some affinities, slid, according to them, into opportunism toward the Party, as if to compensate by his flirtation with Stalinism for his past apoliticism in respect to the Nazis. His famous essay on the reappearance of Stalin's ghost with the entry of Soviet tanks into Hungary had not resolved the point of contention with my friends: the adjective "Sartrian" always retained on their lips a reproving, pejorative resonance.

Consequently, Camus's attitude toward me was cold and distant, although he had a keen interest in Spain and sustained an honorable attitude toward the Régime, to the point of turning his back on UNESCO when a representative of Franco joined that organization. I occasionally bumped into him on the stairs or in the corridors at Gallimard, and I was rather disappointed when he just nodded politely in my direction. Living as I did with Monique, and consequently linked to the Mascolo clan, he mentally included me in the group that had aligned itself with Sartre during the polemic around *L'Homme révolté*. As Monique told me later—when her ideas had developed and she willingly admitted her past injustices toward Camus—the latter had gone into the office where she and other members of the Gallimard staff had just read aloud and underlined in pencil the harshest sections of Sartre's reply to his open letter to *Les Temps Modernes*, and he asked whether they had the latest issue of the magazine in which he, apparently, came under attack. Camus picked up the copy that lay visibly on the table and glanced at the pages marked by her while those present kept an embarrassed silence. The painful run through Sartre's text—a read that, according to numerous accounts, deeply affected Camus—was thus associated in his memory with the initial context in which it took place. From then on, the author of *La Peste* drew a dividing line between the people surrounding him: faced with a majority that supported Sartre's brilliant but often mistaken arguments, he took refuge in a warm nucleus of faithful friends.

During this period, Monique and I regularly visited the flat on the rue Saint-Benoît where Mascolo and Marguerite Duras lived on a knife-edge after their breakup. In an atmosphere that gradually filled with smoke and suppressed tensions, we talked into the early hours of literature and politics with Edgar and Violette Morin, Robert Antelme, André Frenaud, and Louis-René des Forêts. I can remember Marguerite's intense, impassioned, fascinating voice, that subtle magic she communicates to the characters in her novels and plays, the deliberate high drama she brings to the pettiest discussions. We drank a lot, and although we did not entirely share the group's past affinities, they gave us a most generous welcome. After my recent probing of the work of Genet and Violette Leduc, I passed a fine-tooth comb through our friend's poetic world: guided by Monique, the editors of Seix Barral were quick to sign Marguerite up and translate her works into Spanish. Later on, the success of her baptismal incursion into the cinema—the script of *Hiroshima mon amour*, directed by Alain Resnais—would accentuate with charming spontaneity her unquenchable tendency to narcissistic egocentrism. One day when we had debated in turn the relative merits of her books, plays, and cinematic enterprises, one of the guests, as we started our desserts, timidly deflected the conversation toward the latest events in Algeria, and Marguerite retreated into an aloof silence before exclaiming: "Well, since you're having a technical conversation, I'm off!"

I met the novelist Elio Vittorini, the only member of the clan not

resident in Paris and on the periphery of the group, when I traveled with
Monique to Venice in January 1957 and we spent a few days in Milan. It
is impossible to forget that attic where the writer lived on the Viale
Gorizia—a gray avenue some distance from downtown, running alongside
a gloomy, dull canal. Vittorini's face radiated a captivating sense of
beauty; his serious features, gray hair and mustache, the gaze that penetrated his interlocutor with an inquisitive warmth; that embarrassed,
unsophisticated smile of his which revealed, in spite of his sharp wit, the
roughness of his background: an extraordinary combination of strength
and intelligence, wild appearance and gentle domesticity, seduced whoever had the opportunity to chat with him at home, while in the company
of his wife and Sicilian friends he talked, laughed, or played an animated
game of cards, just as in his native village. By his side, Ginetta shared in
his delicate, fierce majesty: tall, serene, noble-featured, her voice had an
incantatory power curiously related to Marguerite's. Basking in the glow
of their startling beauty, Elio and Ginetta presented the image of an
emblematic Castilian couple, lion and lioness resting peacefully; I have
not seen, nor shall I ever see again, such a perfect luminous combination
of male and female. Ginetta and Elio welcomed us with open arms: they
had known Monique ever since her divorce and were obviously pleased to
see her with me so happy and full of vitality. Vittorini had traveled
through Spain two summers before and was interested in speaking to a
Spaniard of my age about the situation in the country and the future of
Francoism. Later his literary work would exercise a momentary influence
on mine: when he read the Spanish text of *Campos de Níjar* he suggested
the idea of extending it with a slight narrative plot and, in the light of his
experiment in *Il Sempione strizza l'occhio al Frejus*, I wrote the fictional
documentary *La Chanca*, the Spanish edition of which I dedicated post-
humously to him. On our return from Venice, we visited his house again
like old friends. Ginetta honored us with her gastronomic specialities, and
Elio conversed with a genial simplicity rare in the tinsel circus of those
infected by literary madness. His death, eight years later, profoundly
saddened both of us; of all the writers I have met beyond the confines of
my own language, Vittorini was, alongside Genet, the one who inspired
me as a person with most respect and appreciation.

While I was getting to know the Mascolo crowd, Monique introduced
me, through her doctor, to a group of writers and artists more or less
linked by their roots to the Surrealists. Doctor Théodore Frankel had been
one of the founders of this movement and appears in the paintings of the
time with Breton, Crevel, and Aragon discreetly in the background.
Monique used to lunch with him once a week; he would occasionally
invite us both to dine with his old friends. Frankel was a bachelor and
inveterate womanizer, whose devouring flame of passion for the compa-

nion of a famous writer had, in a legend difficult to verify, impelled him
to pursue his rival all over Paris with an avenging or justice-seeking
revolver: the crime was never consummated and, after a time, frustrated
sharpshooter and would-be victim made their peace and saw each other
again without any resentment. At these dinners I met Alberto Giacometti, Georges Bataille, Michel Leiris, and other creative artists. Unfortunately, the narrowness of the ideological space I inhabited also reduced
the span of my own literary interests and projects: the writers on the edge
of the mainstream, the successors to Gide's humanism and Malraux's
historic compromise, sometimes seduced me with an attractiveness I
deemed to be unhealthy and which I strove to resist. My models were, and
continued to be for some time, Sartre and Camus: Artaud, Bataille, and
Michaux were thus consigned to the purgatory of the illicit and imper-
missible until, freed from the straitjacket of my literary-political theories,
I could unashamedly surrender to the magnetic pull of my own taste.
Although my quintessentially Hispanic resistance or mistrust of new
trends from outside—at the opposite extreme of the *plus parisien*-than-the-
Parisians-themselves syndrome that frequently befell writers and artists
from Latin America—meant I avoided the trap that snared some of them,
of worship of all things Gallic, it also made it difficult to approach the
work of some writers with whom I conversed quite unprofitably. Giacometti's overwhelming vitality and radiant ugliness, thrust by his genius
to a new aesthetic dimension, created a startling, unforgettable contrast to
Bataille's pale, apparently bloodless face, the blue of whose eyes reminded
me of Grandfather. From the shelter of his thick, bushy eyebrows, Doctor
Frankel, with the hieratic patience of a fawn, could not take his eyes off
his latest girlfriend or mistress.

My relationship with Raymond Queneau, whom Monique had known
for some years, was more original and unexpected. A building-worker—
whose life story I included in a report on emigration published in *Tribuna
Socialista*—came from the community of Valencian immigrants, relatives,
friends or neighbors of our housekeeper and her husband, whom we would
visit on the odd Sunday in their Rueil-Malmaison shacks. José was in his
way interested in politics and spoke admiringly of an overseer in the
building firm that employed him. A refugee from the Spanish civil war,
Jadraque was, José said, a pleasure to talk to, and José often visited him in
the hospital, where he was recovering from an accident at work. Jadraque
was still youthful in appearance, ruddy, well-built, attracted by culture,
and endowed with a subtle sarcastic sense of humor. As a member of the
CNT or FAI he had suffered the trial of French internment camps and had
joined the anti-Nazi resistance before adapting to the grayness of life in
exile by getting the job of overseer in the firm that employed some of my
Valencian friends. Jadraque quite rightly lamented their political ignor-

ance and lack of interest in trade unions: his vision of Francoist Spain was bitter and lucid; he did not share the others' fantasies of an imminent return home. Convinced that the Régime had castrated young people, he sought refuge in the classics of acratic thought and discussed Marx's authoritarian tendencies with me. I remember how one day out of the blue he mentioned Queneau and asked if I knew him. I told him that Monique met him daily at Gallimard. "I also see him a lot," Jadraque commented; "his novels are very amusing." The reasons for this unsuspected relationship became clearer days later. Jadraque cohabited with the housekeeper of Queneau, who was very fond of him. As my compatriot had mentioned me to him, the author of *Les Dimanches de la vie* told Monique he wanted to meet me and invited us to supper in his Neuilly flat. Behind his easy smile and defensive irony, Queneau seemed an affectionate, timid man, full of secret crannies and corners, with a gently exuberant character and a heterogeneous, limitless culture. His unusual literary exploration, which I gradually assimilated as I got to know him, seems now unique and seminal. An anarchist in ideas and temperament, the writer treated Jadraque almost paternally. My links with him, which owed nothing to the literary world of Paris, had been the best route to the secluded space of his private life.

This peculiar bottom-up relationship, through our housekeeper's friends or fellow countrymen who had migrated to France after the frosts had ruined Valencian agriculture for a time, would provide me for a period with an unanticipated vision of some aspects and habits of the indigenous intellectual bourgeoisie. After placing a good number of them on the sites of Jadraque's firm and in the homes of writers and journalists more or less known to Monique, on Sundays our flat became a meeting place where the newcomers from the district of Gandía could noisily swap stories of their respective employers. Thus, quite undeliberately, we discovered that a famous literary critic on *Le Figaro* padlocked his refrigerator when he went away on the weekends or that a renowned author made her Spanish *bonne* eat her leftovers. This indirect, involuntary prying—which would have delighted someone more into gossip than I was—nevertheless revealed the existence of a sordid penny-pinching that until then I had thought the exclusive property of our underdeveloped lugubrious middle class.

Just as a villager from the Bierzo or the Batuecas miraculously introduced into a harem would gradually shed his wonderment and adapt naturally with a few doses of ennui to the delights of his dream made flesh, so my sudden admission to the Olympus of the great had the predictable consequence of quickly curing me of the provincial desire to scale its peaks. Monique had established friendly ties not only with French writers published by Gallimard but also, thanks to her good knowledge of

English, with foreign authors of the stature of Faulkner. The day I met her, the latter was talking to her in her office and laughed when he learned that she was leaving him for a few minutes to say hello to a young Spaniard of "Belmontian" appearance. The friendship of Monique and her ex-husband with the author of *Wild Palms* dated back to the time when he passed through Paris after being awarded the Nobel Prize.* She and the novelist had been writing intermittently to one another ever since: in flight from the relentless pursuit of the professional Faulknerians, he would forewarn Monique of his private visits to France. When Carole was born in 1952, Faulkner asked to be godfather and insisted on giving her as a present a silver cup engraved with his name and an inscription; in the rush to return home, he did not have time to order it and entrusted the right money to Monique, who instead of spending it on that showy, rather absurd present, preferred to lavish it on something more interesting and substantial. Months later, when she learned of the godfather's sudden arrival, she would be forced to hastily buy another cup and dent it to remove its new, unused look: it was a deception that Monique herself would uncover to Faulkner when he came to see his goddaughter. At the start of our relationship, she had asked me if I wanted to meet him, but my absolute ignorance of English at the time would have forced me to play the role of the dumb guest or spoil the conversation with a painful exercise in translation and persuaded me sensibly to reject the offer. Nevertheless, even apart from the cases when my reticence obeyed an objective situation of inferiority, my sudden, dizzy nearness to the big names of the day made me soon understand that, with the exception of singular examples of communication, as with Genet, the role of peeping tom bored me and was at odds with the inclinations and preferences of my real character.

Thus, when on 1 August 1959, Monique, Florence Malraux, and I crossed paths with Hemingway in the bullring in Málaga, at a bullfight with Diego Puerta, Manolo Segura, and Gregorio Sánchez, I gave a lukewarm welcome to their decision, especially that of Monique, romantically in love with Spain as a result of her youthful reading of *Death in the Afternoon*, to accost the writer as he left the arena; I just followed them on an adventure, the ramifications of which would spread, as in a serial story, to a family dinner with an unpredictable ending on one of my stays in New York as a visiting professor, a number of years after the novelist's suicide.

---

* Monique published a piece evoking her friendship, "Une apparition," in the issue of *Le Magazine Littéraire* devoted to Faulkner.

You were in a middle row and he was a quarter of the ring away at the most visible point of the front row, in his shirt-sleeves and wearing a peaked cap to ward off the sun. Forgetting past rancors, the press had given wide publicity to his presence and spectators recognized him, *toreros* dedicated their performance to him, and to the applause of onlookers he drank, arm held high, a jet of wine from a leather bag someone had handed him. He was following Ordóñez in his *mano a mano* with Dominguín around the bullrings of the Peninsula: the period described in *The Dangerous Summer*.

You lost sight of him at the end of the fight, but Monique would not give up: you found him in the bar of the city's best hotel. You headed without haste to the now defunct Miramar and asked after him. Tell him André Malraux's daughter wants to see him. The ploy bore immediate fruit: within a few minutes, the writer appeared in the lobby and gave you a warm welcome. He talked in a strange mixture of English, French, and Spanish and introduced you to his retinue: from the old acquaintance from Pamplona portrayed in *Fiesta* to the wife of a degenerate and alcoholic Peruvian millionaire. He spoke to Florence about her father and the civil war as if wanting to justify his return to the country. It was a pleasant evening that ended in bear hugs. You don't remember now if Valerie Danby-Smith was among those present.

The day after, Hemingway departed to meet up with Ordóñez and you had to return to Paris, now that the holidays were over. However, the writer noted down your address and promised to tell you if he was going to France. At the end of September, he kept his word, forewarned Monique of his visit to the Midi and generously sent three train tickets to Nîmes. You had the opportunity to see him there for a couple of days totally living up to his reputation, surrounded by his faithful followers— Ordóñez, Domingo Dominguín, Valerie, the Franco-Peruvian million-airess: discussing bulls and joking about Shakespeare with Ordóñez, drinking nonstop from midmorning an exquisite Tavel rosé. His affectionate, almost father-daughter relationship with Valerie channeled his dissipated energy: although no conventional beauty, Valerie was a very young, subtly delightful Irish woman who, months earlier, had gone to interview him in his hotel and had accompanied him on his travels ever since. The novelist and storywriter you admired in your youth had become a living monument to himself: that Papa Hemingway that anyone on the make could treat familiarly and whose literary rigor and moral alertness had shipwrecked in a sea of publicity and self-interested flattery.

While you journeyed to Spain with Dominguín and Ordóñez, Monique and Florence would see him again on the Auteuil racecourse, and in his Parisian lair at the Ritz. Monique received several letters that winter from the United States written in his most idiosyncratic trilingual patter:

Hemingway seemed depressed and touched at length in one of them on the question of suicide. After a year's silence, during which one or two letters from Monique met with no response, you heard on the radio the news of the shot with which he killed himself on 2 July 1961, just after you had driven across the Franco-Spanish frontier, on your way to Torrentbó.

Over the next ten years you had indirect news of Valerie: the unexpected marriage to Brendan Behan, his alcoholic death agony, her widowhood. In 1974, after an article on *Don Julián* appeared in the *New York Times*, the newspaper sent you a letter in which she affectionately described past meetings and gave you her address and telephone number. You got in contact with her and she invited you to dinner. On the agreed night, you reached the door to her apartment building only to realize that you knew neither the number nor letter of her apartment. In the conversation she mentioned that she had remarried, but you did not know what the hell her husband's surname was. You looked in vain for a Danby-Smith on the list by the entry phone: there wasn't one. When you were just about to go and call her from a telephone booth, you spotted on the list the existence of a Hemingway: an odd coincidence or had she been legally adopted by the writer before his suicide? You rang the bell: her voice answered. Moments later you were in the small apartment where Valerie and her two sons welcomed you. The elder was called Brendan and was her first husband's. The second, a tiny lad, seemed to belong to the other one, whose absence she apologized for: Gregory finished his consultancy very late and would perhaps arrive after dinner. During the meal you recalled friends held in common, yet the mysterious husband made no appearance. When he finally came and you were introduced, you began to put two and two together and establish the real nature of the situation: one of the sons from Hemingway's second or third marriage was a doctor and was in fact named Gregory. As the plot unraveled and you mentally reconstructed Valerie's extraordinary life story, her husband poured himself a straight glass of whiskey, showed you the manuscript of a book that, he said, he had just written about his father, separated out twenty or so pages and handed them over to you. You settled down in an armchair and, while he downed glass after glass until he had emptied the bottle, you skimmed over, first in surprise, then with unease, finally, with fascination, some sections where, according to your host, Hemingway had boasted to him that he had precipitated his mother's death by a brutal telephone call to the hospital where she was convalescing from a serious heart attack: *I got her*, or words to that effect. Gregory seemed to be waiting anxiously for your verdict and, trapped in that unforeseen situation, you felt a curious impression of unreality thicken: was this scene real or was it a dream? You felt him staring at you, you listened to him muttering about the suicide. Valerie, his wife, remained impassive: she cleared away the plates, talked lovingly to her children. You don't know what you managed to say to Gregory about the manuscript, nor can you remember how you bid farewell to the couple. You can see yourself back in the street, returned to the nocturnal bustle of the city, about to be swallowed up by the powerful jaws of a subway station, threading together the absurd chain of events that had led you there from a chance encounter in the Málaga bullring.

R EGRETTABLY, IN THE *literary circles you know best, writers have a very marked tendency to take themselves more seriously than their own work: as you said years ago in* Don Julián, *genius is confused with appearance and appearance is the key to genius: the greater the genius, the greater the façade; the greater the façade, the greater the genius: since then the situation has worsened both in and outside Spain: while the number of clowns proliferates, the number of authors who take their work seriously, instead of lovingly putting on airs, seems to be in steady decline.*

The writer's physical presence obstructs a proper evaluation of his work by introducing factors outside specific literary criteria: the living author, if he is a smart operator, throws dust in the eyes of those who are looking at him and seeks positions of fame and prestige far beyond his real merits: consequently, when one of these live wires dies he seems to deflate, as you deflated yourself, and falls rapidly into oblivion: having been exalted to excess, he is now brought down with excessive disregard: only the unfashionable never goes out of fashion: as the surrealists said, any triumphant idea or person is fatally on the road to ruin.

The attacks directed at a writer are very often the proof that his work exists, that it wounds the moral or aesthetic convictions of the reader-critic and, subsequently, they provoke his reaction: in short, they enter a dynamic relationship with him: you yourself see them usually as a paying of respects and, fortunately, there is no lack of professional swashbucklers: an innovative work stirs up a defensive response from those who feel threatened or under attack from its power or novelty: the phenomenon is as real today as in the day of Góngora.

The novel that avoids the easy well-trodden paths inevitably creates a tension, collides against the unformulated expectations of readers: the latter are suddenly faced with a code they are not used to, and this code poses a challenge: if that is accepted and the reader penetrates the meaning of the new artistic system, the victorious hand-to-hand combat with the text is itself the prize: the reader's active enjoyment.

If your books were one day welcomed with unanimous praise, that would show they had become harmless, facile, and anodyne, very quickly they would have lost their power to repel and their vitality.

In general terms, writers divide into two classes: those who conceive of literature as a career and those who don't: the first can be easily recognized from their behavior, which follows a strategy of advancement halfway between Macchiavelli and von Clausewitz: they look for glory and jobs, praise those who praise them, read those who read them, practice a barter form of economy, are professional congress attenders and introducers, they serve all governments, climb doggedly to the peaks of the Establishment.

For your part, rightly or wrongly, you believe that the author's labor demands in a free, permissive society do not concern you: you have defended and are ready to uphold the economic and union rights of any trade or job with the exception of that of writers and artists: the activity of the latter is, in your opinion, the result of a vocation that is at once a state of grace and damnation itself: if you are a writer because you cannot be anything else, writing is an essential part of your life, as might be, for example, your family background, your native tongue, your sexual orientation: to professionalize yourself as a writer would be for you as incongruous and ridiculous as doing so because you are male, expatriate, bisexual, or morally a gypsy.

You do not propose to live from your pen: your position in this respect is the exact opposite of the career writers: you do not write to earn a living, but earn a living in order to write: from nourishment, literature is transmuted into an obsessive vice: an incurable form of addiction: however, as it has recently provided you with a decent income, your literary addiction is today self-sufficient and, thanks to the distribution of your books, you have moved from the category of a mere addict to that of peddler or dealer.

THE ATTENTION PAID to Spain by French publishers has almost always been mean, out-of-focus, and intermittent. Apart from the special case of García Lorca, glorified *ab initio* by the publication of his complete works, neither the most representative authors of the 1898 Generation nor of successive pre- and postwar generations were given even average exposure in the 1950s, nor were they the object of selective, accurate translation. If critics and readers in the neighboring country are still unaware in general of a novel of the stature of *La Regenta*,* why should one be surprised that more than a quarter of a century ago, they only knew a handful of works, already sometimes out of print and unobtainable, by Baroja, Unamuno, Machado, Valle-Inclán, and Ortega? I can remember how when the first of these died, just after my arrival, I was telephoned by several newspapers and literary magazines asking after "that Spanish novelist whose funeral Hemingway attended." Later on, when Buñuel's film *Nazarín* received its première, a refined Gallic reviewer would spawn an ineffable paragraph graciously granting Galdós Mexican nationality. This traditional contempt for or lack of interest in what is written beyond the Pyrenees—so similar to our own in relation to Portugal and the Arab world—had been reinforced by the fairly widespread conviction that Spanish culture had died with the war. Francoism had converted Spain into a barren waste; no fruit, however wizened, could spring up there. The writers in exile—novelists like Barea and Sender, poets like Alberti and Guillén—attracted a small sympathetic audience beyond the circles of Hispanists but, in spite of the propaganda activity of the Communist Parties on behalf of their members, martyrs, or sympathizers—from Antonio Machado to Miguel Hernández—the mental barrier erected around the Peninsula stood its ground: Max Aub was translated only in the last years of his life, and when Cernuda died, not even the poetry magazines gave him an obituary.

When I began to read books for Mascolo, Gallimard's only permanent reader of Spanish was Roger Caillois, the editor of the series *La Croix du Sud*, devoted to South American narrative. As a refugee in Buenos Aires, like Gombrowicz, during the Nazi occupation, Caillois had connected with the group around the magazine *Sur* and had the honor of introducing Borges's work into France. In contrast, his knowledge of modern Spanish

---

* Clarín's novel was finally published in 1987.

literature was vague and behind the times; as he himself admitted to me, he had no recent serious information on the slow resurgence of letters in the Peninsula. Maurice-Edgard Coindreau's discovery of the new writers encouraged Claude Gallimard to consult with me on the matter and, in agreement with Coindreau, we drew up a list of works that were in our opinion worth translating. Over a decade, they published more than twenty novels of unequal value, representative of the literary panorama within Spain. Although, as I shall later examine, ideology and personal friendship influenced the choice, the latter also took Coindreau's tastes into account, and if anything it suffered from being too easygoing: not all the authors included reached an acceptable level, but certainly the country had nothing else to offer. The only significant regrettable absence from the picture is that of Martín-Santos: his novel reached me late and, when I read it, it had already been contracted by le Seuil. The translated works almost all received favorable comments in the press; however, with two or three exceptions, they all failed commercially. When Monique resigned from her post and I accompanied her to Saint-Tropez, Gallimard's interest in the matter declined. Quite rightly, the new readership was turning toward the growing Latin American boom, and although I intervened sporadically in favor of authors who would soon be famous, like Carlos Fuentes or Cabrera Infante, and contributed to the publication of Valle-Inclán, Cernuda, Max Aub, and Mercè Rodoreda, my opinion ceased to be decisive. The atmosphere at the publishers had changed in my absence and even though I continued my links there for some years, the eclipse of some well-known faces and meddling by the woman who was Cortázar's companion made me feel vaguely distanced and detached from my old haunt. Long before my friendship with Sarduy brought me to the literary haven of le Seuil, visits to the publishing house where I met Monique and Genet, and which so influenced an important stage in my life, began to seem forced and uncomfortable: prisoner of an image prior to my change of skin, I was forced to assume a role there that was no longer mine. Rid of this double or "inopportune guest," I would realize to my relief, when *Juan sin tierra* was rejected, that, for good or for ill, I had definitively ceased to belong to that world.

Although your function as a consultant was more than modest, the importance attributed to it by the Francoist press when they nicknamed you the customs officer, and the relations you wove at the time with those in charge of the cultural pages of various left-wing newspapers and magazines, finally did grant you, willy-nilly, a small patch of power. While you had plenty of scope to select works for translation in line with your literary tastes, political sentiments, and personal affinities, the fact that you could rely on good friends on *Le Monde*, *Les Temps Modernes*, or *Les Lettres Françaises*, and that you could make yourself at home in the offices of *France-Observateur* and *L'Express*, placed you in the advantageous position, so common in literary circles, whatever the epoch or climate, from which to obtain reviews and critical articles based less on the value of the work than on godfatherly influence and exchange of services. The compliments that today greet *urbi et orbi* the offspring or progeny of those with some sort of influence, or those from whom the flatterer expects a favor, bring a smile to all who, voluntarily or not, put themselves outside the system and don't aspire to climb the ladder. Nevertheless, in the first phases of your life, you took them at face value, at the risk of changing yourself by this attraction into one of those self-sufficient barrels brimming at the rim, always ready to bring their light from under the bushel. As the years passed, only self-criticism and experience would show you that, on Parnassus, one thing is what people think, another what they say, quite another what they write and publish. There is an enormous distance between these limits, and there are authors whom nobody admires in their thoughts and very few in what they say, yet in the press and media they are literally covered in flowers. Others, on the contrary, like Cernuda up to his death, are secretly admired, but nobody or almost nobody expresses this admiration in writing. As you will later be amused to conclude, a work's real impact, whether it is Clarín's or Américo Castro's, is measured by the attacks—the more vicious, the more personalized they are—that the author arouses in his life and, in a more underhand, hypocritical fashion, by the resounding silence of the professional eulogists and adulators.

The old invigorating air of Spain!

As the consultant to Gallimard on the list of Spanish novels included in the publisher's catalogue, the task often befell me of guiding their authors' steps through the undergrowth, tracks, and byways of the indigenous cultural jungle: interviews, press conferences, encounters with Hispanists, and the other usual ways of getting publicity. My role was reduced to telephoning journalists and critics who might eventually be interested, arranging a meeting with my fellow countrymen, and translating the questions and answers if, as often happened, they knew no French.

In the spring of 1958, to coincide with the launching of *La colmena*, we had a visit from the author. Camilo José Cela already belonged to the pantheon of Spanish literature; the creator of such works as *Pascual Duarte* and *Viaje a la Alcarria* merited my esteem, and his entry into Spain's Royal Academy had conferred upon him, as he crossed the threshold of maturity, the support and respect of official circles. For two or three days I introduced him to the main editors at the publishers, escorted him to interviews arranged by the press service, acted as a transmission shaft for self-important or awe-inspiring specialists and fervent groups of admirers. After a while he modestly, quite plainly, told me of his great desire to meet Sartre.

I confess that his request surprised me—however I wracked my brain, I could not imagine what might be the link or point of contact between the two men—but I yielded to his friendly insistence and telephoned the philosopher's secretary. The latter gave us an appointment a few days later in Sartre's old home on the corner of the rue Bonaparte and the place Saint-Germain-des-Prés, which he would later be forced to abandon by the threats and attacks of the thugs and crusaders of *L'Algérie Française.* I gave Cela the message and my colleague asked me rather uncomfortably if he could take Sartre a bottle of cognac. I thought that it was a present and agreed, adding, if I remember rightly, that the author of *La nausée* was following an alcohol-free diet on account of his arterial hypertension. Oh, it's not for him to drink, Cela explained: I want him to sign it; when Hemingway was in Spain, he also signed it for me. I told him that that type of gesture in no way fitted Sartre's style and that he had better let the bottle rest in peace. Cela demurred to my arguments and didn't mention the matter again. Some time passed and, although I still did not understand the motive behind the interview, I was telephoned by a compatriot whose name I have forgotten. Mr. Cela, he said, has asked me to contact you in order to arrange for me to take some photos of his meeting with Sartre. I was bowled over and replied curtly that there was to be a meeting of the two writers, but that he had not been invited to attend: knowing as I did Sartre's suspicious attitude toward journalists, I did not want to see myself implicated in an episode that would upset him and that he would hold me responsible for.

Without these decorative frieses and architraves, the would-be tête-à-tête of the great turned out to be a stale, limp affair. I accompanied Cela and our common friend Eugenio Suárez to the flat and translated as best I could an exemplary dialogue of the deaf, with its dodges, feints, and blows on target. At the start, Sartre seemed interested in finding out about the real position of the writer under Franco, the nature of his literary and political problems, his struggle against censorship, but his conversation partner deflected these issues with jokes and anecdotes, some of which were humorous in Spanish but inevitably lost their spark in translation, although I strove to catch the humor in French. After several laborious exercises in "sonorous inanity," Sartre hinted that the interview was at an end and we said goodbye to him. He always found Cela's reasons for seeking this exchange rather mysterious. Aware of Sansueña and its rites, I was not amazed by the episode: the tribal remnants in the literary world, evoked so lucidly by Cernuda in his poem on Dámaso Alonso, are an integral part of our folklore, and anyone who, out of idiosyncrasy or temperament, does not wear them for the gallery would appear anti-pathetic and sulky in the eyes of its televiewing citizens—a rare specimen from a solitary, unsociable subspecies, probably on the path to extinction.

The same motives that nourished my presumption as *chef de file* of the new Spanish generation contributed in a pettier way to the growth of my *cacique* inclinations under the disguise of an ideological, political cause. Even though my reader's reports for Gallimard were usually fair-minded and took the literary value of the works into consideration, I undoubtedly showed greater indulgence toward the writers of my generation who were Party members or fellow travelers than toward those who were on the right. That is to a certain extent normal, and I do not reproach myself. But my zeal as the guardian of Spanish anti-Francoist orthodoxy dis-played, if not at the publishers, in the publications and media where I had influence now seems, of course with hindsight, regrettable and dubious.

I remember how Arrabal, furiously assailed at the time by Benigno and my friends in the Party, had managed to get to Sartre, through Nadeau, one of his first plays, which was to appear in their magazine with an introduction by the philosopher. The news made me really bad-tempered, as if an intruder had invaded my territory and his talent might over-shadow my own; alongside my commentary, it similarly scandalized my companions in struggle. Following their advice, I went very democrati-cally to Simone de Beauvoir to prevent the "outrage": Arrabal, I told her, was a reactionary idealist and repudiated our struggle; if Sartre promoted him, that would confuse many people and would, in any case, damage the anti-Francoist cause. As a result, Sartre did not write the prologue and my friends and I unblushingly savored our mean victory. Only when I cast off, among other things, the feeling of sordid rivalry of those who conceive of literature as a dogfight and the aftertaste of the arbitrary Manichaeism of the Spanish media, did I realize my ephemeral but sad role as a censor. As I tried to express in *Señas de identidad*, the ideological and cultural police were a perfect match for the peculiar code of the tribe. Five centuries of inquisition and denunciation had shaped the structure of the psyche and, to a greater or lesser extent, the inquisitor, informer, and spy had insi-diously infiltrated everyone's mind. The institution forged by the New State in the midst of the civil war would thus engender a kind of can-cerous growth, courts issuing sentences under different signs. I was ashamed to discover later that the difference between the paid censors and those of us who acted spontaneously was a mere question of detail.

AS YOU NEVER *tire of stating, the only moral imperative for the writer, against which there is no recourse, is to return to the literary-linguistic community to which he belongs a fresh, personal style of writing different from what previously existed and which he inherited when setting out on his task: to work on what is given, to follow accepted models is to be condemned to impoverished insignificance, however much applause the writer gets from the public: the work of whoever does not innovate might as well not exist, for its disappearance would not affect the development of his culture at all.*

The giving of narrative or poetic form to the general ideas of the time—freedom, justice, progress, racial and sexual equality, etc.—lacks artistic interest if the author, as he does so, does not simultaneously set them a trap, charge them with gunpowder or dynamite: all ideas, even the most respectable ones, are double-edged, and a writer who ignores this works on a photograph of reality rather than on reality.

The enterprise of a novelist, as conceived by you, is an adventure: to say what has yet not been said; explore the potentialities of language; launch oneself into the conquest of new areas of expression, of those few meters of land that, as Carlos Fuentes said, the Dutch reclaim patiently from the sea: the writing of a novel is a leap into the unknown: to land in a place unsuspected by the writer when he flings himself into the void without safety net or parachute; when a technique has been mastered or you have reached the end of an experiment, they must be abandoned for the search for what is still unknown: in the field of art and literature, a hundred birds in the hand are worth less than the one that—to our torture and delight— continues flying, inspired, mobile, light-winged.

Literature extends the field of our vision and experience, is opposed to all that reduces or anaesthetizes our perceptive potential, conditions us culturally, ideologically, and sexually, brainwashes us and dulls our senses: the counterdiscourse against discourse: against the inevitable incorporation of what is new and repellent, the parody of what has become conventionalized or respected with sheepish deference: like Bouvard and Pécuchet, literature draws up an inventory of the commonplaces of the day and mockingly revivifies the universal map of idiocy.

Our association as a couple with literary life—conversations, meetings, dinners, etc.—embraces the period between my arrival on the rue Poissonnière and our move to the Midi at the end of 1964. From the diagnosis of Monique's mother's cancer to the cannibalistic digestion of her death, a reading of the diary in which Monique briefly noted the days' events reveals a rapid succession of professional or social dates with publishers, intellectuals, and journalists, as if the drama and internal pain she was suffering had forced her to seek refuge in a whirlwind of lunches and receptions. This agitation, covering up the real anguish of a death agony lived like a process of emotional catharsis, described with restraint in *Une Drôle de voix*, coincided with a personal crisis within myself and in my links with her and with an unsettling sense of alienation and detachment in respect to our milieu: a furtive awareness of being an impostor, a result of not matching up to the role you were playing; the tedium of nighttime living, only tolerable thanks to the use and abuse of alcohol. My recent political disappointments and the bitter certainty that I had created a work that had perhaps satisfied my civic responsibilities but fell totally outside that dense, purifying, initiatory zone forged by literature was now joined by the sudden realization of my homosexuality and the distressing clandestine nature of relationships, which I will describe later. The combined essence of all this could be summed up in one word: weariness. Weariness with the bustle of literary publishing, political militancy, functional writing, my ambiguous image and usurped respectability. So I felt more and more sharply and clearly the need to concentrate my physical, intellectual, and emotional energies in those areas I deemed vital and to throw all else overboard.

In a passage in the last volume of her memoirs, Simone de Beauvoir mentions the fact that a dinner with Sartre on the rue Poissonnière restored their enthusiasm for parties. Two years later, these would be regular events throughout Monique's distressed countdown. I can remember one when, overwhelmed by the weight of the tensions of my incipient schizophrenia, I crept out for some fresh air, to the great annoyance of our guests: French and American publishers, the Semprúns, and Simone Signoret had talked or danced into the early hours and, unable to assume the host's mantle, I kept a rude but eagle eye on the clock, as I waited for the moment of liberation when I could stretch out in bed.

However it was, our crowded dinner parties began to try my nerves with sometimes lasting effects: my portentous ability to absent myself, by putting a million miles between me and everyone else, developed at that time and would sharpen over the years till it became part of my character and hardened my thick skin. It probably began as a defense against others' interfering in my deepest reality, and it allowed me to maintain an albeit flawed façade of correct social behavior, without being torn from the secret pull of the binomial that ruled my life. Fleeting, futile words, subdued smiles, convoluted discussions: "reality" was only the cortex that could be destroyed in a moment by a fertile, incandescent metaphor or the imaginary representation of a body. The stunning, palpable universe evoked lit up the nocturnal opaqueness of the ritual—like a silent, brilliant flash of sheet lightning. Only the woven texture of literature could create that sudden burst of splendor which illuminated the world. When you read Góngora's *Soledades*—the fierce, seering glimpse of those fighters "restrained by mutual knots/like hard elms entwined by vines"—the ophidian lasciviousness of the phrase and copulation of word-made-flesh revealed to me the transmutation of Góngora's daily anguish in the still of his poetry: his generative ability to harness, in polysemic harmony, sexuality and writing.

Reduced to a gradually residual presence—did my friends at the time notice the radical nature of the change? my mental flights in mid-conversation, the signs of a hardly hidden impatience at the prolonging of an evening, the evasive expression on my absentminded or sealed face? Something of my state of mind must have filtered through, since the distancing and abandon were soon reciprocal. In autumn 1964 the rue Poissonnière dinner parties became less frequent, and when we returned after eighteen months away, some of the regulars had forgotten them entirely: the nucleus of friends was significantly reduced without the magnet of influence in publishing. From then on, in the company of Monique and a few others, I would rake the forbidden ground for all that had remained wild and implicit.

The terrain I was slowly penetrating demanded complete rejection of all that did not connect with it. The alienation was further accelerated by an awareness of pathetically wasting time on things that were of no interest and on people who were of no importance to me. My new conception of literature demanded absolute surrender, the total erasing of my previous universe. A change of life, a change of writing. The creative pride developed while you composed *Don Julián* would darken henceforth the glow of your conceit. As I would later see formulated in Flaubert, I would not from then on be sufficiently modest to be flattered by rewards or fame.

Monique's decision to break with Gallimard, Paris, and our sociability fell on me like an April shower. Although it created difficulties for the secret bond tying me to Mohamed, it enabled me to escape from a stifling atmosphere where day after day my alienation intensified. Travel, isolation, a new departure in literature and life were worth more than Paris and all its glory. Monique's grief at her mother's death fitted in with my desire to move well away. United in our sadness and need for a change of scene as we had not been for some time, we packed our bags with almost ecstatic feelings of relief for the pacific backdrop of provincial existence in Saint-Tropez.

Sometimes when she left her Gallimard office, Monique and I would meet alone or with others involved in her work, in the comfortable, quiet underground bar of the neighboring Pont Royal Hotel. The design of the place, the sensitive distribution of luxurious, comfortable armchairs, and the dimmed lighting created an intimate, secluded atmosphere, suitable for whispered confidences and exchanges. The clientele was mainly intellectual, with the regulars keeping at a respectful distance from each other, each group to its own corner or den. I had often seen him there, dressed with distinguished simplicity—a polo-necked jersey and English tweed jacket—and the jagged tufts of hair and unmistakable face that appear in the rare photos of him. He used to sit a long way from the bar and the stairs, at the other end of the small lounge, with a rather younger woman or some translator. His shyness, reserve, evident fear of interference from others established around him a kind of inviolable sacred space, like the one opened up in the street by a blind man's white cane. The impossibility of invading it and stamping like some simpleton on the frontier of his invulnerable modesty turned the mere thought of approaching him into a sacrilegious act. The writer and his female friend conversed isolated in their transparent bubble. Although I knew and admired his work, I respected, like everybody else, the integrity of his territory. It was Samuel Beckett.

I thought of Beckett, precisely of Beckett, in my room at the Hotel Habana Libre the day I was visited by another colleague. The poet Yevgeny Yevtushenko had been living there for some time in the room adjacent to mine: he had fallen into relative semidisgrace through some whim of Khrushchev and had been sent to Cuba to a kind of gilded exile, and he awaited impatiently, champing at the bit, for the moment to make peace with his leader and once more lay his prolific muse at the service of the official creed. Fond of notoriety and flattering attention, he was hard pressed to tolerate his stay in a place where his work and person were unknown. Informed by friends on the daily paper *Revolución* that I was a neighbor, he appeared at my bedroom door one night, very tall, fair-haired, with childish features, and tiny blue eyes that after a few minutes' examination revealed a curious similarity with those bifocal lenses, made for seeing far and near: naively Siberian above and cunning and mischievous below, or perhaps vice versa. Yevtushenko spoke in broken English and Spanish, and in his picturesque gabble explained to me that our respective fame predestined us to earthly or sempiternal friendship. He wrote, so he told me, dozens of poems in the solitude of his room, deprived of the comforting presence of an audience, the deference of his admirers, the din of applause: the ozone that allowed him to breathe. After various pauses and the odd linguistic *quid pro quo*, he suddenly disappeared into his room to reappear with a bundle of sheets of paper, the first fruits of his poetic impulse. He said he was going to read them to me; I firmly rejected his offer: I understood not a word of Russian. No matter, he retorted, you look, you listen. He adopted the theatrical pose of a bolero bard: it was a grotesque scene that I quickly cut short. I explained how I didn't have an ear for other languages and how I hated recitals ever since I had seen Berta Singerman; when his poems were translated into Spanish, I would be tremendously interested in reading them. Visibly upset, the poet made a change of plan: he wanted to go with me to some dance hall and drink a few iced daiquiris. I cannot remember exactly whether we went first to the Red Saloon at the Capri Hotel or directly went into a noisy bar, where he was apparently a regular, as he was immediately accosted by a beautiful mulatto and began to entertain me with an energetic, almost acrobatic exhibition of the twist lit up by the swirling glare of a rainbow strobe. I left him engrossed in the contemplation of his own spectacle and made my exit. But the minstrel from the taiga was stubborn and would not take a hint. Days later he returned to my room, this time poemless, and looked at me with the wan gaze of an orphan child: You don't admire me, why not? I must have smiled as I told him that you could not have admiration by decree. If you understood my poetry, he assured me, you would admire me. Unfortunately for him, that was not so, and my thick Hispanic skin tortured and filled him with despair.

When we left Cuba, he to the official rallying cry of his anti-Chinese muse in the pages of *Izvestia* or *Pravda* and I to a much more obscure life in Paris, I thought we would not meet again. However, on 8 February 1963, during the terminal stage of Monique's mother's cancer, we had a telephone call from our friend K.S. Karol, at the time on the editorial board of *L'Express*, headed by Jean Daniel. Yevtushenko was in Paris and wanted to see me. In our state of mind at the time, the idea of a nighttime spree with him seemed most opportune; it would momentarily distract Monique from her anguish and we could enjoy the man's grandiloquence. I am still unaware of the reasons for his second, and visibly unfruitful encounter with me: as I later discovered through the indiscretions of another journalist, the bard's greatest aspiration—intoxicated by the same provincial, servile spirit that impelled his colleague and rival Voznesensky to write poems to the glory of Jacqueline Kennedy—then centered on rubbing shoulders with De Gaulle and Brigitte Bardot.

Whatever the motives behind his friendly persistence, we went with K.S. Karol to meet him at the Louvre Hotel and, escorted by a female functionary from the Soviet Embassy, we went as he desired to a show at the Crazy Horse. The striptease acts were ingenious and attractive: at one moment of the performance there was an amusing parody of a kind of military parade. Some girls in combat jackets, belts, and boots comically took the stage and Rouget de Lisle's popular tunes were given a burlesque airing. Unexpectedly, to everyone's amazement, the poet got up, stood to attention as stiff as a brush, to the full length of his undeniably Siberian one meter ninety, in a laudable demonstration of respect for the sacrosanct national anthem. People mumbled, smiled, and coughed: What was behind that attack of patriotism? Perhaps it was part of the show? The rest of the evening was less colorful and although, as a result of Monique's bad advice, it ended hours later, much to the bard's dismay, with brazen transvestites at the Carrousel, the image of Yevtushenko doing his Eiffel Tower act while the smiling girls stripped to the tune of the *Marseillaise* attains that degree of exemplary representativeness when anecdotal and general combine to sum up the spectacular romantic conception of the demiurge poet complete with the slippers of Empedocles. Don Yevgeny or Beckett, Don Camilo or Cernuda, Don Ernesto or Lezama: authenticity and myth, critical passion and egotism, moral knowledge and emblematic projection. Two opposing conceptions of literature and life: the sober acceptance of both or the theatrical, clownish accoutrements of the seer on the flies of kitsch and expansive word-weariness.

Monique recounted this anecdote to you.

On her return from Corfu, she was waiting in the sun of Athens airport for the plane that was going to take her to Paris. The loudspeakers announced the arrival of the Air France flight, and as she was absent-mindedly looking at the runway and the preparations of the staff around the recently becalmed machine, she suddenly noticed a round of frenetic activity. A dozen journalists and photographers ran to the steps and crowded around the bottom waiting for a celebrity. The passengers slowly emerged from the doorway and, soon, she spotted the unmistakable silhouette of the Sartre-Simone de Beauvoir couple. The writers walked down the steps onto the runway and walked through the hungry pack of paparazzi without anyone noticing their presence or paying them any attention. Seconds later, a kiss-throwing, hat-waving Eddie Constantine would be the target of an ecstatic welcome and, for someone witnessing the scene and its different actors, one really difficult to forget.

S ET ONESELF THE *Genetian ethic of the* malamatí *as a difficult literary and human ideal: openly practice what laws
and customs reprove, infringe norms of prudence and respect, brazenly accept the
insults and pinpricks of gossip: renounce the prestige of behavior based on conformism or the exercise of official bounty: on the contrary, protect oneself behind a
shield of disdain in order to preserve secret virtue, sacrifice advantage and honor to
scrupulous fidelity to oneself: live in a world without diference or disciples in the
burnishing and perfection of purity.*

*Scavenger from a sudden shipwreck, a jubilant Robinson on the shores of alien
lands: your writerly affinities let you compensate precarious blood ties with the pull
from magnetic fields far from your soil and seed: able to choose ancestors and
relatives, jettison the poor hidalgo's shield, forget all that was destroyed: forge a
genealogy to fit and include therein those accused of rejecting the fatherland who
eluded the common model and its ominous centripetal force: trace the literary
constellations around which you orbit, endow your new trunk with thick branches
and foliage: the gallery of portraits that to advantage replaces the old one includes
thieves and deserters, heretics, sodomites, the proscribed: no possible auction or
outrage because of family mishap or change of fortune: their levity spares them a
roof: they travel freely with you.*

*When you scandalize family or tribal morality and this surfaces profusely on
the printed page you accept the stings as an oblique, involuntary homage to the
proud rigor of your independence: the decision not to respect consensual norms and
zealously preserve your deviation from the praise or reproval of others delivers you
the opportunity to transmute into a source of energy the disorder in your emotional
life, the solar gravitation of its fire: desire to carry your savage wrestling with the
word to the limit of artistic consummation: ardor, plenitude, incandescence, gentle
fierce, body to body, lascivious entwining prey elongated in embrace and con-
junction: bliss and exaltation at the discovery, syncopated swooning of epiphany,
grace of possession: the space where you take refuge, as to the bosom of the sacred,
shelters you from storms: the sweet excludes not the rough: the self-absorbed
pleasurer perceives not the prowling dogs of night.*

My Lailat-ul-Qadr fell one 8 October, perhaps in the sacred month of Ramadan, on the night I first went to the place where I now write these lines and met both Monique and Genet, two people who in different ways decisively influenced my life, an encounter like a new dawn. I owe my later development mainly to them, to their efforts to drag me from the suffocating narrowness of my milieu. Genet's appearances and eclipses over two decades showed me a new moral territory: after the closed confines of the bourgeois world of the Barcelona district of Bonanova, with its family ghosts and emotional devastation, I will gradually, cautiously penetrate, led by their hand, that fertile space, stripped of notions of country, state, doctrine, or respectability, of my medina-commonland in la Bonne Nouvelle.

· III ·

The Poet's Territory

A FEW WEEKS before revising these pages, I had on one day two or three telephone calls from a man with a vaguely foreign accent who wanted urgently to talk to Monique. When she returned home and took the phone, the stranger anxiously besieged her with questions about Genet. Where was he? Had something happened to him? Who could get him his address? Monique explained how we had had little news of him for some time and that only indirectly: all she could advise was to write to his publishers. But her interlocutor seemed upset and would not give up. Neither he nor his wife understood what had happened: the day before, Genet had lunched with them and asked them to telephone him without fail the day after; however, in the hotel where he was staying they said he had paid his bill and left without leaving a message. It was impossible he had forgotten his date with them; perhaps he had suffered some upset; perhaps . . .

The man's sad disarray was nothing new to us: it reproduced a Genetian situation that we had known for decades. After living with this man and his wife for a few days or weeks, granting them the fortuitous gift of his presence, Genet had suddenly disappeared from their lives, from the friendly haven where he had camped down and fleetingly felt at ease. Suddenly abandoned for no apparent reason, deprived of his exuberance and state of grace, this stranger was unable to comprehend that the writer's momentary well-being, the impression that he was being integrated into the heart of a family, had probably been the cause of his flight and exile. His name and his wife's would thus be added to the long list of those seduced by Genet's personality and intelligence, then brutally abandoned by the side of a path that upped and downed, turned sharply, forked and changed direction. Bewildered and incredulous, he would gradually, bitterly realize that Genet had ceased to exist for them except in the hypothetical case that in the future he might have recourse to their services or find himself forced to ask a favor of them.

It was 8 October 1955 precisely. Monique Lange, whom I had met a few days before in the entrance to Gallimard, had invited me to have supper in her flat on the rue Poissonnière, adding at once, fearing, as she later confessed to me, that her warm and beautiful smile would not be sufficient motive for me to accept her hospitality: "Jean Genet is coming as well. Do you know him?"*

Yes, I knew him from his books or, rather, the last of his books published at the time, *Journal du voleur*, which a friend had lent me two years before on my first brief stay in Paris. The reading of that book had an enormous moral and literary effect on me. The author's strange, personal, fascinating style accompanied an introduction to a world totally unknown to me; something I had sensed darkly from adolescence but that my upbringing and prejudices had prevented me from verifying. I can remember the person who gave me the grubby copy of the work once pointing out an individual in his thirties, looking defiant and insolent, heading for the café terrace exactly opposite ours—it was called and I think it's still called La Pérgola, next to the Mabillon métro station—and muttering knowingly: "That's Genet's friend." Days later, when I returned the book, he asked me whether I had masturbated as I read it. I said I hadn't, and he looked taken aback, a mixture of disappointment and incredulity. He said, "I did dozens of times. Every time I read it, I jerk myself off."

I have never liked this kind of confidence and I cut short the conversation. As Genet told me years afterwards, he found nothing more irritating than the inopportune homage to the pornographic virtues of his work: he gave no credit to the opinion of homosexuals and appreciated only the praise of those outside the ghetto described by him, who took his novels for what they were, that is, an autonomous world, a language, a voice. As for the so-called friend singled out by my initiator into the novels, it must have been Java or René, considering the date. "But neither of them used to go around Saint-Germain-des-Prés," Genet observed when I mentioned the incident to him, "both of them were pimping in Montmartre or robbing queers in lavatories or in the Bois de Boulogne."

Ten days after our first encounter on the rue Poissonnière, I go to see him with Monique. Genet is ill from something or other, and she has a bag of food and medicine for him. We climb up to a small studio on the rue Pasquier, where he welcomes us from his bed. Other visitors soon arrive: Madeleine Chapsal and Jean Cau, then secretary to Sartre and later the faithful spokesman for the fears and phobias of the right.

The daily papers print more and more disturbing stories of the repression in Algeria, and Genet has the idea of celebrating in his way the

---

* See *Forbidden Territory*, above page 177.

forthcoming All Saints' Day. He has prepared a statement addressed to those visiting the graves of their loved ones, to be handed out at the cemetery gate. Genet looks for his glasses on the bedside table, sticks them on, and with that inimitable voice—grave, serious, full of intense, restrained anger—reads the reproachful statement, which, with great poetic violence, urges the recipients to think of the other dead, those who fall daily, mown down by the criminal bullets of *their* army and *their* police: old people; children; women; humble, illiterate peasants . . .

I am moved by the text, but Jean Cau immediately pours out a bucket of cold water: the tone is too aggressive, he says, and its effect will be counterproductive. He then proposes drawing up another in more measured, practical language, the usual sort for that kind of manifesto. While he discusses the phrasing with the visitors now packing into the studio, I notice that Genet seems completely to lose interest in the conversation, as if the action planned to fit the political line of a respectful, always defensive opposition does not concern him.

The text is never given out and, as Monique writes me in Barcelona, where I return a few days afterwards, Genet's proposed act of poetic agitation never happens.

A year goes by. Monique regularly informs me of her contacts with the poet and meanwhile I read all of his work in the last months of my military service. When that is over, I return to Paris with Monique and settle down with her on the rue Poissonnière.

Genet drops in without warning—Monique's flat is a kind of canteen for him—and although I want to talk to him about his writing, I soon notice that he is appalled by the prospect. Used to the preening vanity of the Hispanic literati, I am surprised by his attitude. Genet imposes an unbridgeable distance between himself and his work, avoids like the plague those who admire it for the right or wrong reasons, and assumes the aloof detachment of a Rimbaud trafficking on the desolate steppes of Harar. When he later asks for my opinion, he does so with modest self-restraint, without the customary layers of aggression and irony with which he defends himself against untimely veneration or inquisitiveness.

Among those who similarly turn up from time to time is René, whom Monique has known from the period when he saw a lot of the poet and was seeking a modus vivendi by stealing from homosexuals at night in the usual pick-up areas. That friendly relationship, punctuated by comic incidents, has been amusingly portrayed in Monique's first novel, *Les Poissons-chats*. René is in his thirties; he is tall, stout, and coarse, and his rough, ungainly face immediately reveals his past life as a petty criminal;

he is now married, with two children, and cleans bedspreads, sofas, and armchairs in people's homes, which allows him to earn an honest penny as well as to lay numerous servant girls and housewives whenever the opportunity arises. As a way in, he insistently inquires as to the origin of stains unresponsive to his energetic therapy, dryly discards confused and heated hypotheses, and gradually centers suspicions on the spermatic origin of the libation. His visits to the rue Poissonnière obey as much the desire to remember old times with Monique as the aim to bed down Hélène, the domestic help who lives with us and takes Monique's daughter to school.

Hélène talks sixteen to the dozen, wears too much makeup, and goes out dancing every night. From her extravagant stories we gather that she is in with some pimp, since she has been invited to work as a beautician in Casablanca; she is a single parent and has entrusted her three children to Social Security. Her continual verbal diarrhea irritates Genet: while she serves out the food, he orders wax pellets for his ears. One day, at his wits' end with her chatter, he exclaims: "For God's sake! Aren't you able to express even one general idea?"

Some of the encounters during those months have been preserved thanks to Monique's little diary.

We accompany Genet to the quai de Conti, where he is to attend Jean Cocteau's entry into the Academy: it is the first and last official event I ever see him go to. He is visibly annoyed by the ceremony and goes reluctantly to talk with his colleagues, apologizing to us and furious with himself. He does not belong to their physical, moral, or literary world: Genet, in the guests' gallery at the Institute, is a falcon mistakenly let into an assembly of peacocks. What he sees and hears there feeds all he holds in contempt: feelings of disgust, a desire to throw up.

Cocteau had made a decisive contribution to getting Genet out of jail twelve years earlier and he felt a debt toward him. However, Genet avoided personal contact whenever he could; he was offended by Cocteau's worldly ways and exhibitionism. When the author of *Les Enfants terribles* died, Genet spoke to me about him and the superficiality of his work quite mercilessly, but without rancor.

At another time, the diary briefly notes a "Genet-Violette Leduc dinner in a Chinese restaurant," which I don't remember at all.

Violette Leduc had just left the psychiatric sanatorium where, thanks to Simone de Beauvoir's generosity, she had recovered from one of her half-

Monique and I were back in Spain with Florence Malraux,
the filmmaker Claude Sautet ... (221)

Genet now calls me *l'hidalgo* and seems to feel at ease
in my company ... (283)

Abdallah's feet hardly seem to touch the rope while he shakes to a calypso
rhythm about two meters above the ground ... (286)

I leave the Bonne Nouvelle underground, immediately locate the
Rex cinema ... (178)

real, half-imagined attacks of madness and depression. We went to see her with Monique—who had a profound admiration for her work and made me read her books, which were unknown at the time—in a beautiful villa on the outskirts of Paris, surrounded by a large park full of yellowing, almost leafless horse-chestnut trees. Violette—whose terrible physical appearance Maurice Sachs drew so unforgettably—cried over her loneliness and isolation: she suffered or pretended to suffer from a persecution complex, but at times she would calm down and her vulgar face broadened into a cunning grin. She was a "play-actress and martyr," according to the expression coined by Sartre, and waxed ecstatic at the "happy couple" of Monique and myself. She wanted me to pass on to her an old pair of trousers, "with a drop of semen on the fly," she said plaintively, since she lived alone, without a man, and that souvenir of me would warm her up a bit. In the absence of any available jeans, she got a few photos of us in Spain: with those she would sleep better, would feel less lonely, and could create the illusion of participating in our happiness from a distance. A few days later she telephoned Monique, still from the clinic: while she walked round the garden, someone had slipped into her room and torn all our photos to shreds. "Tell Juan there's obviously someone with a grudge against him."

Outside the lesbian relationships so beautifully described in her books, Violette had had two passions in her life: Maurice Sachs and Genet. Loves that were impossible, if it can be said, because of the difference of sex; she would later relate in masterly fashion their failure, sadness, and humiliations in *La Bâtarde*. Years earlier, as Genet confided to us one day, she had invited him to supper with his friend Java in her small flat near the Faubourg Saint-Antoine. Violette had prepared a dish with a sauce, which she insisted on serving up although Genet was not hungry. As he refused, she adopted a rather whining tone: "I see now how you despise the poor" or something similar. Genet was furious and upset the table and everything that was on it: the sauce fell on her low-cut dress and ran between her breasts. He left with his friend, slamming the door behind them, and the next day he had found her sobbing in front of her door still covered in sauce. From then on he implacably resisted her admiring approaches, and I am not sure why he lowered his guard and dined with us and her on the day indicated in Monique's diary.

At that time Genet keeps intact his desire to be a provocateur: as minstrel of crime, thievery, homosexuality, he continually exacts payment for the debt that society has contracted with him ever since his conception in his mother's womb; now that he is respected and famous, he makes up for the unhappiness and injustice suffered as a child and youth. He responds rudely to admiration from the establishment, displays a crude frankness to hypocrites, unscrupulously extracts money from the rich to give to those who like himself have not enjoyed good fortune and upbringing from the start. His anger is sudden and violent: his first publisher, the North American translator of his work, Jean Cau—who came to justify being fired by Sartre—will all at one time or another be on the receiving end of his caning attacks.

When invited to attend an official dinner organized by the world of culture in homage to a minister, he replies by asking whether he has been invited in his capacity as ex-jailbird, pickpocket, or queer. Once, on the terrace at the Flore, he is furtively greeted from another table by a shamefaced homosexual and assails him with the cry: "Hey, did your fancyman stick it right up the other night?" In a restaurant where we are having lunch, an overpainted lady is talking and slobbering over her lapdog at the table next to us; Genet gives a look of disgust and the woman asks him: "Don't you like animals?"

"Madame, I don't like people who like animals."

I can equally remember the time when, a number of years later, Monique and I accompanied him to see a fervent admirer of his, the wife of an important state personage, whom he wanted to have intervene on behalf of a friend. To please him, the woman quotes from memory a sentence of his that had for some reason been aired in the newspapers some time ago. "You know," she says, "when I read or hear something intelligent, I always retain it." "And when you hear something stupid, you always let it out," responds Genet. She takes the jibe without flinching and, showing real magnanimity and self-control, notes down all he asks for and intercedes favorably on his behalf.

The performance of his plays was beginning to pay dividends, and for the first time he was living fairly comfortably. After the worldwide success of *Le Balcon*, he distributed his royalties among his protégés and kept for himself only what was strictly necessary.

Until then, his strategies for getting loot could have filled an anthology of tricks and wiles, worthy of a hero of the Spanish picaresque novel: loans, sponging, hotels abandoned without bills being paid ... Genet performs on these occasions without remorse; his morality works at a different level. Once at this level, his behavior can be, on the contrary, a model of scrupulous rigor. But the level varies—and I notice this only later. His absolute surrender to friendship does not exclude the seed of possible, unexpected betrayal.

His usual recourse when he has no money is to sell publishers the titles of books that do not exist: *Le Bagne, La Fée, Elle, Splendid's (La Rafale), Les Fous* ... When Gallimard acquires the publishing rights to his "complete works," Genet swindles money out of Gaston by promising wonderful things: *Jean la Folle, Les Hommes, Football* ... The founder of NRF, who has a literary scent as keen as a real hunting dog's, has moreover a weak spot for Genet: while he is always able coldly to refuse help to an aged or hard-up author, he always falls into Genet's continuous traps with ill-concealed excitement. He derives intense satisfaction from the certainty he is being deceived. Old Gaston is a "law unto himself," under whom Gallimard will never be a mere book-producing factory: his personality, whims, and imagination then exercise a healthy influence, and the poet, with his carefree insolence, enjoys untrammeled his protection and approval.

Genet now calls me *l'hidalgo* and seems to feel at ease in my company when he turns up on the rue Poissonnière. Monique is his mailbox and helps to solve the small but annoying problems of daily life: arranging meetings, avoiding troublesome encounters, and obtaining the sedatives Nembutal or Supponéryl.

He lives alone in modest hotels nearly always situated next to a train station, as if thus to underline his light-footed mobility. His belongings fit into a small or average-sized suitcase: a change of clothes, a few books and notebooks, sleeping pills and medicine, and his manuscripts. At the time he is still writing: months earlier he published *Le Balcon; Les Nègres* and *Les Paravents* will soon follow. He reads the newspapers and comments on political events: the Algerian war, the last stings in the tail of French imperialism...

His monastic austerity and seclusion suggest the idea of sanctity: a real detachment from property and possessions. He eats frugally, hardly drinks, and the only luxury he allows himself is the small Dutch cigars in metal tins, which he smokes continuously. Apart from satisfying his modest personal needs, money burns his fingers: he always keeps it in small bundles in his trouser pocket, ready to give it out to his protégés, someone he just gets on with, or the lad or tough he has just picked up.

We talk above all about politics. Although I am physically in Paris, I continue to live mentally in Spain. My brother Luis and a large number of my Barcelona friends have joined the clandestine CP, and I am a fellow traveler on the fringe, but a useful coordinator from outside the country of press campaigns and cultural activities against the Franco régime. I am beginning to get to know the work of writers like Céline, Artaud, Beckett, and I know in my inner self that their literary expression, like that of Genet himself, is much more beautiful, rich, and daring than the one my colleagues and I have as our goal, but at the same time I am convinced that it is a luxury we cannot afford. The situation in Spain, I then think, demands that we be clear and practical (read "facile and Manichaean") as in the realist documentary novel (*Karl Marx, l'éternel voleur d'énergies!* as Rimbaud would have said). Thus, I steel myself for years against Genet's *dangerous* political influence (which will not, how-ever, prevent it later from seeping through to me in a slower, more lasting fashion).

Genet sympathizes with our political options and likes to discuss them with Luis and his friend Octavio Pellissa, when they come to Paris to inform or get instructions from the leadership. As I discern later, he is attracted and fascinated by the discipline, impenetrability, and secrecy inherent in the hierarchies of the Communist parties and their perennial "besieged fortress" mentality. He feels above all instinctive hatred for the social system within which he lives and the ethnic, cultural, and economic inequalities engendered by its power. However, our exclusive support for Spain equally shocks him and is the target of his irony. Genet knows the Peninsula well and finds Spaniards resigned to their fate, sentimental and bland, in a word, incapable of repeating the revolutionary deeds of 1936.

Machado is then our bible and I lend Genet a translation of his poetry and *Juan de Mairena*. He returns the books to me after a few days and rattles off a string of criticisms: he thinks the writer's human and literary horizons narrow and limited; his obsession with Castile is a way of nar-cissistically contemplating his navel and resurrecting the retrograde values of the countryside. Machado not only writes in Spanish—as Genet writes in French—but wants *to be Spanish*, a cultural identification that Genet cannot understand and labels as chauvinist. He is left totally indifferent by the moral landscape of France: neither the gardens of Versailles nor the cathedral of Rheims stir any emotions in him. So why, then, that love of Soria, Castile, the trees on the riverbank, the slow procession of poplars? The fatherland, he will say much later, can be an ideal only for those who don't have one, like the Palestinian fedayeen.

"And when they get one?" I ask him.

He is silent for a few seconds.

"Then they will have won the right to throw it down the lavatory pan and pull the chain, just like me."

After one of his frequent absences, Genet reappears one day on the rue Poissonnière with a youth in his twenties. Abdallah is the son of an Algerian man and a German woman, has worked in a circus from childhood, and can perform as an acrobat. His very seductive face reveals a harmonious blend of female and manly features. He has a gentle voice, a gracious and elegant manner, and always speaks with great delicacy and self-restraint.

Their relationship is as father to son. Genet has decided to turn him into a great artist and invents tightrope-walking tricks for him that require patient, disciplined training. An admirable poetic text, *Pour un funambule* will be the result of the coming together of their wills. Abdallah enthusiastically surrenders himself to the task, Genet seems very pleased with his progress, and their friendship radiates a wonderful moral beauty.

When Genet is traveling, Abdallah comes to see us, and both Monique and I are very happy in his company. After a few months, Genet tells us that his friend has received his draft notice and, faced with the prospect of being sent to "pacify" Algeria, they had both agree he must desert. Abdallah does not respond to the notice and comes to say farewell to us with a glowing smile: he is excited by the adventure and knows it stimulates the vitality and energy of Genet, for whom desertion is an absolute value. Rootless from birth, a child of the foundling home, he preaches the virtues of exile by example. Living near him implies getting rid of one's own parameters, throwing off the habits of upbringing, breaking with past feelings and attachments, living like a foreigner in a perpetual state of moving on. To match the image Genet wants of him, Abdallah takes on his nomadic ways, constructs his own life around a risk-filled enterprise, and walks the threadbare tightrope without any harness or safety net. But he is young and strong; Genet's will sustains him, and he cheerfully trusts that fortune will smile upon him.

When we accompany him to the Gare de Lyon, where he takes the train to Bordighera with his acrobat's gear, I do not realize that the situation will be repeated with Ahmed and Jacky. Monique and I kiss him on both cheeks and he waves smaller and smaller goodbyes from the window as the train moves away.

Genet travels for several months: he follows Abdallah through Italy, Belgium, and Germany and closely supervises his training. L'Arbalète has just published *Les Nègres*, soon to be staged by Roger Blin. His good-humored messages and telephone calls show he is going through a creative phase: his only complaint is about the difficulty of getting sleeping pills.

Monique mails him some from time to time, but it is a dangerous operation. When he settles down in Amsterdam with Abdallah we decide to go and see them and leave Paris by road along with Octavio. Monique's friend, Odette, will follow on by train the next day.

Genet shows us the city, jokes about De Gaulle and his *folies de grandeur*, saying that "France is drooling over his big fat cock." I have never seen him so happy to exist as then, and I'll never see the like again. He eats with an excellent appetite, clowns around when Monique is taking photos, takes an interest in the situation in Spain and Octavio's recent exile. Then he leads us to the hall where Abdallah rehearses his dance number every day.

The lad is wearing a garment designed by Genet himself and emphasizing the slender grace of his body. He climbs up to the wire stretched between the two posts and begins to sway with an unreal agility and lightness. His feet hardly seem to touch the rope while he shakes to a calypso rhythm about two meters above the ground. When he reaches the moment for the lethal jump, we all hold our breath, contemplating his incredible defying of the law of gravity: his acrobatics is a form of levitation. *Sévère et pâle, danse, et si tu le pouvais, les yeux fermés*, wrote his friend. The tightrope walker keeps his eyes open: when he finishes and jumps down on the carpet beneath the stuccoed ceiling of the dance hall where he practices, I suddenly notice his tense concentration, the sweat bathing his forehead, and the fragility of his beautiful smile. Genet hides his Pygmalion's pride and says that Abdallah has improved his technique, but that the act is not ready; he must forget the spectators, concentrate entirely on the dance, lighten his movements even more. Abdallah listens to him, tired but satisfied, and we wait for him to change his clothes before going out for dinner.

I shall follow the coherent disorder of memory rather than a strictly chronological account of events.

We—that is, Monique and myself—go to the first performance of *Les Nègres* at the Lutèce theater. Although I am not at all fond of theatrical events—they nearly always bore me and I no sooner settle down in my seat than I get an irresistible desire to cough, my legs get pins and needles, or I get a backache—I am fired by the poetic density of the text, the wonderful stage set, and the delivery and mimicry of the actors: the play is even more beautiful and provocative than *Le Balcon*, and I prefer Blin's production to Peter Brook's recent version of the latter at the Gymnase.

One member of the audience gets up halfway through and leaves, obviously displeased: it is Ionesco. The next day Gaston Gallimard's secretary, who has witnessed the incident with us, asks him why. "I felt I was the only white in the theater," the writer replies, "and I was happy to accept the challenge."

Genet continues living in Holland in flight from prying journalists, but when I see him again he agrees for the first time willingly to discuss literature and the theater. The writers who are then the center of attention, Malraux, Sartre, Camus, are a matter of indifference to him. He says the literature of ideas is not literature: those who cultivate it have got the wrong genre. Their language is flat, conventional, predictable. Their enterprise is no adventure, but just a local bus journey. Why do they waste so much energy?

In fact, he prefers poets: Nerval, Rimbaud, Mallarmé, and, unexpectedly for me, Claudel. His desire to be a writer came to him in prison after reading Ronsard. He has equal respect for Céline, Artaud, Michaux, and Beckett. Years later, when he has withdrawn into total, irrevocable solitude, he will talk to me with real feeling about Dostoevsky and *The Brothers Karamazov*.

We go back to Amsterdam with Florence Malraux and a friend. Genet has booked rooms for us in a central hotel, but we are surprised to find that the management will not let us stay: we are not "legitimate" couples. Genet laughs complacently: in contrast, Abdallah and himself have no problem. Blessed Holland, the homosexuals' paradise!

Abdallah is now training with Ahmed, a childhood friend also working in the circus. It is Christmas and we spend the day walking up and down by the canals. The two lads show us the red-light district, the dance hall frequented by the Guyanese and Curaçaoans, prostitutes on the watch behind their windows like sirens spotlighted in an aquarium.

On New Year's Eve we go to Haarlem and see the *Regentesses* by Hals. Genet is a passionate admirer of the work and declares that in it the painter discovered *goodness*. He is moved by the paintings of the Dutch masters, is a constant visitor to the Rijksmuseum, and a good many years after writing on the genius from Leyden, he confides to Monique that, after seeing himself naked in the mirror, his aged body reminds him of Rembrandt's *Bathsheba*.

The rue Poissonnière continues to be his *point de chute*. He suddenly turns up, between trains, to collect his sleeping pills and correspondence or arrange a meeting with his publishers. He avoids worldly fame and recognition like the plague. One day, on a visit to Gallimard, he sees a stack of books in the room where authors sign books reserved for celebrities, booksellers, and critics: it is a work by Montherlant. After making sure that nobody is watching, he changes the author's set phrase of *With the compliments* into a startling *With the compliments of that twat Montherlant*. The volumes will be sent to their destinations and some academics and distinguished minds will ring up to protest at the outrage and send their copies back.

Meanwhile Abdallah has perfected the tightrope dance that he begins to perform successfully in Belgium and Germany. We receive optimistic news of his tour. "You who are aflame, who last a few minutes, you shall be that fiery wonder," Genet has written for him; and the audience, "unaware that you are the incendiary, applauds the blaze." The photographs that we receive show him slender and graceful as he hops along the tightrope in his tight-fitting, dazzling costume. One day we learn indirectly of his accident: he has taken a fall during his act in Belgium and broken his leg. A subsequent operation is satisfactory, but he has to embark on a lengthy period of therapy. Genet remains at his side to encourage him. Abdallah wants to get back to his dance, darkly foreseeing that if he doesn't, he will cease to delight his friend: he perhaps knows that the enterprise is greater than his strength; nevertheless he insists on triumphing over destiny. The life he knew and appreciated before meeting Genet has lost all attraction for him. He has deserted not only the army but also everything that usually satisfies the "normal" individual: routine work, hobbies, friends, the family circle. His moral and emotional surrender to Genet is a journey of no return: a burning of bridges, a scorched-earth policy. So he will continue to dance on the tightrope, will accept the total solitude of its challenge, will fuse with that brief, precise image that keeps the audience on tenterhooks as he boldly executes his lethal leap.

Genet's territory is discontinuous: it displays crevices, ups and downs, breaks, sudden disaffections. He patiently constructs sets that he will suddenly abandon, leaving his actors alienated and orphaned. He is unselfish, faithful, generous, on the surface submissive to his lover, but at the same time, voluble, possessive, demanding, capable of harshness and cruelty. That discontinuity nevertheless tends to repeat itself, obeys subtle cycles of chance and acquires with time a strange coherence.

When Abdallah falls for a second time, the moral fullness of his friendship with Genet is cast down into a gray, inhospitable reality that has no future: the tightrope walker with the pure, delicate gestures, endowed with miraculous precision will never dance again. It is difficult to settle down to an ordinary life: the experience has marked him forever.

He is henceforth condemned to be a deadweight in Genet's life, the irritating reminder of a frustrated dream. Neither attempts the futile process of reinsertion into society. By way of consolation, Genet gives him a Giacometti painting, and with the proceeds from the sale of that he can travel for months around the Far East: escaping from himself, exiled from the world, he has begun, probably unawares, his implacable countdown.

Genet is then active in the struggle for Algerian independence. L'Arbalète published *Les Paravents*, which will not be performed for many years because of the burning relevance of the main theme.

He often comes to our place with Jacky. The youth is the stepson of Lucien, that *pêcheur de Suquet* to whom he dedicated some of the novels and poems of his early writing. Genet has continued to see Lucien after his marriage, helps him get established, and has known Jacky from childhood. The latter soon reveals an irresistible passion for cars: at the age of thirteen or fourteen he breaks into them whenever he can and drives off at top speed. The police arrest him but release him straightaway as a minor. His spontaneous contempt for legality, his boldness and brazen attitude amuse and captivate Genet, who discovers an incipient spiritual affinity with the boy. Some time earlier, Jacky had left home and we gave him shelter for a few days. By the side of the bourgeois, conformist Lucien, his precocious deviations give him in Genet's eyes the attractive allure of the marginalized.

As I write these notes I am rereading *L'Enfant criminel*. Genet's childhood experience of prison, that *moral region*, which is both cruel and fascinating, of corrective centers for minors will never cease to obsess him. Informed on by the blind musician whose guide he was—Spain with its splendor and rags soon crosses his path—he will be sent to one of them to be reformed because he has spent the small amount of money the blind man entrusted to him on the stalls and sideshows at the fair. Genet will tell me once that when he realized his "crime," he thought of committing suicide. Instead, he gets to know that savage world which sows his dreams with abjection and glory, creates an unbridgeable distance between crime and punishment, and keeps intact his stubborn, rebellious pride. The severity of the sentence forces upon him behavior that is its equal: he will strive to live up to it. From then on, the boy trained in the hypocritical mimicry of an acolyte can surrender to the hard tool of his Senegalese lovers, steal, beg, prostitute himself, accept his idealized image as a professional delinquent with arrogant panache.

Once he is invited, as a famous writer, by the director of a Swedish youth institution to speak to the adolescents on the path to rehabilitation.

After the visit to this "humanized," open center, Genet's speech will so appall the philanthropist that he breaks off his translation: Society wants to castrate you, turn you into gray, harmless people, strip you of all that distinguishes you from it by drowning your rebelliousness, taking away your beauty; do not take the outstretched hand, do not fall in the trap, take advantage of this bloke's stupidity to clear off and leave him to it . . .

As Genet told me when he related the incident, the youths listened without understanding a word, the director was furious, and, forgetting his liberalism and noble sentiments, drove him out with all manner of threat and insult.

The adolescent who breaks from his family and heads instinctively to him for help does not belong to that class of rebel who will settle down. Jacky does not aspire to a home of his own, nor a comfortable existence, nor a job, but a difficult and dangerous livelihood where he can spread out and have faith. He is lively, persistent, pleasant, and not without physical charm. When he matures and becomes a man he will naturally enter Genet's life.

It is not my intention to narrate the events that might frame a biography, but to define and delineate with the help of a number of facts and details the poet's physical and moral space: his vitality, humor, whims, playacting, his anger, simulated and real: the singular grace conferred by knowing him—and also the penalties.

His affinities and fits of pique are immediate and unpredictable. The presence of someone whom he finds unpleasant encloses him in a prickly, repellent silence that will force the blighted individual to leave his field of vision. He likes to contradict commonplaces and so-called truisms, to dismantle cheekily the most solid certainties. He greets in icy silence taxi drivers' clumsy attempts at conversation or replies to their trivial comments with biting irony. When the porter in a big luxury hotel draws the balcony curtain to reveal to him the sublime panorama that can be contemplated from there, he orders him to close the curtain again and bring, if he has one, a screen or panel with the photograph of a factory. The peacocks of the literary world bring on immediate nausea: one day he is leafing through one of their novels and exclaims: "Why the hell don't you copy me and shut your trap when you haven't got anything to say?" But if he feels at ease, among people he appreciates, he is affectionate and responsive to their problems, establishing restrained, respectful relationships. He is upset by aggressive use of the *tu* form: despite our long, deep friendship we always use *vous*.

He sometimes writes to me from Greece, Morocco, Spain, or some

French provincial city. On the envelope he adds under my name, "Monique's friend" or "concubine." On one occasion—now I'm leaping ahead several years—I accompany him after lunch to the Gare du Nord: in the compartment of the carriage where he sits down is a middle-aged lady who recognizes him and starts up a conversation. As it is departure time, we say goodbye and I get out. Two days later I receive a letter from him:

> Juan, here you have the visiting card of that idiot in the train ... She adores the *End of the Romanov* and is deeply moved by Anastasia's adventure. She voted no in the referendum. Her hero is Tixier-Vignancourt. "He's the best lawyer in the high court" and "his voice is like bronze." May '68? God forbid that '69 turns out the same ... her husband is a fat pig waiting for her at the station. This pig is the mayor of a tiny seaside town.
>
> But ... when we arrived at A., where she was getting off, I noticed that there was an enormous suitcase on the luggage rack; it was enormous, most likely very heavy: that's what she was hinting, that she was young but beginning to feel her age and feeling weak, there wasn't a porter on the station at A.
>
> Well, then!!!
>
> I laughed sarcastically and took my two minuscule cases and walking stick in one hand. She had to grapple with her big case and wait for the old pig to come and help her.
>
> And thus, as the Popular Front used to say, we both went *un bout de chemin ensemble*.

When Genet takes hold of someone's life he also embraces responsibility for his family: first Lucien's wife and her children; then Abdallah's mother, a stout, semiparalyzed German who lives alone and whom Monique occasionally visits when Abdallah is away: she speaks in difficult, broken French, complains about her isolation, and one day lifts her skirts to reveal an enormous hernia. Soon to follow will be Jacky's very young wife, their son, and Ahmed, Abdallah's childhood friend. As I find out much later, he took equal care of Mohamed's home in Larache and the future of his son.

To sort out his innumerable problems over passports, residence permits, visas, criminal records and reprieves, Genet unscrupulously uses his reputation and the snobbery of the powerful; he has recourse to Pompidou, Defferre, or Edgar Faure and writes a flowery letter to the Chinese ambassador. When he needs some support, he displays incredible energy and tenacity, and mobilizes the weight of his friendships. He demands absolute dedication: he wants everything immediately.

He likes to arrive home at lunchtime, rush into the kitchen, and there help himself, without wasting a moment, to the *petit salé aux lentilles* simmering in the saucepan. Then he gulps it down, sitting anywhere, like a hungry, badly brought-up child, a smile dancing in his eyes.

Jacky will also avoid military service. Genet travels with him to Italy, where he practices on the racetrack at Monza, and when the lad has mastered the steering wheel, he buys him the hot rod necessary for a career as a professional driver. For months he accompanies him to trials and competitions in various European countries. On 2 June 1963 Jacky is driving at Chimay, close to the French border, and we go with a couple of married friends to see him. Genet is as nervous as a father on the night before his son takes an examination decisive for his future: he ensures that Jacky eats and rests properly, swamps him with advice. He stays with Jacky on the track until the starting flag is up, and when his Lotus wins the race, Genet's face radiates happiness.

In the meantime Abdallah has returned from his trip to Japan and the Near East. Genet has got him a pardon and shows a watchful concern for him, but inevitably their relationship deteriorates: Abdallah will never be the "rare and precious" artist that fires the poet's passion with his bravery. He has withdrawn from all that ties him to life and knows that his place has been filled by a rival.

He will attempt suicide in Casablanca, and when his friend visits him, he will testify how he has returned specterlike from the "compact squadron of shadows."* Abdallah is having a stormy relationship with a hard, humorless Greek girl, Erika, whom Genet can not stand: he acts aggressively and vengefully toward Genet and makes him responsible for his own failure. We often see him, with him or her—but never with both of them—fragile and vulnerable like a condemned man with a temporary stay of execution. Alone he is still the intelligent, sensitive, delicate, and modest youth—now a man—who captivated us from our first meeting. But he has an anguished, precarious air about him. Genet has the unfortunate idea of making him Jacky's trainer and having him go to his competitions and practices. He makes a pathetic attempt, but gives up immediately. There are frequent squabbles, and Abdallah leaves the phone off the hook the night Genet is to call him at home. That is what he confessed to Monique afterwards, but Genet is probably right when he retorts: "Not so, he was really afraid I would *not* call him." When none of us has news of him, Ahmed slips away from the barracks to find he is still awaiting execution. He breaks with Erika one day and comes for some Nembutal saying it is for Genet. On 12 March 1964, forewarned by the latter, the owners of the *chambre de bonne* in an attic on the rue de Bourgogne force open the door to find a corpse.

After the police inquiry, we meet at the morgue with a small group of

---

* José Ángel Valente, *Poemas a Lázaro.*

friends. Abdallah is unrecognizable: the poisoning caused by the sleeping pills has blackened his face: he is a black. Genet will tearfully say he has returned to Africa, has got rid of all that is alien to his origins, that had deceitfully clung to his skin...

It is a gloomy burial in the small Moslem cemetery at Thiais. Genet can hardly stand up and stumbles along after the mufti. Suddenly we spot among the tombs Ahmed, who has in turn deserted and is hiding from the police. A bitter wind blows and, as befits these melancholy circumstances, the drizzle does not miss its appointment.

I frequently go to see Genet in his hotel on the boulevard Richard Lenoir. He looks calm on the surface, but Abdallah's irrevocable gesture has unleashed within him a series of inner springs previously hidden. His brilliant, original, ever surprising way of arguing suddenly coalesces in a mysticism of surrender, an absolute leap into godless transcendence. With his self-immolation, his friend has won the last, most difficult battle, toward which his singular tightrope-walker's art inexorably led. His physical annihilation is the victory that cancels out past failures: Genet reads there the symbol of his strength and purification.

It is difficult for me to follow him along those paths: I know he is waging an intense debate within himself in terms of exultation and guilt. I respect and share his grief but realize in my powerlessness that I can be of no help to him.

Genet returns to Paris after an absence of several months. On 22 August he asks me to come and see him by myself in the Hotel Lutecia. When I get to his room, he is dressed as if to go out, but tells me straightaway to sit down, that we will eat later. I do as he says, surprised by his solemn tone, and listen to his voice—that grave, severe, inimitable voice for great occasions—as he announces his irreversible decision to commit suicide.

To my great dismay, he explains he has destroyed all his manuscripts, his essays, the two plays after *Les Paravents*. Never again will he even touch pen or pencil. He has written, and handed me, the holograph will in which he leaves his wealth in equal shares to Ahmed and Jacky and designates Monique and myself his executors. When he concludes his brief statement, he seems calm and cheerful, as if he has removed a great weight from his shoulders. He makes me promise not to tell anyone and invites me to lunch.

For some time I see him regularly and try to show him the futility of his self-punishment. Genet will not listen: he speaks of Abdallah's gesture in the beautiful language of a Mawlana or San Juan de la Cruz. Although the obsession with death is intense, I nevertheless sense that his inner resistance is just as great. To tell the truth, I know no one with as much vitality or attachment to life: his physical energy is awe inspiring. His use and abuse of sleeping pills would have destroyed anyone else's health, though it hardly makes an impression on his. I can remember the time when, stuffed with painkillers and injections to combat his toothache, he jumped like a rabbit out of the dentist's chair when the nurse exhorted him to a little more patience as he proceeded to another interminable extraction: he hit the street like a whirlwind, to everyone's astonishment, and crossed over Paris, charged like an electric battery, until he found another dentist.

Although I had promised him I would keep silent, I tell Monique everything. Genet's decision is obviously absurd, but we don't know what to do to reason with him. She then has the idea of talking to Sartre: he alone, she says, is sufficiently intelligent to argue convincingly with Genet. As she will tell me after seeing him, Sartre is less anxious than we are: he is sure Genet will not kill himself. He tells Monique that he does not know what growing old is and that Genet's remorse owes less to his sadness than to a lack of it. If he has burned his manuscripts, he adds, that is not to punish himself but simply because he does not judge them to be at the level he requires.

His opinion gives us some relief, but Genet is still obsessed by the idea of committing suicide. He does not even read the newspapers, seems to have lost interest in everything, and his rejection of putting pen to paper goes to the extreme of refusing to put his signature to checks and documents. He has obtained a considerable sum from his publishers and gives this out to his protégés and Abdallah's mother. Gradually I am filled with the uneasy impression that he is using me as a sounding board, that my presence acts only to strengthen him in his intentions. It is a difficult situation and I am unsure how to end it. One day, while we are having lunch near home, I abandon my restraint and tact, seek a way to provoke him and brutally hand him a pen. Genet throws it to the other side of the dining room and shuts himself up in a curt silence. It is a breaking-off, and I will not see him again for almost two years.

Monique and I go to live in Saint-Tropez, where we learn of Genet's two suicide attempts, in Domodossola and Brussels, and of the serious car accident that puts an end to Jacky's dreams, like Abdallah's years before. From the news we get from various friends, we deduce that Genet is slowly emerging from the tunnel. On a trip to Paris, Monique sees him a couple of times by herself and recounts the change in our relationship: Arab passion has erupted in my life, the most secret part of myself escapes her. Genet seems delighted by the occurrence; he is tremendously pleased by my homosexuality and wants to see me. When we finally meet, he is once more friendly, ironic, and incisive, but we are neither the same as before: by mutual agreement we will in the future avoid all mention of Abdallah.

Apart from fleeting bouts of luxury—when he stays in five-star hotels—the poet's room is small, modest, totally bare of decoration: a bed, a couple of chairs, bedside table, and washbasin. Also: an ashtray with his cigar butts, a few newspapers, his suitcase and walking stick.

He now walks along leaning on it fairly coquettishly and bypasses the areas where people recognize him. He has lunch anywhere, walks, reads the Paris press in bed. He has a paradoxically monogamous relationship with French: Genet is completely resistant to other languages: he understands only Italian and the coarsest expressions in Spanish.

At night he hardly eats and goes early to bed. He takes his dose of Nembutal, and overcome by sleep, it is as if he sinks slowly into a well or the grave: his nightly journey to darkness with the rigid face mask of death. Every day, at dawn, he will arise like Lazarus.

Genet has come back to life, but does not write. At times, he seems indifferent and alien to literature, like a believer who has inexplicably lost his faith and state of grace. His prodigious intelligence still functions but works only on barren land: the electric charge, the generating spark of his work will resurge, miraculously, only in the terminal phase of his cancer.

His previous lyrical transports—"I know no other criterion of the beauty of an act, object, or being," he had written, "than the song it rouses in me and that I translate into words in order to communicate it to you: that's lyricism"—are replaced by more humdrum, routine feelings and reactions: like a father, he scrupulously worries over the errant ways of his protégés. Ahmed is preparing a horse-riding act in Spain; Jacky is divorced and will follow in Abdallah's footsteps to Japan. Genet has for many years not been to the cinema or theater or read any literary works: he has always lived on the edge of the fashions and interests of the literary world, but now he does without literature. His inner song—if there is one—is not translated into that beautiful, repellent flame that flares up and spreads like fire ever since the miracle of *Notre-Dame-des-Fleurs*. He too is living on after the mutilation of his transcendent impulse, like Abdallah after his fall from the tightrope or Jacky after the accident that almost cost him his life.

In a strange delight in symmetry, destiny has reduced all three to the same level.

The scandal aroused by the performance of *Les Paravents* at the Odéon briefly rescues him from his state of protective anonymity. However, if he again takes up his pen, it is only to support the revolutionary groups he favors: the Palestinians, the Black Panthers, the Baader-Meinhof gang.

The May '68 events restore his old combativity and energy. Genet goes to the Sorbonne, is overcome by the applause of the occupants, and goes back into hiding. One day while we are having lunch at home, we hear shouts from a demonstration opposite the nearby *L'Humanité* building. The day before, they were the leftists hostile to the "prudent, responsible" line adopted by the French CP. As we realize at once, these demonstrators belong to the far right: they are waving French flags and shouting against "Moscow gold." Unhesitatingly, Genet grabs hold of the soup tureen and tries to throw it through the window onto the demonstrators reassembled at the foot of our block. Monique snatches it from him: it belongs to a neighbor! He then picks up a plate, which soon smashes against the beret, the skull of a fifty-year-old individual who looks like a member of the Action Française invented by Buñuel. His forehead bleeds slightly as he looks up at the furious genie who is insulting him. *Grossier personnage!* he spits out.

During my stay in California, Genet bombards me with telegrams: he wants me to help him pass illegally over the Canadian frontier in order to meet up with the Black Panthers. Just as I am getting ready to meet him in Toronto, I hear it is unnecessary. The immigration official to whom he has handed a passport that does not belong to him had fought in France during the world war and loves Paris chic and French *esprit*. He can even whistle *la Marseillaise*. Genet smiles and whistles with him. The policeman forgets to look at the photo and date of birth, which are patently false, and twixt smiles and patriotic whistles, Genet slips into the United States, to the perplexed dismay of the FBI.

He then pursues his wandering life: he stays for several months in Jordan and Lebanon with the PLO guerrilla fighters, travels to Pakistan and Morocco. He writes to me from Tangier, complaining about the heat, "just when I feel like rain," and his recent stay in Barcelona: "Oh, the Mediterranean, that big salt lake—all that makes me want to crap!" Later he will turn up again in Paris with Mohamed, a physically attractive youth, whom he helps to climb out of poverty and settle down in the city of his birth.

Finally, I no longer see him but receive news of him through others:

discontinuity repeats its irregular but predictable cycles. I glimpse, as I write these lines, the mysterious coherence that infuses everything he touches, that extends beyond his work and weaves into the very life of the poet the complex pattern of attractions, rejections, orbits, circles, tensions, ruptures of a kind of solar system with its fixed stars, satellites, dead planets, and shooting stars: a zone at once moral, poetic, and physical, the Genetian universe, whose subtle laws have yet to be deciphered.

To know Genet intimately is an adventure from which no one can emerge unharmed. Depending on the situation, he provokes rebellion, self-awareness, an irresistible desire for sincerity, the break from old feelings and attachments, disarray, an anguished void, even physical death.

If in my youth I imitated more or less consciously some literary models from America or Europe, he has in fact been the only adult influence on the strictly moral plane. Genet taught me to cast off my early vanity, political opportunism, my desire to cut a figure in the life of literary society, to center in on something deeper and more difficult: the conquest of my own literary expression, my subjective authenticity. Without him, without his example, I would perhaps not have had the strength to break from the hierarchy of values accepted on the right and the left by my compatriots, to accept proudly my predictable rejection and isolation, to write all I have written from the time of *Don Julián*.

In January 1981 I bumped into Jacky by chance in Marrakesh, next to the square of Djemaa el Fna. I had not seen him for years and took some seconds to recognize him: he had grown thin, his features were purer and more expressive, and his thick black beard gave him the severe, almost forbidding appearance of a mountain Moroccan.

As our conversation soon revealed, it was not just a physical change: his intelligence and sensibility had sharpened. He had just accompanied Mohamed to the Sahara and was unhurriedly returning, sometimes on foot, stopping to rest in the villages. He led a solitary and ascetic life. He sometimes painted and wanted to learn Arabic, as he had previously learned Japanese. He had very little money but seemed happy.

As I was writing these pages, a journalist gave me the bad news of Genet's accidental death in one of those anonymous hotels he frequented near a train station or on the road to an airport: in recent years he had exchanged the train for the plane, but his readiness to depart, his permanent transitoriness remained the same. I had lost sight of him since his throat cancer and successive chemotherapy treatments: his group of friends was limited to Jacky, Mohamed, and the Palestinian comrades. Stays in Rabat and Larache alternated with brief visits to Paris, where he went only to get his royalties or a medical examination. He had lost interest in Europe in its entirety and was at ease only among Arabs. He met his end on one of those trips to the France he so hated, when he wanted to correct the proofs of his last book, *Un Captif amoureux*. His wish to be buried in Morocco, to leave no trace of himself in his country apart from his beautiful, repellent, and poisoned prose, apparently complicated the formalities of the funeral. As with Abdallah twenty years before, his body remained several days in the morgue; and as Abdallah blackened by poison had returned to his African origins, Genet would in turn be reintegrated symbolically in his adoptive land: as I later learned from his Palestinian friends, the customs official asked those accompanying the coffin whether it was the body of a migrant Moroccan worker. They proudly proclaimed it was.

The solitude of the dead, he had written in relation to Giacometti, is "our surest triumph": Genet, the honorary Moroccan worker, rests in the old Spanish cemetery in Larache—it is presently abandoned and can be reached only by crossing the town rubbish dump. His tomb looks to the sea significantly from amid the graves of our forgotten compatriots, again and forever that *Gênet d'Espagne* who rises from the pages of the *Journal du voleur* like the glow from a blazing fire.

· IV ·

A Black Cat on the Rue de Bièvre

A T THE END of April 1982, after a short get-together to launch a book of mine at Ruedo Ibérico's now historic bookshop in Paris, I went out for dinner with a group of friends in one of the many North African restaurants in the area: a cheap eating-house where they served up an excellent couscous, according to José Martínez, the publisher of anti-Francoist books around whom we had gathered twenty years earlier to create the magazine *Cuadernos de Ruedo Ibérico*. We went round the place Maubert-Mutualité, across the boulevard Saint-Germain and, deep in conversation, turned down a narrow side street, on the left of which, some fifty meters from the corner, was the bistro: a square, reasonably sized room whose shape, as I sat down, suddenly reminded me of one I already knew. Only then did I notice that we were on the rue de Bièvre—now famous for being the street where President François Mitterrand resides—a small street that years ago was much visited by me over a number of months. In Arabic I asked the waiter looking after us the number of the restaurant: "*Setta u aacharin, yasidi*, twenty-six, sir." While my companions were choosing the menu, I began to reconstruct mentally, behind the Moroccan décor of the moment, the layout of the furniture in the old office of the magazine *Libre*, censored by me to such an extent that I failed to recognize it when chance led me back inside. Nonetheless, those few square meters at 26, rue de Bièvre had played an important part in my life and that of a handful of Spanish writers: the critical quarterly magazine of the Spanish-speaking world that should have welded us together became, in fact, for a series of imponderable reasons, a weapon pitting us against each other, till in the end we were enemies. The personal relationships that united its initiators—almost all of them protagonists of the misnamed Latin American *boom*—went sour and, in some cases, ended there. Feelings of doubt, mistrust, and even outright hostility replaced the old warmth and camaraderie. A black cat had inopportunely passed through the magazine's home: the famous Padilla episode. The consequences of this shattered our original attempts at dialogue and discussion. Hatred, aggression, and attacks would henceforth transform the Spanish cultural community into a world of goodies and baddies worthy of a Wild West film. *Libre* thus meant an end to many friendships and illusions. Ever since its closure, for financial as much as political reasons, after a year and a half of tense, floundering existence, I had not been back to that intersection on the boulevard Saint-Germain where the future president of the French Republic already resided in 1971. I thought it was not only a joke on me but also a sign of fate that eleven years later our premises had undergone a metamorphosis into a humble couscous restaurant. That night, throughout the meal, I couldn't take my mind off the forgotten chapter of the magazine and, still savoring the familiar taste of mint tea, I decided to return there in print when time and opportunity allowed.

In the spring of 1970 a journalist active in the fringe movements that sprang up from May '68 telephoned me that a friend of hers, who closely followed issues in Latin America, was prepared to finance a political-cultural magazine aimed at a Spanish-speaking readership. She gave me her address and phone number, and after a brief telephone conversation I went along with the journalist to see her in her elegant residence on the rue du Bac. Albina de Boisrouvray was then a very young, exceedingly beautiful woman, with a passion for literature and the cinema, whose origins—her maternal grandfather Nicanor Patiño had been the famous Bolivian "king of tin"—explained her familiarity with the real problems in the world. A recent trip to Bolivia—where she would later return to collect eyewitness accounts and material on Che's capture and assassination—had brutally revealed to her the oppression, injustice, and backwardness dominating the majority of our countries and inspired the idea of creating a medium of expression for those striving to denounce them in the fields of politics and literature. By way of a visiting card she modestly referred to her articles in magazines and weeklies like *Il Manifesto, Politique-Hebdo*, or *J'accuse* and defined the exact limits of her involvement in the enterprise: she agreed to advance the sum of one hundred thousand francs to set up the magazine and to respect scrupulously its independence. I filled her in on the broad outlines of my idea for the future publication, its aims and ambitions, the list of possible collaborators who could advise me. Albina responded affirmatively to my plans, and we agreed to meet again once I had taken the first steps and spoken to my friends.

During the weeks after this meeting I explained the project by letter or word of mouth to a dozen writers, including Cortázar, Fuentes, Franqui, García Márquez, Semprún, Vargas Llosa, and Sarduy. I can remember Severo Sarduy listening to my panegyric to Albina—"young, beautiful, refined, a millionairess, and moreover, left-wing"—and exclaiming in his inimitable accent: "It's not true! Or else she's got cancer."

As my contacts were so geographically scattered, we decided to postpone all discussion of the proposal until some timely event brought us together. This appeared only months later with the première of a play by Carlos Fuentes at the Avignon festival. We friends of his had promised to be there, and on the day of the first performance we gathered to discuss the magazine in Cortázar's summer residence in the nearby locality of Saignon.

I had driven from Paris with two journalists, and as we reached the Provençal village where we had our rendezvous, I spotted straightaway the coach that had brought Carlos's many friends from Barcelona. Donoso, García Márquez, Vargas Llosa were waiting for us in the garden to Cortázar's small chalet: the latter was now separated from Aurora, and his companion at the time, Ugné Karvelis, acted as hostess. Cortázar had just returned from Cuba—where he had numerous relationships with writers and bureaucrats from the world of culture—and passed on to Vargas Llosa and myself the best wishes of the already "controversial" Padilla.

When we tackled the subject of the magazine, my colleagues agreed with me that the enterprise was both interesting and opportune: its central goal, I emphasized, should be that demilitarization of culture which Sartre had proposed years before in a gathering of writers in Leningrad. The radicalization of the Cuban revolution and intensification of political and social conflicts in Latin America tended to create a cold-war atmosphere in the field of Hispanic letters and enclose the island's writers in a besieged-fortress mentality damaging to their interests. A magazine like the one we were proposing, determined to lend critical support to the Havana régime from outside, would not only help to avoid the cultural isolation of the latter but would also strengthen the position of intellectuals who from inside were struggling, like Padilla, for freedom of expression and real democracy.

The *Mundo Nuevo* operation—immediately denounced by Cuba as a cover-up for the CIA—had aroused the suspicion of Castro's cultural appointees toward any initiative stemming from Europe. Although the image that was then broadcast of Emir Rodríguez Monegal, dangerous superagent, brought a smile to the lips of those who knew him, the fact is that the past connections of *Encounter*, *Preuves*, and *Cuadernos* with United States secret services had shrouded the magazine that succeeded the one Gorkín edited for many years in a cloud of suspicions difficult to dispel. Rodríguez Monegal declared that the magazine's source of finance was completely private, and, as facts testified, he was telling the truth. However, the links existing between old and new publications—symbolized by their remaining in the offices of *Cuadernos*—maintained an air of ambiguity that we were all fully aware of, no one more so than Emir himself. If authors later associated with the *Libre* project—like Paz, Fuentes, García Márquez, Donoso, Sarduy, or I—had published texts or interviews in *Mundo Nuevo*, others, like Cortázar and in general those collaborating with the Casa de las Américas magazine, kept at a prudent distance. The suspicions of the group in the leadership of Cuban culture increased two years later because of our dismay at the attacks by the Armed Forces journal on Padilla, whose criticism of Lisandro Otero and defense of Cabrera Infante's novel caused a furor. The famous interview with the author of *Tres tristes tigres* in *Primera Plana* in August 1968 was like a time bomb going off: the idea of a dark conspiracy against Cuba began to take shape. Coinciding as it did with the then surprising support from Castro for the Soviet invasion of Czechoslovakia, the cultural policy of the revolutionary government progressively retrenched and hardened. The disillusion and worries over Cuba, shared by myself and a nucleus of fellow travelers, echoed an increasingly harsh and sectarian policy from the revolution. Although it was a risky business, the idea of building a bridge between ourselves and the latter, of favoring dialogue between Cuba and the non-Communist left in Europe and Latin America, was, nevertheless, a tempting one. As events soon demonstrated, it was to prove unviable. Inevitably, during our informal conversation on Cortázar's garden stairs, the issue of Cabrera Infante's participation in our project provoked the first revealing confrontation: while Vargas Llosa and I were in favor provided it were strictly literary, our host categorically declared that if Cabrera Infante came in through one door, he would leave by the other. I can't remember opinions expressed by others present except for Donoso's words in the bus taking us to Avignon, as shocked and irritated by Cortázar's veto as I was. However, political arguments that seemed convincing persuaded me to give in: I see now that our idea of a publication should have been buried there. The need to keep up contact with the Cuban revolution and to help the friends who from within, and in more and more difficult conditions, shared my ideas and views overcame my hatred of proscriptions. *Libre* was born out of deals and compromises: the future involvement of Cuban writers demanded the sacrifice of Cabrera Infante, and both Cortázar and Vargas Llosa, our permanent links with the Casa de las Américas, who became our ideal intermediaries, promised to defend our proposal to their colleagues at the next annual meeting of the editorial board. As we gathered around Carlos Fuentes, in the splendid papal precinct that was the showcase for his play, the future promoters of *Libre* innocently drank to the success of the endeavor.

A PRODIGIOUS CONDENSING OF *impressions, images, rhythms, smells, immediately on alighting from the plane in an airport where against all expectation nobody was waiting for you: the island accent sweet to your ear, the instant warmth of the air, dark, smooth-skinned or bearded faces, olive-green uniforms and caps, diffuse aromas of vegetation, the royal palms' slender trunks and lethargic fronds. Irregular flights, clearly an untimely arrival, radiograms aimed at no one. You went through police formalities, got a taxi, hesitated between the address of the Casa de las Américas and the one of the newspaper run by Carlos Franqui. Chose the latter and wound up with suitcase in the entrance hall to* Revolución *guarded by armed militiamen. Franqui came and welcomed you simply, joked about the functioning of the Cuban postal service, and accompanied you to the Hotel Habana Libre, where your room had been reserved.*

It seemed as if the plants from all the greenhouses in Europe had suddenly fled to a rendezvous in Havana: frambesia, bougainvillea, aracaurias, species with lobular leaves of rubbery consistency, ficus with enormous knotted trunks, their ophidian roots airborne. Bustle in the street, a wealth of gestures and movements, a mulatto girl walking along in tight trousers, her hips trembling, just like a crème caramel in an old man's clutch, the taxi driver said.

There are cities that take over a traveler from the moment he arrives, and others that require careful treatment, react unpredictably. There are also those where a foreigner will never settle, and their encounter will be like two strangers chatting in a café or train compartment and then going their different ways.

The subtle Havana breeze, bathed in a unique, luminous glow: gusts of wind from the Malecón, Empyrean calm of the Prado, protective wind on the quayside, somnolence of an alley shaken by the slight tremor of a fiesta.

The human tide of the Revolution invading the streets of Vedado. A demonstration against the murder of an infant brigadista; *an endless procession of volunteers, array of angry, patriotic placards, hymns spluttered out over the loudspeakers, satirical ditties, slogans, and messages.*

You and Franqui make your way through the mass of people present at the event, all there to hear the words of their Leader. Suddenly, an ice-cream seller in an understandable rush entrusts his cart to your companion; to your wonderment, the director of Revolución *gleefully takes over the business and dispatches ice creams to his customers with the speed, enthusiasm, and efficiency of someone who has been doing it for a lifetime.*

Your letters to Monique communicate your feelings of blissful joy, soaked in an atmosphere of solidarity favoring lyrical transport: the people have regained their dignity, which they proclaim; happiness is within the reach of everyone; despite the boycott and threats, nobody is prepared to give in. How can one live, after so many frustrated dreams, without Cuba's warmth and fervor? What better token of love than to invite her to share the Island with you?

Curious sensation of experiencing a prismatic acceleration of time. The spontaneous popular reaction to the Punta del Este conference and exclusion from the Organization of American States: swaying syncopated movements, circles of raised hands, thousands of throats clamoring against unacceptable foreign interference. Third anniversary of the fall of Batista: high-pitched speeches, phrases chorused to a pachanga rhythm, a determination to die defending the conquests of the Revolution. Your trip to Santiago and the Oriente province: a sumptuous splendor of vegetation, white sandy beaches, militia troops dancing under coconut trees, the harvest freed from the slavery of centuries, peasants happily cutting sugarcane, political discussions and conversations with a Caribbean musical lilt.

The literary experience of Pueblo en marcha, *your contradictions and ancestral guilt exorcised, the application of moral deconstruction to a past that fascinates, captivates you: the appropriation of a mulatto universe into whose sweet charm you sink in innocent ritual beatitude.*

In your besotted, confused state of mind, impossible to distinguish the complex superimposition of layers: Spanish, African, the truly insular, created and imposed by the Revolution; the simultaneous presence of a residual past condemned to extinction and a future transmuted into present with hasty, jubilant fervor.

Fruitful discovery of the lucumí *and* abakuá *brotherhoods: litanies of the* ñáñigos *tiny dancing devils, mysteries of the* fambá *room, religious syncretism, ritual sacrifices, ceremonies and altars from the* santería *shop. Instinctively you homed in, headed for promiscuous areas with knife-edged existences; salty nights on the quayside, supper at the San Román tavern, musical soirées with irredeemable, leathery sirens, infinite cuba libres on the curbs of Jesús María, fertile, porous commingling in the working-class districts. Capillary action, osmosis of the two levels: the militiamen of the defense committees are simultaneously ñáñigos, prostitutes become literate and join in the re-education programs.*

The itinerary for your wandering, paralleling those of a deceased infante, commune with his premonitory vision of Bulwer: meticulous trawl through a seductive, worn-out world before the Pompeiian torrent of lava, the purifying fire, sweeps it away before your eyes.

Medullar belief in a shared destiny, free from all notions of social class, economic power, racism, exploitation, surplus value. Evening chats in the Central Park, captivating incursions into Regla and Guanabacoa, exchanges oiled by rum and jukebox music, a leveling familiarity, an immediate tú. Personal gravitation toward fresh magnetic fields, tacit subterranean affinities, burning ideals still uncorroded. The siege the island suffers instigates the closing of ranks, erases and abolishes the frontier between public and private. Leaning on your balcony on the eighteenth floor, you contemplate the panorama of the city transfigured by the dusk in apprehensive excitement: captive horizon, cowardly, wan light, gently iridescent breeze, evanescent labors of a tortillon, *slow, gentle palpitating of a gigantic wounded panting animal.*

In your watchtower, your lame devil's vantage point, you are lost in your solitary thoughts: the intermittent flickering of aerials on some skyscraper, crouching shadows, confused silhouettes, an all-embracing blackness, the muffled whelp of an animal about to be swallowed by the whirlpool, to disappear with you into the night, into the vortex of the abyss.

Like that innocent wisp of white cloud that naively appears in a smooth, gleaming sky and gradually gathers around nebulas with brilliant, expansive, voracious contours, dull and threatening in their presence, the arrival of the first symptoms of decay will pass you by, be cast aside as meaningless and uncertain, despite the cautious forecasts of the meteorologists.

Through different channels and avenues, your friends carefully communicate their message: Lunes *has been closed down, Party functionaries are taking up leading positions, culture has lost its autonomy and little by little bows before the directives of obtuse new commissars. An embarrassed silence at your questions, conversations broken off at the arrival of strangers, worries regularly silenced by your wish to counterbalance possible defects against the enormous benefits brought by the Revolution.*

Walterio Carbonell, Padilla, and Cabrera Infante come to say goodbye in Rancho Boyeros on 21 February, and the prophetic photo of you and them, preserved in your archive at Boston University, appears the day after on the pages of Carlos Franqui's daily newspaper.

DURING MY LAST fleeting visit to Cuba—invited along with fifty-odd writers and artists to the anniversary celebrations of the assault on Moncada, in July 1967—I found myself in a very different situation than the one I had experienced on previous stays. The difficulties created by the comprehensive United States blockade and by the mistakes of the Cuban leadership itself were compounded by a climate of reserve, if not fear, which those of us who had been brought up in a dictatorship scented more easily than people accustomed to the rights and freedoms of democratic society. It is not my aim to delineate here the transformations suffered by the Cuban revolutionary project from its inception to the historic failure of the giant sugar harvest of 1970: I have referred to them in another context and I won't cover that ground again.* I shall point out only that the popular enthusiasm that I had known had been replaced by a sloganizing enthusiasm, which was hard pressed to hide its forced, purely official character. The warmth of our welcome, Franqui's bustle of activity to ease our path and give a touch of spontaneity to the festivities were not enough to hide the presence of a ubiquitous, all-powerful bureaucracy that was discreetly tracking our movements from behind the scenes. I can remember how during a happening organized by Franqui opposite the old Caballero funeral parlor I was interviewed live on television, and while we were preparing the outline of the eventual interview, the journalist in charge asked me not to mention the name of Cabrera Infante when referring to Cuban narrative, although he had not as yet broken with the revolution: I obeyed his advice on the surface and refrained from naming him, but I did remark that the most important Cuban novels in recent years were *Paradiso*, *Tres tristes tigres*, and *El siglo de las luces*. The next day, I had a telephone call in my room at the Hotel Nacional: it was Lezama Lima. He thanked me for having referred to his novel and added: "Do you know that it is the first time in my country someone has spoken about it on television?" But for the majority of the guests, especially those who were visiting Cuba for the first time and had no knowledge of our language, it was a successful trip. My friends—Marguerite Duras, Nadeau,

---

* See my essay "Cuba, Twenty Years of Revolution," *The New York Review of Books*, 26 April 1979, 17–24; "Neither God Nor Master," an interview with Ernesto Parra, *Black Rose*, Spring 1979.

Guyotat, Schuster—were delighted by the predominant atmosphere of freedom that, in the eyes of Dionys Mascolo, dwarfed the freedom they enjoyed in Paris. Castro's honeymoon with European intellectuals— described by him in a famous speech as Cuba's only real friends—had reached its high point. In 1967 the Supreme Leader willingly allowed their observations and criticisms. K.S. Karol, who was then writing his book on the revolution, was the object of Castro's individual attention; he accompanied him by jeep and helicopter in his journeys around the island. Surrealists like Leiris and Schuster thought they had discovered the libertarian revolution they dreamed of: when they bumped into a hardened Stalinist like Siqueiros at the opening ceremony of the May Art Exhibition, the poet Joyce Mansour gave him a tremendous kick up the backside "on behalf of André Breton."

For someone who knew Cuba well and had many friends among its writers and intellectuals, the outlook was quite different. During my stay in Havana I managed extensive conversations with Franqui, Padilla, and other companions whom I will not list since they still live in the country: as a result I found out about problems and obstacles they met with, the continual police presence and the ravages of self-censorship. I was also visited at the Hotel Nacional by Virgilio Piñera: his worsening physical state, the signs of a life of panic and distress were quite visible. Frightened like someone on the run, he wanted us to go out to the garden to converse freely. He related in detail the persecution suffered by homosexuals, the way they were being spied on and rounded up, the existence of the camps run by the UMAP (Military Units Supporting Production). Despite repeated moving evidence of attachment to the revolution, Virgilio lived in constant fear of betrayal and blackmail: his voice trembled and even when walking within the beautiful, well-kept hotel grounds, he could speak only in whispers. When we bid farewell, I found the impression of moral solitude and misery emanating from his person quite unbearable.

My feelings and opinions on the Cuban revolution were perceptibly modified in the course of that rapid and exhausting trip. The ideal of a more just, egalitarian society that was also free and democratic originally proclaimed by the 26 July movement had been replaced by a schema I was well acquainted with from my visits to Soviet-bloc countries: that "real socialism" where, as the Berlin student leader Rudi Dutschke once said, "all is real except for the socialism." From then on, my external support for the revolution lacked enthusiasm and conviction. With Franqui's discreet exit just before Castro's speech in the Chaplin Theater in August 1968, my rather vague hope for some modification in the sectarian *caudillo* approach diminished even further: in the space of two or three years, Cuba had ceased to be my model.

While I ate my share of couscous at the Moroccan restaurant in the old

Libre office, I began to review internally my gradual alienation from the Castro régime: the descent from that "lyric effusion" I detected in my fellow travelers in 1967—like the "revolutionary tourists" in Hans Magnus Enzensberger's masterly description—to the more prosaic, lucid attitude of someone who has ceased to see the world through the blinders of ideology and has shed a number of scales on his eventful journey.

On 8 November 1968, just after 2 P.M., I went down the boulevard Bonne Nouvelle to stretch my legs and buy *Le Monde*, when a report from the paper's Cuban correspondent suddenly caught my attention: "The organ of the Armed Forces denounces the counterrevolutionary maneuvers of the poet Padilla." The article, signed with Saverio Tutino's initials—also the special envoy of *Paese Sera*—reproduced some passages from the *Verde Olivo* diatribe against the poet, whom it accused not just of a catalogue of literary-political provocations, but also—and this was much more serious—of having "happily squandered" public moneys during his time as the director of Cubartimpex. According to the author of the editorial, Padilla led a group of Cuban writers who allowed themselves to be swept along by sensationalism and foreign fashions "by creating works whose effeminacy was mixed up with pornography and counterrevolution."

Padilla's polemic with Lisandro Otero, the vice-president of the National Arts Council and the old and new editorial boards of *El Caimán Barbudo*, in the summer and autumn of 1967 over the relative merits of *Tres tristes tigres* and a now rightly forgotten novel by Otero had split the Cuban intellectual coterie into two irreconcilable factions: with a rashness verging on blindness—the casual attitude that would lead him to play a game much beyond his strength and for which he was clearly unfit both morally and physically—Padilla had set the literary talent of the emigré against the mediocrity of the official writer, dubbed the Writers' Union "a pathetic puppet show" and railed against "the false hierarchies established by the degree of give in a writer's backbone, his age, and posts in the government"; in Cuba, the poet concluded, "it is a fact that a humble writer cannot criticize a novelist-vice-president without being attacked by the short-story-telling director and the poet-editors entrenched behind that generic title, *the editorial board*."

His sarcasm at the expense of the docility and conformism of his colleagues brought a series of reactions from the "young revolutionary authors" grouped around *El Caimán Barbudo* and Otero himself. When the echoes of the polemic had still not faded, Cabrera Infante's break with the revolution and the prize obtained by *Fuera de juego* in UNEAC's annual competition put the spotlight back on Padilla. Placed in an uncomfortable position by the violence of the attack from the man he was defending, Padilla reacted with characteristic ambiguity: if on the one hand he disassociated himself from Cabrera Infante in a letter sent to *Primera Plana*, on the other—from an official perspective—he kept on with his "provocations." Whatever the state of play, he was obviously vulnerable and his friends were extremely anxious when they read Tutino's note in *Le Monde*.

On Franqui's advice, I got into contact with Cortázar, Fuentes, Vargas Llosa, Semprún, and García Márquez and tried to talk by telephone with Padilla from Ugné Karvelis's Gallimard office. Given the futility of the telephone calls—his number never answered—we resolved to send a telegram signed by us all to Haydée Santamaría in which, after declaring "our consternation at the slanderous accusations" against the poet, we manifested our support for "every action undertaken by the Casa de las Américas in defense of intellectual freedom." Haydée's telegrammed response—received two days later—filled us with amazement:

> Inexplicable how you can know from so far away whether accusation against Padilla slanderous or not. The cultural line of the Casa de las Américas is the line of our revolution, and the directorate of the Casa de las Américas will always be as Che wished: guns at the ready, firing on all fronts.

After that I heard little or very little of Padilla and a group of friends who, like Virgilio, Rodríguez Feo, Lezama, Arrufat, Walterio Carbonell, or Pablo Armando Fernández, seemed under direct attack from the *Verde Olivo*, UNEAC, and the appropriation of cultural power by that group of unashamed opportunists who had distinguished themselves three years earlier with their ridiculous, pitiful invectives against Neruda. The number of trustworthy visitors had been considerably reduced since Franqui's demise, and the coded messages or letters I sometimes received already pointed to the almost paranoid atmosphere of mistrust so eloquently described by Jorge Edwards in his controversial account:* Marx's justice-bearing fraternal project had undoubtedly been replaced by the tangible reality of Orwell's universe.

---

* Jorge Edwards, *Persona non grata*, 1973.

THE UNFORGETTABLE ATMOSPHERE *of expectation during the missile crisis: general uncertainty, diffuse apprehension, unusually authentic human relationships, hazy reading of signs leading to the cataclysm. But calm and good humor prevail: the last drop of life is squeezed out. Scarcity of products, liquidation of small street-traders, egalitarian austerity imposed by decree, accepted with resignation or heroic glee.*

You are preparing a filmscript for ICAIC and survey possible locations with Gutiérrez Alea and Sarita Gómez. The saltpeter wind of the Caribbean not only corrodes the fronts of buildings and battered wooden houses, car bodies, and metal railings: it also eats into the faces and looks of those dwelling in poor districts, devotees of Ochún, Yemayá, and Changó: wrinkles transformed into crevices, sudden old age, sickly smiles, sidelong glances, opaque, glazed eyes, rusted tone of voice.

One Sunday in November 1962 Franqui takes you to an agricultural development near Havana frequently visited by Fidel. After a time spent looking around the plots, a procession of official cars warns you of his arrival: el Comandante is there surrounded by other comandantes smoking cigars like him, chorusing his every word. Franqui goes to greet him and introduces you: here's a Spaniard, he says, with a smile, he's had the bright idea of paying us a visit rather than rushing off like other writers you know. Fidel jokes with you and while he explains his plans for cheese and milk products with a passion that would have delighted your father, you give him a good looking-over. He has a bright, cunning, roaming expression: out of the corner of his eye he spies the effect his words are having, and at times you catch a mistrusting, evasive expression of instinctive suspicion.

Unfortunately for you, he decides on the spur of the moment to show off his shiny vinegar tanks: although you go in cheerfully prepared to follow his guided tour to the bitter end, your innate allergy to acetic acid is more powerful than your own strength of mind and forces you to leave the cellars sick, at the point of suffocation. He seems upset by the violence of your reaction, and after a lordly tour of the estate leaves without saying goodbye.

From then on, you see him only from a distance and in public, on his impromptu visits to Franqui's paper, jumping out of a jeep or perched on his orator's podium, speechifying with a magisterial sweep of the forearm, wagging a hypnotic index finger, in his extremely didactic style.

A scheduled meeting with the volunteer coffee-planting brigades in Havana's future green belt. The collective enthusiasm seems real and people sign up to sow before or after their normal work hours in factories or offices. Some of your writer friends join in the campaign with great energy and gusto. The scene impresses you favorably, but Franqui takes it upon himself to turn on the cold shower. Coffee will never grow there because the land is not suited to coffee bushes.* He is of peasant stock and sees the gap between reality and slogan. You are surprised and ask why they are wasting so much time, effort, and persistence in an activity doomed to failure.

It was Fidel's personal decision. Who will bell the cat?

In the entrance hall to the ICAIC, where you have gone to pick up your check, you bump into its director, Alfredo Guevara, and take the opportunity to talk to him. You are alarmed by the attacks on him from the leading group in the old Cuban CP because of his so-called softness for decadent bourgeois art. Blas Roca, Vicentina Antuña, Edith García Buchaca criticize him for allowing the screening of Accatone *and* La dolce vita: *their sour confrontation with the ICAIC perhaps augurs the arrival of difficult times, of a period of narrow-minded, puritanical sectarianism. Guevara listens, his smile never fading, modulating his s's with sybaritic delight: they can shout as much as they like, he says, what Blas and these people don't realize is that before passing a script or buying a European film, I tell the plots to Fidel, and if he likes them, that's the end of the matter.*

Your first interview with Che, organized by the Casa de las Américas, comes to nothing: the person allotted the task of accompanying you gets lost, and you reach the Ministry of Industry out of breath only to be informed by the orderly that Che is busy with other people; he uses your regrettably late arrival to justify leaving you in the lurch.

For the moment you are happy enough to survey him from the guests' stand during the great revolutionary celebrations. Fidel has the power; he is in temporary attendance. Unlike Fidel, Che distances himself ironically from any attempt at servile flattery. His subordinates admire and fear him: he wears a halo of obvious charisma and seems to defend himself from it by digging himself in behind a barrage of taunts and barbed comments.

When you finally meet him it will not be in Cuba, but Algiers, where you have

---

* It never did grow. Years later not another word was heard of Havana's wonderful green belt.

been invited with a group of French sympathizers to the ceremonies commemorating the first anniversary of independence. Che Guevara is there, en route from a long trip to the USSR, and Jean Daniel has an idea for a magnificent scoop: interview him for L'Express *on the recent, undoubtedly instructive, experience. You phone the ambassador "Papito" Serguera and get an appointment at the embassy for that same night. Having learned your lesson, you show up on time, but he in turn keeps you waiting in a modestly furnished room where, on a low table in the middle flanked by a sofa and two armchairs, stands out in all its glory the cheap edition of a book: a volume of Virgilio Piñera's plays. Che and Serguera have hardly arrived when, before saying hello and settling down on the sofa, Che imitates you, takes the book, and immediately poor Virgilio's work goes hurtling through the air to the other end of the room, as he aims a peremptory bewildered question to all gathered there: Who the fuck's reading that pansy?*

Did you foresee then what would happen, what was going to happen, what was happening to your brothers in nefarious vice, the reviled crimine pessimo, *and along with them, santeros, poets, ñáñigos, lumpens, idlers, and scroungers, unadapted or incapable of adaptation to a monochrome reading of reality, to the implacable, disciplined, icy glare of ideology?*

Rescue the scene from oblivion, resurrect the brief, dazzling transfiguration.

    The raw morning light of the tropics, a halt on the road, time to put gas in the car that is taking you or bringing you back from somewhere, a small kiosk with little cups of coffee and fresh fruit juice, a quiet spot, early morning or late-night customers, and the eruption, his unreal, titivated, tiny, ageless, baggy-eyed eruption, all atremble, my boyfriend, where is my boyfriend, soft, tremulous tones, but piercing, almost challenging, a leaf blown down by a gust of wind, swept along by panic, where is he, what'll become of me, questions fired at no one, only at his own terror, amid the embarrassed silence of the sleepless café, of the customers silenced by the spectacle, frantically tidying his scant hair, combing without a comb, no face powder, no lipstick, only winks, nervous tics, Saint Vitus's dance, a ravaged smile, feverish contortions, uncoordinated, uncontrolled gestures.

An impression of the black district of Jesús María, leaving your favorite spot early in the morning: small bars and shops shut up, deserted pavements, tumbledown houses, as if emptied of all substance, drunks arguing crossly in a dark alleyway, old propaganda posters torn down by the wind. Cuba is not the Congo, is not the Congo, the Congo.

    But no clue or indication as to what Cuba is.

Before, afterwards, some day or other when your friend the poet Navarro Luna fetches you from your hotel to take you to the closing session of a political education course for hundreds of young girl volunteers, to what promises to be—yet will not be, as you later realize with the lucidity of hindsight—a routine, anodyne soirée.

I MADE THE FIRST steps toward eventual publication of the magazine on my return to Paris in December 1970 after a three-month stay in Boston. The quest for a suitable person to be editor-in-chief led to some friction. Apparently, Ugné Karvelis had a candidate for the post, but Franqui deeply mistrusted her: sunk in a Kafkaesque nightmare in which reality and neurosis came together to the point of total fusion, Padilla had sent us various messages to put us on our guard against her "double game." Julio Cortázar's former partner had gradually woven a net of privileged relationships between the literary coterie on the Rive Gauche and the leaders of the Cuban revolution, and although I was not then aware of her uncontrolled aggression, limitless thirst for power, and incredible, almost Florentine capacity for intrigue— characteristics I would experience at my own cost years later—our differences of opinion on the evolution of Castro's régime and the future role the magazine should play encouraged me to keep her at a distance. The candidates I toyed with had the drawback of being Spaniards or Latin Americans long resident in Europe and consequently out of touch with the real day-to-day problems in their countries. While we drew up a short list of writers suitable for the job with Severo and Albina, García Márquez suggested the name of a close friend of his, whose ideas, political and cultural perspectives, he pointed out, were very close to my own. Days afterwards, Plinio Apuleyo Mendoza came to see me, and after an open, informal conversation we agreed on the focus and options for *Libre*: support for Allende's socialist experiment and liberation movements in Latin America; critical backing to the Cuban revolution; struggle against the Francoist régime and all other military dictatorships; the defense of freedom of expression wherever it was threatened; the denunciation of American imperialism in Vietnam and Soviet imperialism in Czechoslovakia. Plinio was, moreover, on very friendly terms with the leaders of the Venezuelan MAS—at the time the liveliest, most dynamic political group in Latin America—whose involvement in the project I judged to be indispensable. This detail, and the interest shown by García Márquez, persuaded me he was the person I was looking for. I introduced him to Albina, and after agreeing on the material basis for his work with her, he immediately began to carry out the duties of chief editor.

The selection of a secretary was less onerous: Cortázar put forward the name of Grecia de la Sobera, at the time married to his friend Rubén

Bareiro Saguier. The office where the magazine was to be based was supplied by Albina: small premises situated in the basement of 26, rue de Bièvre, belonging to one of her former employees. The room looked straight out onto the street and had a washbasin and back room. After furnishing it with bargain-priced office equipment—tables, armchairs, filing cabinets—we discovered it was useless for receiving visitors and even for just walking round: the pompously titled *Libre* news office in France was really a pleasant cubbyhole. When describing the minute area of the future couscous restaurant, and perhaps alluding humorously to the stormy personal relations of its former occupants, García Márquez would quip years later: "That small space was only fit for fucking in."

As we had agreed in Saignon, Cortázar and Vargas Llosa took advantage of their trip to Havana in January 1971, on the occasion of the annual meeting of the committee of the Casa de las Américas, to explain the idea of *Libre* and try to enlist the support of Cuban writers. The independent nature of our enterprise and impossibility of controlling it from afar aroused the latter's suspicions, despite the fact that the statement of intent and list of collaborators constituted the best possible guarantee of our favorable attitude toward the revolution. As both informed me on their return, the Cubans had listened politely to their arguments and made no promises of active participation.

During the following weeks—packed with gossip hostile to *Libre* and alarming news filtering through from Havana—Plinio and I wrote a note that, with the backing of Cortázar and friends resident in Barcelona, later appeared in the first issue of the magazine:

> Present circumstances in Latin America and Spain urgently demand the creation of a means of expression open to all those intellectuals who critically face up to the requirements of revolution. *Libre*, a quarterly publication with totally independent sources of finance, will offer its columns to writers struggling for the real emancipation of our peoples, not just political and economic but also artistic, moral, religious, sexual emancipation [. . .] *Libre* will engage in revolutionary tasks at all levels fundamentally available to the printed word: "to change the world" according to Marx's program, and "to change life" following Rimbaud's desire.

Albina's social life and family background—that "dirty Patiño money" soon to be thrown in our faces—had surfaced right from the inception of the magazine: those who tried to tar our friend with the original sin of her ancestors seemed to be unaware, on the other hand, that a revolutionary bourgeois like Marx had lived almost all his life on the appropriation of the surplus value of Engels's workers. Such accusations, however grotesque and unjust they were, nevertheless succeeded in their objective: namely to put us on the defensive from the start and force us to justify a modest economic contribution that really required no justification whatsoever.

As we were assembling the contents of the first issue, which carried contributions from Vargas Llosa, Cortázar, Paz, Donoso, Fuentes, and my brother Luis, together with some of Che Guevara's unpublished writing with a prologue by Franqui and a study from Teodoro Petkoff, the small office on the rue de Bièvre buzzed with life and activity. Plinio had a flow of Latin American visitors interested in the project, while Grecia held court with her retinue of admirers. The worries I had felt on my return from Boston concerning the risks inherent in the venture—worries that brought me to the point of throwing the project overboard after a most painful attack of shingles—gradually dissipated as the magazine took shape. For the first and only time in my life I experienced the joy and problems of collaborative work—work that, I should make clear, was carried out in a totally disinterested way. Through Marvel Moreno, Plinio's wife at the time, Plinio himself, and Rubén Bareiro's wife, we corresponded with our future collaborators, laid the basis for *Libre*'s distribution in Europe—entrusted via Sarduy to Editions du Seuil—and discussed its possible impact on Spanish America. The storm gathering over our heads caught us completely unawares. One day I was woken up by the ring of the telephone to be told very excitedly by Plinio that Padilla had been arrested.

On that gray March day in 1971, the *Libre* office telephone rang continually. Heberto's friends called from Spain, England, Italy, asking us what they should do. The naked brutality of what had happened came as confirmation of the fears we had been harboring for months and suddenly confronted us with our own irremediable impotence.

At Franqui's insistence, I contacted Cortázar in order to draw up a letter of protest to the Supreme Leader and request he intervene. The author of *Rayuela* set a time for me to see him in his home on the place du Général Beuret, and we composed together what would later be known as the "first letter to Fidel Castro," a letter that won the approval of Franqui, to whom we had spoken while drawing it up. We then decided it should be a private letter, so the recipient could consider our case without the inevitably damaging impact of a blaze of publicity. Our only proviso was that if we had no reply after a given period we reserved the right to send a copy to the newspapers.

In respectful, measured tones the statement proclaimed the signatories' solidarity with the aims and principles of the revolution, expressed our worries over the use of repressive methods against intellectuals exercising their right to criticize from within, and sounded the alarm as to the negative repercussions of such actions on writers and artists throughout the world "for whom the Cuban revolution is both symbol and banner." Once we had collected some fifty signatures, including those of Sartre, Beauvoir, Claudín, Calvino, Fuentes, Moravia, Nono, Paz, Anne Philippe, Susan Sontag, Semprún, and Vargas Llosa, we sent the letter to the Cuban embassy, pointing out we would at some time in the future publish the letter. Plinio had tried in vain to track down García Márquez in Barranquilla and, in the mistaken belief that we had his approval, included his name on the list. This detail would be disowned later by the author of *Cien años de soledad*. With his consummate skill in wriggling out of tight corners, Gabo would carefully distance himself from his friends' critical position while avoiding confrontation with them: the new García Márquez, genial strategist of his own enormous talent, victim of fame, devotee of the great and good in this world, and promoter at the planetary level of real or would-be "advanced" causes, was about to be born.

A few days later, Vargas Llosa called from Barcelona to announce the visit of Jorge Edwards, whose diplomatic mission in Cuba had come to an end and who was now to take up his position in Allende's embassy in Paris. Edwards wished to see me and Cortázar, and his startling account of recent months, later brought together in the pages of *Persona non grata*, convinced me that Heberto's arrest might be much more serious than we had thought at first. The Padilla case was not simply an unfortunate episode in a struggle of internal tendencies, but the fruit of a political decision taken personally by Castro. For reasons that he alone knew, the Supreme Leader had decided to put an end to any form of dissidence and establish the intangibility of his "ideological monolith."

When our letter appeared in the newspapers, I was traveling around the Sahara, Algeria, and Morocco. I read the summary of Padilla's retractions at the UNEAC shortly before my return to Europe in one of those collective taxis that ply between Tetuan and Tangier. I had bought the *Herald Tribune* and the contents of the brief news item from the United States agency made me fume in angry indignation. After telephoning Plinio, I decided to stop off in Barcelona, where Vargas Llosa now had the complete text of the "confession" and wanted to discuss the matter with me.

It is an unreal, grotesque exercise to review with hindsight the *Prensa*

Latina transcript of Padilla's statement at the UNEAC. The extravagant staging of the act, Dostoevskian revelations of the accused, the palinode of his supposed accomplices, the cultural commissars' references to the "beautiful night" ruined by Norberto Fuentes's obstinacy are not only a parodying remake of the Stalinist trials but a really Ubuesque setup that would have sent Jarry himself into fits of ecstasy.

Beating his breast, Padilla confessed he had been "unjust and ungrateful toward Fidel, for which he would be eternally repentant." He admitted that the revolution could not "continue to tolerate that poisonous situation with all those disaffected little groups from intellectual and artistic areas of life." Against the mistaken, embittered posturing of his friends, he counterposed the "humility, simplicity, sensitivity" of the very "intelligent" State security police, a "group of most valiant comrades working day and night to ensure moments like this" through "long, intelligent, and extraordinarily brilliant forms of persuasion" that had made him see "clearly every single one of my errors." After revealing he had written a "clever little novel" that would fortunately never be published, "because I have torn up and will tear up each little bit I might come across some day," he declared he felt "so fed up, so sick, so pathetically sad, so damagingly counterrevolutionary that he could not bring himself to write." In that bankrupt state, he had experienced his detention within his heart like a "just, moral imprisonment" where he had written "pretty pieces, new poems"—on Spring, for example—"in a kind of desperate catharsis."

For those of us who knew Heberto and were aware of his literary and political interests, that distressing caricature of a confession seemed sown with snares and traps for his guardians and coded messages aimed at his friends. The poet knew by heart the official discourse imposed on Trotskyists and Bukharinites during the great Stalinist purges and had taken over its formulas and clichés, exaggerating them to the point of absurdity. The abject mea culpas, the typically Vishinskyan references to "the French Pole Karol" or "the old counterrevolutionary agronomist René Dumont," his boundless licking-up to the system that oppressed him might deceive the state functionaries who had organized the act, but not the readers of Swift or Brecht. Apparently giving in to force and using their language, Padilla had recourse to the cunning of a Mark Antony in his harangue on the assassination of Caesar. If, as one of Valle-Inclán's heroes says, "Spain is a grotesque reflection of European civilization," the theatrical staging of Padilla's surreal confessions of guilt at the UNEAC was a grotesque Caribbean reflection of the infamous Moscow purges.

I have often wondered how the leaders of Cuba's cultural life could have fallen into such a clumsy trap. The whole proceedings constituted a bloody mockery of the principles of freedom, dignity, and justice that the revolution was trying to defend and no doubt had defended at the beginning. That its protégés could not see this has always filled me with incredulous amazement. When Padilla says, "You have to live this experience" and adds, after correcting himself and mercifully hoping that the present company "won't have to," that "you have to live it, to really feel it, to be able to understand what I am saying," the message he was transmitting to us could not have been clearer.

That having been said, with the greater objectivity brought by retrospective vision of the facts, if the Poet's extravagant palinode lay bare the mechanisms of oppression within Castro's "Leninist-caudillista" régime, it also betrayed a series of idiosyncrasies and traits in the accused that fostered the farce he had to perform. When Heberto spoke of his character defects and grave psychological problems, his words introduced a brief note of sincerity into the oneiric context of the ceremony. Together with the warmth, generosity, wit, and humor that so seduced and seduces his friends, Padilla would sometimes surprise us with his frivolous, narcissistic behavior: he loved to adopt the airs of an *enfant terrible*, throwing himself into irritating or pathetic histrionic attitudes. Incomprehensible carelessness and thoughtlessness pushed him into a game from which he would necessarily emerge the loser. His intelligence was often cynical and corroding: irresistible vertigo seemed to drive him to the abyss, to that "moral and physical self-destruction" he had mentioned in the course of his speech.

On his return from the USSR, where he had lived for a year working as a proofreader on the weekly *Novedades* in Moscow, he had a perfect knowledge of the mechanisms of "real socialism" as practiced in Soviet-bloc countries. He had been traumatized by his internal analyses of that society of zombies. I remember how when he stopped off in Paris he accompanied me to a literary cocktail party in the gardens at Gallimard and, while contemplating the cheerful, complacent writers and intellectuals prancing on the well-kept lawn, glass of whiskey or champagne in hand, he had exclaimed with a sarcastic roar of laughter, "Oh, if only they knew!" He had come back from the society of the future *and he knew*. However, he had continued his journey to Havana, into the lions' den, without taking the elementary precaution of donning the protective mask of conformity. Just like my friend Martha Frayde, he had continued to express his ideas at the top of his voice; like her, he had reaped the punishment his rashness deserved.

The shocking, ridiculous ritual of the famous soirée at the UNEAC is, of course, one of the greatest blunders of the Cuban revolution: all those involved, whether as judges, accused, or mere witnesses, were inevitably marked, and the blight similarly reached those who felt obliged to react after reading the transcription of the official Castroite news agency.

In spite of my great repugnance at the idea of setting foot in the Spain of the time, I made a short stopover in Barcelona. Vargas Llosa lived in an apartment on the Vía Augusta, not far from the Bonanova district where I was born, and when I reached his house, I found him in discussion with a group of friends who, at one time or another, had traveled to Cuba and proclaimed their solidarity with the revolution: Castellet, Barral, my brother Luis, Hans Magnus Enzensberger ... It was there, together with the complete text of the UNEAC session of self-criticism, that I learned the recent breathtaking news from the island. The Supreme Leader's violent speech against the "libelous, bourgeois, intellectual, CIA agent gentlemen ... the brazen pseudoleftists who want to win their laurels in Paris, London, Rome ... rather than in the front-line trenches" and his declaration at the National Congress for Education and Culture, held at the end of April in Havana, where, in his desire to preserve the "ideological monolith" of the revolution, he launched the hunt for all forms of deviationism and heterogeneity, indicated that Castro's régime had decided to weed out its hesitant or lukewarm supporters. These were dubbed as "rubbish," "intellectual rats," "minor agents of colonialism," etc. In the great clear-out of "foreign fashions, customs, and extravagances," homosexuality in all "its forms and manifestations" was to be eliminated, African religions were dubbed "seedbeds of delinquency," and rebellious youths were to be condemned to forced labor in the pursuit of norms of moral hygiene that astonishingly recalled those dictated by Fascist régimes.

Our measured, respectful letter to Castro thus earned the signatories a terrible diatribe in which the most worn-out clichés and stupidest accusations came together. Such a disproportionate reaction—on top of the tragicomic masquerade performed by Padilla—forced us to take the bull by the horns and reply to the flood of insults. Our second letter to commander Fidel Castro, written on that 4 May afternoon in Vargas Llosa's flat, was not a response that matched up to the challenge: rather than analyzing point by point the accumulation of regressive decisions that over recent years had transformed the Cuban revolution into a totalitarian system, it concentrated its reply on the UNEAC spectacle, although toward the end we partially made up for our mistake by adding, following Enzensberger's advice, a paragraph that should have really been at the center of our thinking:

> We are not alarmed by the contempt for human dignity shown in forcing a man to accuse himself ridiculously of the worst betrayals and vilest acts because he happens to be a writer, but because any Cuban comrade, peasant, worker, engineer, or intellectual might also be the victim of similar violence and humiliation.

Although none of us had the slightest illusion as to the impact of our protest, we decided to gather the greatest possible number of signatures at the foot of our letter before sending it, this time to *Le Monde*. The following day, with the text of the letter in my pocket—while Vargas Llosa wrote his resignation from the Casa de las Américas committee—I returned hotfoot to Paris.

When I reached the *Libre* office, it looked as if it had been hit by a hurricane. Latin American writers and press correspondents wanted to know our position on the incident, and the telephone would not stop ringing. Although the varied points of view of its collaborators prevented the magazine from taking a stand, with Plinio's agreement the office became our center for co-ordinating the collection of signatures for the second letter. With a delightful, inexcusable lack of awareness, we telephoned the four corners of the earth, forgetting that our publication's limited budget did not cover such expenditure. But our moral indignation at the time and solidarity with our Cuban friends on whom the trapdoor had just closed meant more than any arithmetic calculation. A year later, as a result of Rubén Bareiro's momentary arrest by the Paraguayan police, the passionate Grecia would equally move heaven and earth to get help, in one of her frequent attacks of remorse inspired by her real or imaginary infidelities. Among other reasons, *Libre* died from its telephone bill. The political vicissitudes of the day and the defense of writer friends led us to take on a humanitarian role that we were not equipped for. If the magazine closed after four issues, it was due not only to the crisis within its staff but also to our generosity, lack of foresight, and light-headedness.

The great majority of those who subscribed to the first letter and others who, like Resnais, Pasolini, or Rulfo, had not had the opportunity to do so approved the contents. Yet there were defections as well, including some important ones. Cortázar, who when we wrote the first protest letter had told me to include Ugné's name, had called hours later to ask me to withdraw it—after taking a quick look at the text, he said that he could not back it. Her friends similarly decided to withdraw, and the day we were preparing to send it to *Le Monde*, Barral telephoned me from Barcelona to get his signature removed. Although he was a close friend of Padilla, with whom he had transacted some good publishing deals when the latter was in charge of Cubartimpex, I was not at all surprised by his decision: by that time I knew only too well the strength of his convictions and his noble idea of friendship.

The letter, with sixty-two signatories, appeared when I was in Syria, where I participated with other European intellectuals in a broadcast on the Palestinian struggle. On my return to Paris, on 27 May, the statement had caused an enormous stir in the Hispanic world. Letters from writers opposed to our position, bristling with accusations and invective, had been published or were circulating in Cuba, Chile, Mexico, Peru, Uruguay, Argentina, and Spain. Luigi Nono, who had visited the rue de Bièvre weeks earlier with a message from Franqui, was to reveal signs of an uncouth *qualitative leap* in the direction of stolidity and ideological lunacy by way of a mouth-watering telegram sent from Chile that invited me to "suspend publication *Libre* magazine financed by Patiño real mortal insult to Bolivian miners and all Latin American comrades in struggle."

Predictably, the prodigious, irrepressible lie-machine went into action at once. The presence among the signatories of some of the most outstanding, respected writers from Europe and Latin America had unleashed a groundswell of frustrations, envy, and rancor, which, under the varnish of revolutionary inflexibility, concealed the crudest possible settling of accounts. The Supreme Leader's decision to pillory us gave the green light to attacks on all fronts, in which every weapon and method was legitimate: the history of the last fifty years is littered with similar cases whose victims have been symbolically or actually hurled into the Great Dustbin of History.

"Accusations rain down on the imprudent who dare to violate taboos," writes Maxime Rodinson, the veteran third-world militant, summing up his own experience. "Analysis becomes insinuation; description, slander; criticism, attack. Your past, background, private life, anything that will bring discredit without requiring a great effort—that necessary to understand and impugn your ideas—will be dragged out. Doubt will be cast on your sources. Who wrote the book you are quoting? Is it a Trotskyite, Bukharinite, a bourgeois? Who's the publisher? Where does the money come from? Why now? What's their tactic?"

I remember how some journalists—"with good intentions" or simply after a sensationalist story—turned up on the rue de Bièvre to photograph the *hôtel particulier* or mansion where *Libre* was produced. Their amazement and annoyance when they discovered the magazine's microscopic fief were truly comical. Did the dangerous imperialist publication financed by Patiño come from that little hole with its secondhand furniture?

Parallel to opportunist proclamations of loyalty and enforced collection of signatures, the would-be orthodox revolutionaries had launched a ridiculous campaign—a tissue of lies—against us: on my stop in Algiers weeks earlier I had happened to come across Régis Debray in the street; Debray had just been on a quick visit to Cuba, after pressure from left-wing intellectuals in the West got him released from a Bolivian jail. When I asked him what he knew of Padilla, who had quoted him as his "fine example" of a revolutionary intellectual in his polemic with *El Caimán Barbudo*, Debray replied that Padilla was but a CIA agent getting his just desserts. Later on, when I was back in Paris, Simone de Beauvoir indignantly related to me how she and Sartre had bumped into Alejo Carpentier on the boulevard Raspail and how he had brusquely turned his back on them and stuck his nose up against a shop window, worried and afraid he might compromise himself just by saying hello to them. Friends had told them that the Cubans were spreading the rumor that Sartre was also a CIA agent.

Even before *Libre* saw the light of day, the magazine was enveloped in an atmosphere of suspicion and espionage. However, as we were able to confirm over the following weeks, that atmosphere was not entirely without foundation. One day a North American "professor" appeared on the rue de Bièvre, speaking in perfect Spanish and expressing great interest in *Libre*; after interrogating Plinio on our political position and cultural orientation, he said he could give us material help, if we had any problems, through a private foundation whose funds he controlled. But in the course of conversation the would-be professor revealed an astonishing ignorance in matters literary. His insistence in getting Franqui's address and the wonderful philanthropy he exhibited convinced Plinio that he really was a United States secret agent. He too must have scented the reticence, since, despite his promises, he failed to show up again.

About the same time K.S. Karol, whose book on the Cuban revolution had enraged Fidel Castro, told me of an incident that befell him a year earlier and that related to the Leader. The wife of an important official personage, whom he had seen a lot during his stay in Cuba, had just separated from her husband, and after establishing herself in Paris, had come to ask him to help her find some work connected with Latin America. Karol was not at all suspicious of her and entrusted her with the typescript of his manuscript *Les Guérilleros au pouvoir*, in which he set out a series of criticisms of regressive decisions in the areas of police repression and censorship alongside analyses and commentaries that were very favorable to the revolution. On the occasion of the annual reception offered by the Cuban embassy every 26 July, Karol turned up at the banquet rooms, not worrying that he had not been sent an invitation that year. As soon as the ambassador saw Karol, he told him he had no reason to be there, since he had written an anti-Cuban, counterrevolutionary work. When Karol expressed surprise that he could know the contents of an as yet unpublished book, the ambassador maintained an embarrassed silence. On the basis of this episode, the writer reached the conclusion that the friend who had requested the pleasure of typing it had secretly passed a copy on to the embassy.

Days after Karol related this anecdote, Plinio told me that while dining with friends, he had met a very interesting woman, the ex-wife of a Cuban dignitary, who seemed very close to our perspective on the magazine and was offering to work gratis for us. I was alarmed and asked what her name was: it was the same person.

"I hope you didn't agree!" I exclaimed.

"No. Why?"

"She's a spy!"

When I brought him up to date with what had happened to Karol, we broke into wild fits of laughter. Our beautiful conception of a revolutionary vanguard cultural magazine had imperceptibly been transformed into a mediocre, well-worn plot for some pulp novel.

The first issue of *Libre* was ready for the printers just as the Padilla case burst upon us. The burning topicality of the affair and the role that the magazine's main collaborators played in it persuaded us to postpone publication until autumn in order to include a dossier of documents, eyewitness accounts, and other background articles indispensable to a correct appreciation of the problem. With Cortázar's agreement, we added a short introduction in which we declared:

> Many of *Libre*'s collaborators believed it incumbent on them to state their position on this question. The opinions expressed show to what extent there exist shades and differences of opinion in the evaluation of the same event among those on the left. A critical magazine, *Libre* considers it helpful to discuss the Padilla case because of the ideological implications it has for problems in our time, such as the way forward for socialism, artistic creation within the new kinds of society created, and the position and commitment of intellectuals in relation to the revolutionary process within our own countries.*

The dossier reproduced in its entirety the UNEAC session in self-criticism, fragments of the declaration from the Cuban National Council for Education and Culture, Castro's speech at the closing ceremony there, the text of the two letters that we had sent to the Supreme Leader, the correspondence between Vargas Llosa and Haydée Santamaría, as well as a number of disquisitions, open letters, and comments from European and Latin American writers. After all these years the latter offer some meaty lessons: by the side of the dignified ludicity of writers like Paz, Fuentes,

---

* My apologies to the long-suffering reader for the part I played in the composition of this stodgy paragraph.

Revueltas, Ponce, Valente, or Enrique Lihn, the reactions of others evoke the twittering of those "well-trained budgerigars" that Bataille once ridiculed. Julio Roca's interview with García Márquez is a remarkable feat of juggling, whose virtuosity earns admiration rather than respect. But now, as then, the first prize for grotesque slipperiness goes to the famous "Polycriticism in the hour of the jackals."

When Cortázar submitted his text, our immediate reaction was one of rank incredulity. Could the subtle author of *Bestiario* and *Las armas secretas* have written those lines of crude doggerel, which deserved a place on their own merits in a Ukrainian or Uzbeki anthology from the glorious days of Zhdanov?

As Marvel Moreno said, after reading the "poem" in the *Libre* office, it seemed like "a tango to words by Vyshinsky." But worse than the accumulation of insults and clichés against "the pinko liberals ... signatories to self-righteous statements," who until then had been the author's friends, were the lyrical outpourings and bombast to that well-known Shining Future that awaits us.

It was only later, when we read the *Libro de Manuel* and other works that followed, that we were disappointed to find that their author was really the *cronopio* we had read and been dazzled by fifteen years earlier.

To give our endeavor an appearance of unity in diversity, we strove to keep associated with it people, like Cortázar and his friends, who had adopted a position opposed to the one we defended. This wish to preserve our pluralistic team of *Libre* collaborators brought in its wake, however, a number of concessions that I would soon find unacceptable. I can remember the distinguished English Hispanist J.M. Cohen—who had been a member of the UNEAC jury the year it awarded its poetry prize to Padilla's book—sending on to us Lisandro Otero's letter, a response to another one from him protesting against the humiliation inflicted on the poet. This epistle—an incredible hodgepodge of eschatological references, insults, and obscenities—faithfully reflected the hysteria then dominating the official Cuban media and, consequently, in my view was worthy of publication. Cortázar disagreed. For my part, I had written a parody comparing Padilla's ordeal to that experienced centuries before by an Andalusian poet, Abu Bakr Ben Alhach: he was guilty of writing satirical verse about the eminent judge Ibn Tawba, who condemned him to a liberal flogging and to being put on show in the marketplaces, a public abasement, "with town criers in front and the rod behind." Such an act of justice inspired the favorite court poet, Abú Ishaq de Elvira—a favored precursor of the official bards of our day—to write a magnificent work translated into Spanish by García Gómez, which includes these lines:

A whip is more eloquent than any telling-off,
or the deceits churned out by some lout . . .
It makes a man dance a dance without music,
although its hide is heavier and harder than an elephant's.

This conceited fellow has had a good taste of it,
tearing off strips of skin like broadbean pods . . .
Tell him, if a satirical verse crosses his mind again:
"Remember when you were walking around with your breeches undone.
Recall the punishment meted out for your stupid slanders
of our glorious leaders and exalted chiefs,
people upon whom the Merciful One
bestowed great prerogatives,
allowing them to be honored with great veneration.
They are the finest flour among all people
and everybody else is in truth leftovers in the sieve."

My congratulations to the new Caudillo and Sublime Chief did not reach the pages of our second issue: foreseeing Cortázar's reaction, Plinio persuaded me to withdraw it. Gradually my physical move away from Paris and the rue de Bièvre—my university lectures in New York, my stays in Morocco—was compounded by a moral distancing from *Libre*, whose hesitating direction and defensive attitude were less and less in keeping with the original ambition behind the idea. The four issues that came out—coordinated after mine by Semprún, Petkoff and Adriano González León, and, finally, Vargas Llosa—undoubtedly contain worthwhile creations and essays, exemplary interviews and surveys, but, at the same time, texts and articles that were obviously the fruit of compromise and which I am ashamed to read today. In the end these accommodations turned out to be futile: when the final issue went on sale, the likes of Cortázar and his ilk no longer figured on the list of collaborators.

The growing difficulties caused by production costs and postage expenses to Latin America, the ban on sales in Spain and other dictatorial régimes, the Cuban boycott, internal dissension, and our amateur, rather lastminute approach to organization intensified throughout 1972 until they killed off the magazine. The offers of economic help we received meant giving up our independence, and Vargas Llosa, Plinio, and I agreed that it was better to close the magazine down.

After almost two years of effort, tensions, fleeting successes and abundant reverses, we gloomily had to admit that our ambitious venture had been a failure.

The history of *Libre* as it passed through my mind during that dinner in the couscous restaurant on the rue de Bièvre is much more than a mere anecdote: to the extent that it repeats, with a minimum of variants, a combination of situations experienced by Western left-wing intellectuals over the last fifty years, it belongs to a historical trend of which examples abound. Many of the supporters of the Cuban revolution, who thought they saw there the model for the society of the future, were familiar with the sad path trodden by Barbusse, Romain Rolland, Éluard, Aragon, Alberti, or Neruda—all eyewitnesses to the brutal truth about the Soviet system and the deportation, murder, or gagging of their writer-colleagues but who kept silent when they did not applaud the parody of the trials, who carried on with their journeys as revolutionary tourists enjoying privileges that ordinary people lacked, having perfected that "habit of lying knowing that you are lying" denounced by Enzensberger in one of his essays. But the idea that something similar could happen again seemed impossible. When we visited Cuba at the beginning of the sixties, we had more or less come to know Lezama Lima, Virgilio Piñera, Padilla, Reinaldo Arenas, César López, Walterio Carbonell, Arrufat, Luis Agüero, and other authors who years later would suffer UMAP sentences or be reduced to silence. And the adoption of Soviet-style repression by the leadership of the Cuban revolution filled us with bitterness and anxiety for the fate awaiting our colleagues; we were amazed to see how the brand-new rivals to the processional oxen, indifferent to the destiny of the Bielys, Pasternaks, or Akhmatovas—not to mention now those who perished—refused to admit the reality of the new persecutions and the physical or moral suffering of the victims, as if both were the price to be paid for the construction of their utopia. The rationalizations for their pitiful deaf-and-dumb game—we mustn't discourage comrades in struggle, supply the enemy with weapons, etc.—were the same as before. Sitting comfortably in their bourgeois democracies, the standard-bearers of their so-called revolutionary causes, entertained by the unmovable leaders of the latter on their periodic visits to get an "overview," celebrated or covered up with their complicity every one of their oppressive measures, even the most distasteful. Their outright defense of "real socialism" and the adoption of postures that were militant in word alone also ploughed along the same furrow as their European predecessors. As Vargas Llosa rightly says, exposing the terrible consequences of their Manichaean attitude, "Latin American intellectuals have been the main instruments of Latin American underdevelopment." The bloody, reactionary dictatorships in the Southern Cone and in Central America would justify their unreserved support for Cuban autocracy. The frightening "essential" distinction established by one of them in a memorable interview between "the mistakes and even crimes that can occur within a socialist context and the equivalent mistakes and crimes that may occur within an imperialist or capitalist context" would logically lead to the equally "essential" difference between the corpses of the Vietnamese, Guatemalans, Salvadorans, and Afghans: the absence of the three Latin American members on the Russell Tribunal when it met in Stockholm to judge Soviet crimes in Afghanistan—after condemning in previous years North American crimes in Southeast Asia and Central America—an absence publicly criticized by its president, Vladimir Dedidjir, would be the inevitable consequence of that peculiar Thomist or Zoroastrian sally into metaphysics.

As we would see later, to our surprise, the followers of the official Cuban line, who stigmatized the inconsequentiality and frivolity of pinko liberals, would keep well clear of any analysis, in line with Marxist doctrine or basic honesty, of their own relationships and social practice, their own actual style of everyday life: the fact that they preferred, for example, United States scholarships or professorial years in California to a prolonged sojourn without any kind of privilege in that political laboratory where their dreams of harvests without slaves or imperialist powers, nourished at the cost of other people's suffering, would run the risk of fading into nothingness. My experience in those months at *Libre* thus showed me that the high level of artistic awareness of some of my colleagues did not necessarily match their level of moral and intellectual rigor.

"On the morning of April 16, Doctor Rieux left his office and stumbled over a dead rat in the middle of the stairwell," writes Camus in the first chapter of *La Peste*. From those now-distant days in which I too spotted my first rat, a lot of water had flowed beneath the bridges of the Seine, one bank of which passes by the street where the magazine had its home. The expulsion of my friends from the CP, my trips to the USSR and Czechoslovakia, my brief visits to Cuba with writers and artists in the May Art Exhibition, the frustrated *Libre* venture, and incidents in the Padilla case would gradually swell the invading ranks of rodents till it too became an epidemic. Reality is sometimes strangely symbolic: I remember how as I left the Moroccan eating-house where I had dined with my friends, I suddenly spotted the mementolike corpse of a genuine little mouse opposite 26, rue de Bièvre.

· V ·

Monique

WHILE I WAS going through my sergeant's routines in the Mataró infantry regiment, we promised each other in our letters to live as an open, mobile, undomesticated couple whose relationship would not be affected by my frequent absences nor by our mutual carefree "infidelities," but our somewhat illusory aspiration not to fall into the trap of humdrum bourgeois existence, to love each other without living together every day, and to respect our individual freedom of movement immediately clashed with the insidious inertia of habit. Once I was settled in the pleasant, modern, comfortable flat on the rue Poissonnière, I ceased to be tempted by the idea of the occasional return to my small hotel on the rue de Verneuil. Home comforts and work rituals, the desire to be near Monique, our daily renewed complicity were stronger than my theories of independence and apprehensions as to the hermetic knot of a couple. The trial period that we set ourselves for a few months was imperceptibly transformed into life together, and when our time ran out neither of us made any reference to the fact. The precautionary measures dictated by the failure of Monique's marriage and my Gidean rejection of the notion of family succumbed to the quiet persistence of daily reality, to the complex, subtle web of emotions created by that physical nearness. When I went to Spain months later, I did so knowing that it was a fleeting visit at the end of which I would return to Paris: it was disconcertingly easy—in light of my youthful aversion to the bourgeois couple—the rue Poissonnière had become my home.

I remained inflexible on only one issue: my firm decision not to have children, not to extend under any circumstance our family tree. The origin of this obsession is obscure and deeply rooted in my childhood: a desire to leave behind me only my books, not to submit to paternity's hazardous fatalism. Of all the arguments I have mulled over when analyzing this question, not one satisfies me entirely nor totally clarifies the instinctive source of the feeling. Was it a wish to prolong the giddy irresponsibility of adolescence, not to mortgage forever the precious gift of freedom? A desire to ensure my eventual progeny should avoid the experience I had to endure as a child? Was it an anxiety of existential or even metaphysical proportions? Was it an exaggerated, sickly fear of passing on the fragility and psychological disequilibrium from my mother's side, as revealed in the lives of my grandmother and Aunt Consuelo? Whatever it was, the anguish certainly existed and pursued me for years. I can remember one day as we were leaving a cinema on the Champs-Élysées, Monique suddenly felt queasy and wanted to throw up, and the friend with us began to joke and was quick to offer his ironic congratulations: although we were taking every step to avoid such an outcome, the possibility of an error and a subsequent abortion filled me with horror. A few months after we met, Monique had endured this experience in order to terminate a pregnancy by someone with whom she could not and did not wish to live, and the detailed description in a letter sent to Mataró moved me to tears. From that point, I knew what it meant to place oneself at the mercy of a stranger, the moral and physical torture of brutal, clandestine, rudimentary operations often carried out without anesthetic; however, my gut rejection of paternity was even stronger: I would not have hesitated to force abortion on her at the risk of irrevocably endangering our real, if fragile, relationship. Fortunately, it was only a false alarm and I was not compelled to push the privileges of my egoism to the extreme of cruelty. As time passed and the danger diminished, my neurosis associated with the fear of having children gradually faded until it vanished entirely at the time I began frequenting Arab haunts and we moved to Saint-Tropez.

The abrasive harshness of the destiny imposed on women, the unflinching calm and courage with which they often face up to it, will make you always doubt that the terms *weak* and *strong sex* have even a margin of precision. As you could later verify in the texture of patriarchal societies, as much in the Spain of thirty years ago as in Latin America and the Islamic world, the surface strength of the male usually masks thoughtless, even childish attitudes, insecurity concealed by arrogance, a pitifully real feebleness in the trials of existence, while as a natural reaction of self-defense, the female's inferior status endows her, in contrast, with a capacity for thought, magnanimity, and fortitude wrongly attributed to the other sex: when tried by pain, old age, and the other burdens and setbacks of life, her resistance is usually more lucid, spirited, and less complaining than the male's. To be truthful, your fear and even repulsion at the idea of becoming a father cannot be imputed only to masculine feelings of weakness and egoism: they also reveal a healthy mixture of skepticism and detachment, shared by a growing number of women and men, from the servitude of the species. By choosing writing and the gestation of books as a substitute, you saved yourself from the contingencies of the chance law of genetics, you willingly broke the chain of cause and effect. The debt and respect owed to parents came to an end with you: you were not and would not be responsible for the existence of anybody else. This decision not to propagate the species on a planet with limited resources and armed to the teeth with destructive weapons earns your unconditional approval more than two decades later. Shoddy creation is not prolonged through any fault of yours: the surprise of beauty will come to you as an extra. When life presents you in your fifties with the sparkling gift of a young girl, your attachment to her will be free and light: an almost divine offering or manna, the gracious enjoyment of which will be intoxicating.

These first months of life together stand out in my memory with diaphanous precision because of their exhilarating, fertile novelty. The move from Pablo Alcover to the rue Poissonnière, from the dull life of a son at home to a radiant conjugal state, and subsequent changes in scenery, characters, and action confronted me with a combination of novel, unexpected situations and responsibilities. When I arrived, Carole was four years old: her parents' early divorce had spared her the tensions and traumas usual in children from broken marriages, but I had to work tentatively and carefully to integrate myself in her life without disturbing or upsetting the paternal image. On the rare occasions that she called me daddy—absentmindedly and no doubt unconsciously—I immediately corrected her, insisting she call me Juan, pronounced Spanish-style. We related well together from the start, perhaps because of the imprecise nature of the family bond. When she entered puberty she went through a stormy phase, and circumstances forced me to act repressively, yet she bore no grudge against me. Even at the toughest moments in her youthful straining at the traces, she always kept up normal communication with me.

After a few weeks of this life, our process of three-cornered adaptation received outside help from an unexpected quarter. Hélène, our home-help who went out dancing every night in the hope of catching a boyfriend unblemished by the stigma of Arab or African origins and got telephone calls from suitors named Tony, Dédé, Jojo, and others of identical exemplary stock, began to feel vaginal pains and suffer hemorrhages—frequently described, hélas, as she brought us coffee in bed—until one day her condition worsened and we had to call an ambulance at midnight to take her to hospital. Freed of her presence—her chattiness had the knack of riling Genet—we decided to search out a Spanish woman whom a friend had recommended. Vicenta was waiting for us in a café on the rue de Buci: small, gentle, dressed in black, around forty, she had just arrived from her village of Beniarjó, where she had left behind her husband and a large collection of brothers and sisters, in-laws, nieces and nephews, and cousins. We were pleased by our first impressions of her, and she came back home with all her bits and pieces.

She was overjoyed at the idea of looking after a girl: she didn't have any children and her later solitary pregnancy, a few months after Antonio's arrival, ended sadly in a clinic from which she wrote us a moving letter, which I still have among my papers. Although she knew not a word of French, she immediately enveloped Carole in her noisy country affection: carrying her in her arms, covering her in kisses, humming carols and lullabies. At the beginning, the little girl was overwhelmed and irritated. *Tais-toi*! she would say to her. Tetuan and Melilla, Vicenta unflinchingly replied. While we had wrongly imagined that she would soon learn the language of the country, we soon realized that communication was operating in the opposite direction: Carole was starting to speak Spanish, at times interpolated with turns of speech and swearwords from Valencia. Within months, they understood each other perfectly. Vicenta took her on Sundays to the Piles bar on the rue Tiquetone or to someplace off the rue de la Pompe where she used to meet her friends from Valencia, and Carole amazed them all with her childish charms and surprising linguistic know-how. Vicenta's role in her upbringing was central and in any case softened the inevitable problems created by her parents' separation and my erup-tion, however discreet, into her world. The practical intelligence and instinctive wisdom of that simple woman, whose horizon remained within the bounds of her native district, were a constant source of wonderment to me. I remember the day when Carole came back upset from the Champ de Mars gardens, where she had gone to play with some other girls, to tell us of an individual who, we deduced, had masturbated in front of them; before Monique and I could embark on our futile, embarrassed com-mentary on the incident, Vicenta swept her up in her arms, exclaiming joyfully: "That's right, it must have been fiesta-time in his village!"—an unexpected explanation that had the virtue of calming Carole down while making her immediately forget the episode.

The quiet, pleasing warmth of Vicenta's presence on the rue Poisson-nière did not benefit only the little girl: it was a blessing for all three of us. Like Eulalia, she was a woman of strong personality; but, as I realized at once, Vicenta did not suffer from Eulalia's whims or coquettish ways, nor from her apprehensive, insistent melancholy in relation to her own or the family's destiny. In contrast to the tenderness impregnated with anguish that suffused my relations with Eulalia from the day I left Pablo Alcover, my affection for Vicenta was cheerful and straightforward, based only on pleasant cordiality. Apart from us, her world verged entirely on Beniarjó and surrounding districts. When we went for a drive in the car, Monique had attempted to show her the beautiful spots of Paris and "la Francia." A waste of time: Vicenta looked and saw nothing, making immediate comparisons with scenery or places near her village from which the French points of reference always came off badly: the place de la

Concorde had an illuminated fountain like the one in Beniarjó, but the latter was always changing color; the Loire reminded her of the half-dry but better-shaded river that flowed next to her neighborhood; people in Paris went out dressed anyhow, whereas in her village they really smartened up on Sundays. In the field of morality she was similarly strictly bound by the standards of her own world and remained alien to all she observed in France: over the years she spent with us, she saw pass through our house couples coming together and falling apart, women changing husbands, homosexuals (solitary or paired-off), and she showed the greatest possible ease and lack of concern—easy come, easy go, she would comment imperturbably on learning of some divorce or breakup—but such jovial condescension came to an abrupt halt at the approach to the Beniarjó area. There, the most rigid, austere tradition reigned supreme: any transgression brought down on the heads of the guilty the fulminating sanctions of society. I remember her once referring to a girl whom we had placed with some friends, hinting she would never find a husband—that is, she added, unless she hooks a Frenchman—and when we tried to find out why the girl was being ostracized, she explained how the young girl's uncle had interfered with her as a child and that the whole village knew about it. Wasn't it ridiculous to reproach her for something so far back in time for which she was not at all to blame? In France, it would be, replied the unruffled Vicenta, but not in Beniarjó.

Some weeks later her husband arrived and I went with her to meet him at the Gare d'Austerlitz: dry, reserved, rather rough and ready, he had been a goatherd in Extremadura up to the day he arrived in Valencia, where he devoted himself to the orange harvest and was soon to meet his bride-to-be. The three of us caught the métro, and after settling him at home, I suggested to Antonio that he should go for a walk with me to get to know his way around the city. "No, don't worry, señor Juan, I've seen enough," he calmly replied. As I realized at once, his only worry was about finding work as soon as possible: after several frustrated attempts in various factories, he managed to get a job as a porter with a fruit-importing firm in Les Halles. Despite the fact that Monique's flat at the time comprised just three rooms, a kitchen, and two bathrooms, we adapted as best we could to the new situation. I wrote in a tiny cubbyhole that was once the kitchen, and Carole slept alongside us in the dining room. When Monique was coming back from work, Antonio would leave to load and unload trucks, returning home only at day-break. This promiscuity didn't bother us, and Vicenta's cheerful, irrepressible character was a perfect match for our irregular, disorderly existence. Whatever time we turned up, she would quickly get our supper without losing her cool or good spirits: we've got meat, eggs, anything. She cooked as she had been taught at home, not at all impressed by the refinements of French cooking. One weekend when we went to the Mont Saint-Michel and came back determined to savor an exquisite foie gras given as a present to Monique, we discovered to our dismay that the delicacy of our dreams was not in the refrigerator. We asked Vicenta what had happened to it. "It's there," she said, pointing to the trash bin. "We were stupid enough to open the tin, and threw it away after a mouthful. It's not a bit like our rabbit *fuagrá* back home! Now *that's* really tasty."

Antonio and Vicenta's setting up home in our flat soon drew to the rue Poissonnière a good number of relatives, friends, and neighbors from their area; the responsibility for that soon becoming a veritable Sunday invasion was not truly exclusively theirs. In the neighboring compartment in the train that brought us from Spain to Paris, there was a group of emigrants eating, drinking, singing, clapping—the dust of their country still clinging to the soles of their shoes—who remained supremely indifferent to the reproving looks of the natives, visibly upset by a din and hullabaloo outside their notion of civilized behavior. One of the emigrants had gone to the lavatory before me; when I went in after him, I discovered he had left his passport next to the automatic washbasin tap. I glanced at his name (José), place of birth (Lora del Río), and home (a village in the Valencia region) and popped into his compartment to give it back. José chatted with us for a bit (it was the first time he had left Spain), asked for our address, and some while later, after Monique and I had forgotten the incident, he turned up with a group of Valencians. Apparently they had found work on a building site in Rueil-Malmaison: the following Sunday, they were going to cook a paella and wanted us to come and eat it with them. At the back of my mind I had the idea I was preparing a novel or documentary on the emigration that was depopulating whole regions of Spain, and we accepted their invitation. That autumn I went several times with Monique and her daughter to eat in the wooden shacks where they lived, shacks that were very similar to those I would visit alone years later at the invitation of North African friends. The meals were noisy but pleasant: surrounded by compatriots exiled for economic reasons, I felt more in Spain than I did when in Spain itself, enveloped in an atmosphere of warmth, spontaneity, and stimulating straightforwardness. Monique would later confide that she was fascinated by my attitude in that exclusively masculine world of manual laborers: as she would then discover, my intellect and emotions were always seduced by men not belonging to my own social class—never by men or women from our own social milieu. Although I am sure she was correct in her observation, my instinctive affinity with men who earn a living by the strength of their arms and who lack those "bourgeois" stigmas that, like the sacraments of the Church, make their mark, did not include at that time a sexual component except in a sublimated form. This innate attraction, which confers on social inequality a very similar role in the interplay of the complementary and opposites to that normally played by difference of sex, would later deepen, become sexual, as it reached out and went beyond the limits of my language and culture into the incandescent brilliance of Sir Richard Burton's Sotadic Zone. But at that stage it represented only a strange trait perceived by some third person as a whim or eccentricity. Monique was passionately drawn to the world of masculine friendships: to the extent that she did not feel rejected, she was attracted by my ambiguity. On the beach at Peñíscola she had once seen me tipsily caress or let myself be caressed by one of our fisherman-friends who had stretched out next to me by the side of the boats, and the spectacle really stirred her up: it didn't go any further and I made love to her in the hotel—still smelling of him, she said—while my friends drank and dived in darkness, drunk and naked. The Sunday meals in Rueil-Malmaison went on for some months: once or twice, in response to our friends' invitations, we invited them to the rue Poissonnière. Monique's diary for 2 December 1956 pinpoints a detail: seventeen Spaniards in the house! Vicenta and Antonio prepared paella for everybody, and the banquet went on till very late, much to the excitement and happiness of Carole, spoiled and entertained by those nostalgic expatriates separated from wives and children.

Along with this chance invasion by José's worker-friends began another, slower, more furtive, and interstitial: Vicenta's brothers, sisters, and relatives gradually disembarked in Paris, appearing at our flat with their bags and big old suitcases. We had to help find them jobs and accommodations and, through Jadraque and Monique's friends, we managed to salvage some of them. The fresh migrants from Beniarjó trundled leisurely along from the rue Poissonnière to the Piles bar and from there to the vast pavements of the rue de la Pompe. Sometimes, Vicenta extended the sphere of her recommendations to other villages in the region: the girl dressed in mourning who came to our flat asking after her, she's from Benifla, Vicenta said, but she's a good soul. After a time, we had combed the entire field of our friends and acquaintances, and closed down our free employment agency with a feeling of relief. The untimely appearances and visits became less frequent. We had been drained by those months of intense Spanification and, as we admitted to each other, laughing at the end of a particularly hectic, rowdy day, we'd about had enough of it.

Your immense vitality allowed you to ride roughshod over the needs of sleep, take on the boreal rhythm of arctic nights: writing a novel or following the timetable at the publishers, reading for pleasure or out of duty, chatting at length after supper, drinking calvados in your favorite bars, going to transvestite haunts, getting drunk and making love. While you devoted the weekends to visiting Rueil-Malmaison or towns on the Normandy coast with Carole, you finished off your respective days with a tour of the cabarets on the rue de Lappe, next to the hotel where Genet was then staying, or with dinner in one of those modest Vietnamese eating-houses in the environs of the Gare de Lyon. Then night seemed young and somnambular, and you did not notice the first signs of aging and wrinkles till the early morning. Your body obeyed every caprice and decision without rejecting any, as if it were a mere appendage or instrument of your will. There was no such thing as tiredness, and you bravely fought off the impact of alcohol with Alka-Seltzer in the course of the long evenings. At that time Monique professed a real worship of queens. Guided by her cousin Frédéric, you began to explore their lairs and hiding places: you sometimes went to dine at Narcisse, a restaurant where you joined in an extravagant *réveillon* with streamers, confetti, and hysterical shouts from a group of Spanish males decked out in mantillas and combs, as if on the lookout for the hero of *Sangre y arena* or some remote, improbable Escamillo; at other times, you dropped in on the dance at the Montagne de Sainte-Geneviève, where a huge, brazen queer, also from your country, performed a number of acts with a profusion of obscene gestures, propelling, whirring his tongue round as fast as an electric fan. Genet later told you that the most audacious, provocative queens he came across in his wanderings and stays in the prisons and red-light districts of Europe were always Spanish. Whether beautiful or repellent, pathetic or derisory, their rejection of any notion of decency, their defiance of all norms and good manners, the waggles and grimaces of their laboriously recreated bodies endowed them with an exemplary moral hue. The fact that Spain forged and exported the most outrageous specimens was no product of chance: it revealed the great power of the taboo, the social stigma that marked them. Their excessive response was directly related to that excessive rejection. Unlike the Sotadic Zone, where an extended, diffuse bisexuality erases and removes the frontiers of what is illicit and becomes secretly and implicitly integrated in the marrow of society, the gravitational pull of the Hispanic canon determines the existence of centrifugal, extreme, disproportionate reactions. The plentiful numbers and aggression of the queens, Genet explained to you, were in response to the oppressive atmosphere that shaped them: it was the reverse of constrained official machismo, its lower, lunar, cleft face, its other visage.

In the company of Frédéric and Violette Leduc, who had been recently discharged from the sanatorium where she had been held, you made for the rather sordid haunts by the Gare de Lyon or Montmartre in preference to the more bourgeoisified, elegant dives on the Champs-Élysées. When Monique discovered Michou, the basement on the rue des Martyrs became her favorite port of call. You often went there with other couples or married friends: there was a promiscuous atmosphere, and one night Monique was invited to dance by an individual who, deceived by her short hair and black trousers, was hoping for a good time with someone of his own sex. "I was taken for a transvestite," went the triumphal entry in her diary. A trip to Hamburg, at the invitation of Rowohlt, the publisher, stepped up your interest in the leafy glades, shady arbors, and exuberant foliage of this nocturnal jungle. From the sixteenth to the twenty-second of April, you inspected with him the notorious establishments on the Reeperbahn and St. Pauli: the Rattenkeller, Katakombe, Rote Kotze, Mustafa. The German and Spanish transvestites were more insolent, exaggerated, and bare-arsed than the Parisian variety: you were set alight by a women's wrestling match on a hard-earth pitch, surrounded by customers drinking whiskey or champagne with bibs to keep off the splashes. After a few weeks, Rowohlt paid a return visit and wanted you to take him to a spot for masochists; but none of your friends knew of the existence of such dens, even through hearsay. In this predicament, Monique had the fortunate idea of posing the problem to Gaston Gallimard: it seemed he had dealings with an inspector from the vice squad who quite obviously ought to have been well informed on the matter. Old Gaston was greatly excited by anything that broke the monotony of his publishing kingdom and hurried to meet the request: days later, he gave Monique the address of a restaurant on the rue Guisarde where, according to his friend, his colleague-publisher would find the atmosphere he sought. Monique gave the details to Rowohlt and we headed there with him, after taking the precaution of reserving a table.

The delectable, troubling Sadian emotions that besieged you on the way there vanished as soon as you arrived: the entrance to the joint, a tiny doorway, forced the customer to stoop down to get in, and while he clambered in, head lowered and back bent, someone on the other side hung a cowbell around his neck like a scapular to the hoots of laughter of those who with similar ringing chimes observed in delight the newcomer's humiliation. Inside, the childish, rowdy, rough atmosphere would have horrified the author of *Justine*. The waiters were arrogant and insolent, decided the order without taking into account the customer's wishes, and if the opportunity presented itself, regaled the latter with an elbow in the ribs and a string of insults. The sepulchral silence and seriousness of a torture chamber had been replaced, to your friend's consternation, by the festive shouting match of some paunchy, bald-headed schoolboys. Although Rowohlt hid his disappointment, you realized that what Paris had to offer in the genre was false rather than mediocre, no more than a pretense. Accustomed to greater rigor and depth, he went back to Germany convinced that the French still had a long way to go to reach the level of his fellow countrymen in matters of self-knowledge.

If Genet avoided nightlife and took himself off early to bed, Violette Leduc longed to accompany you and break, if only fleetingly, the oppressive solitude that enclosed her. Monique's diary recalls a few evenings with her in the course of 1957: her extraordinary ugliness and playactress manner had the virtue of disarming the usual misogyny of the queens, delighted to exhibit themselves to that ingenuous, cunning woman who was amusing, eccentric, and above all incapable of overshadowing them or arousing feelings of jealousy. When Violette, with the success of *La Bâtarde*, suddenly met fame and fortune, she surrounded herself with the flamboyant retinue of homosexuals of her dreams: a queen in dazzling Carita wigs and suits made by the best designers, whose apparitions at Laurent's or other elegant places would be welcomed with murmurs of derision, curiosity, or wonder.

Divided among politics, writing, social contact, and nocturnal habits, your life was none the worse for the wear and tear. Your physical relations with Monique would never reach a more satisfactory level, and you had cast aside one by one the old hankerings after independence, carefree mutual "deceptions." Monogamous, a possessive, subtly jealous husband, you gradually adapted to the classical, conventional partner's role: holidays in the Midi, plans for trips to unknown countries. For a time you would consider your latent homosexuality as something belonging to a distant past: but love for Monique was not accompanied by physical or emotional interest in other women. At a sexual level these were still the object of an indifference that you would strive to hide. Your amorous life was restricted to Monique and the tiny bubble encapsulating you. You were worried by the precarious, fragile nature of your happiness. What would happen if the bubble burst, if she or you suddenly stopped loving the other? Entrenched in your tepid but pure heterosexuality, you discarded the idea of repeating your second-rate experiences in the Barrio Chino and began to avoid situations that could refresh your magnetic attraction to those the Party dubbed "our exploited comrades." But your distance and withdrawal from the female world gathered apace. The exception you triumphantly lived confirmed the rule learned in adolescence. If to the outside world you were the same as everybody else, you were and continued to be so for some time, in a unique, unusual style.

My trips to Spain opened more or less extensive parentheses in our life together. While the "concubinage" was consolidated and displayed the characteristics of a stable matrimonial bond, the brief visits back to Barcelona and incursions into the Almería region momentarily reestablished my elemental condition. Monique and her entourage soon got used to my disappearances: although I was not yet that "ever absent" husband she would describe later, my political involvement and the bedazzling scenery of my adoptive province often transformed me into a fugitive from domesticity. Customary French ignorance of Hispanic realities, which reached the point of confusing the tattered screen of the Pyrenees with the cement wall or curtain of Stalin's vice-regencies, wrapped these trips in an aura of anxious expectation. With her innate love of melodrama, Marguerite Duras never missed an opportunity to ask Monique if I would come back, if the Francoist authorities would allow me out again, if this eclipse from Paris and her life was or would be final, period. Another friend at the publishers, equally worried by my absences, had summed up her repeated, almost morbid curiosity in very Parisian fashion: "I don't want him to leave you, you know. But if he were to, I'd like to be the first to find out!" All in all, the gaps as we planned them never went beyond that halfway house between fleeting pleasure at my recovered freedom and incipient nostalgia or melancholy. Just as when I had been on military service, we wrote or telephoned each other daily: but, unlike then, my letters mentioned only in passing my odd coitus with a whore and assumed a joking voyeuristic tone in respect to my nocturnal sorties with Luis, María Antonia, Jaime Gil, or some other friend to homosexual bars or areas. Implicit censorship excluded my solitary adventures in those dens in the Barceloneta or Barrio Chino where, as on Raimundo's floating shipyard, I took a dip in that warm camaraderie between men while highlighting and piling up anecdotes and details of my folkloric fondness for queens. Even more significant: the letters no longer refer to possible mutual "infidelities," the happy *calafells* we allowed ourselves. Unsure of myself, conscious of the fragility of our links, my attitude had perceptibly changed. I am jealous of her, and my lack of interest in women of her background, whose attractiveness, culture, and intelligence could compete with hers or foment potential rivalries condemned me to a position of inferiority. The freedom that we theoretically granted each other when we parted was in my case a dead letter: keeping as I did a careful watch on my latent homosexuality, my so-called unfaithfulness was limited to encounters with whores, generally under the influence of alcohol. But it was not the same in her case, and there was that risk it might firm up, as in the months of my stay in Mataró. In spite of my protestations of permissive liberalism, the idea disturbed me: insidiously, my inner responses had become, without my noticing at first, those of a traditional Spanish husband. I discovered I was extremely vulnerable and in turn that intensified my dependence on Monique and the suspicious cunning and close-mindedness of one who felt the legal owner of a body. Although I fought to hide my anxiety and repress symptoms of my possessiveness, the submerged tension influenced our relations. If my ambiguity seduced Monique and created that opaque, secret area that had impelled her from youth into the world of homosexuals, my unsure but exclusive hetero-sexuality, the anguish of which began to overwhelm me from autumn 1958 on, symmetrically altered her bonds with me. I knew that her adventures and infatuations did not endanger the link between us: however, my inability to make a practical response—by arousing in turn a feeling of jealousy toward another woman of her type—introduced an element of imbalance that would worsen over time. I feel now that her acceptance of bisexuality could have diverted the course of events: our relationship could have recovered its lost harmony, its dimension of strangeness and mystery. My oppressive espousal of the criteria and pre-judices predominant in the Spanish world around which I gravitated frustrated any such possible outcome. The more uncertain and cloudier my impulse toward women became, the greater would be my external parade of starkly heterosexual behavior. Trapped in that mire by my own mis-takes, I clutched with all my strength to the safety of a branch, a would-be erotic normality, at the very moment it was beginning to fail me and the branch was giving way. Determined to hide the source of my anxiety from Monique and everybody else, I erected obstacles and barriers against the desirable solution. On our now-routine visits to homosexual bars I showed no signs of sympathy or affinity: my condescending, mocking attitude was that of an uptight Spaniard, like the political militants I went about with. I adopted as my own the jokes and reproving opinions toward the queens that I heard daily around me: I dropped in on the sordid misery of the ghetto, but I belonged to the planned, clean city outside.

Monique could not correctly interpret the symptoms she perceived: I had painfully swallowed the key. Our life would continue to be the same on the surface; however, she was increasingly weighed down by my deficiencies and excesses, the scenes of jealousy when she took an interest in other men, and the inevitable recourse to alcohol on our daily *calafells*. She wrote to herself in her diary, "I still love Juan." Holidays in Spain and Italy, a change of scene and friends for a while restored to our bond its former luxuriant freshness. But the degeneration and weakening I so feared continued to filter through. One day I read F. Scott Fitzgerald's *The Crack-Up*, and I felt cast down by cosmic pessimism: it was impossible to return to Spain, I had no future, I did not even know whether I would be able to maintain my heterosexual front. I had set up camp on precarious ground, rife with uncertainties, and, or so I believed, perhaps I could only be rescued by the flame of Revolution.

In an interview granted some time ago, Jaime Gil de Biedma perceptively observed that from a particular moment in time a stable amorous relationship usually brings us the bad tidings about ourselves: that we aren't really as we thought we were or, to put it more sharply, as we imagined we were. The shock ought to have a dampening effect, but it does not or will not, except retrospectively. The discovery that we are worse, much worse than we supposed—subject to jealousy, pettiness, incongruous attitudes, passionate outbursts, emotional ambivalence, sickly self-pitying, bad faith, irrationality—is not usually accompanied by feelings of shame or by good resolutions. The visitor who lives within us and acts in this way enjoys absolute impunity. His real name is Mr. Hyde.

The process favoring his installation in our inner being is not fortuitous and, as I know from experience, follows a path that any honest, competent cartographer could trace out, whatever its sharp bends and diversions. The leafy proliferations that, from the initial buried seed, conceal the reasons for our behavior from others, do not prevent us from reaching the root of the evil, if we so wish. If I had confessed earlier to my repressed homosexuality and been completely sincere with Monique, I could have been spared the state of tension and crisis in which I lived with her for four years, the concealed anguish I communicated to her, the consequences of my frequently aggressive, incoherent behavior. Lacking both the necessary lucidity and courage, I did not follow the only path that might have led me to resolve the problem, and I was gradually snared by a trap of my own setting. Although I could add in my defense that at the time I had still not yet gotten to know any of those immigrants whom I passed daily in the street and whose violent, imperious figures matched the one that with periodic belligerence stalked my dreams, the fact was that, fearful of their power over me and the danger they evoked in relation to Monique, I tried to avert my gaze from them, although my heart, pinioned in their grasp, beat quickly at every chance moment of those fleeting, brutal, unsettling encounters. The deliberate rejection of openness, at the behest of a combination of social, political, and moral pressures heaped up from childhood, pulled me into an untenable, painful situation where, sucked down by my own contradictions, I saw neurotic irresponsibility as a possible refuge and value. My family's propensity to allow ourselves to be trapped by circumstances in moral prisons or swamps from which escape verges on the heroic; to fabricate with total sincerity compensatory fantasies providing momentary relief, however much they remain unrealized; to set ourselves deadlines to ensure they become fact and *a posteriori* justify our failure to meet them; to run away from the naked truth and shirk the Gordian knot by projecting our own frustrations or dissatisfaction onto other persons or places—the whole pathetic inheritance of subterfuge, weakness, resignation, evasions, and spinelessness that ruined our maternal grandparents' life or mental health—has at different times hung over my destiny and that of my brothers but has never exonerated, if I keep to my own example, an incomprehensibly tardy reaction. Disturbed by my frequent moods of equally exaggerated euphoria and depression, Monique put me in touch, through Dr. Frankel, with my compatriot Ajuriaguerra—at the time the director of a psychiatric center in Geneva who also held private consultations in Paris; my obstinate hiding of the truth, of the central cause of my lack of equilibrium, made our conversation a tissue of deceit: lying to him as I did, he could not help me, and he must have understood that, for when I did not keep the next appointment he did not even bother to call me to find out what had happened. The plethora of events I have already referred to—absorbing political militancy, Luis's arrest, the Milan affair, etc.—distracted me from the tension and anguish that oppressed me without, however, erasing them entirely. When I was at my most active and involved, relations with Monique improved: I felt close to her once more, we recovered our lost complicity, and my passionate surrender to the cause of revolution, first the Spanish and then the Cuban, brought us together again, allowed a cautious exchange of warmth. Our joint trips to Spain, full of suspense and novelty, and the sorties to Italy, to the beaches where she always felt happy, gave breathing spaces in which the perceptible worsening of things was halted. On the sand dunes of Guardamar or in Garrucha we experienced unbridled enjoyment of scenery swathed by the sea mist, the quiet, luminous sea, the warm, penetrating protection of the sun: reptilian lethargy, sips of iced wine, fertile, enclosed, succulent siestas. But our return to Paris, social life, contact with friends who held a passing interest or attraction for her, brought me back to the reality of the blind alley in which I was trapped, the dilemma I dared not confront. My reading at the time betrays a morbid delight in works soaked in pessimism and authors imprisoned by the gentle music of impotence, the dawn melody of suicide: Pavese, F. Scott Fitzgerald, Larra, Ganivet. My despondency and inability to drag myself up succeeded, as was my intention, in making Monique feel guilty. When I came back after going out I sometimes found on my desk messages from her, like bottles hesitantly cast into the sea. Aware that my neurosis was progressing, she lamented the fact that her vitality, energies, and love were of no use to me and that, despite her efforts, she could not communicate them to me. Her sadness was searing, but it filled me with secret satisfaction. The help she could have given me depended on cooperation that I withheld. In such conditions and states of mind, the small hell to which couples often descend hovered threateningly on the horizon. The bad tidings about myself would leave me indifferent rather than surprise me: the patient clinging to his sickness finally found no other consolation than to scatter the seeds of his illness.

Seen from the vantage point of time, my behavior in those years now seems unreal. The duality of my relationship with Monique inevitably affected relations with everybody else, tinged my whole life with a diffuse irrationality. Taciturn and powerless, I acted like a spectator at my own jealous outbursts, absurd accusations, shocking eclipses of moral sense. If my travels and absences at first brought me relief, they soon became a fresh source of friction. Deprived of my sullen, menacing, hypochondriac presence, Monique would feel relieved of a deadweight, pleased to feel free to move around. Consciousness of my own weakness spurred on my wily, tortuous imagination: the unconscious desire to snare the woman responsible for my distress in a web of ominous culpability. A comparison of the letters written on my first visit to Cuba with the ones I sent on my second reveals a sharp growth in my self-pitying recriminatory attitude, in my desire to prevent her from being happy, from breathing far from me. The discovery of her mother's throat cancer in January 1962, during my impassioned, elated stay in Havana, had frustrated any possibility of a trip, of her following my suggestion that she share the feelings of intoxication and enthusiasm the island aroused in me. On my return to Paris, I found Lucienne with a tube down her throat, voiceless and shriveled up, forced to endure a torture that worsened daily, the sterile contemplation of which was overwhelming her daughter. As she adjusted to the certainty of her mother's death, Monique seemed prey to a compensatory agitation that intensified my neurosis and ate into our already corroded ties. Although she had different reasons, with a base in reality, she swung, like me, from periods of illusory hope and forced happiness to others of gloom and despondency. My behavior toward her did not help matters: our parallel, superimposed unhappiness was a cruel repeat of the old situations in my own family. Rather than help her withstand the painful trial she was experiencing, I criticized her for her moments of forgetfulness, her emotional generosity, indomitable vitality, and, unable to take reality by the horns, I sought refuge in militancy as if in a protective religious order: but neither Marx nor Lenin nor the working class had anything to do with my real worries. In truth, my case was quite similar to those middle-class youths who, as Octavio Paz would later write, "transformed their personal dreams and obsessions into ideological fantasies in which the end of the world takes on the paradoxical form of a proletarian revolution without a proletariat." During my second stay in Cuba, while her letters told me extensively of her mother's daily torment and her fortunate discovery of Jorge Semprún's book, I threw in her face "the irreversible distance between us," the "dialogue of the deaf" that we sustained, my lack of attachment and indifference to the world around me: I drank a lot, I fucked two women, and "I don't know where we fit in, nor what's left to us." The letter's bitter tone was sincere, but my factual account purposely leaves out the little "matter" that, apart from the two women, there was the owner of a small bar in the Jesús María district, a cheerful, festive mulatto whom I twice went to bed with in a drunken state. Although that relationship was of no importance to me and did not meet my expectations, its omission from the letter shows my attempt at the time to make it difficult for Monique to diagnose the causes of my neurosis. As she was writing in her diary *cafard atroce*,* I was consciously covering my tracks.

The latent disquiet dictating my behavior—not mentioned here in any kind of self-justification—was the certainty that I must irrevocably enter turbulent waters full of dangerous currents where I would have to swim alone: like someone deceived by the weakness of the current who loses his footing and disappears under a high wave, I was afraid of leaving behind all that made up life till then, afraid of getting lost on the open sea. Mine was not the pleasant, jocular, likeable, carefree homosexuality of the queers Monique had dealings with. The ambiguity that attracted her was no doubt the result of a female ideal of man that is much more widespread than is generally believed, which is both insensitive and hostile to the features, traits, and attributes of extreme combative virility; more or less explicit effeminacy was at the antipodes of my own desire. At different stages in my life I have had occasional or sporadic sexual relations with women, but never, absolutely never, with queers or heterosexuals from my own cultural and social background, those who are classically attired, well brought-up, elegantly mannered; later, I would extend this rigorous demarcation line to my own ethnic group: from 1963 my passion and longings would be aroused only by the rough, sunburned sons of the Sotadic Zone. Nevertheless, even before my initiatory meeting with Mohamed, I could mentally delineate, with the detail and precision of a miniaturist, the masculine image that had attracted me ever since it had magically erupted into my childhood; intermittently and unconsciously it had crept into my dreams until it finally harassed me with hustling determination. As Ibn Hazm beautifully said, I was exchanging a green and pleasant land "for one hedged in thorn." Monique could not follow me there; I knew that only too well. My persistent lying was thus a last futile attempt not to leave her before facing up to that forbidden territory where "by implacable decree" and absolute rule of love "from which no one can steal himself," I would soon enter.

---

* January 1963.

The most unhappy period for you both undoubtedly came after your second trip to Cuba. Lucienne died just after you had returned under no illusions as to your future as a couple. When her suffering came to an end, you accompanied Monique and a group of friends to the sinister cremation ceremony. The urn containing her ashes, which the undertakers handed you after a tense hour's wait, bore a symbolic value in your eyes: they summed up seven years of life together; Lucienne's scattered atoms epitomized the history of your relationship. Nine days later you were in Venice, where Monique decided to go in search of distraction and alleviation for her distress. On your previous visit in 1957 you had walked along the canals, explored the labyrinth of side streets and *cuppo di sacchi*, zigzagging in a *vaporetto* from jetty to jetty, in an ecstatic feeling of aesthetic delight and mutual fulfillment. In March 1963 your walks along the Via Garibaldi, against a luminous backdrop of stagnant water and ruined mansions, testified to the change in the interval—your solitary, icy lack of communication. The room in the Hotel Montecarlo, near San Marcos, would be the scene of disputes and recriminations. Prickly, unapproachable, you carried things to the breaking point while ensuring it never materialized. Like those people who destroy domestic property in apparently uncontrolled fits of anger but let loose on objects of little value, making certain not to touch anything valuable—clearly revealing some vigilant inner mechanism at work—your double behaved with a selective irrationality that tempered, but did not destroy, your exercise of will. This attitude, which you would later see painfully repeated in relatives and friends, now exemplifies for you those very ambiguous notions, madness and reason: that vast intermediate area in which the neurotic sets traps and tripwires for everyone else only really to run away from himself and rush headfirst into the sea, all the time wearing his life jacket. But the retrospective lucidity with which you now judge yourself did not then come to your aid: for a hateful length of time you would live irremediably in the shadow of your Mr. Hyde.

Suppositions, nightmares, a split existence: the impression that you were a powerless witness to the wiles and maneuvers of a character who looks like you, acts in your name, carries your documents, writes your signature, wears your clothes and shoes, is identified with you by the neighbors, the tenant in your flat, that you embody his crimes and betrayals in a fading dreamlike unreality. You evoke his oneiric, spectral exploits, are his judge and memory, grapple with the upset of his fleeting reappearance: your desire to wash your dirty linen, pillory him, separate yourself out from him. You peer into the hidden corners of a distant schizophrenia and observe with relief that he has gone for good. The morbid product of passing mystification or a real being, swept away in a healthy, vigorous cleanup? Faced with the threatening dislocation, you are unsure of your ground, don't know what to reply.

On my return to Paris, I found the tensions in our life together unbearable and went on one of my habitual flying visits to Spain, but with characteristic ambivalence, I persuaded Monique to meet up with me and, two weeks later, we were swimming together on the beach at Torremolinos in a state of deceptive contentment. It was there I would learn by phone both of Benigno Cordero's death and the sudden worsening of the "Grimau affair."

On 17 April I was back in France. It is not my intention to recount here the futile activity of that period: collection of signatures, acts of protest, hopes that Franco would suspend the execution of the death sentence against Julián Grimau at the last moment, would not go through with his iniquitous act of vengeance. Our failure intensified my feelings of indifference and distance from my public persona, my grating awareness of its absurdity. Monique was to leave for Corfu with the Gallimard delegation to be present at the meeting of the jury that would days later award the Formentor prize to Jorge's book. The night of her departure, I went for a walk around Barbès. Ever since Algerian independence, the police had slackened their siege of the area, and it was possible to wander around without coming across their somber hostile patrols. I can remember how, as on other occasions, I examined the Arab cafés from the outside, their customers leaning on the counter or sitting at tables, absorbed in a game of dominoes or a Spanish hand of cards: a compact, homogeneous world, but also one that was attractive and lively, from which I felt painfully excluded. No European ever set foot there, as if an invisible frontier forbade entry and, despite my attempts to overcome my timidity, I finally resigned myself to walking by. Weren't any possible awkward approaches doomed from the outset by my total ignorance of their language, culture, patterns of behavior, and idiosyncrasies? Given their bitter experience of persecution and the discrimination of which they were victims, how would they look upon a *nesrani* who nervously peered into their ghetto? The strange, captivating music of their record players invited me to hover around their territory. What were those intense, tormented voices that they listened to with such fervor and nostalgia trying to express? After tramping, like an intruder, around the rue de la Goutte-d'Or, rue de Chartres, rue de la Charbonnière, I walked down to the boulevard de la Chapelle, thronged by indigenous promenaders, and sat at the bar of a café on the corner of boulevard Barbès, which vibrated regularly as the overhead métro rushed by. To my left, with his back to me, a young man was talking to a friend in Arabic and, suddenly, when his friend went off, he turned to me. Thin, sinewy, of average height, dark-eyed, a big black mustache, his face radiated a lively sense of strength and warmth. He asked for a light, and noticing that my hands were trembling as I handed him a match, he gently calmed them in his own. He said, *Merci, khuya*, in a mixture of French and Arabic. I don't know what we talked about or have the slightest idea what we drank: perhaps two or three rounds of beer, quickly replenished by the waiter when I caught his eye, with the aim of prolonging this chance conversation that promised so much. I was afraid to break off the thread, that we would each go our own way; but, belying my apprehension, my new acquaintance waited for the waiter to give my change and left with me. "I don't know where I'm going to sleep," he said. "Do you know anywhere we can spend the night together?" Trying to conceal the fact that my heart was pounding furiously, I just replied that there were many hotels in the area, that we would find a room in one of them. We went up the boulevard de Rochechouart and immediately hit upon one, at the top of the rue de Clignancourt. It was a poor, shabby room, with one double bed covered over with a long bolster. While I undressed, Mohamed slipped, eagle-eyed, between the sheets, his fleshy lips smiling beneath his wild mustache. My slow descent into pleasure was accompanied, in the disturbed slumber of the night, by the lucid regaining of serenity.

Mohamed had to get up early and, as we woke up late, I took him by taxi to Porte de la Chapelle, where he and a gang of immigrant miners were digging out an underground gallery for a public works firm on the first stage of the future motorway to the north. As we got up, he had told me simply that he wanted to be my friend, and we agreed to meet at six o'clock that afternoon, when he left work. For a few days, while Monique was away, I carried on, going with him to work in the early morning and picking him up hours later in a large café on the rue Ney, opposite the entrance to the métro. We drank, dined, fucked in some down-at-the-heels old hotel in the shadow of the Sacré-Coeur, in a mood of frank, happy complicity. The terrain I was penetrating was deceptively easy: in spite of Mohamed's naturalness and warmth, expressed in hoarse, jumbled French—the bodily immediacy uniting us, our nightly colluding connection, rested on precarious foundations. Our reciprocal lack of knowledge about each other did not seem to bother him very much; but the recondite strangeness of his world, sheathed in the magnetism radiating outwards, forced upon me the challenge of clarifying and determining the reasons for my captivation. My later desire to get to know, explore step by step the universe where his life unfolded, to intoxicate myself with his language and culture, to delimit the imprecise boundaries of the exotic were then given life. My tardy vocation as linguist and ethnologist, which has made me devote an apparently absurd amount of time in recent years first to the study of North African Arabic and then of Turkish, was the result of my resolution to draw nearer to a physical and cultural bodily ideal, the white heat and refulgence of which guided me like a beacon. The act of transforming the stigma inherent in my deviation into a fertile curiosity for what was alien would thus open the way to a state of grace beyond the reach of the bourgeois trapped in the conventional rigidity of his petty world. By suddenly conjugating sexuality and writing, I could in contrast forge a new language, decanted and purified in the harsh, combative expression of my desire, a long, seminal process originating in that initial chance encounter: Mohamed, and his box of Gitanes, drinking at the bar in the café on the boulevard de la Chapelle, a bar I had entered before I had even seen him.

My lack of experience of his world, reactions, and character required the choice of an emotional strategy: rather than spelling out the questions crowding in upon me, I allowed him to answer them himself as I gained his confidence. Was he married? Did he have any children? Why did he live hand-to-mouth with no fixed abode? Who looked after his suitcases of clothes, and where did he go to get changed? Gradually, he explained to me that his wife and children lived in a mountain village near Oujda; in recent months he had shacked up with a *kahba* whom he had rowed with the day before we met; although his idea when emigrating to France had been to improve his family's lot, it was all a miserable waste of his time: not only had he squandered his family's money on that evil whore but also, through her, he had got himself into some tight corners. What were they? Mohamed related the confused story of a pistol sold by a *pied-noir* police inspector who had infiltrated the Arab ghetto; apparently, he had slightly wounded a rival with it in an act of legitimate self-defense. As a result he spent a few days in prison and was still waiting for the trial, perhaps a summons from the police. If they imposed a fine, he would find ways of paying it; but if he were deported to his own country, what would happen to his wife and children?

Converted by circumstance into a good samaritan, I helped him find a *chambre de bonne*, renew his labor permits, answer the worried letters from his family. My naïveté at the time was limitless; however, although Mohamed, with his peasant mixture of innocence and cunning, often lied to me as one lies to a wife, he never took advantage of the situation. When, on Monique's return from Corfu, I went back to sleeping on the rue Poissonnière and waited for him at dusk in a café or inside his poky garret, I spotted unambiguous traces of the visit of an unknown woman. Mohamed allowed himself to be loved by me and then used my conjugal state to disappear in turn on lengthy tours of the Barbès bars, where he met up with fellow countrymen. On some occasions, he took me with him and would lead me by the hand into those dense, compact, exclusively masculine preserves, possessed by a sudden, voracious hunger for knowledge. I was slowly learning the gestures and movements, greetings, polite formulas, guttural words haloed in subtle magic, which I furtively scribbled down or tried to commit to memory. The only European in the place, I shared the privilege with several Algerian prostitutes. Mohamed's introduction allowed me the quiet corner for observation that I sought: once the first moment of curiosity had passed, my presence went unnoticed. Nevertheless, my cultural superiority, centered on my knowledge of French, would soon turn me into a kind of public scribe, to whom Mohamed and his companions would give their Social Security forms to fill in or would dictate messages to their families. In order to keep Monique away from my new friendships, I had invented for myself the plausible profession of a printer obliged to go on frequent visits to the provinces: but no one, apart from Mohamed, ever asked me about my private life, work, or home. For the regulars in the half dozen cafés on the rue de la Goutte-d'Or I frequented while our relationship lasted, I was only an anonymous Spaniard with a smattering of their dialect who wrote their letters for free.

Monique mentions in *Les Cabines de bain* the "margin of perversity" arising from the fact that, though a writer, I have loved or had an interest throughout my life only in illiterate men or in men with only a rough elementary education. It is an accurate observation inasmuch as sexuality feeds on emotions, fantasies, and "perverse" ideas. But, without dismissing their incidence in my case, the primordial factor in my friendships with hillsmen, peasants, or Moroccan infantry soldiers whose features corresponded to darkly ancestral tastes was my need to compensate for the mental refinement required in the act of writing with their exhilarating, pervasive rawness: possessed by them and their rough pleasure, I instinctively looked for a way to counterbalance my physical submission with an intellectual domination capable of establishing an equilibrium between both scales. The enjoyment this indemnification provided me—the sly secretive sensation of taking control of their lives and destiny while they entrusted to my pen the messages to their families—would be as great as that reached through communion with their virility: the act of writing and taking on their voice with the same fullness with which hours or minutes before they had disposed of my body would frequently intertwine the apparent benevolence of writing with the secret delights of erection. This and other discoveries during that brief period of my life had lasting consequences: the framework, backdrop, situations, places in which other more or less ephemeral adventures would arise were then fixed once and forever. Not only the powerful call of faces and features hinted at or dreamed of from adolescence, but also a combination of elements the repetition of which would belie their supposedly circumstantial character. Those who sat beside me clumsily dictating their letters would change over time; but the immutable pleasure-seeker disguised as public scribe would patiently extend his mastery of conventional, more or less accurate French to the wanton, jubilant appropriation of Arabic script.

My friendship with Mohamed was threatened from the start. The wheels of the administrative machine set in motion by his earlier conviction turned ominously on the horizon, despite my efforts to stave it off by getting the sentence suspended. With a fatalism that often irritated me, Mohamed placed his destiny in my hands; but if that relieved him of all responsibility for his future, it burdened me with the duties of an irksome moral guardian. The battle with the administration, marked by defeats and victories, was to last several years; forced to abandon French territory during my stay in Saint-Tropez, Mohamed would obtain, thanks to the good offices of my lawyer, a trial period that was abruptly ended in 1969, a long time after our intimate bonding had ceased, by a second and definitive deportation order. By that date, my experience and knowledge of the Islamic world had broadened and deepened. My choice of comrades with whom to maintain more or less lasting ties no longer obeyed as before the whim of the chance encounter; it was also a response to obsessive and stricter criteria that were as much physical as emotional.

The entry of North African society into my life favorably influenced my turbulent relationship with Monique. Placated, lucid, conscious, I gradually gained in self-confidence and assurance what I lost in relation to her in sickly dependence and aggression. Although my decision to hide what had happened and keep my precious secret was condemned to failure, our life as a couple calmed down. For the first time in years, our holidays in Venice and on the Dalmatian coast were peaceful and happy. My uncontrolled dark reactions gradually disappeared. The silence I kept momentarily conferred an exceptional lightness on my existence. The accursedness associated with the nefarious crime was suddenly transformed into grace. Like a slithering serpent, I was sliding toward new wells and fountains in search of the propitious time and place for that delayed change of skin.

Our relationship reached a plateau in the spotless wintry frame of Saint-Tropez. We rented a small house on the rue de la Citadelle, but weeks later Monique found a more pleasant duplex, with views over the port, that belonged or had belonged to Dominique Éluard. So as not to miss my tiny study-kitchen on the rue Poissonnière, I chose for my office a cubbyhole where you could hardly fit a table, with a small window from which I could contemplate the reddish roofs of the town and where I felt isolated and afloat, like at the top of a dovecote. I worked there regularly in the mornings while Monique read on the beach or put some order into the notes she had taken during her mother's cancer, notes she would later include in *Une Drôle de voix.*

Her decision to move out, to abandon her publishing job, to run away from the literary scene that had been her life till then corresponded to what I had secretly been hoping from her for months. The eruption of virile pleasure into my world demanded body-and-soul surrender to the abyss of writing; it was not only mutual convergence or adaptation but something more complex and far-reaching: the introduction of a personal universe and experience of the world, areas as yet hidden away, into the text of the work that was emerging, until they and I were integrated into it as just extra ingredients. The change my life was undergoing would thus be articulated within a globally generative process; my existence would lose its autonomous character and merely exercise a dynamic function in a world conceived as a space for writing, in the omnivorous textual whole. My daily struggle with successive versions of *Señas de identidad* would stand out qualitatively from my previous skirmishes with literature; it was to be a text marking a break and leap into the void; initiatory, genesic, foundational. As I noticed later, when rereading the novel in print, I only half attained my goal. Both a compendium and a transcending of past narrative, *Señas* turned out to be a hybrid of my newly acquired subjectivity and a formal structure that I did not manage to escape entirely.

Rapidly acclimated to a place that suited us for a variety of reasons, Monique and I lived in apparent serenity. The tensions brought on by my sexual insecurity, periods of depression, ravages of schizophrenia had dissolved in a tranquil working atmosphere favoring an intimate coming together. There, the physical anguish and suicidal fits that had tortured me disappeared forever. When I finished writing, good weather permitting, I would stretch out by her side on the beach; at dusk we would walk down to the town and sit in a small bar, frequented by fishermen and sailors, with whose owners we had struck up a friendship. In winter the port sheltered several cruisers: the guards or supervisors of the odd one were Spanish sailors who, on discovering we were fellow countrymen, came and had a drink with me in our favorite bar or visited me up at the house when they saw the dining room lights were on. The Saint-Tropez rhythm of life with its small-scale rituals intensified, on the other hand, our tiredness and coolness toward Paris. For months we trawled the region in the company of real estate agents: with a neophyte's enthusiasm, Monique forged plans to sell her flat, settle down for good in the Midi, and buy a small house or plot of land there. Her mother's horrendous death agony, which she still had not assimilated, was impelling her toward a break, which she believed to be definitive, with her haven on the rue Poissonnière. Carole was pursuing her studies in a school in Sainte-

Maxime and also seemed entirely happy with the change.

Just as everything was apparently getting on course and our fragile, unstable life together was experiencing a blissful interlude, an untimely, though predictable, factor sent my plans awry and overturned that precarious happiness. By sacrificing my links with Mohamed to the project of provincial life dedicated to work and Monique, I had omitted one essential detail: while the anonymous confusion of Paris allowed for clandestine sexual activity that attracted no one's attention, the social transparency of Saint-Tropez, where the nucleus of North African immigrants lived in their ghetto, visible and marginalized by the rest of the population, doomed from the outset any attempt at a discreet approach. The locals' crude racism, as instinctive and deep-seated as their professed attitude to the guild of *enfoirés* or *sales tantes* to which I secretly belonged, not only distorted my relations with other people but also imposed on me the yokelike torment of homosexual chastity. As at other times in my life, but in a more abrupt, tyrannical fashion, a blind force drove me to meet up with men shaped in the tangible, effulgent image I had mysteriously formed as a child. In the small bar where we got together with our neighbors, I noticed one day a sailor who was "tall, broad-shouldered, of storm-tanned complexion, whose pure Arab features, energetic chin and mouth" were in retrospect extraordinarily similar to those I would later find in the iconography of Richard Burton and the detailed description of his wife Isabel. Although from North Africa, the customer was a *nesrani*, married with a large family. Hardly had we been introduced than we felt a shock wave of sympathy: he liked his drink and willingly accepted my invitations and, seated round a barrel-shaped table, we soon got into the habit of downing two or three bottles of wine a day. My friend was sensitive to the interest I displayed toward him but, brought up in a *pied-noir* environment hostile to that kind of affection, he allowed himself to be courted in muffled tones in view of everyone, yet he avoided any opportunity to be compromised. The other regulars were in on our libations and chats but harbored not the least suspicion: we were both married and our masculine behavior and ways saved us from any malicious gossip. Alcohol favored our coming together but reduced it to a mere shadow. The Tavel rosé—which Hemingway abused so much—acted as a substitute and had a discouraging effect on me. I was drinking now like I did before I met Mohamed, and the Saint-Tropezians were astonished at my staying power. Monique had obviously noticed the ambiguity of a situation that reminded her of my past bouts of drinking in the Varadero or with the Valencian workers from Vicenta's village, in the course of their Sunday paellas in Rueil-Malmaison. That aspect of my personality attracted her, and sometimes she would venture to mention it and question me. Months later, she would harshly reproach me for not having taken advantage of those opportunities to speak out clearly, the unforgivable cowardice that beset me when facing up to the truth.

I was often possessed, in a glaring limpid trance, by a feeling of alienation and strangeness toward all around me, as I engaged in anodyne conversation with friends, or in the family arena: the certainty I was different from everyone else, with an inner life a million miles away from them, a symbolic statuesque presence at their alien, absurd ceremonies, assumed at times almost physically tangible dimensions. A traitor ambushed in a world of smiling appearance, I was suddenly invaded by a savage desire to act profanely: desires to slash with a knife the tranquil canvas of my life, to declare my violent inner repulsion toward it. My subsequent self-absorption, the mental deafness that preceded by fifteen years the onset of physical atony, developed from that moment; my ability to withdraw into myself when surrounded by people, to be present at the social comedy while inwardly laughing, to elaborate *in situ* compensatory fantasies at the antipodes of such a universe would thus become fixed traits of my character. Becoming taciturn and furtive, my distance and reserve would soon earn me my solid, deserved reputation as a prickly customer. But rather than these traits, which were suffered or perceived by an immediate circle, I was worried by the frequent ruptures or short circuits produced in me by the most unforeseen circumstances. I can recall how Roger Vailland had told us the story of a regular caller at a brothel who once a week chose the same prostitute and how, once alone with her, he undid a small packet of sauerkraut and handed the varied contents to her for her in turn to put into her vagina. The client watched this to-ing and fro-ing without masturbating, returned the cooked dish to its packet and said goodbye to the woman after giving her a generous reward. As he in the end revealed to her, he then headed home with the sauerkraut, handed it to his wife and with an ineffable smile shared in the family feast. The anecdote, or rather the protagonist's attitude, reflected accurately the sudden blackouts in my social self and the mocking duality with which I intervened—and sometimes still intervene—in supposedly intimate or serious public or domestic scenes: an evening with helpful neighbors, a visit from a relative, an official reception with under secretaries and ministers, a jolly birthday tea. A thought or nomad fantasy detector would have led or would lead in such cases to my immediate expulsion from the place where my visible ventriloquist self acted out of a mental furtiveness similar to the refined client's in the story.

The concentration required by work no doubt contributed to my isolation and the emergence of that touchy ego trapped like a genie in its box. Perhaps the phenomenon is consubstantial with a vocation that is lived like a permanent voracious devouring; however that may be, its effects would still live on even once the genitive cause disappeared: a pleasing indifference to everything outside my personal affections, likes, and obsessions; a pressing awareness that only amorous emotion, sex, and writing are real, that the bourgeois, ordered social world disturbs and interrupts that subjective authenticity which, with the absorbing power of a whirlwind, would henceforth suck me into the privileged substrata of literary creation, personal communication, or complaisant bodily submission. In the face of these patiently conquered dominions, everything else—social ties, involvement in literary and cultural life, vanity, reputation—lacked importance, did not justify any burning of energy. My moral outlook underwent a change and became more pragmatic: the quest for intensity in the triple area just mentioned would then become my basic aim in life.

But I anticipate events: in those first months in Saint-Tropez, dual awareness of the impossibility of avoiding the law of the body and establishing my life with Monique on lies and deceit came painfully to the surface till it swept aside the mediocre array of defenses. The sublimatory arguments behind my refusal to act openly seemed false and even monstrous: a shameful tribute to the iniquitous ethics of Catholicism, like the one Grandfather paid. What tormented me was not the act of revealing the truth to everyone else—convinced as I was that by removing the ambiguities behind which I sheltered myself, I would be freed of a burden whose weight grew daily—but the risk that the situation thus created might ruin and put an end to my close relationship with Monique. The renewal of her happiness with me, after the stormy tensions of Paris and Havana, moved and paralyzed me. Never since our get-togethers in Spain had I seen her so radiant and diaphanous, involved in her work, generous and warm toward friends new and old. Several times throughout the spring, as the climate got milder and we stretched out in the sun in one of the bays near the town, I had tried to be frank with her and reveal what had happened with Mohamed. But for one reason or another, the words stuck in my throat, my heart beat violently, and after an exhausting struggle with myself, I pitifully abandoned the attempt. In my mind's eye, I had written various scripts in circumstances and settings favorable to a clarifying conversation: a walk through La Garde Freinet woods; dinner alone in some restaurant in the port; the relaxed togetherness of postcoital calm. However, when the moment of truth came, things happened differently: not even alcohol succeeded in unleashing my tongue or sparing me the rage and humiliation of failure. Monique's trusting smile, the vulnerability of that smile, her sweet love for life after the trials of her mother's illness made my position cruel, merciless: the idea of dealing her such a blow was unbearable and forced me to waver. I knew from that moment that a man is capable of the worst deceptions or extremes out of mere cowardice.

I now view that indecision and diffidence with a feeling of shame. No woman was in a better position than Monique to understand the problem and dilemma facing me: a devotee of Genet's world and author of *Les Poissons-chats*, she harbored authentic sympathy of feeling for homosexuals, and her reaction would have in no way been cutting or small-minded. She often aired the question with me, as if unconsciously she guessed my anxieties and wanted discreetly to give me a helping hand. As she would later say, it would have been very easy for her to grasp the opportunity to discuss our future calmly. An insistent, ridiculous, inexplicable fear frustrated time and time again favorable opportunities and, full of self-hate, I kept leaving the decision for later. During the months of May and June, I solemnly fixed half a dozen definitive dates, only later to acknowledge my impotence and accumulate new, more wounding fiascos. Was that stubborn resistance caused by my distant upbringing in Spain or was it a response to some concealed ambivalence, a selfish desire to have my cake and eat it? Whatever the truth was, the waiting dragged me down: of all the difficult decisions I have taken in my life, this would certainly be the one that would cost most.

While I was struggling with my contradictions and fears, I received an official invitation to visit the Soviet Union with my family. We were all three won over by the idea of traveling in the summer during Carole's holidays. I was to go to Paris at the end of June to get the visas and sort out the tickets and, to save Monique and her daughter the predictable trying professional commitments on arrival in Moscow, we decided I would see those out of the way by catching a plane a few days earlier. The idea of explaining myself by letter, carefully debated after the failure of various other attempts, seemed suddenly a blessing from heaven. Among the numerous discarded scenarios was the one with an envelope left in an obvious place on her desk as I went on a fishing trip in the bay with one of my fellow countrymen; but diverse reasons—Carole's presence, the lack of a period for reflection before she could discuss the issue with me—persuaded me finally to discard it. If, however, I was to write the letter in Paris, on the day before my flight to the USSR, the inconvenience of a sudden passionate or depressed reaction disappeared. Separated from me for a week by thousands of miles—and the Iron Curtain!—Monique would have time to think and develop a defensive strategy. Certain knowledge of the brutal quarantine I was imposing on her did not dissuade me from that course. I thought that the temporary distancing would allow her to decant her emotions, accept the challenge of this new chapter in our life with greater calm and equanimity.

In a state of anxious confusion, I took a whole day to write the letter in my study-kitchen on the rue Poissonnière. I was afraid of being both too clear and not clear enough: I was distressed by the idea of hurting her without really needing to. To make matters worse, a last-minute change of plans was to complicate life even more: my plane left on 3 July—twenty-four hours before Monique's arrival by car from Saint-Tropez—but in her impatience to see her Parisian friends after such a long time away, she moved up her return by three or four days. Her unexpected rush back upset the scenario I had fashioned so laboriously and forced me into a final regrettable pirouette: I would also deceptively advance my departure so that when she arrived, she would think I was in Moscow. The new scheme meant I had to leave home immediately and settle down for two days with all my luggage in a small hotel on the rue Lafayette near the Gare du Nord. I read and corrected the letter several times before I thought it acceptable, and after a gloomy stroll through that district where anonymity hid me like some miscreant, I grasped my inglorious *alea jacta est* and threw it in the mailbox.

I HAD FOR SOME *time been intending to write and to confide to you something that touches me to the quick, but the impression I was heading down a path leading nowhere and a mixture of fear and shame had postponed my decision day by day. I similarly feared that in conversation I would get nervous, not express myself fairly and exactly, lack the necessary sang froid, communicate poorly. Nevertheless, I have decided to make the attempt, although I know—and I am now sure of this—the real affection you feel for me, the strong and lasting ties binding us together. I know what your feelings are and in a way I also love you much more than I did: with an intensity that I had not experienced and will not experience again; and when I say "in a way," I mean moral love, feeling for your person and your truly unique qualities, all you have represented to me over the last nine years and which you represent beautifully today in your need for love: generosity, tenderness, unlimited friendship for those around you. I would like to have added "physically," in the way I loved you for years—although I loved you less then than I do now—but I cannot lie at the very moment I am trying to see clearly and am trying to bring my behavior toward you and others in line with reality. I know this letter will not surprise you; you yourself touched on the issue, especially over the last few weeks, in relation to————.* Your instinct did not deceive you as to the deep interest I have felt for some time in a particular kind of man—an interest, I suppose, that was obvious, in spite of my embarrassed evasion. The certainty of my love and desire to preserve it prevented me from talking to you as I would have preferred. Over the last three months I had determined to do so but never found the opportunity. Don't throw it back at me that I haven't done so before. I was full of hesitation before taking this step, and I needed to gather together all my strength. I repeatedly weigh in my mind the thought of the pain I shall inflict on you. It will be hard for you, but it is even harder for me. I feel totally bound to you, and my letter is the confession of profound defeat and unhappiness. I would prefer never to have written it, but I cannot continue without writing it. I must explain to you why and how I came to realize beyond any shadow of doubt my liking for men and the reason that I had not revealed it to you before.*

In reality, I have always been attracted by a particular type of man that you yourself are now familiar with, and I do not think my falling in love with you or your reciprocity were purely chance occurrences. I found in you what I needed but

---

* The dashes and bracketed ellipses correspond to people's names and paragraphs that have been cut to avoid unnecessary repetition. The original letter is in French.

*could not find in other women: "masculinity" and an independence that allowed us
to live together. My previous homosexual experiences were negative, and from the
time we started to live together up to a year ago, I had no relationships with men,
nor did I even contemplate one except fleetingly. Your love had inspired me with a
self-confidence that I lacked, and for a long time I thought my homosexuality was
a thing of the past. You attracted me physically and I felt secure in myself. Things
began turning sour when————came by, when my cycles of depression and
impotence started as a result of my jealousy and loss of that previous certainty—in
spite of the ephemeral nature of your adventures and my conviction that you
preferred me to everybody else. Consequently, I lived through some difficult years
and, on the rebound, I made you suffer them too. Don't think I attribute to you the
least responsibility for what then happened: circumstances, as I see now, only
contributed to showing the precariousness of my physical relationship with women.
You should think rather that without you I would probably never have known a
female love that was requited. There were many ups and downs, periods of calm
and relapses. The jealousy got worse in my case because after the first cycle of
depression I again fucked women but with difficulty, and two out of three times I
was impotent. For months, as you know, I went to bed with whores from Saint-
Denis until repeated failures made me bring the experiment to an end. In those
circumstances, the feeling you were in love, even only transitorily, with other men
was unbearable for me. I seriously contemplated suicide and loathed myself for not
having the courage to go through with it. Afterwards there was Cuba, the need to
hold on to something, to find another door. With————————, I reached a
point of intense jealousy, depression, desire to throw everything overboard. I had no
release with women and lost control of my actions: the only things I am ashamed of
in my life are a product of this phase; I was not responsible for myself yet was
nevertheless aware of the moral degradation. Then, gradually, I had the
impression I had touched rock bottom, realizing that henceforth I could not be
jealous of you. The day I saw Luis, I explained the situation to him and told him
the only possible way out was some kind of homosexual life. It was then that he
spoke to you, and you mentioned the conversation to me, but I was still probing and
was unable to respond with any certainty.*

*It must be about a year ago that I started to go out with Arabs and I needed a
few weeks to recognize the evidence: I did recover my equilibrium and coalesced
with you once again; but I also discovered that I was totally, definitively, irrevocably homosexual. From then on, as you must have realized, our relationship
improved; although differently, I began to love you more than before and reached a
kind of happiness that I had not attained in the past. I felt at peace, pleased to
share life with you, to have you and Carole at my side. As you can imagine, I
wanted to tell you what had happened; but our well-being seemed so fragile that I
was afraid of undermining it. Then there was your need to leave Gallimard, to
write about your mother: I wanted to support you on both fronts, not to wreck a
decision that was central to your future. Despite my secret, life in 1964 was*

happy, the year when our relations firmed up and I recovered my lost peace of mind. I then decided to keep my silence, to help you cut loose from Paris and the publishers, to support you as you support me. I went to Saint-Tropez prepared to renounce the new life I had discovered, content to dedicate myself to the novel, you, and Carole. The months we have spent together have shown me how far I feel morally and emotionally united to both of you {. . .} But they have also shown me that I cannot do without real homosexual life. The {ambiguous} friendships I have woven are not enough and, although I am happy in your company, I am choked by this chastity toward my own sex. In Paris I could have kept my secret without arousing suspicion; in Saint-Tropez it is impossible, and if at times I wanted to go to bed with —————, I put the idea to one side because of you, your status in the town, the possible scandal that could flare up, the gossip. The reality of life there has rendered impossible the dual sexual life I was leading and confronted me with the need to confess the truth to you {. . .}

I could not care less about what others think. Since I have been sure of my homosexuality, the only problem worrying me is in relation to you and Carole— the damaging impact that its discovery would now have on her. I am the opposite of an exhibitionist, and my sense of shame and attachment to secrecy are deeply rooted; but I am not afraid of the truth, and the few people I can rely on are you, Carole, and Luis. I told him all about this on my last trip. It remained only to tell you.

This letter explains my anxiety. I know too well what effect it will have on you, and yet I am forced to write it even with the risk {. . .} I am thirty-four, I love you, and I love Carole, I cannot live without you, I feel a boundless affection for you. What should I do? The void that life alone would be terrifies me, but I will accept it if that is what you decide. I would have wished from deep down that things could have been different, that my deviation had not happened {. . .} but what I know of myself now is eating me away and, surrounded by our Saint-Tropez friends, I am suddenly aware that I am a usurper, that our friendliness is fictitious and based on deceit, that I must cast off the esteem of those who would be disgusted if they knew the truth. How often I have wanted to walk out slamming the door behind me when they were talking about me as if I were one of them, to clear off and live friendless in a country where no one understands me, in total isolation. I am obsessed by the destiny of Jean {Genet}. Sometimes when I wake up at night I want to shout out. I then say to myself that this is my truth, that all the rest is fabrication, facile deceit. That if I am to do anything morally valid, I should make a clean break with everything.

I am now on a knife-edge. I can suggest nothing, promise nothing at all. Your reaction fills me with anguish, but secretly I want to know. I realize I am destroying my happiness close to you, yours when you are close to me, which I feel to be so strong. I have begun the letter time and again with a timid heart. I pray you do not see it as a breakup although I am powerless if you do. I am afraid of life without you: your face, your capacity for love, your eyes, your affection. I have never been closer to anyone than I have to you. You are the farthest I have gone in love.

Although I have written this letter exclusively to you, you can show it to people who love us and want things to go well between us {...} I know that the involvement of others would not help you and would be a futile complication.

It only remains for me to add my desire that you find the happiness, friendship, and esteem that you deserve and that I would like to be able to give you forever.

I shall be waiting for you on the tenth in Moscow with all my love and I shall also be waiting for Carole. With tenderest love...

THE REPLY, so impatiently awaited, finally arrived. A telegram addressed to the Sovietskaya Hotel relayed a succinct message: AN INHUMAN WEEK I STILL LOVE YOU. Three or four days later, after meeting her at the airport with Irina, our interpreter, and Agustín Manso, Monique handed me a text, written in fits and starts during her cruel quarantine, which included a long postscript written and dated in mid-flight. Her reflections, questioning, reproaches, formulated in difficult, anxious solitude, revealed at once her strength and vulnerability, nobility, love, openness, generosity, doubts, torment.

The basics had been stated: henceforth the success or failure of our relationship—her adaptation to everything she had just discovered—depended on our wish to continue together. The idea of becoming a normal couple had sunk without a trace, and we were posed with the challenge of creating something new. But were the love, understanding, and mutual respect that we could count on enough to preserve the strength of ties that we saw as essential? Was there not the risk that the precipitous, difficult area I was penetrating, and to which she would have no access, would spread and reduce our joint life to a kind of pretense? The danger existed and we were both fully aware of the fact. The decision to hide nothing from each other clashed in practice with mighty obstacles: the desire not to hurt each other, not to make ourselves suffer gratuitously. Gradually, we would establish the rules of a game in which rigor in relation to what was considered important would be tempered by a sense of restraint informed by affection. Although we would carry on a physical relationship for a number of years, the center of gravity in our union moved to the sphere of shared values and feelings. Monique knew that my Arab friendships were not testing out my love for her: the sex and characteristics of my companions excluded all potential rivalry. My existence was unfolding on two parallel planes that did not cross or interfere with each other: without Monique I would have been reduced to half of my personality. Liberation from the shackles that tied me down in this way modified the nature of our links. I ceased to be the insecure or grim lover of the early days and became quite different, and, in the end, more tolerable: a man resolved to integrate writing into his life and his life in writing, whose circle of interests and affections would gradually be bound only by essentials. Our agreement to preserve what bound us together from passing storms and disturbances would have a triumphant outcome. Darkly, but accurately, I guessed that the act of not yielding to social pressures and of bringing my behavior into the open implied progress in relation to the customs of the time, thanks to which my bonds with Monique and the world were purified and acquired greater integrity. In opposition to the frustration, hypocrisy, and sordidness of a great many marriages, what we were proposing was that we should both forge a modest victory against destiny. Monique's prophetic fascination for the universe of Genet, her swiftness in tearing me from the dilemma with which I was struggling would be crucial to the conquest of that new moral territory.

On 17 August 1978, fourteen years after the date reached in my narrative, I contracted civil marriage with Monique Lange in the mayor's office in the second arrondissement in Paris.

· VI ·

The Time Machine

I T WOULD BE difficult for me to express exactly my state of mind on that 3 July 1965, when I embarked for the USSR from the old, down-at-the-heels airport at Le Bourget. A sensation of exceptional weightlessness, as if in a sudden change of cabin pressure, wrapped the red tape and formalities of the flight in a hazy cloud of unreality. Freed from the burden that had been depressing me, I felt I was acting under the subtle influence of marijuana. The anguish of the last few days, given over to the painful writing of the letter and preparations for the journey, had waned little by little from the moment I had irrevocably entrusted my fate to the mailbox. My roaming around Barbès, la Chapelle, the Gare du Nord, very close to the place where Monique, on her return from Saint-Tropez, was going to find the bulky envelope and read and reread pages that would shake the foundations of our precarious life, bathed me in a daydreaming haze, almost a state of levitation. I calculated the time of her arrival with Carole on the rue Poissonnière—cheerful, at ease, sunburned, the usual load of bags and suitcases; apprehensively, I imagined her surprise at the letter, her unpredictable reactions to reading its contents, her shock or panic at the setting out of a problem that, although surmised by her, was suddenly going to blind her vision and abruptly stand between us. My disturbed slumbers in the hotel on the rue Lafayette, knowing she was near to me and yet distant and unapproachable—I could not communicate with her, since she thought me already in Moscow—drained me of all life. Reduced to a pale shadow of the traveler who had embarked supposedly two days before, I killed time as best I could, walking around familiar areas in whose anonymity I found shelter, waiting for the moment to merge with the other on the sunny runway at Le Bourget. Once seated in the Aeroflot plane, I let myself be taken over by a kind of fatalism: aware I had burned my bridges, cut myself loose, gone to war against my false image, was moving into a difficult future full of incentive and novelty. My rebirth at the age of thirty-four with an imprecise identity, determined only to end my previous opportunism and lies, was leading me to a chain reaction of ruptures that would gradually contract my circle of friends; the predictable solitude awaiting me would be bearable, I knew, only with Monique's support and understanding.

Mixed feelings and emotions, relief at terminating the ambiguity and fear of inconceivable rejection, accompanied me while I moved away from her, flying to where we had agreed to meet two days later, the new, exotic world of the country of the future: that bastion of scientific socialism, cradle of the glorious October Revolution, hope and Mecca of the exploited—the feared, admired, hated USSR, object of ephemeral youthful nightmares and no less fleeting adult adherence, to that Moscow whose very name would send my father into a rage and which, with the freedom granted by my flamboyant change of skin, I was finally about to tour and examine without blinders of any kind.

Unlike my journeys to Cuba a few years earlier, I was heading for the Soviet Union determined to be receptive and open, aloof from both the primeval anticommunism inculcated in my adolescence and the credulous innocence of past Castroite enthusiasms. The rumors that had filtered through from Havana and my bitter political experience in 1964 helped to make me more wary and cautious: under attack simultaneously from the right and the left, from the Communist Party and the régime of Franco, I had lost my previous political innocence and moved firmly forward in a kind of no-man's-land. Reality, as exemplified by my expelled companions, was much more complex and trickier than I had previously thought. I was amazed by the parallels and symmetries between the methods of ruining opponents employed by friends and enemies alike. Accustomed for years to looking at the world from a single angle and dividing humanity into two perfectly delineated camps, I experienced moments of confusion and helplessness before healthily reacting with resolutions to change my ways: to stop keeping my head in the clouds, to act in the future with greater discernment and lucidity.

I was to go to the USSR without forebodings or preconceptions, endowed only with the curiosity and interest of a voyeur wishing to adopt if not a neutral position, at least one that was cold and balanced. To become a movie camera and tape recorder for all I saw and heard, punctually to note down facts, incidents, conversations. To write for the first time in my life a kind of diary.

Although I did not fulfull that last resolution, Monique did so on my behalf. In her notebook, day by day, in minute, almost undecipherable writing, she summed up each day of our visit, and her notes, even in their bare telegraphic density, allow me today to evoke without anachronism or error the scenes of our fêted bourgeois life in the world fatherland of the proletariat.

The excitement of my first days in Moscow suffered the consequences of corrosive anguish: Monique's delay in answering the telegram carrying my address and the growing, stifling anxiety of my wait. Contrary to expectations, police and customs formalities were completed surprisingly quickly. Being, as I was, a guest of the USSR Writers' Union, the airport functionaries showed no interest in the contents of my suitcase. At the passenger terminal I was greeted by Agustín Manso, a Soviet citizen of Spanish origins, a member of the group of Asturian refugee children in Russia during the civil war, whom I had met in Paris months earlier, and Irina, a welcoming, attractive comrade acting on behalf of the Union. I went with them to the Hotel Sovietskaya, which was reserved, as I discovered later, for select guests.

While Agustín got me acclimated with his circle of fellow countrymen and friends, Irina was busy guiding me through the labyrinths of officialdom and bureaucracy: protocol visits to her colleagues and chiefs at the Writers' Union, interviews with writers and editors of cultural magazines, collection of my substantial royalties, decisions about the itinerary and stages on our journey. To avoid the bother of organized tours of model farms and factories, I emphasized our particular interest in churches and historical monuments, with the paradoxical result that I have never seen as many religious images, churches, and chapels as during my stay in that supposedly atheist world. Knowing how keen Monique was on beaches, I managed to add to the list of planned excursions a few days' rest in the Crimea. Following the rule of countries with "real socialism," a *pirivocho* was to take charge of us and escort our every step. I had suggested Agustín's name to Irina but, as he had predicted, someone else was chosen: a small, lively, bespectacled Lithuanian lad, rather Disney-like in appearance, by the name of Vidas Silunas, whom Agustín had known from university and whose later companionship was as pleasant as it was unburdensome. Vidas, Agustín, and Irina took me to the offices of the editors of the *Foreign Literature Review*, which had published my works; the publishing houses specializing in the translation of Western novelists and writers; the editorial board of *Novy Mir*, where Alexander Tvardovsky welcomed me with open arms, introduced me to his collaborators, and startled me with the frank honesty of his questions. The first and only publisher of Solzhenitsyn in the brief period of Khrushchevian thaw, although previously awarded a prize by Stalin and a distinguished member of the nomenklatura, the poet stood out from his peers because of his greater spirit of independence and praiseworthy openness of mind. I can remember how he immediately wanted to have my opinion of Neruda. The poet or the man? Both, he replied. I told him that 20 percent of his work seemed splendid, 60 percent rather average, and the rest was detestable; as for his personality, I added that objectivity was impossible since he embodied in my eyes everything I hated in other people and in myself: opportunism, self-worship, a cheerful, fatalistic acceptance of a linear concept of history. Tvardovsky's reaction was unexpected: he got out of his seat, embraced me, warmly patted me on the back. While he remained editor of *Novy Mir*, he would never publish a line of Neruda's poetry. He forcefully explained to me how in the era of the purges and Zhdanov's pedantry, Neruda had been the dictator's international custodian, the willing guardian of his ideology. Then, he gave the word to his advisers, and questions and answers turned to issues in contemporary literature in Spain, Paris, Cuba, and countries in Latin America. But Tvardovsky was a *rara avis* in Soviet officialdom. In the other cultural centers that I had occasion to penetrate, the dialogue with those in charge inevitably went along different paths. Outside the field of the universal classics, my hosts' literary tastes revealed an amalgam of incredible ignorance, obtuse dogmatism, complacent, desperate mediocrity. They hardly advocated a single modern writer whom I admired: neither Proust, Joyce, Kafka, Svevo, nor Borges were circulating in Russian, nor were they then in the course of being translated. The advisers for the Spanish section were making known the work of Celaya and Marcos Ana, but not Cernuda; that of Dolores Medio, but not Martín-Santos. I remember asking one of them why they were not publishing *Tiempo de silencio*. I was astonished by my female informant's reply: it was, she said, an overly complex novel that the Soviet reader would not understand. I should have replied—since I did not at the time—that with such criteria literary and intellectual progress were impossible and the readership in her country would in the year 2000 still be legally underage and deprived of the most significant, enriching works.

When at one of the readings or cultural events in which I now participate, someone asks me the hackneyed question of why I write such sybilline, hermetic texts as *Don Julián* or *Makbara* if an average reader cannot manage to comprehend them, I flourish this anecdote as a reminder of the real, deep contempt for possible improvements in public taste implicit in the paternalist, demagogic attitude of those who take it upon themselves to lower the creative level and arrogate the right to decide what the people understand or do not understand in matters artistic and literary. The history of literature—as of all manifestations of the human spirit—comprises a succession of difficult enterprises that often go unrecognized at the time of their conception: to be grasped in all its depth and complexity, any original, innovative work requires at times very lengthy lapses of time during which it will find a way through. An extreme example of this is the great poetry of Góngora, which has only become accessible to readers three centuries after being created. But one would merely have to extend the discriminating criterion adopted by the bureaucrats in the field of literature to the area of the sciences to reveal at once the arrant nonsense of their position: since the people do not understand either, for example, the discoveries of physics, then the State should logically ban them as well. If it does not, that is clearly, strictly a matter of profitability: science, in its practical application, can be mobilized on its behalf; literature, on the other hand, cannot and will never be. Principles based on the political-social function of art are the death of art itself. Of all the literary and artistic doctrines formulated over the last two centuries, that of socialist realism has one really exceptional distinguishing feature: it has not produced a single work of value in fiction, poetry, music, or painting. When Tvardovsky's collaborators asked me for my preferences in modern Russian literature, they smiled at my list of writers—Blok, Essenin, Babel, Akhmatova, Mandelstam: all had composed their work outside and in the teeth of official doctrine and some had paid with their lives for their audacity. The magnitude of the punishment and risk immanent in any act of defiance explains the fact that both writers and readers in the USSR take literature extremely seriously. If the composition of a work different from that propounded by the state creed leads a writer to civil death and to being ostracized; if the majority of printed books are mere moralizing tracts, a hybrid of conformism and propaganda, this situation sheds light on the eagerness of an alert, active minority for those works that are difficult to find even on the black market and that, if they are published, disappear immediately from the bookshop shelves. People in line in the street for a whole night to buy a book of poetry, as happened months before my journey to the USSR when a small selection of Akhmatova's poems were given authorization, is one indication of the high value bestowed on literary creation by a ravenous readership and, inversely, of the censors' justified fear of outbreaks of enthusiasm produced by their own absurd blind policy. The different status enjoyed by the artist in the Soviet sphere and in Western countries testifies to the religious respect and admiration with which readers surround the figure of a writer whose trajectory moves away from set canons and harnesses literary and artistic demands to uncorruptible moral rigor. The search for new artistic forms of expression, the exploration of virgin linguistic territories can be dubbed a game in the West; in the USSR, because of the external sanction they incur, such matters assume in readers' eyes a surprising and shared gravity.

In the interval between my arrival and the date of Monique's flight, I also visited Agustín Manso's friends and the nucleus of Spaniards whose addresses Claudín had passed on to me. Some were Party members and were more or less integrated into the rigid, compartmentalized strata of the Soviet hierarchy; others, like the theater director Ángel Gutiérrez, encountered serious obstacles in their professions or lived entirely outside the hierarchy, like Dionisio García. The latter had recently been divorced from a gypsy and had lived a long time with the monks of Zagorsk, spent his time restoring icons and professed a real love of literature and philosophy, although his knowledge of the latter was minuscule: his ignorance of languages other than Spanish and Russian and the difficulty of obtaining a supply of related works in either language limited the range of his reading to a short, eccentric list of authors. I can remember his curiosity and interest in the works of Kierkegaard, Bergson, and Berdayeff, whose theories he knew only by hearsay, and his radical mistrust and contempt for politics. Thanks to him, I managed a few glimpses of aspects of Soviet reality that were different from, and even contradicted, those on show on official circuits: the flat he shared with several families or neighbors where he had only one modest room filled with books; the existence of anti-Semitic groups, where, as a Spaniard—from the home of the Holy Inquisition and the Catholic Monarchs—he was welcomed one day with a round of flattering applause. Although sentimentally inclined to things Russian—culture, customs, scenery—my new acquaintances revealed signs of a truly praiseworthy independence of ideas. They had a subtle, fair-minded vision of the USSR: they spoke affectionately about the country but did not hide its defects. My royalties, paid in non-convertible rubles that I had consequently to spend on the spot, allowed me the luxury of inviting them to the most expensive restaurants. For the first and probably only time in my life, I had sufficient means to offer a group of friends a real banquet and, awaiting the day when Monique and Carole were to meet up with me, I fleetingly savored the pleasures of acting like a millionaire. With her daughter and wearing a light white raincoat, Monique finally emerged from the passengers' arrival channel after going through police formalities. My companions did not suspect the deep emotion of that meeting nor the change wrought in our life by my letter. Her warm smile, tender manner and gestures really disguised her loneliness and uncertainty before the riddle I had set her. On that rainy but brightly luminous afternoon we took their suitcases to the Sovietskaya before going for a stroll around Red Square and the walls of the Kremlin. Irina and her colleagues at the Writers' Union had worked hard to smooth out all the problems and ensure we had a comfortable stay. Monique was delighted by the program for the holiday, which had been drawn up according to my wishes. The novelty of the perspective—friends, décor, pace of life—facilitated cautious mutual adaptation. Without the excitement of exploring that vast, alien, extreme world, things would have been different for both of us and probably more arduous.

My brief diary and notes on the USSR, worked out from Monique's diary, has only one aim, to restore the freshness of my impressions at the time, while adding indispensable later thoughts. Their deliberate super-ficiality and *parti pris* of carefree humor might upset both enemies and defenders of the Soviet system, but they reflect the vision of an observer like myself struggling to cast off the cobwebs of ideology. The fact that I was examining "real socialism" with the simplicity of a nursery child was not the fruit of some capricious decision or arbitrary point of view; it was part of a chain of circumstances that involved my break with the past and a desire to make a clean sweep of all that was stifling me in order to forge myself, counter to everybody—friends, enemies, those nearest to me—a new identity and, in conflict with myself, to impose a new direction on my life.

I

In the entrance to the Hotel Sovietskaya, Monique bumped into a friend with whom she had had dealings years before, for professional reasons. She too had just arrived in Moscow, knew no one in the city, and asked if we wouldn't mind taking her out for dinner. Monique said we wouldn't, and we agreed to pick her up later from her room. She was on a different floor, and at the agreed time I took to the stairs, walked past a stout woman who sat impassively at her small table looking after the keys to the bedrooms. I went down the corridor and knocked on the room door she had earlier indicated. However, for some unknown reason, my gesture infuriated the hall porter: she stood up immediately, shouted, ran toward me, and began to wave her arms threateningly. At that very moment Monique's friend opened her door, and the scene she surveyed astonished her; the matron repeated, "Nyet, nyet" and, not satisfied with that, suddenly pulled me by the sleeve.

"What's the matter? Has she gone mad?"

I said I didn't know, but the message was clear: unwittingly, I had committed a most serious crime. It was an unusual situation and we couldn't stop laughing. In order to bypass a trial of strength from which we would clearly emerge as losers, we agreed to meet up in the lobby. When I recounted the episode to Monique and my friends, there was general hilarity. Rather embarrassed, Agustín told me that the rules in some hotels prevented guests of a different sex from visiting each other, in order to stamp out immoral behavior.

Spanish Catholic Action, which I had met in my years at secondary school, would no doubt be proud to see the seeds of their preaching unexpectedly blooming on the distant shores of the Moskva!

2

The restaurant food was excellent, but the waiters seemed to be unaware of the notion of time and often remained absorbed in mysterious thoughts, not paying the slightest attention to a customer's futile signals and calls. An incredible interval could elapse from the moment one sat down at a table until one actually received a menu, and on the surface this did not seem to be justified by any other tasks.

My preferences went to the Uzbekistan and the Tibilisi, where the waiters seemed more awake and pocketed their tips without blinking. However, writers favored places reserved for their own guild, in which stars like Yevtushenko had a *right to a table and could theatrically welcome the arrival of a distinguished visitor by throwing a glass of champagne to the floor. (The "distinguished visitor" writing these lines would be submitted to such an ordeal in the course of a second visit and would search in vain for a hole or corner in which to hide from the bard's flamboyant gesticulations.)*

My hosts toasted the family reunion with vodka and white wine, and when it was time to get up and leave the drawing rooms of the Artists' Café, Monique and I felt cheerful, if slightly tipsy.

Less fortunate than restaurant-goers, ordinary people got drunk standing up, in solitude. During our first tour of Moscow, my friends pointed out a line of silent men, vaguely sad and unkempt like Salvation Army regulars, outside a liquor store. As I noticed on other occasions, the bottle of vodka was often paid for by two or three people who then swigged it down in the street without exchanging a word. The communion brought by alcohol was replaced by a ritual whose insularity I found disconcerting: the drinkers remained anonymous, and after briefly coming together to drink, each staggered off, pie-eyed, by himself. The price of vodka was relatively accessible to the pocket of the average citizen and, as I was informed, the system ensured that there was an uninterrupted supply.

3

Vidas Silunas offered us a sightseeing tour of Moscow with stops at the Kremlin, Red Square, Lenin's mausoleum, Gorki Street, the monument to Pushkin. At Dionisio's suggestion, we stopped off to visit the subway, built in the time of Stalin. Our guide led us to an imposing, cold, awe-inspiring station, with glass lamps in the ceiling and an escalator that went down to platforms adorned with statues of heroes of the Revolution; these had been cast in bronze, were larger than life, and represented soldiers, sailors, commissars, militiamen in impetuous, bellicose, triumphal poses. Uniforms, belts, and boots were reproduced faithfully to the tiniest detail, and one fine figure even waved a real revolver in a monstrous attack of rage. We decided to go for a ride and with Vidas got on one of the trains. The train cars seemed more spacious, more comfortable, and cleaner than those of the Paris métro, and the passengers, who were few, given the time of day, went in and out easily, serious, patient, disciplined. We sat down in a row, both curious and the object of the curiosity of those seated opposite: villagy women in head-scarves, middle-aged ruddy-faced men, almost always wearing a hat or cap. One of the former's perverse stare in Monique's direction suddenly attracted my attention: just as I was about to mention it to her, the woman suddenly got up and, without uttering a word, pulled down the edge of Monique's skirt until her knees were completely covered. The gesture left us tongue-tied and Vidas Silunas was quick to pacify us: peasant women, he said, were not used to foreigners' ways of dressing; any anomaly, however innocent, clashed with their exaggerated sense of modesty. On successive days we would have occasion to verify that widespread mixture of harshness, warmth, and brusque behavior of the Russian people: the driver of the vehicle that took us to Suzdal showed a lively interest in us, bombarded us with questions through the interpreter, laughed like a child at our candor, and continually turned round to look at us, to the point that we feared he would let go of the steering wheel and crash into a tree. Monique went with her daughter to the GUM department store to buy some small keepsakes; the customers, she said, pushed and elbowed their way through with incredible brutality. Later, in the Crimea, when she went one day to the bathroom in a pharmacy or a shop, an employee slipped in with her and without ceremony seized the opportunity to examine her underwear, ask her about and comment on the origin and quality of her bras.

4

A visit to Vladimir: the city had just been opened up to foreigners and my Spanish friends urged me to go. We went by train, with Vidas Silunas, and for two or three hours we passed through a land of oaks, firs, and birches. When we arrived at the station, a small group of men and women were waiting conspicuously on the platform with bunches of flowers. Fears that I was the victim of such a glorious welcome were confirmed at once: forewarned by Moscow, the local organizers of the Writers' Union had come en masse to welcome us. Monique, Carole, and I greeted our respective bouquets amid smiles and bows. I handed mine to Vidas and asked him whether they had confused me with Aragon or Alberti.

A journey to the hotel, where a banquet awaited us. For more than an hour we remained seated in a small drawing room with our hosts. The usual vodka was inexplicably delayed, and we all kept ceremonially silent in an attitude of stiff awkwardness. To bring some relief to the heavy atmosphere I was forced to ask a few questions: How long had the provincial branch of the Union been in existence? How many members or affiliates did it have? What literary genres did they cultivate? How did artistic life proceed? What were their main activities? Their replies were detailed, mechanical, and boring, and when the translation was broken off and the silence thickened, my questions again steered toward gratuitous extravagance and inanity: When was the library opened? How many volumes did it contain? What kind of books did readers prefer? The figures floated about, useless, unreal, absurd, and when I was about to discover the number of cultural— or philatelic, or financial—magazines they subscribed to, the announcement that the table was ready fortunately brought the nightmare to a close. The Siberian gastronomic speciality heralded by the president turned out to be a kind of ravioli. But the vodka finally arrived, and with their mouths full, nobody felt obliged to prolong the incongruous dialogue.

After bidding farewell to that lethal group of writers, we walked out into the street. It was a Sunday or a holiday and the pavements were packed with people: introspective, gloomy, inert, they brought to mind those described by Jovellanos in his upsetting, unforgettable pages on the atmosphere of exhaustion, sadness, and desolation in the villages of Castile. The men and women we saw looked more like a pack of soldiers suddenly abandoned by their officers. Street-sellers wandered along the main avenue and gathered around some enormous billboards inscribed with the names and photographs of the most meritorious workers of the month. The contemplation of this display appeared to be the only diversion in the city and kept attracting new groups of spectators. Nobody laughed, joked, or spoke in a loud voice: silence was obligatory. From time to time, music from a transistor radio ephemerally broke the almost physical density of that hybrid of alienation, lethargy, and monotony.

The churches were splendid and, as they were celebrating worship, full of the faithful. The canticles of the priests, smell of incense, solemn ritual of the offices created a strange counterpoint to the grayness and conformity outside. The massive church attendance did not necessarily reflect, however, the religious feeling of the population: as far as I could see, Vladimir was without cafés, cinemas, or other places for recreation. In such circumstances, any novelty inevitably attracts people's attention and, like our appearance and clothing, becomes a source of distraction and curiosity.

5

We continued to trawl churches and monasteries in the region. Their architecture was noble and majestic, though slender and light in design. The gold of the Byzantine domes stood out in its purity against the compliant blue of the sky.

In Suzdal we spied in the distance a pitched battle fought by hundreds of horsemen. We were not too surprised by the anachronism; however, we stopped to inquire. As we got out of the vehicle in which we were traveling, Vidas approached a group of technicians and drivers involved in the shooting of the film. As he then told us, they were filming Tarkovsky's now-famous film on the life of Andrei Rublev. The preparations for the scene, with great movements of the masses and deployment of armies, were harmoniously integrated into countryside that seemed to have changed very little since the time of that famous painter of icons.

These rapid incursions into "deep Russia" revealed, however, the disturbing backwardness of agriculture; the survival of conditions and ways of life profusely described in literature from the times of Gogol, Turgenev, and Tolstoy. The small isbas with their stoves and indoor plants fitted quite easily into the scenery in Tarkovsky's film and, almost fifty years after the Revolution, were probably still the same as they had been centuries ago. When I went to Uzbekistan and the Caucasus, that apathy and immobility, the almost mildewy existence of peasants only two hours by car from the capital would seem even more intriguing. It would be unjust and mistaken to blame everything on the Soviet régime, which had witnessed spectacular improvements in the standard of living of Georgians and

Uzbekis, which was now much higher than under their former masters and occupiers. Rather than being a colonizer, the Russian peasant gave the impression he was vegetating, poverty-stricken and colonized. The peculiar features of his history would perhaps clarify such a striking contrast and the tenacious attachment that numerous layers of the population of the Socialist republic, in towns and in the country, had to traditional norms and practices.

A tendency to make the countryside a place to escape to: all my acquaintances, both Spaniards and native Russians, spoke blissfully of the forests of larches, oaks, and birches, to which they fled as often as possible and that apparently contained the decanted quintessence of all they identified as Russia. They were filled with emotion by the evocation of firs, snow, sledges. The disparity between my tastes and theirs was as abrupt as it was extreme: when I told them I was an urban animal capable of walking dozens of kilometers through the streets of a city that excited me, but incapable of taking a step in a setting whose peacefulness irritated me, they looked surprised and incredulous. Didn't the quiet and silence of the countryside favor work and inspiration? Without any desire to be paradoxical, I retorted that the latter were associated, in my case, with the lively bustle of the city: while the urban hum and fury hardly bothered me, the gentle rustle of leaves or the trill of a bird distracted me and made concentration impossible. Didn't any kind of scenery appeal to me? The desert, I replied; I found lush vegetation depressing and appreciated greenness only when it was sparse and bare, when placed against mineral splendor, the creation of arduous, laborious toil. A few fig, olive, or almond trees in a parched landscape, the persistent wavy hedge of oleanders along the dry bed of a stream move me much more than sixty thousand square miles of Siberian natural park. That mutual insensitivity to our respective preferred haunts finally made us laugh. Dionisio told me—in reference to his recent reading of Campos de Níjar—*that I had become an incorrigible specimen of Almería man.*

6

Visit to Leningrad: we stroll tirelessly around the streets near the beautiful Winter Palace, the age-old, now self-absorbed aristocratic districts, the bridges and banks of the Neva, the quayside where the Aurora was still moored next to the dark, intimidating fortress of Peter and Paul.

We enjoyed the sweet suspension of time, the ethereal subtlety, penetrating luminosity of the white nights in the company of two intellectuals living in the city, both former volunteers with the International Brigades: Dr. Pritkere, professor of Spanish at the university and a Larra specialist, and Ruth Zernova, a Jewish translator who had an equal command of Spanish and French and whose mother—whom we visited for a few moments in her tiny central flat—happened to be an old Bolshevik who had divorced Karl Radek before he fell in one of the purges and was executed by Stalin. Both Ruth and the professor displayed a warmth and spontaneity that were unusual in that hardened, scaly intellectual

world, and we immediately felt a wave of mutual sympathy. When we inter-
rogated them on the period of the terror, the Spanish civil war, the siege and
resistance to the Nazis, their replies were direct and honest. We visited the Pushkin
museum with them; walked along the gardens belonging to Yussopov Palace, where
Rasputin was killed; we followed the route of Raskolnikov, drawn with such
detail by Dostoevsky. Ancient Petersburg, beautiful and mournful as Venice
sometimes is, watched over us in an unreal heady atmosphere of fading light; our
presence seemed oneiric and false. Tenuous, lifeless, tired, the sun finally hid at
midnight behind a panorama of sleeping palaces and deserted squares. From the
hotel window we would see it reappear, still through mists and yellow haze, at
half-past three in the morning.

7

As we knew from Paris, Sartre and Simone de Beauvoir were also
in Leningrad, in the company of Lénina Zónina, a young attractive woman with
whom Sartre had a discreet, emotional relationship for a number of years.
Monique, Carole, and I visited them in the Hotel Astoria and dined with Castor
and Lénina in a Caucasian restaurant. Sartre had another engagement, but had
lunch with us the day after and related some salacious anecdotes on China-phobia:
at one of the meetings of the World Council for Peace, to whose leading or advisory
committee he belonged, one of his Soviet hosts, who was apparently rather drunk,
had jokingly whispered to him that although peace was of course extremely
desirable, a small hydrogen bomb aimed at Peking, close to Mao's residence, would
not be a totally bad idea. This bitter animosity—so accurately forecast by my
father—was not limited to the well-known anti-imperialist rhetoric of official
circles: on the contrary, as we were able to ascertain throughout our journey, it
embraced the whole population. The number of anti-Chinese jokes, gags, stories
that we heard was unending: while the average Soviet displayed a mixture of envy,
admiration, and indulgence toward North Americans, they reserved scorn, sar-
casm, and hatred for their comrades in the East. When a heroine in the world of
the Guermantes sighed "la Chine m'inquiète" in one of her society gatherings,
she could not imagine that half a century later her opinions would be shared by a
huge country whose official doctrine would be none other than so-called proletarian
internationalism.

As we were eating dessert, we had an unexpected visitor. Luis Miguel Dom-
inguín was on a business trip to the USSR and, having learned from a third party
that we were there, he came to say hello. I knew his brother Domingo and his
brother-in-law and rival Antonio Ordóñez: the time I went to Nîmes with
Monique, during the period we saw something of Hemingway, they took me to
Spain with them, and the frontier police were so intent on their rapturous welcome
for the bullfighter that they didn't bother to find out who was in the car or to stamp
my passport. On the journey to Barcelona, perhaps to keep sleep at bay, Domingo

and Ordóñez had sustained an amusing political discussion. The former, at the time his brother-in-law's manager, insisted on converting him to his Communist ideas, but the bullfighter was not at all convinced and counterattacked with ad hominem *arguments: if he was so proud of being red, why did he keep charging him a 10 percent commission? Was that not a form of bourgeois exploitation? Of course it was, Domingo answered. The capitalist's only moral rule was to appropriate the surplus value of others. The more he exploited, the more he would help to dissipate reformist illusions and objectively nourish revolutionary consciousness. Class collaboration, social democratic fudging would lead to the revisionist vices so severely condemned by Lenin. Ordóñez's arm would not be twisted and he burst out laughing: What the hell, you're no Communist! You're just on the make. Domingo's attitude—that I would later see reflected in the language and behavior of some Latin American magnates as they opened up their luxury umbrellas under the luminous firmament of Mexico or Caracas the moment they heard it rained in Moscow—was a characteristic product of the Manichaeism and confusion of those years and expressed very clearly the contradictions and shortcomings in our political and cultural world. Dominguín had hardly gone when I related the anecdote to Sartre, who laughed heartily. As Monique later reminded me, both he and his friends maintained an attitude of reserve toward bull-fighting, if not of discreet moral disapproval, as was the case with his companion. Fortunately, neither introduced that issue, and as we said goodbye we agreed we would meet up again in Moscow on our return from the Crimea and Uzbekistan.*

8

Luis Miguel invited us out to dinner, and we went with Vidas and Ruth Zernova to the Europa Hotel, where he had reserved a small drawing room. The bullfighter traveled with a tiny retinue of Spaniards, including Lucía Bosé, elegantly dressed in red and more beautiful than in her early films. Despite the vodka and champagne from the Caucasus, conversation languished, but Estela, a Soviet interpreter and translator of our social poets, unknowingly took responsibility for enlivening it. With that burden of moral sentiments often exhibited by the comic characters in Chekhov, she asked the bullfighter if the Spanish people were suffering a lot under the chains of an oppressive régime like Franco's. "What on earth have they got to suffer about? It couldn't be happier!" "Happy?" exclaimed Estela. "Yes, happy, the Spanish adore Franco and so do I." "But Franco has killed lots of people, he's very cruel and unjust ... " "All governments kill people and are cruel and unjust: if the people obey them, what difference does it make?" "I thought the masses in Spain ..." "Look, miss: the masses follow those who give them orders and quite right, too; who gives the orders in Russia? Is it the Communist Party?" Estela said it was, but then she got mixed up and had to get it right: well, it was really the Supreme Soviet. "If I were Russian, I would go along with the Supreme Soviet; but as I am Spanish and Franco's in charge in my country, I'm a supporter of Francoism." "But that's terrible," mumbled the upset Estela, "your views are selfish and cynical ..." "Exactly," he agreed, "that's exactly right, cynical, yes sir, cynical."

We were cheered up by the exchange: Dominguín's sarcastic aplomb and Estela's consternation delighted the party, especially those who were forced to put up with the funereal gravity of official speeches and their usual stock references to humanist values. Laughter plays a liberating role, and where the suffocating orthodoxy of a political or religious doctrine reigns supreme—as Bahktin taught me years later in relation to the world of Rabelais—the truths of the jester are like a breath of fresh air, the escape valve thanks to which life becomes more bearable.

9

Our stay in Leningrad—the walks along the streets of a somnambulant, sleeping-beauty city, in an atmosphere of hazy luminous tranquillity—seemed too short. The Petersburg, or Petrograd, that is so wonderfully described in literature survived specterlike on those white nights steeped in nostalgic memories. The desolate splendor of the city, the uncertain brightness of the night suddenly immersed the traveler in the atmosphere of the Russian novel. We decided to reread Pushkin, Dostoevsky, Tolstoy. Biely was little more than a name to me at the time: the decadent writer Trotsky fulminated against. But my efforts to meet Akhmatova would not bear fruit: they told me she was getting over a long illness and had gone for a few weeks' rest far from the city.

In the airport, after checking our luggage, we had a drink with Vidas while waiting for our plane to depart. We became entangled in a discussion of Soviet sexuality and did not notice the time go by until our guide was startled by a loudspeaker announcement demanding we present ourselves immediately on the runway. We ran after him to the foot of a small staircase where a dozen people were packed together, hoping to secure empty seats at the last minute. Our untimely arrival frustrated their attempt, and there was a chorus of muffled shouts, badtempered expressions. To make way for us amid those who hadn't yet given up and were waiting in vain for a miracle, a couple of militiamen pushed them aside with uncalled-for brutality: some of them lost their balance and thudded to the floor. Surprisingly, the expeditious intervention of the forces of law and order provoked no reaction. The disappointed travelers moved back, and we slipped between them and our protectors with heads lowered in shame. Such a scene would perhaps not be shocking in Calcutta or Bombay but, given the context in which it took place, Monique and I were filled with vague, if persistent, disquiet.

10

We spent a day in Moscow, en route to Tashkent. Agustín, Ángel, Dionisio came to see us in our hotel, and Monique pursued with them her survey of

Soviet youth. What's happening to couples? What are their moral attitudes? Was the puritanical restraint that dominated press, television, books, and films a relic of the old peasant tradition or did it reflect customs and social codes as well?

Although censorship excised any reference or allusion to the sexual act, my friends said, the attitude of boys and girls was fairly lax. According to them, the greatest obstacle to intimate relationships was rooted in the penury and packed nature of housing, a lack of space. In summer, people copulated in the woods, but in winter only the fortunate owner of a private room could allow himself the luxury of enjoying himself alone with his partner; everyone else had to be satisfied with the occasional loan of room keys from their more fortunate colleagues. Those who had influence or means also used the cabins on the boats that plied the Volga or the sleeping cars on the train to Leningrad. As to homosexuality—on which Monique playfully insisted—their response could not have been more disappointing; they had all heard about it as something way-out and extravagant, but declared that they personally knew no "perverts."

Apart from these exchanges of opinions with my Spanish friends and exceptional personalities like Ruth Zernova, conversations with Soviet intellectuals who were accessible to foreigners very soon became a painful ritual. Forced to keep quiet on essentials—their absolute dependence on the system that lodged, dressed, fed, and found work for them and, in cases of good behavior, granted them the privileges of daschas, cars, and permission to travel—in their dialogue with Westerners they pursued a continuous exercise in reserve, trivial comment, and avoidance of the truth. Knowing they could say only what they ought to say, they strove to compensate for their individual barrenness with a series of declarations exuding vitality or vague, general, humanitarian political propositions. Their propensity to sudden raucous laughter, in slightly more strident tones than normal; their recourse to rhetorical clichés and facile sentimentality; the habit of relating anodyne jokes about the régime as proof of their illusory independence; the need to rapidly drown in alcohol any attempt at potentially dangerous communication—all these tendencies betrayed a self-censorship or inner repression that gave their slightest gesture or movement an air of forced stiffness. Contact or acquaintance with one of them allowed one to spot the syndrome in all the rest. As I would verify years later, these marks stay with even those who have had the courage to break with the system and, still in exile, display the scars and traces of their traumatic apprenticeship and cultivation of mental wariness and restraint.

I I

First impressions on leaving the airplane: bustle, warmth, sensuality, immediacy of human relations; a greater variety of faces, clothes, colors; sudden increase in temperature; refreshing stereophonic voices.

The cavernous, imposing Writers' Union car thundered along the dusty road, passed and left behind a motley succession of vehicles of all shapes and sizes. The

Uzbeki driver, wearing a kind of biretta, seemed to be driving happily along, following the musical rhythms on the radio: an intense, warm, heart-rending Turkish-style melody I then heard for the first time. His steering wheel and windshield were decorated with rosary beads, photos, and lucky charms, just like those of his Arab colleagues. He sometimes greeted a friend through the window and laughed to himself, either at the chance encounter or the wit of his own words. On the journey we contemplated family scenes or set pieces, open-air cafés shadowed by vines, customers stretched out lazily on rush mats. Some were crouching, lost in their tea tray or game of checkers. Idleness was a way of life. I felt that I was, I am an integral part of that scene.

Tashkent looked like a modern city, with its functional, graceless architecture; but the contrast of its inhabitants' temperament and character with those of their Russian comrades could not be more extreme. The aura of alienation and gloom that enveloped the pedestrian masses in Moscow or Vladimir was dissipated here by the dual impact of Islam and the sun. The population's standard of living was clearly what it ought to be. If Russian ethnocentrism existed, as I would later see myself, Uzbekistan had not, on the other hand, been beset by the devastation and thieving of the booty-hunting régimes of the old Western protectorates and colonies. Poverty had been efficiently swept aside: people dressed better than in Moscow, notably with greater variety and imagination. No beggar was there to upset visitors, unlike in Moslem countries. Their indolence was not the fruit of destitution but of a particular relaxed casual style of life. An almost unique example among peoples subject to capitis diminutio, *the Uzbekis could pride themselves on material conditions far superior to those in the distant but all-powerful metropolis.*

This dip into a nation of Islamic culture, annexed by force of arms by the czars and then inserted against its will into the multiracial conglomerate of the USSR, would allow me on my return to Moscow to distinguish the purely Soviet from the Russian and not repeat the mistake made years earlier in Cuba when I erroneously attributed to the Revolution elements of happiness, spontaneity, and dissipation in fact inherent in the Cuban people. The oppression, melancholy, silence that startle the visitor to Tula or Vladimir cannot be attributed, as one might think at first sight, only to the hermetic immobility of the régime, but also to a centuries-old tradition and experience; the creation as much of Ivan, Peter, and Catherine as of Lenin and Stalin. After an open-air party, when we went for a walk with Vidas and Valeri, the Uzbeki guide, amid gardens, pavilions, meadows, and ponds in a municipal park full of families, couples, bathers, chess or checkers players, a vague sense of well-being impregnated the atmosphere and finally intoxicated us with a gentle, frivolous felicity. The heat was extremely dry and healthy: Monique's persistent rheumatism, a result of her winter bathing in Saint-Tropez, would disappear within hours of her stay in Uzbekistan. At night the temperature drove sleep away, but after showering a dozen times all in vain, I finally nodded off like Marat in the bath, nibbling the slices of watermelon that we had providentially bought in a market.

12

      Vidas's tact and care reduced our official contacts to the necessary minimum: nevertheless, I was the first Spanish writer; apart from Alberti, to visit the country, and we could not avoid a natural feeling of friendly curiosity toward us. The leaders of the Writers' Union proudly showed me several brochures of political tourist propaganda in Spanish and inquired after the rigor and accuracy of the translation. I politely examined the pages of one of them—The Progress of Uzbeki Woman Under Socialism—*and had to make an effort not to burst out laughing. Rather than a traitor, the genial translator seemed to be a fan of Ionesco and his dialogues in* La Cantatrice chauve. *Threading together like beads the unknown words extracted from the dictionary, his dronelike activity had created a stodgy, amphibious prose—subject to the breaks and dislocations of a fierce tor-turing steed—but one that was also incredibly comic. Referring to the traditional Islamic custom of wearing the veil, abolished by the Soviets, he had produced an inspired phrase that verged on the sublime: "The women would walk along upheld by their impenetrable velaments." When I read the most amusing Cervantine chapter in* Tres tristes tigres *devoted to translation, I remembered that anon-ymous though elegant rival to Riné Leal and her ineffable adaptation of the story of Mr. Campbell and his walking stick . . .*

    The same strand would be repeated soon afterwards in the hotel dining room with an overdressed folkloric singer who was also anxious to try out on me the tuneful perfections of his Brazilian or Caribbean accent. As I gathered on the journey, a number of Uzbekis were aware of the diplomatic mission of Ruy González de Clavijo, Henry IV's envoy to the court of Tamerlane: the words Spain, Castile *had then a familiar and exotic ring in their ears. However, days later a youth who looked like a peasant sat next to me in the airplane, stared, and then spoke to me. His brief dialogue with Vidas, whose help I sought, went something like this:*

    "Which country are you from?"
    "From Spain."
    "Where did you say?"
    "Spain."
    "Spain, Spain . . . Whereabouts is that in the Soviet Union?"

13

      We were dazzled by our arrival in Samarkand: although a great number of mosques and medresses were in ruins, the city as a whole was splendid and confirmed my presentiments of immediacy, familiarity, and harmony with the old Moslem civilization. Tall slender minarets, gilded domes, gloriously blue mosaic façades blended together with effortless symmetry; street life was dense and full of bustle, a subtle invitation to wander. On foot we visited the various markets sheltered from the sun by awnings and shades; we entered one of the few mosques still devoted to worship. The faithful were few and, generally, very old. Valeri, our local guide, commented that young people did not usually go. His explanation—"they don't have the time"—was not entirely convincing and was soon corrected by another Uzbeki youth who whispered in our ear in English, "Believers can't get into university."

We visited one of Tamerlane's palaces. The cicerone responsible, stuffing us with her profuse historical knowledge, was a middle-aged Russian woman, dowdy and expressionless, wearing a hat-cum-parasol, her face covered in a thick layer of powder. She halted at every step in the heat of the sun to explain in her monotonous, dull voice unimportant anecdotes in the life and customs of the Mongolian emperor, his love of letters and astronomy, the number of his wives and concubines, his frequent after-dinner conversations with his astrologers. The heat was unbearable, and I looked in vain for a shadowy tree to stand under. The lady kept on speechifying at us, obviously something learned by heart, breaking off from time to time only to enable Vidas to continue his slow, deadly translation. A mini-lecture on the different turquoise shades of the zellijes, or tiles, lasted for several minutes: in the days of Tamerlane there were only eleven; now, thanks to the progress of Soviet industry, there were forty-three. Or was it a hundred and twenty-three? On the brink of committing a criminal act, I looked at that white, jellyfish mask whose pallid lips kept articulating that flow of inane, vacuous, incomprehensible words. Would she ever stop? She seemed not to notice the symptoms of my impatience and launched into a prolix story about Tamerlane's favorite wife, of which I can remember a few words translated by Vidas: doe, ankle, fall. Able to contain myself no longer, I pointed at the inexorable, hieratic face. Tell her to shut her trap, I snarled at the guide. Vidas obeyed and his translation clearly did not beat about the bush: the woman looked at me in amazement, and suddenly a double river of tears streamed down her cardboard cheeks. Monique was upset, turned to me indignantly: I had just humiliated that poor woman, who was only doing her duty; I was an odious Spanish snob. Ashamed of myself, embarrassed by the tears, I begged her through our guide to continue her fascinating talk. The woman gathered herself together at once, wiped her face with a handkerchief, and resumed the anecdote of the wife injured when playing with the doe, exactly where she had left off. The glare of the sun was like a real furnace; even the air seemed to catch alight and flame up. Almost ready to melt, I tolerated the lecturette as best I could, with my shirt around my head. When we finally bid farewell to the monster, we all felt nervous and exhausted. Back at the hotel where lunch awaited us, I dampened my brow and temples for some time in order to deaden, albeit tardily, the effects of sunstroke.

14

To avoid a repetition in Bukhara of what had happened the day before in Samarkand, I advised Vidas midjourney to inform the Intourist representatives at the airport of our desire to do without local art and history experts. Hardly had we touched down on the runway than a group of people, agents or guides, rushed to welcome the passengers. Vidas exchanged a few words with one of them, a tall, spruced-up European, looking like a hussar or officer in the Kaiser's guards, who turned out to be—the height of bad luck—the cicerone himself. Visibly upset by our interpreter's message, he escorted us silently to our minibus and, after crossing the city with unnecessary speed, deposited us by the entrance to the hotel, with a smiling, enigmatic farewell.

Then began the endless waiting: the minibus had vanished into thin air with the hussar, and Vidas's efforts to track him down were futile. The entire morning went in telephone calls to Intourist and a phantom delegation from the Writers' Union. The bar and lounge in the hotel where we waited remained shut; we had no room where we could make ourselves comfortable and a temperature nigh on one hundred and twenty degrees ruled out any possibility of a stroll outside. Not knowing what to do—sorcerers' apprentices in a situation of our own making—we hung with growing dismay on the result of Vidas's feverish negotiations: his looks, manner, glasses—the messenger bringing news of our Waterloo—confirmed at a distance the refined, subtle hussar's revenge. Shipwrecked by an insistent, lusty sun, helplessly stranded in a gloomy corridor, we saw the hopes raised by our visit fade like mirages or a magician's trick. The delicious Uzbeki meal that we were served when the dining room opened—a cold soup similar to gazpacho, a rice-and-meat dish called plof—did not make up for our imprisonment. Intourist promised to send transport after lunch, but it didn't arrive until almost five o'clock, leaving us only an hour before we had to be back at the airport. We got into the minibus with the chauffeur and an evil-looking Intourist representative. As we drove off, I told Vidas to take us quickly to a few mosques and monuments that were on our way. Our friend spoke to the Intourist woman, and from the sharp, lively tone of the exchange I deduced that she had refused. Her assignment was to accompany us to the airport, she said, not to show us the city. Fed up, impatient, I told her we had caught the plane to see Bukhara, not to put up with her bad manners and hysteria. Vidas translated my words literally and the impact was devastating: the woman ordered the driver to stop and got out of the minibus shouting and gesticulating. We also shouted and gesticulated, and while the driver drover off, abandoning her on the pavement, we celebrated our delightful victory with an outburst of general hilarity. The Uzbeki driver gave signs of appreciating our daring and took us amid laughter to half a dozen abandoned or deserted mosques whose ashen, withered beauty will always be with me: a pure, intense emotion that I relived years later in Cairo, in the symmetrical, desolate splendor of Ibn Tulun.

We had a cheerful return to Tashkent: accustomed to escorting gray bureaucrats or gullible sympathizers, Vidas was obviously enjoying himself and confessed that he had never suspected till he met us that writers existed who were as irreverent and undisciplined as we were. Did all French or Spanish people behave like us, or were we an exception? He had innocently thought he was looking after an exemplary progressive family and suddenly discovered that we were very dangerous anarchists!

As our departure date for the Crimea drew nearer, Valeri looked somber and gloomy. During our stay he had become infatuated with the beauty of Carole, who at thirteen was heading for puberty with alarmingly attractive allure: he wanted to ask for her hand, invite us home, introduce us to his family. When we said goodbye to him, we had to console him. We had been captivated by Uzbekistan and would return again to Bukhara, we promised, but without the hassles or setbacks of that first, incident-prone visit.

15

On 23 July we flew to the Crimea and landed at Simferopol. As it was nighttime, we took ourselves to a motel near the airport. The Intourist car fetched us early and we traveled by road to Yalta, through a lush green landscape whose inhabitants seemed to be soaked in the warm caress of the sun.

Yalta had all the appearance of an antiquated city on the Riviera, with villas and mansions built by aristocrats and bourgeois before the outbreak of the Revolution. Our car meandered upwards along a road bordered by woods and gardens. Instead of being lodged in a hotel, we went to the Writers' Union summer residence, magnificently situated in a park, on the crest of a hill. On arrival, once our luggage had been deposited in our rooms, we were welcomed by two smiling matrons in nurse's uniforms, who rushed to weigh us and then insisted on submitting Monique and myself to an energetic therapeutic massage. Politely but firmly we refused—our health, Vidas told them, was absolutely perfect—and we went for a walk in the gardens to await lunchtime. Monique wanted to go for a swim straightaway, but the bus that went to the beach left very early and was now about to come back.

We strolled around the park, the object of the discreetly curious gazes of the other guests: we then realized we were the only foreigners, and some of them turned round to look at us as soon as they noticed us. The writers gathered there looked fairly unintellectual, a disturbing sight: corpulent couples with closed, inscrutable expressions, clad in shorts and sandals; one tall, strapping individual wearing athletic garb; a kind of aged Japanese, diminutive, engrossed in himself, wrapped in striped pajamas, looking as if he had just escaped from a penal colony or asylum. When the bathers' bus arrived, we looked in vain for some familiar or sympathetic face. I had a faint hope that I would come across Victor Nekrassov, whom I had met at an assembly of European Community writers held in Florence and whom I had got on with immediately; it seemed that since then he had fallen *into disgrace. I was told he had turned to drink and wrote "things that were unpublishable." In Moscow they had informed me he was resting in Yalta, but, as I found out through Vidas, he had finished his holiday early and returned to Kiev.*

Apart from a couple with two children, whom I shall mention later, the guests with whom we shared the nutritious but insipid meal served up at lunchtime belonged quite obviously to the omnivorous, proliferating state bureaucracy. Judging from what one could see, no one knew any foreign languages and the pensioners' reading was limited to the stodgy pages—true printed bedsheets—of Izvestia *and* Pravda. *In any case, my soundings came up with no well-known names. That imposing materfamilias, with cellulitis thighs and a plastic sheath over her nose, sprawled out on the lawn, was she a writer or a writer's wife? The imperturbable gymnast, hands on hips, absorbed in his repeated loosening-up exercises, did he write as well? After a brief gossip around, Vidas informed us he was in the militia. What on earth was a militiaman doing in the writers' rest home? It was a swap, he explained: a novelist wanted to write a novel devoted to the exploits of the militia and, to get the right atmosphere, he requested a stay in their rest center; in exchange, with that strict, fussy symmetry of engineers, ideologues, and geometricians, the militia sent one of their own to the writers' mansion. The dreamy Japanese of the striped pajamas was in fact, in contrast, a specimen of a most rare species: the official bard of a country, the Yakut, situated in a remote confine of Siberia and whose language had yet to be codified. He had been writing a grammar or dictionary for years and was preparing to write a poem with thousands of lines on the mythology and history of his people: their* Odyssey, *their* Iliad. *Weighed down by that giant responsibility, the Yakut Homer wandered in a day-dream along the paths in the park, in his anachronistic pajamas and incurable gloom. I was frightened by his unusual fate, and when I came across him I imagined the blind poet and his pathetic jarring reincarnation in this pleasant Chekhovian theatrical setting in which text, production, and actors took us back unwittingly to the world of Kafka.*

16

When the afternoon bus came to pick us up, we got on with fifty-odd fellow writers who rushed to sit down and exchange noisy jokes as the vehicle panted slowly down a winding road till it finally came to halt in a pleasantly treey square. We got out and I walked to the beach with Monique and Carole, but the group of matrons in front waved at me, signaling I shouldn't go on. The place I was going was for women only; to reach the men's beach I should go in the other direction. Confused by such an unexpected event—not yet understanding that rigorous segregation worthy of our ultramontane bishops—I was forced to desert them and look out with my peers onto a rocky shore, covered by a uniform mass of pallid, naked, paunchy bathers. Rather than a concentration camp for nudists, the place looked like a colony of penguins with protruding bellies, flashy glasses, rubber sandals; the uneven ground strewn with pebbles and crops of rock hindered even more their waddling movements; penises and testicles hung down sadly, flaccid, lifeless, and unprotected. The spectacle evoked the prints of both Bosch and Doré, heightened by some surrealist touch: while dozens of individuals plunged and surfaced walruslike in the water, others stayed motionless on the side, their arms stretched out in the sun as if in surrender or worship, with their plastic eyeshades and goggles. Was this limbo a nightmare, a hallucination, a forerunner of a future extraterrestrial society of Selenites and Martians? Where were the slender, taut, athletic youths, the splendidly formed Tadzios immortalized by Thomas Mann? On the other side of the wire fence separating the beaches I spotted Monique and Carole, who had laughed themselves silly and had come to console me. The vision in their patch, they told me, was not any more comforting: Soviet men and women were unaware of dieting, and once youth had passed by, there was physical flab in abundance.

Back at the residence, we communicated our comic misfortune to Vidas, and after several calls and consultations, we obtained a special pass to the difficult, sought-after artists' beach where, he assured us, we could swim together. Dinner was served at six, and with no appetite we resigned ourselves to the same strenuous, tasteless menu we had suffered at midday. Monique timidly requested Crimean wine, but we were told there wasn't any. A drop of Moldavian or Caucasian wine? The establishment does not dispense alcoholic drinks, translated Vidas: writers came there precisely to dry out. We were not alcoholics, we objected. Our polite observations were of no use: the regulation was unbendable. Dinner was over at once, and as it was still daylight we went out into the garden. The pajamaed Homer; materfamilias, readers of Pravda, the brave militiaman were engaged in their usual occupations, already part of the scenery. Not knowing what to do—there were no cafés in the vicinity and it was not time to read in bed—we also wandered through the park, talking about Chekhov and Kafka. A distinguished, elegant man wearing a panama hat and simply dressed in white came along arm-in-arm with his wife from the other direction, and as he passed us gently nodded at us. His discreet manner and style—the opposite of the other guests in the residence—intrigued and whetted our curiosity. When we met up with Vidas, we found out that he was a well-known translator from Spanish and French who had rendered nothing less than the Quixote and the work of Rabelais. In corroboration, his two children came to say hello and welcome us on his behalf, to express his pleasure at seeing us there. In our innocence, we thought that their embassy was the prelude to a visit, but that was not to be. Despite his mastery of the languages we spoke, the translator would content himself with distant greetings and communication with us through his offspring. Boris, the boy, was the same age as Carole, and during our stay and even after he chatted to her in English about books and poetry. Thanks to those conversations, we would discover that his father had translated À la recherche du temps perdu knowing that it would be accepted by no publishing house. From various references in their adult conversa-

tion, well beyond their years, we deduced that "he has had problems." But neither Carole nor myself dared question him. The day someone mentioned his past imprisonment by Stalin we would finally see behind his wariness: knowing that he was being watched by one of his so-called colleagues, he preferred to smile at us from afar and thus avoid running the risk of a relationship with a foreigner without the corresponding permission from the authorities.

17

The artists' beach did not offer the same depressing spectacle as the day before had: the majority of the bathers were young, and some slim, attractive girls, apparently dancers, were going through rhythmic, gymnastic exercises at the edge of the sea. By the empty space where we stretched out, a group of actors were silently listening to a lean, dark colleague, oozing in suntan lotion, mercilessly declaim a speech or press editorial. A bit further away, Vidas told me, there were half a dozen Egyptian Communists just released from Nasser's prisons: they had brought with them a fair number of books in their beachbags and, as I walked past them to dive in, I looked out of the corner of my eye and made out several novels in French.

Seaside passenger boats, like the old pleasure boats in the port of Barcelona, slowly edged along the coast, linking up the different spa stations; the next day, rather than staying on the beach, we boarded one of them and went along several miles of shore, contemplating from a distance the crowds of vacationers who splashed on the bank like a shoal of sardines. As Vidas explained, the different trade unions and professional associations availed themselves of their respective beaches, reserved for their own exclusive use. In between the two monumental workers' residences was an almost deserted fenced-off area occasionally dotted with awnings and sunshades. With the help of binoculars, we made out small bands of bathers comfortably spread along the coast: it was the beach for the Party hierarchy and foreign guests of honor, the same perhaps where, two or three years earlier, my friends Claudín and Semprún, then still members of the Politbureau, had consoled themselves in the sun for the Party's failure and difficulty in adapting to the new, disconcerting realities of structural change in Spain.

The stay at the writers' rest home was in all ways becoming unbearable: the diet, times of meals, park stuffed with bureaucrats and materfamilias, indirect, almost clandestine communication with Boris's parents were injecting drop by drop a mood of claustrophobia, and we decided with Monique to have a change of air, break the daily monotony, escape for a few hours, in a word, breathe. Airports, hotels, Intourist offices displayed striking posters with alluring invitations to visit Sebastopol, la ville héroïque. Although unenthusiastic about patriotic tours, we begged Vidas to organize the excursion. It seemed a simple project that in principle posed no problems, but our friend returned downcast from Intourist: traffic between Yalta and Sebastopol was provisionally halted by roadwork on a stretch of the road and, for the moment, it was impossible to go. We were rather incredulous but discussed other possible trips when, on looking at the map of the Crimea, I realized that another road going inland linked the two cities. I communicated my discovery to Vidas and accompanied him to the Intourist offices. He had a few minutes' discussion with the female agent before coming back crestfallen: the inland route was also cut off. We would go by boat, I said: there was a jetfoil service. Another brusque half-whispered exchange with the representative: the timetable had been suspended! Annoyed by the amazing accumulation of obstacles, I asked Vidas to ask her frankly why on earth she did not want us to go to Sebastopol. Our friend translated my words and her only response was to fold her arms haughtily in an eloquent mixture of anger and disapproval.

Days later, in Moscow, when commenting on this strange episode with Sartre and Simone de Beauvoir, we were amused to discover that on their earlier journey to the Crimea they had had exactly the same experience: they too, despite their insistence, could not reach Sebastopol. There was probably a new regulation forbidding foreigners access to the town; but if that were the case, what was both intriguing and beyond explanation was the abundance of polyglot posters inviting you to visit. The gap between reality and propaganda defied any rational or logical schema. What was the secret of this city? What was behind that ridiculous contradiction? The most plausible of the hypotheses offered by Sartre was the possible secret dispatch of arms to Cuba. However, twenty years after these events, *this* I never got to Sebastopol *is and will continue to be one of the enigmas of the trip that, I fear, I will never manage to solve.*

18

The prospect of spending one more day in the aseptic "writers'" residence forced us into new schemes and strategies for escape: a drive through the outskirts of Yalta, a visit to the Livadia gardens, where Roosevelt, Churchill, and Stalin agreed on the redistribution and future of the world. Fortunately, Vidas mentioned to us the nearby presence of Nicolai Tomashevsky, whom I had met with Nekrassov in Florence, at a COMES congress: a son of one of the founders of the famous formalist school of Brik, Jakobson, Shklovsky, and Tynyanov, the young Tomashevsky had been a Russian lector in Naples, spoke Spanish perfectly, and brimming with vitality was fond of a drink; his spontaneous, frank character was a million miles from the reserve and officiousness of the majority of his colleagues. Tomashevsky was taking his summer holiday near Yalta and laughed heartily when he found out we were staying with those most cultured, intelligent bureaucrats of literature. With the exception of Boris's family, he said, not one of the guests in that place wrote anything but bureaucratic reports or really liked reading: what evil Trotskyite agent had had the perverse idea of sending us there?

Piloted by him, we went up to a beautiful mountain spot and sat down to have a drink in a picnic area. What's happened to the famous white wine of the

Crimea? asked Monique. The wine of the Crimea is no more, he said: in the old days the Tartars used to produce it, but after their deportation they were replaced by Ukrainians, and the secret of its exquisite bouquet was lost. The present wine was on the bitter side and he did not advise it. Although connoisseurs now drank wine from the Caucasus, the favorite wine of czarist times belonged exclusively to the world of myth. Relaxing in a clearing in the wood, we spoke at length about literature. Tomashevsky admired as I did the work of Svevo and Gadda and spoke very enthusiastically about two Russian writers who had just emerged from the long purgatory where they had been kept under Stalin and Zhdanov and were beginning to dribble through the publishers but had not yet been translated—Platonov and Bulgakov. He was not generally inspired with great respect for the work of his contemporaries: Voznesensky had written some decent poetry, but was the victim of provincial snobbery and a love of fame; the poetry of Bella Akhmadoulina, the author of a delicate evocation of Pushkin and Danthès, the translation of which in Les Lettres Françaises *impressed me, connected, according to him, with the best Russian lyric tradition without, however, reaching the depth and poignancy of Tsvetaeva and Akhmatova. Nonchalantly, trying not to reveal my irony, I asked him about Yevtushenko. Well, he smiled, he was something like our Zorrilla. I remembered Eugenio d'Ors's gloss on him and quoted it from memory: "a pianola; and as he's the one who gets tired of pedaling . . ." "Oh," exclaimed Tomashevsky, "the worst thing is he never gets tired. His readers do, but he never does!"*

The conversation and wine had put us in a good mood: neither of us wanted to go back, and Tomashevsky suggested a visit to an old Tartar cemetery. We went along a mountain road that had sudden views of the Black Sea until we came out at a village with pretty rustic houses not as yet spoiled by modernity. The Ottoman mezarlek *was a miniature reproduction of those I would later look at in Turkey; the memorial stones on the grave monuments, with or without a turban at the top, indicated the sex of those buried, and the symmetrical disposition of the tombs pointing toward Mecca provided a quiet scene, imbued with gentle calm. But something there, alongside the theatrical ploys of twilight, accentuated the feeling of melancholy and surreptitiously added a pathetic, desolate note: the total absence of the living. Transferred thousands of miles away, the Tartars could not come and mediate by the tombs of their forebears, which were decaying in their solitary abandon, covered in grass and moss. Deprived of their community, erased from memory, the dead lived there a second definitive death: no curious visitor even managed to decipher their names cut in Arabic characters. On my return to Paris, I would add the lines scrawled hurriedly on the journey, Cernuda's simple lines:*

> No es el juicio aún, muertos anónimos.
> Sosegaos, dormid; dormid si es que podéis.
> Acaso Dios también se olvida de vosotros.*

19

Although we stayed in another hotel, our third stop in Moscow followed a by now familiar framework, in line with well-established but flamboyant rituals: cheerful dinners at one of our favorite eating-houses, evenings with Sartre and Simone de Beauvoir at the Prague restaurant or in the lounges at the National, strolls with Agustín, Ángel, and Dionisio.

Agustín related to me an anecdote illustrating the recent conflict of factions within the Spanish CP leadership and its bizarre repercussions in the field of literature: Two years earlier, he had been advising the editors of an anthology of Peninsular authors to be published in Russian; the editors were visited by a Spanish "cadre" who demanded to examine the list of those selected. He scolded them severely: "Why haven't you included Jorge Semprún? He must be included at once!" None of the compilers then knew who my friend was, but they managed to have sent to them from Paris the galleys of his novel, hastily translated a chapter of Le Long Voyage, *and incorporated it into the volume. After a few months the book was ready, and the same person returned for a second time. He consulted the contents page again and a look of angry surprise came to his face: "What on earth is Jorge Semprún doing here? He must be eliminated immediately!" Neither Agustín nor his Soviet comrade had understood that nonsensical succession of contradictory orders until through some CP militants they discovered the identity of the mysterious Federico Sánchez, first praised to the sky by his colleague and then thrown into the dustbin of history with equal conviction.*

We went for a walk with a group of Spaniards around the side streets off central Gorki Street, where there were gathered more or less furtively the sellers of secondhand books that did not carry the nihil obstat *of the authorities. They drifted through looking conspiratorial, and when they met an eventual buyer mumbled the password for their merchandise. I heard one fair-haired romantic youth, in a tight-fitting threadbare mackintosh, repeat quietly: Pasternak, Pasternak. The area looked strangely like a spot for picking up males or clandestinely selling drugs: but instead, hash was, to advantage, replaced by authors outside the canon or glowing with the aura of the forbidden. They told me the most sought-after and expensive title was Salvador Dalí's* Secret Life. *A fact that ought to be food for thought for future Hispanic censors concerning the imponderable marvels of their stimulating, beneficent trade!*

As we could see from many small pointers, the country had been biding its time ever since the fall of Khrushchev. The personalities and intentions of the new leaders were still unknown factors: the writers I spoke to were not sure whether the timid thaw Krushchev had begun was to be prolonged or whether they were headed,

---

* You're not to be judged yet, you anonymous dead.
  Calm down, go to sleep; that's if you can.
  Perhaps God has forgotten you as well.

on the contrary, for harsher times. Strangely, while Stalin's name was still wrapped in a halo of fear and respect, his successor was earning the most surprising, ridiculous criticisms and reproaches: he was having thrown back at him his rudeness, his vulgar attitude the day he hit the rostrum at the United Nations with his shoe. Almost no one seemed to grant him any recognition for having freed hundreds of thousands of prisoners and for his denunciation of the crimes and persecutions of Stalin, from which I would deduce correctly that the winds blowing from above and inspiring the supposedly personal comments from the more or less "official" colleagues with whom I had dealings indicated a phase of greater ideological rigidity and a return to the sacrosanct principles of Leninism.

20

As our departure date drew near, the comrades in the Writers' Union and other cultural entities multiplied their friendly overtures. Tanya—the efficient adviser to the Foreign Literature Review*—Irina, always very warm and sensitive, Hispanists, and translators of my books came to our hotel, went shopping with us, tried to make life easy while Boris took Carole out and initiated her in the study of Russian.*

Four weeks at Monique's side had softened bit by bit the blow dealt by my letter, and in various scenarios and moments on the trip we had recovered gestures we thought had died, resumed familiar communication, reached physical intimacy with the same disturbing novelty as on our first encounter in Barcelona. The Soviet Union—model or Aunt Sally for so many writers—had filled us with neither enthusiasm nor horror. Our stay there had been initiatory, warm, and sometimes friendly. Anyhow, our glimpses and taste of the society of the future had injected us with a healthy skepticism in relation to the state planning of happiness and had sharpened, perhaps involuntarily, our sense of humor.

F OURTEEN MONTHS LATER, at the end of summer in 1966, I would repeat the journey under very different circumstances. I had been invited to the festivities commemorating the centenary of a stupendous Caucasian poet—whom I had never heard of before those events and whom I would never hear mentioned again afterwards—and went as part of a group of foreign guests who were mainly French, Communist Party sympathizers or members. The year gone by had been rich in developments not only in relation to my private life—my first stay in Tangier, emotional distancing from Spain, return to Paris with Monique—but also my political connections and feelings of ambivalence toward the USSR: the Sovietization of the revolutionary process in Cuba, the arrest of the writers Daniel and Siniavsky, the abrupt end to hopes of a gradual cultural thaw. In August Carole had spent several weeks at Tanya's house in Moscow and had made great progress in Russian thanks to Boris and his friends. I thought at first I would politely decline the invitation, but the friendly insistence of the Soviets and the short length of the trip filled me with doubts. Rightly convinced that this would be my last visit if I published, as was my intention, a kind of diary of the previous tour, I thought it rather senseless to squander the opportunity to set my impressions against the reality that had produced them. Although I shelved the publishing idea months later, as much through a passing lack of interest in the issue as from fear that my criticisms might be used by Francoism, the argument about testing out my attitude of conscious subjectivism finally persuaded me to accept.

My affinity with nascent Soviet dissidents, my condemnation of the military occupation of Czechoslovakia—where I went, immediately after the invasion, as a guest of the Czech Union of Writers, to work on an article that would appear in *Les Temps Modernes*—would finally terminate my rather ambiguous relationship with the official world of the USSR. The certainty that the crushing of the "Prague spring" was in no way different from the sending of marines to Santo Domingo would in the future enforce upon me a double-edged, more complex militancy in respect to Palestinians, Afghans, and the victims of Castro's dictatorship and the criminal juntas of Central America and the Southern Cone. The cardinal discovery of the last decades, as Maxime Rodinson has seen very clearly, is that revolutions are relative and that the final struggle moves ever away, as we think we get closer, inasmuch as "existing socialism" by a long shot never puts an end to exploitation or oppression but transforms them and sometimes intensifies them; consequently, the methods, objectives, and programs of real or would-be revolutionary states or movements should be examined with a clear-thinking caution. "Unconditional adherence often leads one to approve mistakes and, often, real barbarity." Such experiences, full of setbacks, disillusion, strokes of luck, and relapses, would gradually take me to the conclusion formulated years later in a university session with arts students in Sevilla: that I prefer making my own mistakes to following the right slogan.

Since saying farewell to the Soviet Union in 1966, I have fleetingly seen some of the friends who have appeared on these pages or have found out indirectly about them: Agustín Manso is still in Moscow, busy working as a translator; Dionisio keeps himself rather on the fringes and apparently supports the nationalist and anti-Semitic ideological currents set out in Alexander Zinoviev's latest startling interviews; Ángel, having become a rabid anti-Communist, returned to Spain and works or worked for the Russian service of Radio Free Europe; Lénina Zónina spent brief periods in Paris, faithful to her old friendship with Sartre and Castor, and I am filled with sadness and emotion as I receive news of her death in Moscow as I sit writing these lines; Vidas works in the university and goes about with the usual friends; Ruth Zernova emigrated to Israel when her mother died, and the night she dined in Paris with Monique and myself posed strange arguments—coming from a former volunteer to the International Brigades—against my defense of the right of Palestinians to self-determination . . .

Several times over recent years I have dreamed that I am back in the USSR: the oneiric intrigue is not oppressive or anxious but develops generally in a pleasant and rather unreal atmosphere. A vague awareness of returning to a dead and unrepeatable past that launches me afresh into remembering my journeys and, subliminally and indirectly, to the tardy discovery of how ridiculously happy I was there.

· VII ·

All That Glitters Isn't Moorish

THE NEWCOMER GREETED the concierge for the block and exchanged a few polite phrases: an old woman with her white hair tucked up in a bun and a strong southern accent. Madame had warned her he was coming and given her the keys. The flat's on the first floor; a young man like him, she says, better take the stairs, not the elevator. She apologizes for not going with him; she can't leave the porter's room unattended and the imagined hint of a smell of some dish perhaps indicates that the old lady has also got her coal or gas cooker on the burn.

The foreigner accepted her excuses with an understanding smile: in spite of the pleasant or neutral look on his face, the absentminded re-creator of the scene could imagine that there was even a glint of satisfaction. Perhaps he would rather no third person share his initial glance at what will be his home for some time: the exclusive first fruits of that vision. Perhaps he also wants to keep to himself those gestures that betray his clumsiness, the difficult relationship between his hands and the tiniest objects of everyday use: the inevitable confusion over the keys until he hits the hole corresponding to the lock and the bolt, possibly then stumbling into something as he gropes for the light switch, a less than glorious skirmish with the blind-pull warped with damp. The flat, as he will see, comprises two spacious rooms, bathroom, and kitchen. The furniture is comfortable but impersonal: a suite upholstered perhaps in green, dining room table and chairs, a double bed already made up, more chairs, built-in wardrobes, refrigerator, small framed prints and engravings, standard lamps, a table suitable for writing. The foreigner inspects things as if adapting to them and assessing their exact shape and size before taking them over. For the first time in his life he is settling down in a city that he does not know and where he in turn is a total stranger. He is pleased by the anonymity of the home he agrees to rent hours later: after thirty-odd years of life *en famille*, he is relieved by the idea of camping down amid furniture that lacks history. Appropriation will be cautious, in stages; check that the water heater for the bath is working, that plugs and bulbs are in good order. The objects and clothes he has brought with him fit in a medium-sized suitcase: before nightfall, he hangs up jackets and trousers, puts shirts and underwear on their shelves; inkpot, pen, books, paper on the small table. The refrigerator will continue to be empty and disconnected: the new tenant knows his limits and it doesn't even occur to him to use it. Crockery, saucepans, cutlery will stay clean and tidy, piled up on the cupboard shelves or lined up along the rack. When he draws a summary conclusion to his move, he finds that the flat has not lost its cold, battered look; his presence there is to be anodyne and slight, just a passing visitor. The dining room window, at the front, looks out on a dull block of flats in the unmistakable architectural style that marked his childhood in the forties; a plot surrounded by ruined walls, covered in rubbish and weeds, acts as a store or hiding-place, he later notices, for European and indigenous junk-dealers and kids; from the back balcony adjacent to his bedroom, the newcomer can glimpse, hemmed in between two buildings, a small patch of the port, with breakwater and cranes and, in the distance, like a whitish, misty scar, the blurred coastline of his distant and despised country.

At first sight, the new tenant is a man of sober habits, neat and elegant to an extreme: he gets up early, showers, shaves, and goes out straightaway to stretch his legs and purchase for a few cents some tatty esoteric local newspaper. About fifty meters from home he has discovered a café belonging to a compatriot and has decided to adopt it for the moment, while awaiting a better solution. In midmorning, after writing an extensive letter and sticking stamps on it, he checks all is in order and equips himself with the necessary items for his program of exploration: a conversation manual bought at an airport kiosk, a short tourist guide to the city. Although the manual is not much help and the guidebook doesn't include a map of the small streets in the district that interests him, he embarks daily on his rambler's route armed with them, like some tiny derisory protective barrier. A decision that is all the more absurd given that the expatriate—like his wife years later in Roscoff* —does not really wish to preserve himself from anything and, on the contrary, gives himself over to the adventure with the incentive of total availability. For the first time in his life he too has no timetable or work schedules; his stay in the town is the same as any ordinary gentleman of leisure attracted there—like the tourists he comes across on his way down to the sea-front—by the typical, proverbial local color or the chance enjoyment of evasive, impregnating luminosity. Usually, he stops on the terrace of some café near the bus stop and station, asks for the same aromatic infusion as his neighbors, unobtrusively follows their conversation and from time to time scribbles down a word on a cigarette box or in the margins of his

---

* See Monique Lange, *Les Cabines de bain*, Paris 1982.

conversation manual. Later on, as he loses his diffidence and feels more on home ground, he speaks to the locals, although after an elementary exchange of phrases on weather, nationality, or origins, he is forced to give up his efforts unless, as sometimes happens, his interlocutor speaks his language or, to his greater mortification, responds directly in French.

In retrospect, the expatriate seems like a topographer in his detailed taming of this exotic world. Day after day he wanders through the labyrinth of narrow streets, copies down the trilingual sign in each of them, draws and corrects maps, redoes routes, checks his accuracy.

His meanderings are both obsessive and erratic, as if he were following in someone's footsteps or, in reverse, was being tracked by someone he was trying to throw off course. In truth, he is behaving in the city as circumspectly as he had initially behaved in the flat. He often gives the impression that he feels a need to encompass and measure the space he moves around in in order to fit himself in: before entering the small cafés that attract him, immersed in those shadowy, silent, narrow streets, he explores the nooks and crannies of the alleyways, sketches in beforehand a brief outline of place. His persistence in overcoming his manifest insecurity finally earns its reward: the most arduous, unyielding bastions surrender in turn to his curiosity. He gradually gets acclimated, is recognized by the waiter or owner, savors his infusion, smokes a pipe or two, alternates reading and notetaking with a scrutiny of everything happening about him. Given the lack of the sought-after understanding of language, he strives like a deaf-mute to observe expressions and gestures. The aim is to familiarize himself, melt into this milieu, acquire the privileged impunity of a chameleon.

Daily observation of the expatriate allows one to establish a timetable for his activities that, even though subject to modifications and imponderables, nonetheless pinpoints his basic propensity toward routine: he never leaves home before the mail arrives, then goes down to the porter's minutes later, and when the old lady hands him the awaited letter, he separates it out from the others, the ones that are less important, and keeps it in a jacket pocket so as to read it unhurriedly in one of the cafés on his walk, where he usually sits down before climbing the slope and taking on the steep steps that lead to the old quarter of the medina. If the reply from his correspondent is delayed and the postman has no new ones, rather than rereading the old ones, he heads for the main post office, joins the line for a telephone, and when it's his turn asks for a long-distance call to Saint-Tropez. Apart from that brief, sporadic incursion into the modern quarter, largely inhabited by Europeans, his walks take him exclusively to the small cafés and terraces that he has become attached to: he has lunch by himself in an eating-house, greets or smiles timidly at the waiter, stops to drink an infusion at the crossroads in the old quarter, turns down the labyrinth of alleyways that he trawls doggedly with growing aplomb and confidence. His conversation manual, with its imprecise and even misleading phonetic transcriptions, is now full of words, corrections, and crossings-out. This interest in getting a command of the language contrasts with his slowness or difficulty in finding someone to share it with. Whether in the seaview cafés set in the city wall, the dingy backrooms where he crouches on a rush mat, or the place from which he enjoys a view of the flat roofs and domes of the city, he goes in and out unaccompanied and, often unaware of the voices of the lotto players and the noise of the dominoes, he tries to memorize a phrase he has just learned or the complicated conjugation of some verb. He is satisfied by the novelty of all he sees, hears, touches, tastes, breathes. Unlike other journeys he has been on, he is not seeking to confirm a theory or validate his own knowledge. The ideological monolith where he once lived has given way to a fertile range of petty kingdoms. The vast, changing nature of the area excludes facile assimilation and he prefers gradual annexation, like someone scaling a fortress or walled keep. Only mental appropriation of that world can enable him to forget old errors and learn from new ones, the task of casting off the oppressive experience of the past, the need to extend to himself the investigation he has till then urged on everyone else. The expatriate is convalescing from an affliction that does not appear in any dictionary and against which no medicine can be prescribed. His rejection of all that marks him out assumes the dimensions of an allergy: proximity to his fellow countrymen irritates him and, as far as possible, he flees from their presence. When he returns home, he transcribes in an exercise book the lexis acquired during the day and strives to express his effervescent ideas on notepaper that he sends to his wife.

Although the correspondence is not dated, the content of the letters allows you quite accurately to establish the correct chronological sequence.

> When my bedroom is bathed in sunlight, it's as hot as in summer. I feel happy, I walk around for ten hours a day, I'm seeing Haro [Tecglen] and his wife, I'm not going to bed with anyone and I look at Spain from afar, full of intellectual excitement.

I need to be here: I couldn't stay in Saint-Tropez with no ideas and no will to write and I predict that in Tangier I will recover both. This is what really matters to me, not sex.

One observation that will interest you: while European homosexuals usually reveal themselves by imitating women, here, in contrast, they take on an extra layer of exaggerated virility. That's what attracts me to them and helps me to distinguish them without fail, since naturally there are plenty who aren't.

A little while ago, I was watching and listening to Spanish television (you can pick it up here). Its cretinism and the profanation of our language made an incredible impression on me.

I'm dying to get writing, and I'm not sure yet what about.

I really miss you, but I am afraid to return to Saint-Tropez and get upset. I admit life with me is difficult and you have had to swallow a lot since we came back from Moscow; but in Saint-Tropez, I just don't exist if I'm not involved in something more tangible. Although I detest Spain, this feeling has its positive side: it's useful to me since it helps when it comes to writing. In Saint-Tropez, and I insist that this has nothing to do with you, I'm not in or opposite Spain and I cannot look at her as I can from here in a *new way*. If I'm not working, I'm just growing older in a pleasant climate. I'm not making any moral or intellectual progress.

I have just received your three letters all together: I love you a little-a lot-passionately totally. As I read them in amorous crescendo, I felt happy. But I have since seen that the real order was in reverse. Having said this, you're right and I'll try to be more explicit. You must believe me when I say that if I'm staying here for a while that it has no bearing at all on you. I miss you and I seem to have been without you for a long time; but I've no wish to return to Saint-Tropez to feel fucked up, get drunk, and then blame it on you. I would rather you got annoyed with me than that I feel rancorous toward you. The idea I'm working on is based on the vision of the Spanish coast from Tangier: I want to start off from this image and write something beautiful, that goes well beyond anything I've written so far. Tangier is still indispensable [for] this daily struggle with a theme that is still hazy. [At the moment] I'm immersed in Golden Age literature.

I've just received a letter from Luis. Eulalia died three days ago and she was buried on the second of January.* They preferred me not to go since she remembered me arriving when Dad and Grandfather were in their death agony, and she thought that if I didn't go that meant her illness was not serious and she wasn't at death's door.

---

* This letter was written after my sister-in-law's telegram reached me in Fez.

Perhaps it's all been for the best, but despite the predictability of what was coming, the news had a terrible effect on me. Neither Luis nor I have anyone behind us now—as regards the past and the family—nor in front—in relation to death. The umbilical cord's been cut and we're on the waiting list.

The expatriate has found a friend. Their eyes had met the day before on a café terrace in the main square, and he bumped into him again crossing the road on the way to the post office. The stranger said hello without more ado in his garbled Moorish Spanish: he's wearing a blue woollen hat, and trousers and overcoat in the same color. He looks like a fisherman or a sailor, but isn't; he has worked for several years in the port with Spaniards, he explains; there he learned to get about in the language of Cantinflas and Joselito. After drinking tea together, they went to buy wine in a Jewish shop and quietly closed themselves off in the flat on the rue Molière.

Although the farmhand is about as old as our hero, his appearance is totally different: his rough, solid face and tough, coarse complexion make him look like an oarsman, a sturdy, muscular fighter. His untamed intelligence and uncouth ways are not without their humor or mischievous appeal. When he's talking he laughs, showing off his teeth beneath his thick mustache; his half-shifty, half-confused manner remind the expatriate of Alfredo, the deceased Torrentbó cropper. There's nothing better than wine, he assures him, to lose his sense of shame with him; he makes out he hasn't tasted any for months and gulps it down while answering his questions, your questions, naked by now, but still wearing his cap.

From then on—the end of November—the man from the wilds will often visit your house and escort you with the somber looks of a bodyguard in your trawl of the medina; he usually walks with you up to the small cafés by the Alcazaba, helps you unthread and mix the leaves, initiates you in your fruitful incursion into majoon: thanks to him and his robust protection, you forced entry into the toughest dives and discovered the pleasure of smoking a pipe or two in the hanging garden of the Khafita, scrutinizing the enemy coast from your watchtower or vantage point. After supper, your guide prefers the attributes of the modern city and a thirsty visit to the English bars, in one of which he had worked as a doorman or, more precisely, as a bouncer. Infected by his excesses and nocturnal fury, you will also down alcohol with majoon and grass, you will make up for the deceptive austerity of your first days with the seer's search for the abyss or precipice. You have hit upon the perfect inductive agent and only await the moment that will spark it off. The inexorable gravitation it sets off is light-bringing, horizon-opening. Only by yielding to it will you attain the fullness of the mental space hinted at: raw, cooked, consumed acts paralleling the word as it is purified to the marrow.

It's an evening like any other, just like the others, following your head-strong, worrying wandering path: to and from the Alcazaba, pipes of shared kef, televised course in Spanishry, a rushed meal in Hammadi, nocturnal bustle in a taxi, cheerful disembarking with your guard and mentor on the usual entertaining circuit: out-of-the-way dives and quaysides, Rolling Stones background music, conniving little grins, waltzing around like an African queen, finicky queens, Oxonian accents of some broken-down noble or superannuated lord: cheerful libations in the half-dark, never-satisfied thirst, the expansive euphoria of my Hispa-narabic wildman, the obsessive repetition of old stories of Nasride, trailing in the rear, and the last Abencerraje a navy-blue cap, perhaps pulled down tight, thick, hircine brows, primitive nose, sylvane mus-tache, voracious lips, energetic, crushing jaws, determined to serve him forever, he swears again and again, such a good understanding companion, guide him through the city, ensure his rest and safety, attend night and day to the exact fulfillment of his desires, wash and cook for him, go daily to the market, accompany him to the baths, prevent any trouble, incident, or danger, ready for anything to satisfy his friend, drink a few comforting glasses of wine with him, make up his joints, have a look around the bars far from the dirt and the rabble without faith, religion, or trust, intent only on robbing and kicking their peers up the backside, he's a man to be trusted, his only dream is to get to know Spain one day, to cross the accursed Straits, to clear off forever from Tangier and all these thieves and bastards on the loose, to travel with his friend, greet those friendly Spaniards who toiled with him in the port, loading and unloading oranges, sixty, even eighty kilos of oranges on their back, just touch his body to see it's true, he's not a braggart and a liar like everybody else he's raised his voice, begun to strip so as to show off the tough sinewy muscles of his arms or perhaps it's later, in another setting or, more likely, in the bedroom? you don't know and will never know because everything is misty and unreal and the imagined exchange is the one you heard or will hear afterwards from his lips, stammered out as night advances and the empty bottles of Boulaouane pile up: fifteen years in the service of those bastards, from dawn to dusk, never complaining, then suddenly they shut the firm and throw him out on the fucking street like a cigarette butt, no bonuses or compensation, just a letter of recommendation, look at it, twenty liters of olive oil, a pair of new boots, and a bag of flour, how the hell was he going to feed and look after his mother and sisters with that, suddenly quiet, calmed down, taught a lesson by what happened tonight, ready to laugh or cry, depends how the mood catches him, yes, that's life, brother, time to down another glass and stare at you, on the brink of laughter and tears still in the bar, the cushions and the buzz of the bar, surrounded by evasive presences, anxious creatures fleeing from the light, adding up, perhaps to hold onto something, the alarming way the glasses are replaced, gin cognac vodka, perhaps everything's mixed up, both lost in thick, dark foliage, paths tracks shortcuts simply rubbed out, no memory of them after the storm blowing down and buffeting you, picks you off, pulls you up, kicks you out on foot or by taxi? but finally in the flat, unsure how you have arrived or why you are arguing, did you start it, as he'll say later when facing up to the consequences of the scene, a hidden desire to kindle his fury till you drove him out of his mind? to reach the bitter raw truth in your bitter garden of delights? veiled images, opacity broken by the glaring lightning flash of violence, your stunning communication of energy, the bruising damage of the blow, fall, painfully get up, brutal order to stretch out on the bed, intermittent flashes of consciousness, shriveled up, weighed down, drowsy while he stalks the room like a caged beast, looks for alcohol in the kitchen, drinks from the bottle, fires threats and muffled accusations at you, at the city, at lousy life, stands there not taking his eyes off you, grim alert like a brutal guard, nodding off for minutes hours in the chair till sleep overcomes you and him and, when you wake up, you can see him there lying on the floor, inert, spread-eagled, snoring in the middle of the ravaged room, clothes scattered everywhere, upturned chairs, dirty, unmade bed, gradual perception of the tense scene around you, cruel aggression of day, accusing upside-down time of day, mental and material disorder, painful effort to get up, go to the bathroom, look at oneself incredulously in the mirror and find a face that is not yours, transmuted as well into the fierce whirlwind of the night, still incapable of thought, of understanding what has happened, the chance spark that set off that sudden outburst of virulence, get washed, shaved, hide the swelling behind merciful sunglasses, open the window wide to let the fresh air in and wake up your befuddled guard, he in turn gets up, goes for a lengthy piss in the bathroom, reappears looking flustered, his mustache lank and contrite like a child who has just broken his toy; mumbling pitiful excuses, wishing to make it up, make friends with his friend who is so well-behaved, so kind, a real brother who looks after him and helps him when he hasn't got any money, daintier than lace, softer than cotton, ready to reach the bottom of the pit of self-abasement just like the lover caught erring so beautifully and sharply described by Ibn Hazm but you want to be alone, to digest what has happened, distance yourself, transform humiliation into yeast, rage into power: reach that point of fusion in which the war waged against yourself symbolically transcends, augurs in morals and literature a new departure, vindicates the reason for the mishap, the cataclysm both sought and feared: stern imposition of destiny whose prize will be the written word, the blight or grace of creation.

On the same day you arrived in Marrakesh on a flight initially planned for both of you but that you alone took: a threadbare image of dusk over the palm forest and the ocher land, insensitive, in your state at the time, to the beauty, radiant abundance of a city that in the future will grant you the magnificent gift of the word. Closeted in your hotel room, between Kutubia and Djemaa el Fna, you experienced moments of solitude, elation, and madness, conscious you had broken the cortex round your burning center, reached the depths from which bubbled, poured out, the magma of filth, burnt matter. The sudden, violent exhilaration, the bright, destructive lash glimpsed from childhood had ceased to be a secretive vision, panting to become real: a force tied to your peculiar experience of sex, the animal gravitation of bodies that you had to experience and integrate in the body of your text with the same disenchanted lucidity and calm fatalism with which Fernando de Rojas, the student from Puebla de Montalbán, laid out, for the lovers in *La Celestina*, the recondite laws of their intimate, substantial vulcanology.

Not the same as happened in Madrid years before, that evening you got drunk with Lucho, moral disaster has become a vital source of self-knowledge. Beyond the personal sphere, it reveals, renders diaphanous the latent mechanisms within society, exhumes and rescues from the bone marrow the energy that will propel the devastating invasion you propose: that work not yet written in our language, against it, to its greater glory, to destroy and pay homage, to profane and bring offerings, schizophrenic, oneiric, alienated aggression, integral alliance of imagination and reason, as Malraux says of Goya, beneath the lying appearance of delirium. Strings of resolutions forged dizzily from your flight to the city where today you evoke and transfix on the page what has happened: penetrate the real history of the country from which you felt inexorably proscribed; immersion in a lustral bath of its classics; sieve through the totality of its literary corpus with the same painstaking frenzy as you daily trawled the chaos of Tangier; place the humanistic mass of the epoch—linguistics, poetics, historiography—at the disposal of such an enterprise; reach down to the roots of the civil death you have had to live through; bring out into the light the demons and fears crouching in the depths of your consciousness. Days, hours, privileged moments, lush richness unequaled since, brooding on your anger, insults, thirst for revenge on those windmills or giants by the name of religion-fatherland-family-past-childhood. The mental spring set off by the taunts of your guard proliferates, spreads out: it presents out-of-the-way corners, shady spots, rough edges, a vast field to sound out and explore. For a time, your proximity to the initiator is indispensable and, back in Tangier, you submit to the magnetism of his blind, repellent labors.

Antagonistic parallelisms and schemas: topographic appropriation of the urban nucleus where you have taken refuge and distancing overseas from the land glimpsed as receding outline; clumsy, childish apprenticeship in the new language and irresistible pull of the old, entranced and forever captivated by the incandescent splendor of the word; renunciation of a broad alien space and gradual immersion in the strata of its history and culture; purification, decanting, refining of an extreme, diamantine language against the sterilizing monopoly of an arrogant, all-embracing caste.

Ritual wanderings after spying from your window the arrival of the messenger with news from Saint-Tropez or of Eulalia's cancer, accompanied not just by the conversation manual and gradually amended map but also a modest, dog-eared copy of *Soledades*. Your close, attentive, almost obsessional reading of the text, its rich leafy bowers and twisting tracks interwoven with the pauses and fantasies of kef. Sitting in one of the cafés that you like, you break off your siege of the poem to rise up at will, watch over minarets, flat roofs, and white domes, scrutinize the faded scar of a repudiated, hostile land. Góngora indissolubly linked in your memory to the changing capricious sky of Tangier, as Juan Ruiz will be years later to the bustling forum of Djemaa el Fna: line after line joined together like cherries, metaphors of wily, insidious beauty, enjoyment, subtle beatitude. Waking up at midnight with a quotation on your lips as if you had commended your dreams to the Poet: immediacy, outpouring, impregnation of writing that supplants the world to your advantage, acts as a reference point and, like a lighthouse, beams its light toward you in the midst of the chaos.

Only later, much later, will you establish the existence of a cartography and speleology common to mystic and lover alike that, by transcending and generalizing what you thought was particular to you, will free you of guilt but will also strip you of your precious strangeness: a similarity of experiences translated in identical throbbing images, tightness and breadth, pain and joy, harshness, flame, consummation: the universal law of the subsoil, complementing the discoveries of Kant and Descartes, Marx and Bakunin, Humboldt, Rousseau, thanks to San Juan de la Cruz and Mawlana, Eckhart and Al Hallax, the Marquis de Sade and the obscure Masoch.

Like Mlle. de Vinteuil next to the paternal photo in the love scene, you will incorporate Eulalia's dreaded imagined death agony into the peaks,

ups and downs, precipices of your perverse frame: illuminating assumption of the center and its igneous reality: extending, unraveling, intensifying the friction till you are dizzy associating it with the original
nodule of anguish: counterpointing conflicting visions, slow devouring by
opened jaws, a pallid, worn-out face, sanctified by pain: enigmatic relationship between the intrusive, inductive image, the stubborn dipping
into glorious suffering and the brusque syncopated swoon: magmatic
eruptivity, red-hot volcanic slag surging out of your own Gehenna:
duality, ambivalence, Zoroastrian love and profanation, generating spark
of a secret alternative current.

One meager, greedy January day, winter harshens, Eulalia has died and
the expatriate has digested the news in his way, walked up without his
guard to one of the small cafés by the Alcazaba, dissolved a good dose of
maashun in his glass of mint tea, been delirious, sobbed, moaned for hours
his guilt out in the open, fulfilling the millenary, funereal, anthro-
pophagous rite of the final missing explanation. His stay in the city is
coming to an end and he has written a few lines to Saint-Tropez
announcing his return.* He now has a familiar relationship with his
environment: he recognizes spaces and players and, gradually, in turn,
feels accepted and recognized. He daily retraces his steps with all possible
variants, stopping to drink tea or smoke a pipe in the same places, he
reads a few lines of *Soledades*, notes down words or phrases in the margins
of his conversation manual.

The air of Tangier, imbued with gentle light, stimulates him. Under
its caress people and things acquire relief and liveliness, the street bustle
unwinds in an atmosphere of dense plasticity. Wrapped in their djellabas,
burnooses, or hooded cloaks, women and men move through the shadowy
side street as if it were a theatrical set, the salty damp of the Straits
impregnates the whitewashed walls, light and shadow combine their
effect with subtle skilled harmony. The man of leisure can spend minutes
or hours absorbed in the contemplation of the clouds or following, almost
hypnotized, the cautious movements, in a patio or on a flat roof visible
from his lookout post, of a little old woman wrapped round in a towel
near a minute coal stove. The morning gust of breeze transmits and
spreads voices and messages: greetings, shouts, bits of music, noises and
echoes of çraftsmen, the simultaneous invocation of the muezzin calling
the faithful to prayer. The scattering flight of the birds, their anxious
hovering seem to obey secret, indecipherable signals: the pigeons that
were dotted over the minaret of the nearby mosque abandon it with noisy

---

* Letter of 10 January 1966.

conviction and fly off in a whirl of white patches to the ancient town walls. Visions beyond grasp, fleeting images, drenched in sun and mist: trumpets and drums of a mountain marriage, a procession of religious brotherhoods with their dingy oriflammes, flashy polyglot flocks after the red fez of their shepherd.

The expatriate guides his steps through the labyrinth of the Alcazaba through gardens and green spaces in the Marshan, till he reaches the Square of Motherhood and zigzags up to the haughty vantage point of the Khafita. A warm, indulgent sun invites him to sit at the tables set on the slope along the flowering terraces: thickly verdant nests sheltered from indiscreet gazes, in which loners, groups, couples smoke, read, converse, savor mint tea curled up in a ball of lazy warmth. The coastal scarp is precipitous, and from these heights can be surveyed the panorama of the Tarifa Strait to Gebel Tariq, the bellicose succession of waves that in slow suicidal majesty break and die in foam at the foot of the cliff: repeated realization of the distance separating him from the other shore, the kernel of his aggressive anxiety and vehement desire for betrayal. Gripping his falcon-mentor's book, he awaits the sharp flash whose blinding light will transfigure him; but from Lermontov, and not from Góngora, from a poor Spanish translation read by chance months before, will leap like a hare the refrain in lines that will engrave themselves with their devastating truth: *goodbye, filthy Stepmother, country of masters and slaves/goodbye three-cornered leather hats, and you, the people that put up with them.* New excitement and emotion entrance him at once, fire him with the intoxication of someone who has solved the riddle. The poem he has just adapted to his own obsession is a dawn to something: the feverishly noted phrase triggers off, drives on, the generative furrow of writing.

The one who sees and the one who is seen are one within yourself, says Mawlana; but the expatriate you now bid farewell to is *another*, and when he packs his case and disappears from the city to which he came quietly in the ephemeral sweetness of autumn he could exclaim, à la Flaubert, in the fever of his undertaking, totally at one with the felon in the distant legend: Don Julián, *c'est moi.*

Memory, writes Walter Benjamin, cannot transfix the flow of time or encompass the infinite dimension of space: it is restricted to re-creating set scenes, encapsulating privileged moments, arranging memories and images in a syntactic order that word by word will shape into a book. The unbridgeable distance between act and written word, the laws and requirements of the narrative text will insidiously transmute faithfulness to reality into artistic exercise, attempted sincerity into virtuosity, moral rigor into aesthetics. No possibility of escape from the dilemma; the reconstruction of the past will always be certain betrayal as far as it is endowed with later coherence, stiffened with clever continuity of plot. Put your pen down, break off the narrative, prudently limit the damage: silence, silence alone will keep intact a pure sterile illusion of truth.